ALIENS and DISSENTERS

A Publication of the Center for the Study of the
History of Liberty in America
Harvard University

ALIENS and DISSENTERS

FEDERAL SUPPRESSION OF RADICALS · 1903–1933

WILLIAM PRESTON, JR.

HARVARD UNIVERSITY PRESS

Cambridge, Massachusetts

1963

Distributed in Great Britain by Oxford University Press, London

Publication of this volume has been aided by a grant from the
Ford Foundation

Library of Congress Catalog Card Number 63-10873

Printed in the United States of America

TO

ROGER N. BALDWIN

Foreword

The right to dissent has always been a significant aspect of American liberty. But its development has by no means followed a simple course. The tight communities of the first settlements did not tolerate heterodox opinions; and permissiveness with regard to the unorthodox only slowly became characteristic of the eighteenth century. Even when the First Amendment became part of the Bill of Rights, its scope was quite uncertain. And thereafter the freedom to speak out in favor of unpopular religious, political, and economic views has frequently been tested under the stress of crisis.

Banishment has often been a means of extirpating dissent. The Massachusetts Puritans who could not tolerate Anne Hutchinson or Roger Williams or the Quakers, expelled them. But that ready method of dealing with aberrant opinion could not be used as the right of settlement became established and as the concept of citizenship emerged to protect dissenters within the community.

The status of residents who were not citizens remained uncertain, however. Aliens were present in the country on sufferance; it was by no means clear that the safeguards of freedom of expression applied to them. Indeed they had been the special targets of one of the early assaults, under the Republic, upon free speech. The Alien and Sedition Acts had revealed that attacks launched against the foreigners who were incomplete in their rights could also be extended to citizens.

The significance of this study lies in its examination of the problems of the alien and the dissenter. Professor Preston deals with the critical three decades after 1890. In these years of rapid change that culminated in a great war, the fear of the radical and of the foreigner mounted in intensity. Frightened men unwilling to confront the problems of the new America coming into being preferred to blame the difficulties about them on the heretics and the strangers. Such fears ultimately made the alien and the radical scapegoats for the country's ills.

The precedents established in the treatment of the helpless aliens in the 1890's in the course of the next thirty years would be widely applied against radicals. Professor Preston traces the origins and examines the consequences of the restraints on liberty that resulted. His story has significance both for the period it treats and for our own society which still shows the effects of that heritage of intolerance. But his story also shows that many Americans resisted the dominant trend and maintained a view of liberty broad enough to leave dissent unfettered and to protect the rights of aliens. The interplay of the two sets of forces provides the drama of his account.

OSCAR HANDLIN

CONTENTS

Introduction   1

I   The Immigrant as Scapegoat   11

II The I.W.W. Challenge, 1905–1915   35

III Naturalization and a New Law, 1912–1917   63

IV Military Repression, 1917–1921   88

V   The Day in Court, 1917–1920   118

VI A Winter in Seattle, 1917–1918   152

VII The Labyrinth of Deportation, 1918–1919   181

VIII The Red Raids, 1919–1920   208

IX Holding the Line during Normalcy   238

    Epilogue   273

    Bibliographical Note   279

    Notes   287

    Index   347

ALIENS and DISSENTERS

Introduction

On June 25, 1952, President Truman vetoed a restrictive immigration bill, only to see a security-conscious Congress override him on a wave of twentieth-century neo-Know-nothingism. The McCarran-Walter Act empowered the Attorney General to deport "any alien who has engaged or has had a purpose to engage in activities 'prejudicial to the public interest' or 'subversive to the national security.'" In his veto message, Truman noted the lack of judicial guarantees and called attention to the departure from the "traditional American insistence on established standards of guilt. To punish an undefined 'purpose,'" the President said, "is thought control."[1]

The Immigration Act of 1952 as well as the Internal Security Act of 1950 represented, however, not a deviation from, but an adherence to, the antidemocratic treatment often accorded aliens and radicals by the federal government since the 1890's. Although the United States has long been preoccupied with the deportation and jailing of aliens and radicals, historians have given this problem scant attention. In November 1919 and January 1920 federal agents staged a series of dragnet nationwide raids and detained for deportation several thousand alien members of the Union of Russian Workers, the Communist Labor party, and the Communist party.[2] Those dramatic and climactic events, of which A. Mitchell Palmer, then Attorney General, was chief architect, have become notorious as the "red scare." Their sensational character obscured the fact that the road to these incidents had been charted many years before.[3]

The disaster itself has become the explanation for all

succeeding events. Historians have treated the red scare of 1919–20 as largely, if not entirely, the result of World War I and of the Russian Revolution of 1917.[4] The "deportations delirium" or the "Palmer raids" which climaxed the scare have appeared as an aberration, a departure from normal procedures during an unusual period of antiradical fear and hysteria. The nation went wild and helpless radicals were the sudden victims of officials too frightened to do justice. Attorney General A. Mitchell Palmer has been cast as the main protagonist of red hunting. Such interpretations neglect causal developments for a "devil" or "conspiracy" theory of history. To highlight the Palmer raids is to use dramatic effect at the cost of understanding.

The search for perspective, therefore, must come to grips with two interrelated questions about the events of 1919–20. What gave the red scare the intensity it had when it occurred? And why did it take the particular form it did, namely, a mass attack by the federal government on the alien component of the newly organized Communist parties? The government's postwar crusade was evidence of the fear and antipathy directed against all things foreign and subversive. The problem then is to understand how these sentiments and practices developed — both antialien and antiradical — and why the federal policy-makers tended to conflate and identify them.

While the drive against the nation's political and economic heretics had a certain independent existence of its own, it was also one of the themes in the nativist pattern.[5] As a result, the growth of the federal government's concern with internal security became entangled almost inextricably in the rise and fall of nativism. The former cannot be understood without reference to the latter; in fact, the attitude and techniques adopted by the government are witness to the power of nativist stereotypes among federal officials. Still the story is not that simple. The men at Washington proved anxious to move against radicalism without reference to race and national origin but usually lacked the tools to translate this desire into effective action until World War I.

Within the federal government, as within the nation at large, periods of concern with immigration and radicalism fluctuated with times of tolerance and indifference. When America had confidence in its own institutions and in their ability to assimilate ideas and disarm dissent, then the restriction and repression movements died down. "Economic opportunity, social stability, and international security" produced an optimism and apathy that looked benignly on the problems of immigration and unrest.[6] On the other hand, depression, class conflict, increasing social and geographic immobility, war or the threat of it, and other problems of industrial and urban growth developed tensions and fears that sought release in retaliation against the supposed enemy within, alien or radical.[7]

The ability to retaliate on the federal level differed markedly, of course, from what took place at the scene of the crime. United States history since the 1870's was replete with examples of the hysterical and infuriated actions of the mob against various helpless members of the community. But at Washington the passions were less intense, the time element extended, and the opposition able to marshal its forces. The foreign-born and the radical, whatever their local fate, sometimes found fervent supporters in Congress and in the executive branch of government. Thus, the drive to restrict, exclude, and repress reflected not only the cyclical nature of nativism but also the relative strength of two opposing traditions. This struggle was always dramatic, and the outcome was never certain, as the ultimate reaction to the Palmer raids suggested.

At issue was the very nature of American society. Would it remain largely true to its nineteenth-century character — open, mobile, diverse, heterogeneous, fostering dissent, and welcoming ethnic variety? Or would it abandon this liberal and humane Americanism for the 100 per cent variety, which demanded national unity, conformity, homogeneity, uncritical loyalty, and an acceptance of the economic status quo? Those who fought for the nineteenth-century tradition delayed, diverted, and even thwarted the programs developed by their opponents. But in the end the victory belonged with those who would screen both the alien and the radical out of American life.

The precedents that were to facilitate this victory began to be established in the late nineteenth century. Two developments during the depressions of the 1880's and 1890's long influenced federal policy makers. In an upswing of nativism, the country initiated a restriction movement and established with it immigration and deportation procedures of a summary and nonjudicial nature.[8] At about the same time, a fateful and erroneous identification of alien and radical was firmly implanted in the public mind. The basic conservatism of the peasant immigrant, with his yearning for tradition, status, and authority, had little influence against nativist fears of foreign extremism. Nor did the alien's overt and steadfast repudiation of various radical movements soften the stereotype.[9] The influence of this image became obvious at the time of McKinley's assassination, a tragedy that provoked a policy of legislative repression directed solely against the foreign-born that resulted in the Immigration Act of 1903.

The nativist and antiradical upheaval had thus brought about the first important restrictions on the personal liberties of aliens and radicals. In the investigation of opinion among immigrant arrivals and in the deportation of undesirable aliens, the federal government had indicated a hostility to subversive ideas, a demand for conformity, and an insensitivity to the rights of immigrants. The pattern of suppression, however, still had to contend with democratic and Christian ideals of tolerance and welcome that drastically limited the force and scope of federal activity. Reinforced by the prosperity and optimism of the Roosevelt years, this tradition helped to weaken the power of nativism and the fear of social change during the first decade of the twentieth century.

In the lull of the reform era, a new and vigorous labor organization — radical in outlook and uncompromising in spirit — prepared a protest that revived all the former fears. Founded in 1905, the Industrial Workers of the World (I.W.W.) was the largest, and for many years, the most feared radical organization in the country. Whether the "Wobblies" deserved this reputation or rated this attention was beside the point; from then on the federal government saw the internal security problem largely in terms of the I.W.W. threat.

A revival of nativism in the second decade of the century accompanied and exaggerated the I.W.W. rise to national prominence. Once again, therefore, federal policies took on an antialien as well as an antiradical tone. Demands for more stringent deportation and exclusion legislation, for stricter enforcement of the naturalization law, and for the development of much more summary immigration procedures characterized this revived prewar interest in radicals.

In spite of this focus, federal policy did not see radicalism only through nativist eyes. From 1912 to 1917 the government was quite willing to move against all radicals, but it did not yet see the way to do so. In the great strikes of 1877 and 1894, it had sent in troops; these labor disputes had been easy to classify as domestic insurrections. I.W.W. activity never reached that dimension. California's appeals for aid during the Wobbly resurgence of 1912 and 1915 failed to produce any evidence of an offense against such federal laws as the seditious conspiracy statute. Lacking the tools and the emergency conditions that would justify extraordinary procedures, the national administration could only await more propitious circumstances.

This impotence and the opposition arrayed against the passage of more restrictive immigration legislation indicated that powerful forces still inhibited the repressive tendencies in American life. They gained dominance, however, in the wave of nationalism that accompanied the country's entry into World War I. In that struggle the majority insisted on subservient conformity, total loyalty, and 100 per cent Americanism from all members of the community. In this atmosphere the literacy test finally passed as a "phase of national defense" and any radical dissent became a pro-German threat to national survival.[10]

The I.W.W. chose this moment to launch apparently successful organizing drives in several areas of crucial significance to the prosecution of the war. The lumber, copper mining, and grain and fruit areas west of the Mississippi suffered strikes and shutdowns during the summer of 1917. To many, large-scale deportations under new legislation seemed the obvious response. But the Labor Department leadership was unwilling to sanction a widespread resort to the summary processes that the Immigration Bureau had hammered out over the years. Public demands for relief, however, were not to be denied, and these wartime pressures led the more eager branches of the federal government into a series of emergency repressive measures involving illegal intervention of the army and use of the federal courts. At the same time, the Wilson administration further broadened the immigration law to facilitate the expulsion of I.W.W. aliens arrested but not deportable.

The war both fed upon and extended the ideas and techniques to which the federal government had turned in the past. The fervent nativism of the period reaffirmed the mistaken identification of alien and radical and resulted in the Immigration Act of 1918 that made possible the mass character of the later Palmer raids. The Immigration Bureau also rounded up I.W.W. aliens in the Northwest. The bureau's undemocratic and nonjudicial treatment of these immigrants became a determining factor in the evolution of the new policies of 1919–20. But the war also provided an excuse for the much more effective elimination of radicalism by troops and trials, procedures that previously had been sought unavailingly.

The termination of hostilities turned the antiradical crusade toward deportation again. Little else was now available, for the federal government could no longer justify recourse to the army and the courts. This limitation, however, harmonized admirably with the tempo of the times and the desires of certain federal officials. The unexpected survival of wartime Americanism became intensified by the fears of the Russian Revolution, the failures of international cooperation, and the frustrations of social and economic readjustment. Meanwhile, the Department of Justice and Immigration staffs blueprinted a dragnet roundup that combined the historic techniques of the deportation process with the more recently developed practices of the federal detectives.

If the Palmer raids thus were a sacrificial offering to an intense nativism by certain high priests of repression, they were also the unique convergence of two parallel and often complementary traditions. From the 1890's on, the antialien and antiradical movements had established a series of precedents for dealing with the marginal groups in society. This groundwork was of immense aid to the proponents of the red scare. The intensity of those raids reflected the force exerted when the two traditions fused.

In the shocked aftermath of Palmerism, official differences within the government and a revival of public opposition put a stop to any more such roundups. But both the antialien and antiradical forces lived on, though no longer closely identified. Antialienism culminated in the 1924 immigration restriction and quota system and in the return to "business as usual" by the Immigration Bureau. Antiradicalism most clearly survived in the long fight waged by the federal government over the release of political prisoners and the restoration of their civil rights, but it was also apparent in the army's growing concern with domestic disturbances. Franklin D. Roosevelt's Christmas pardon in 1933, restoring the civil rights of the political prisoners of World War I, ended the phase of a red scare that had started so uncertainly nearly half a century earlier.

The I.W.W. was the decisive influence in the evolution of federal policy. The Communists have since become so dominant that it requires imaginative effort to believe in the existence of an indigenous radical organization with such a militant reputation. Emphasis on Communists in the Palmer raids has also obscured the earlier role of the I.W.W. Nevertheless, in eliminating the Wobblies, government officials passed legislation, evolved techniques, and learned lessons that shaped their later course of conduct. In addition the I.W.W. was the only group with large numbers of political prisoners still in jail during the 1920's. The antiradical temperature of the government could be measured by its willingness to release those men. Thus, the relations between the government and the I.W.W. were most significant in the development of policy and most clearly indicate how and why that policy changed.

The decision of the federal government to enforce an increasingly conformist view of what radical thought and words it would tolerate also created perplexing problems for a generation of Americans. The issues then raised are still of crucial contemporary significance in an age whose own methods are rooted in the patterns established before the New Deal.

The dangers involved in the search for loyalty and security clearly revealed themselves in that earlier struggle with radicals. What standards of justice did the government observe in cases where the excited passions of the community were directed against a despised minority? At such times could constitutional guaranties remain effective? The answer was that too often the federal government responded to the demands of class or selfish interest and proceeded against radicals with little regard for due process and the Bill of Rights. But in a system so responsive to political pressure, could the administration at Washington stay aloof from the insistent requests of its supporters? Would it want to, where radicals were involved?

Furthermore, did the investigation and punishment of ideas and opinions prove at all successful — was it even possible? Congress showed itself incapable of defining with any precision the proscribed speech or belief it considered subversive. Nor could the federal legislature impose its intent on the administrative bureau carrying out this policy. As a result, public officials faced the enforcement of vague and indefinite laws. Men with certain preconceptions and standards investigated the beliefs and loyalties of men with differing values and compared their findings with legislation about whose meaning no one was clear. The attempt by government to uncover and analyze the innermost convictions of the human mind was a tragic failure.

Finally, did the suppression of radicals operate in an atmosphere of bureaucratic responsibility? The answer is a decided "no." Top government officials often lacked the power to impose their policies on subordinates. The conduct and customs of immigration inspectors, district attorneys, and army officers were often the controlling factor, a situation which favored local discretion and administrative chaos. In addition, differences of interpretation and interservice rivalry fostered further inconsistency in the antiradical program. The men of that era certainly did not discover how to maintain a standard of justice, a clear and consistent definition of liability, or responsible administration when striking at the free speech of radicals, although many tried painfully to do so.

The nation's controversy with its political and economic heretics has been a long, bitter, and serious conflict, that has not yet ended. It has been waged on the local, state, and federal level by private citizens, volunteer groups, and public officials. The whole of the story cannot be told in these pages. The concern here is with the federal government. Today its increasing authority and police power dominate the field of antiradical surveillance and control so tentatively embarked upon half a century ago. Once confined to an investigation of immigrant arrivals, the screening process now includes thousands of Americans not only in government but in all walks of life. And it affects many others indirectly by making them fearful of dissent, less willing to champion the values of free speech and free thought. A study of the earlier decades may throw into relief the development of the policies and practices from which the present spirit and structure evolved. There is no better place to begin than with the government's treatment of aliens. Had it dealt with them as human beings, it might have handled the radicals in the same way.

I

The Immigrant as Scapegoat

THE Immigration Bureau brought to the deportation of radicals the same abusive tactics used in the apprehension and removal of all aliens. Contemporary observers were aware of the excessive and devious violations of fundamental rights. The roundup of many innocent people, detentions incommunicado, excessive bail, and denial of counsel until confessions had been extorted were not the product of an unusual nationwide postwar hysteria that denied due process to "reds"; the processing of aliens had been growing more and more summary for years. Yet many of the procedures had remained unchallenged, the powers untested, until they were exposed to public scrutiny during the red scare and fully debated for perhaps the first and last time in immigration history.

Due process in deportation was smashed on the rock of judicial decision in 1893, never to be put together again. In *Fong Yue Ting v. United States*, the Supreme Court determined the future pattern of expulsion in one simple interpretation: Deportation was not a punishment for crime but merely an administrative process for the return of unwelcome and undesirable alien residents to their own countries.[1] The United States deported aliens on the grounds of expediency not of crime, not as punishment, but because their presence was "deemed inconsistent with the public welfare."[2]

Some years later, the high court in the *Japanese Immi-*

grant Case reaffirmed the absolute power of Congress to deport aliens summarily and by administrative fiat if it chose. Because of the "extremely informal and summary character of the proceedings which were followed therein," this case remained "the most emphatic decision" limiting the rights of aliens.[3] An alien resided in the United States at the entire sufferance of Congress and became deportable whenever that body classified him as such. It could do so for any reason at any time as "an inherent and inalienable right of every sovereign and independent nation."[4]

Once deportation had been defined as noncriminal, all else followed. The guaranties of the Bill of Rights applied only to persons charged with crime. Expulsion often involved, therefore, long detention, excessively high bail, unreasonable searches and seizures, the denial of counsel, self-incrimination, and trial without jury. It was difficult for an alien under arrest to realize that he was not undergoing a cruel banishment from a country where he had lived for many years. It was even less comprehensible that few of the rights he had come to associate with American judicial practice were available to him. The Fourth, Fifth, Sixth, and Eighth amendments and section 9 of Article I prohibiting ex post facto laws afforded him no protection.

These considerations did not sway the decisions of more than a minority of the Supreme Court justices. Conceivably, the Court might have decided that deportation *was* punishment. In the 1893 case Mr. Justice Brewer's famous dissent flatly asserted: "Deportation is punishment. It involves first an arrest, a deprival of liberty; and second, a removal from home, from family, from business, from property." He presumed that "everyone knows that to be forcibly taken away from home and family, and friends . . . and sent across the ocean to a distant land, is punishment; and that oftentimes the most severe and cruel."[5] Rejecting the concept that the United States has the inherent power to deport aliens in any manner, Mr. Justice Field once said, "Brutality, inhumanity, and cruelty cannot be made elements in any procedure for the enforcement of the laws of the United States." [6] Although the Department of Labor itself had considered deportation "*more severe punishment* than imprisonment," it never allowed this belief to influence its procedure.[7] It stood by the Court.

Supreme Court decisions have sometimes concealed the true nature of reality. For many years a legal fiction absolved the deportation rites of their penal character. If the act of expulsion was not punishment, then almost any administrative implementation of the act was legal. The Court's interpretation has thus opened the way to practices basically at odds with its own definition of due process. Deportation has been "a system of executive justice, with a maximum of powers in the administrative officers, a minimum of checks and safeguards against error and prejudice, and with certainty, care and due deliberation sacrificed to the desire for speed." [8] In a field largely free from judicial and congressional dictation, immigration officials have evolved procedures that guarantee results rather than rights, deportation rather than due process.

Four techniques came to predominate: arrest without warrant; telegraphic application for a warrant of arrest; preliminary hearing; and denial of counsel until a relatively late stage. Adopted informally, these practices became a normal, if not essential, part of deportation. A generation of officials so trained found it difficult to function any other way. Perhaps they could not even remember there was another way.

Both detention without warrant and telegraphic application came into being out of real necessity in certain unique cases. These procedures then became common practice, the immigration inspectors apparently being unable to regulate such contagiously useful devices. According to the rules, the

Washington office issued a warrant only when an inspector had made out a prima facie case against the alien under the immigration law and accompanied the application with "some substantial supporting evidence."⁹ Yet this was entirely too involved and lengthy in cases involving Chinese aliens and immigrants crossing the border. The Chinese were required to produce documentary evidence of their right to be in the country, yet aliens found without this certificate often disappeared while the inspectors awaited legal authority to hold them. It became customary, therefore, to detain Chinese without a warrant of arrest. Similarly in border-crossing cases aliens caught in the act were arrested without warrant.¹⁰

Telegraphic warrants took root in much the same way. Originally the immigration rules cautioned subordinate officials that "telegraphic application may be resorted to *only in case of necessity*" or "when some substantial interest of the government would thereby be served."¹¹ There was a justifiable fear that the telegraphic warrant might prove the instrument of local hysteria and lawlessness or the cloak for individual incompetence. Yet the terminology was broad enough to tolerate the expansion that began in 1908. The Immigration Bureau was then a part of the Department of Commerce and Labor, and its solicitor approved telegraphic warrants for aliens with criminal records. The government feared that the police might release deportable alien criminals before a written application for a warrant of arrest was received at Washington and returned to the local inspector.¹² In the same year Secretary of Commere and Labor Oscar Straus endorsed telegraphic applications for anarchists "in rare instances" of certain deportability.¹³ In so doing the department made possible an irresponsible autonomy susceptible to local pressure for the roundup of radicals. The Washington office could only hope that probable cause for telegraphing a warrant existed, and that the immigration inspector knew what he was doing.

Very early in the history of deportation the alien himself began to supply the "substantial supporting evidence" required by the rules for the warrant of arrest. While local authorities (when possible) "detained" the immigrant, the inspector conducted a "preliminary hearing," at which the individual was encouraged to tell all. This extralegal interview soon overshadowed all other deportation practices. Evidence secured there was usually sufficient to obtain the warrant and to accomplish the deportation as well. No lawyer was present at the "preliminary hearing." [14]

At one time the Bureau of Immigration had considered the interrogation of aliens before their arrest a questionable practice.[15] Doubts as to its legality, however, disappeared in the self-assurance induced by the Supreme Court. Immigration officials relied increasingly on the authority of the *Japanese Immigrant Case* decision, which upheld proceedings "of an extremely informal and summary character." [16] The Court had decided that the hearing reserved to the alien should be "not necessarily an opportunity upon a regular set occasion and according to the form of judicial procedure, but one that will secure the prompt, vigorous action contemplated by Congress." [17]

Immigration officials could hardly be expected to be self-critical when sustained by such high authority. The average inspector pictured himself as the heroic protector of the public welfare, with the immigrant lawyer cast as villain. While the myth of the dishonest counsel may certainly have had some basis in the fact of immigrant exploitation, it was all too easy a rationale for developing a self-incriminating procedure. The hypocrisy and smugness implicit in this stereotype were depicted in a bureau memorandum of 1910. "The reason for holding a preliminary hearing without the presence of counsel," it explained, "is to enable the immigration authorities to ascertain in their own way the true facts without the intervention of the dilatory tactics which some counsel are disposed to employ, including advice often given the alien not to answer questions put by the immigration authorities." After noting that the proceedings were non-criminal and designed "only to determine whether the alien has the right to be in the United States," the report concluded, "It is appropriate to ask him any relevant questions calculated to throw light on the situation, and if he refuses to reply to any such question the fact may be noted and in the discretion of the immigration authorities taken strongly against him." [18]

Once the warrant of arrest had been served, the Immigration Bureau officially took the alien into custody, notified him of the charges, and gave him an opportunity to be heard. According to rule 22 of bureau procedure, at some time during this hearing the inspector had to notify the immigrant of his right to have counsel. Although rule 22 had changed over the years on this point, its most generous stipulation afforded the immigrant legal aid "preferably at the beginning of the hearing under the warrant of arrest or at any rate as soon as such hearing has proceeded sufficiently in the development of the facts to protect the government's interests." [19] The Supreme Court again upheld this procedure, being unable to find it "so arbitrary and so manifestly intended to deprive the alien of a fair, though summary hearing" as to be unconstitutional.[20] The Immigration Bureau, reading the high court's endorsement as moral approval, saw no need to introduce greater justice on its own authority but instead simply avoided gross abuse.[21] As for the alien's attorney, the bureau suggested that his role might be "to correct any possible error or oversight on the part of the immigration authorities." [22]

The hearings themselves were reminiscent of the Star Chamber and the Inquisition. The examining inspector, often legally unqualified, was detective, prosecuting attorney, interpreter, stenographer, and judge. In his bias, eagerness to win a confession, and desire to make a case, the immigration officer played most enthusiastically and convincingly the role of prosecutor. There was no attempt to conform to the rules of courtroom procedure. Thus the file forwarded to Washington for action might contain unsworn statements, ex parte affidavits, inspectors' reports, personal letters, statements of informers, hearsay or opinion evidence, and extraneous material not related to the charges. The examination itself was a fishing expedition into the alien's life, often an abusive and hostile interrogation characterized by vague or leading questions. In defense the immigrant could insist that there be no flagrant misuse of discretion, and that his lawyer be able to cross-examine government witnesses, introduce those of his client, and submit a written brief. At the end of the hearing, the inspector prepared a recommendation for his superiors. This summary might not be based on evidence in the record, and all too frequently indicated a willingness to deport aliens solely on grounds of their general undesirability.[23]

From the detention by local authorities to the transmission of the file for final approval, the alien faced dangers that Judge Learned Hand found "inherent in a system where prosecutor and judge are one and the ordinary rules which protect the accused are in abeyance." It is an easy road, warned the distinguished jurist, "to the disposition of cases without clear legal grounds or evidence which rationally proves them." [24]

The alien could rarely expect his exit from the country to be interrupted by executive or judicial review. While the file sent to Washington passed from a law examiner to the commissioner general of immigration to the Assistant or Acting Secretary of Labor, theirs was a perfunctory review. This rubber-stamping was routine unless a well-contested case came to their attention through a personal appeal. The deportation of aliens thus remained largely the prerogative of the local inspector.[25]

The federal courts usually supported the government and frequently confused the alien by substituting their own judgment about the meaning of the law for that of the Immigration Bureau. The judges construed individual rights narrowly and broadly upheld the rights of sovereignty and public welfare.[26] If there was any evidence at all under any part of the immigration code, expulsion was certain to follow. As to the fairness of the proceedings, the courts required "only the loosest kind of procedural safeguards," and insisted merely that there be no gross abuse of discretion or due process.[27] Furthermore, a successful habeas corpus action by the alien might be only a prologue to a second arrest. Since the proceedings were not criminal, a dismissal did not operate as *res adjudicata*. The Immigration Bureau could and did issue new warrants, while the court often delayed the discharge of the alien until these had been served.[28]

There were few openings and many dead ends in the deportation maze. Most aliens succumbed during the preliminary hearing; those who carried the fight further did so with the odds against them. One historian of deportation has insisted that "the present procedure affords opportunity for deprivation of rights considered fundamental to Anglo-Saxon law where personal liberty is involved." [29] The immigrant arriving at New York City suffered from a delusion. The statue he might have admired did not symbolize the rights and justice afforded aliens by the Constitution and courts of his adopted country.

In the years before World War I, Immigration Bureau customs became steadily more repugnant to normal judicial procedures and to commonsense notions of fair play. There was neither mystery nor conspiracy behind this trend. It was the natural growth of an administrative technique unrestrained by publicity or opposition.

The government tested and applied its malpractices against a steadily increasing group of outcasts — prostitutes, procurers, lunatics, idiots, paupers, persons likely to become a public charge, professional beggars, individuals suffering from a loathsome or dangerous contagious disease, polygamists, epileptics, persons convicted of felony, crime, or misdemeanor involving moral turpitude, and Chinese and Japanese.[30] These were in the main friendless, despised, ignorant, defenseless people, and, more important, *unorganized*. While anarchists were deportable after 1903, they only had the semblance of organization. As the Immigration Bureau discovered later, "Real anarchists are usually associated together, if at all, simply in groups or gatherings which have no constitution . . . and no officers other than a Secretary and Treasurer." [31] And for various reasons there were very few anarchist cases that might possibly have called into play a vigorous defense by these semiorganized radicals. Thus, the Department of Commerce and Labor and the local inspectors operated almost without check and largely without public notice in the development of the distasteful methods that caused such an outcry after the war. The aliens rounded up had failed to make the protests that might have advertised the procedure and forced its reconsideration by the government.

The alien fared better in the prewar period than he would after 1917. Despite ever-increasing administrative inflexibility, the law itself provided some protections that were later abandoned. Immigration legislation still possessed a minimum number of vague standards and terms. It was quite certain whether an immigrant was or was not a prostitute, a pauper, or an individual afflicted with a loathsome contagious disease. An alien was therefore aware of what brought him within the law. "Liable to become a public charge" and "crimes involving moral turpitude" were the only clauses that defied clear and consistent interpretation.

Furthermore, specific time limits defined the duration of the alien's liability. No one could be wrenched from family and friends if he survived one-, then two-, and later, three-year probation. This minimized as well the menace of nebulous phrases. The later abolition of all time restrictions and the increase of indefinite standards placed immigrants on permanent parole, the conditions of which are not fully disclosed.[32]

The immigration inspector also preferred the calmer and less complicated prewar years. Dealing with resigned, docile individuals whose deportability was easily established, he had relatively few administrative problems. Armed with a signed confession, he firmly believed that deportation could be prompt and vigorous. He had but slight familiarity with the interpretation of vague standards, and he had not dealt with many aliens of long residence. He was thus singularly ill-equipped by training and experience for the coming struggle with radicals.

Often without legal background, the inspector was not prepared to appreciate either the fine distinctions within the same radical philosophy or the distinguishing features among different radical beliefs. If he could, he still had to decide which were legal actions or thoughts according to the law. The few scattered anarchist cases before 1917 supplied him with little practical knowledge of the operations of radicals under fire.

By 1917 a procedure and a state of bureaucratic mind had developed within the Immigration Bureau. When government officials so oriented met radicals, always sensitive to persecution and tenacious of their rights, it was not surprising that the struggle should be poisoned by misunderstanding, fear, and hatred on both sides. Only the time of the contest remained in doubt.

That it came at the end of World War I was a result of numerous factors. Among them the most important was probably the radical's growing estrangement from his fellow Americans. They had not always singled him out for such hostile attention. But beginning in the late nineteenth century, the tide of repression seemed to surge more forcefully and ebb less completely at each succeeding phase of reaction. Had this development been directed solely against the radical, it would have been unnecessary and unfortunate enough. But contrary to the realities of American life, the foreigner became identified as extremist. Nativism thus tended to focus federal policies on immigration, and the alien began to carry the double burden of his foreign birth and of his trumped-up radicalism.

II

In 1886 in the United States, the anarchist movement died.[33] Seventeen years later a frightened Congress passed the first federal legislation designed to suppress this movement by cutting off its immigrant supporters.[34] This law and others like it that followed had their tragic connotations, for however irrational the fears this legislation symbolized, they represented a real loss of nerve and of faith in the virtue of freedom.

It had been many years since the federal government had felt that the country's safety and self-preservation required an attack on the radical dissenter. Apart from the notably unsuccessful Alien and Sedition Acts of 1798, Congress had maintained a tradition of tolerance, yet the seed of repression and the growth it might take lay buried in the American soil throughout the confident decades after 1798.[35]

The fear of "treasonable or secret machinations against the government" during the French crisis of that year had led the Federalist government to pass antialien legislation.[36] Based on the mistaken conservative theory that foreigners were more dangerously extreme than native-born Americans, the Alien Act of 1798 gave the President power to deport

those foreign agitators he deemed a threat to the welfare
and security of the country. What was more, the chief executive could expel an alien "without accusation, without public
trial, without confrontation of witnesses, without defense,
and without counsel." Such summary procedure followed
naturally from the idea that "those who corrupt our opinion
. . . are the most dangerous of all enemies." Precedent for a
nationalistic response to internal insecurity had now been
established. Class-oppressed foreigners, the tradition asserted, were quick to support demands for revolutionary
change. Ignorant of American ways and bred on the European propensity for violence, the immigrant would supposedly resort to license and disorder to achieve his ends.[37]

The Alien Act of 1798 became famous not for the expulsion of foreigners (none were expelled) but for the deportation of the Federalist party from its position of power in
American politics. As the Kentucky and Virginia resolutions
so vehemently pointed out, the unconstitutional and despotic
Alien Act "subverted the general principles of free government." [38] The Federalist, not the foreigner, was the real
alien. Within two years the discredited act had expired, and
with it went the idea of removing those aliens whose views
or political commitments made them "dangerous to the public peace or safety." [39]

Developed during the French crisis, the alien-radical
stereotype soon faded in the face of America's material
growth and geographic expansion. The European laborer
was only too welcome during these years of supposedly
endless opportunity. "For many decades confidence in the
stability of American institutions and in their appeal to all
mankind quieted nationalistic fears of revolution." [40] Only
the influx of German refugees from the upheaval of 1848
shook such self-confidence — and that only briefly and on
a limited scale.

Much more serious were the social and economic changes

of the late 1870's. These transformations revived the latent fear of radicalism, stimulated a new wave of nativism, and furthered the faulty assumptions of 1798. That the United States should single out the alien as an enemy of opinion in 1903 was, therefore, a not unexpected aftermath of such years of tension. But it was ironic that the average immigrant — a staunch upholder of tradition and authority in his castle of conservatism — should be a scapegoat for the radicalism in American life.

The nervousness that gave rise to repression stemmed from the problems left unsolved by an increasingly industrial and urban society. The slums, corruption, and lawlessness in the city and the discontent, labor strife, and exploitation in the industrial community coincided with three apparently fundamental challenges to the Jeffersonian image of America: a series of business depressions, the closing of the frontier, and massive waves of immigration. All these seemed to endanger the historic opportunity, mobility, and material expansion that had long been considered crucial to social stability.

The nativist resurgence had similar origins in the problems of modern capitalism. So many of its evils paralleled the alien influx that it was easy to associate one with the other. The causal connection so loosely established had only the slimmest relation to reality, yet the idea that foreign influence was subverting the promise of American life grew steadily in the 1880's and came to a climax in the economic crisis of the mid-1890's. The first restriction legislation in 1882, discrimination against aliens with public works jobs, increasing pressure for a literacy test, the formation and extension of the anti-Catholic American Protective Association, and development of racist attitudes were indicative of the growing nativist hysteria.[41]

The suppression of radicals during these decades reflected the strength of such emotions — but only in part. Other techniques not representing any antiforeign feelings at all also helped preserve the status quo. As nativism gained strength, however, its influence became more significant at the federal level. Since the country's historic policies of welcome and tolerance were still difficult to change, national antiradical legislation was slow to take shape. The end result of these diverse factors was the Immigration Act of 1903, penalizing a radicalism that was no longer influential and an alien population that had never been radical.

The first of the great industrial crises to test the country's self-restraint was the depression of 1873–1877. Those years witnessed the desperate, spontaneous strikes and riots of the city unemployed and the revolts of armed miners. In Pennsylvania, the Molly Maguires challenged the coal operators on their own terms, terror, and lost. In 1877 the fuse of depression restlessness and exploitation sputtered and caught fire along the railroad network of the country. Many large railheads became battlefields between strikers and militia.[42]

Force dominated both the state and federal reactions to these disturbances, but nativist suggestions also made their appearance. The militia units, proving quite unreliable, found additional support in the federal troops dispatched by President Hayes. When the trains were again running on time, state authorities determined to repair their own defenses. While urging the national administration to build up the regular army and to garrison it in industrialized areas, the states also took steps to establish an effective antiradical National Guard. "The primary reason for its revival was to provide the states with a means whereby their 'laws may be enforced, social order maintained and [protection afforded] against the sudden violence of popular faction.' " Repression of "popular faction" was to be the Guard's *raison d'être* during the tumultuous years ahead.[43]

The 1877 strike revitalized as well a virile but passing phobia toward foreign radicals. A narrow focus on the Irish in the Molly Maguires, on the few union leaders of alien birth, and on the scattered radicals among foreign-born strikers encouraged the idea broadcast by the New York *Herald* that "the railroad riots were instigated by men incapable of understanding our ideas and principles." [44] The reassertion of governmental authority and the continued confidence in the invulnerable superiority of American capitalism soon quieted fears of an alien overthrow. The anti-radicalism of the 1870's thus remained largely free from the nativistic overtones of the next two decades.

The depression of the 1880's, culminating so tragically in the Haymarket riot of 1886, was a historical watershed that sent anarchism into oblivion and raised nativism to new heights. It was a turbulent period. Because of the many strikes — the most noteworthy those of the Knights of Labor — this era has been called "The Great Upheaval." Nearly four hundred thousand workers joined in the movement for an eight-hour day in 1886.[45]

Flourishing socialist and anarchist groups exaggerated the radical nature of the labor unrest. From 1876 to 1880 the Socialist Labor party built up a membership of ten thousand supported by twenty-four newspapers and directed by men who could win election to public office. After 1878 both socialists and anarchists bored from within the Knights of Labor often exercising a dominating influence and giving the Knights in certain areas a very definite radical character. The 1880 split in the Socialist Labor party committed its revolutionary wing to the embrace of the anarchist Bakunin's "Black International," under the leadership of the recently arrived Johann Most. This German agitator for violent anarchism dominated the Pittsburgh Congress of 1883, which demanded the "destruction of the existing class rule, by all means, *i.e.*, by energetic, relentless, revolutionary and international action." [46] The depression beginning in that same year magnified the membership of all these groups, but most significantly that of the anarchists. In 1885 they numbered seven thousand organized in eighty localities.[47]

Then the anarchist movement passed through the crucible of 1886: the strike for the eight-hour day at the McCormick reaper plant outside Chicago, the workers killed by police, the protest meeting at Haymarket Square called by the anarchists, the bomb, the public hysteria, the conviction of eight anarchists, the hanging of four. When it was all over, "the back of the movement was broken." Thereafter, anarchism was Emma Goldman and Alexander Berkman, a small colony outside Tacoma, a dying Johann Most, a crazed assassin of McKinley, a few Italian anarchists clustered as contributors and subscribers around Galleani and the *Cronaca Sovversiva*, some rebels in the I.W.W., here and there a bookstore selling anarchist literature, and a few individualistic Tolstoyans. After 1886, "anarchism faded away completely as a political force in America." [48]

If the Haymarket riot finished off anarchism, it also created nativist stereotypes that lasted for many years and helped implant in the public mind the distorted image of the subversive foreigner. Although the bomb thrower of 1886 was never found, the community and the courts convicted the anarchists. In the future imagery of fear, "a ragged, unwashed, long-haired, wild-eyed fiend, armed with smoking revolver and bomb — to say nothing of the dagger he sometimes carried between his teeth" was to represent the anarchist at work. "No nativist image prevailed more widely than that of the immigrant as a lawless creature given over to violence and disorder." [49]

The apprehensions aroused in the 1880's were further inflamed by both the economic crisis and the haphazard violence of the following decade. With three million unemployed and capital as intransigeant as ever, industrial warfare reached a new peak of drama. Henry Clay Frick and the Carnegie Steel Company locked out the workers at Homestead in 1892 and brought up reinforcements. Three Pinkertons and seven strikers later, the workers had won the first battle, but Frick won the war. The Pullman strike of 1894, which Eugene Debs called "a contest between the producing classes and money power of the country," further underscored the bitter seriousness of the struggle between capital and labor. There were other strikes as well — many of them equally bloody, all part of the same unrest that sent armies of unemployed workers onto the nation's roads.[50]

During these same years anarchist terror reinforced the memory of Haymarket. Assassination in Europe took the lives of a king, a queen, a prime minister, and a president, as if designed to include the whole spectrum of governmental leadership in its attack. In 1892 Alexander Berkman assaulted Henry Clay Frick, reactionary manager of the Carnegie Steel Company, during the Homestead strike. With gun and dagger, the young Russian-born anarchist had hoped to publicize the exploitation of the workers by the murder of their expropriator.[51]

While falling back on the historic technique of military repressions in the face of such serious problems, the nation also turned more frequently to proposals for punitive legislation directed against the foreigner. In 1892 five states turned out the National Guard against the strikers, while federal troops helped overawe and disperse the railroad men at Chicago two years later. However successful these expedients, their temporary nature failed to relieve tensions made intense by nativist fears. In spite of the fact that there were fewer radicals than ever among the foreign-born, their presence seemed more and more dangerous to congressional lawmakers.[52]

During the fifteen years between the bomb at Chicago and the murder of McKinley at Buffalo, federal legislation aimed periodic but unsuccessful shots at the anarchist menace. In 1888 Congressman Adams, representing the Haymarket area, proposed the "removal of dangerous aliens from the territory of the United States." A year later Senator Mitchell would have excluded from the country anyone "who is an avowed anarchist or nihilist, or who is personally hostile to the principles of the Constitution . . . or to the form of government of the United States." Immigration legislation in 1891 and 1893 contained proposals for the exclusion of anarchists as individuals and as members of anarchistic societies. All of these suggestions, however, either died in committee or were dropped from the bills as finally passed.[53]

On June 26, 1894, the House of Representatives voted to adjourn so that it might pay its respects to the memory of President Carnot of France, the most recent victim of anarchist violence in Europe. As one member of Congress observed, the House harbored "not merely, personal grief and anxiety for the wanton murder of a good man," but also felt the graver apprehension that occurs "when social disorder is threatened in so many places." Symbolic of this fear was the bill to exclude and deport alien anarchists then under consideration by both branches of Congress, unanimously supported by the respective committees of the House and Senate, and strongly backed by the administration.[54]

Without defining the term "anarchist" the bill afforded great latitude to administrative officials in excluding and removing aliens that came to their attention. The superintendent of immigration could deport, for example, any anarchist whom he considered "a menace to the government or to the peace and well being of society in general." Despite the vague criteria, the Senate passed this legislation without delay.[55]

The proponents of immigration restriction in the House were unable to match the speed and decisiveness of the Senate. As time ran out at the end of August, the House still waited to consider the bill. The opposition refused to approve it unless the meaning of "anarchist" was more thoroughly explained and until the power of immigration officials was

more closely circumscribed. In 1895 and 1897 Senator
Chandler of New Hampshire introduced legislation to exclude alien anarchists, but these proposals never got out of
committee.[56]

The failure of this early antiradical legislation revealed the
continuing strength of some old American traditions and the
geographic limits of the suppression movement. Its proponents represented the urban-industrial communities of the
North and East, and their demands for action often did not
outlive the hysteria of their constituencies. As Senator Burrows himself recalled after the Haymarket riot, "When the
anarchists were tried, condemned and hanged by the Cook
County authorities, the outraged feelings of the people were
temporarily satisfied and the demand for general national
legislation against the whole body of anarchists infecting this
country, which manifested itself in localities, again subsided." [57] In addition, neither the South nor the West were
as yet fully committed to nativist attitudes and immigration
restriction. With the defeat of Bryan and the revival of prosperity, a reassured and more confident America temporarily
put aside the search for a foreign scapegoat.

The historic belief in freedom of opinion also checked the
antiradical drive. The national could float in the currents of
hysteria without drifting into the shoals of repressive legislation. Other stumbling blocks were the legislators' inability to
agree on a definition of anarchy and a distaste for approving
such undefined terms where administrators exercised much
power.[58]

Without some new reminder of the danger of anarchist
violence, the immigrant might have escaped congressional
attention in the ten years after 1897. These were times when
"the acquisition of an empire fortified the confidence revived
by prosperity, by relief from class conflict, and by a psycho-
logically invigorating war." [59] Yet history was ready to under-
mine this buoyant optimism, for waiting in the wings was

the mentally unbalanced murderer of McKinley, Leon F. Czolgosz, who fatally wounded the President at Buffalo, New York, on September 6, 1901. Ironically, the symbol of anarchism for a generation of Americans had only the briefest and most shadowy association with it. Just enough, in fact, to make his public identification as its executioner plausible to a people reared on the Haymarket riot, the European assassinations, and the career of Alexander Berkman.[60]

The ceremonial rites by which the nation then sought to absolve its responsibilities for the death of McKinley soon manifested themselves. Local police apprehended anarchists, mobs assaulted radicals, and several states passed criminal-anarchy laws. If these were the immediate and excessive convulsions of popular disgust, they also had the transitory quality of such seizures. By 1904 "the issue as a whole ceased to be of public interest." On the other hand, federal legislation inspired by the assassination of McKinley permanently paralyzed a formerly vigorous libertarian immigration policy. The United States was on the road back to 1798.[61]

Federal proposals to curb anarchism fell into two major categories: those seeking to safeguard the President and other high officials from any attack by drastically increasing the penalties for such action, whether successful or not; and those attempting to make such attacks impossible through immigration restrictions. The first assumed that there were citizens as well as aliens whom the law would deter. In this group of projected laws were bills to suppress anarchism, punish anarchism, amend the Constitution to suppress anarchism, punish anarchistic killing, and amend the Constitution to declare anarchism treason. The other line of legislation presumed that the menace was entirely alien and favored the exclusion, deportation, and nonnaturalization of all immigrant anarchists.[62]

The latter bills represented the denial of reality. They ignored the native birth of Czolgosz as well as the unsubstantial character of his contacts with the anarchist movement. What was worse, such legislative proposals renovated the shabby fallacies of nativism and perpetuated the myth of the alien assassin.

The man whom Czolgosz made President also presented detailed and vigorous recommendations for the suppression of anarchism, in part anticipating the future direction of immigration legislation. Believing that "we should war with relentless efficiency not only against anarchists, but against all active and passive sympathizers with anarchists," Theodore Roosevelt set forth a three-point program in his annual message to Congress of December 3, 1901.[63] As the initial tactic in the "war," the President proposed the exclusion of "all persons who are known to be believers in anarchistic principles or members of anarchistic societies. The second object of a proper immigration law," he suggested, "ought to be to secure by a careful and not merely perfunctory educational test some intelligent capacity to appreciate American institutions and act sanely as American citizens." According to Roosevelt this literacy test would "tend to decrease the sum of ignorance so potent in producing the envy, suspicion, malignant passion, and hatred of order out of which anarchistic sentiment inevitably springs." The President struck finally at the environment itself as a cause of anarchism. He advocated "a certain standard of economic fitness" to bar the cheap labor that settled in the slums and gave birth to the "pestilential social conditions in our great cities, where anarchistic organizations have their greatest possibility of growth." [64]

The federal lawmakers transformed this feast of solutions into a famine of results. When Congress adjourned in March 1903, it had agreed only to exclude and deport and not to naturalize certain categories of anarchists. Unwilling to limit debate and unable to agree on a compromise measure without it, the Senate let the bills punishing domestic anarchism die as time ran out.[65] Nor did Congress act upon Roosevelt's proposals for a literacy and economic fitness test, the first not becoming law until 1917.[66]

In the Immigration Act of 1903, the United States for the first time excluded certain immigrants because of their beliefs and associations.[67] Section 2 made "anarchists, or persons who believe in or advocate the overthrow by force and violence of the Government of the United States, or of all government, or of all forms of law, or the assassination of public officials" ineligible for entry. Section 38 prohibited the admission of anyone "who disbelieves in or who is opposed to all organized government, or who is a member of or affiliated with any organization entertaining and teaching such disbelief in or opposition to all organized government," and also barred any proponent of official assassination.[68] Congress did not exclude, however, an individual who believed in or advocated the overthrow by force and violence of any government. Senator Hoar forced the retraction of this provision because of his belief that "there are governments in the world that ought to be overthrown by force and violence." [69]

Any alien who slipped into the country as an anarchist or became one after he arrived was deportable if arrested within three years of the date of his entry. Succeeding legislation in 1907 and 1910 did not change the time limit. This restriction represented the then current belief that the expulsion of a person after a residence of three years was an unfair hardship. It signified as well the willingness of a country still relatively unafraid and humane to accept responsibility for the views acquired by an alien in his adopted home. The government assumed that conditions might well determine beliefs, and it hesitated to banish individuals who were victims of forces beyond their control. The departure from this position would constitute a major ideological retrogression of the succeeding years.[70]

The great wave of anarchist arrests, which some lawmakers confidently expected, never materialized. From 1903 until 1921, the United States excluded only thirty-eight persons for holding anarchistic beliefs,[71] while it deported a mere fourteen aliens of the anarchistic classes from 1911 until 1919, when the red scare deportations began.[72]

The Department of Commerce and Labor, worrying about its poor showing in this field, exhaustively surveyed the nationwide condition of anarchy in 1908. Circularizing every major immigration station and working with the Secret Service and local chiefs of police, the Immigration Bureau sought to uncover deportable resident radicals.[73] The response was overwhelmingly negative. Twenty-three areas reported no cases at all, and some four districts discovered a handful of anarchists who had lived in the country longer than three years. Along with the exclusion and deportation figures for succeeding years, it was indicative of the small role played by anarchist immigrants in the subversion of American life, and suggested that millions of alien arrivals then as in the nineteenth century were bringing with them and cherishing the basic conservatism of their peasant background.[74]

At the end of Theodore Roosevelt's term in office, the menace of anarchy was more fancied than real. What the President had heatedly and excitedly called "the enemy of humanity, the enemy of all mankind" was not a visible threat — in fact not even visible in many American communities. Although Roosevelt thought that "when compared with the suppression of anarchy, every other question sinks into insignificance," it seemed in 1908 in America that anarchy itself had become insignificant.[75] Yet it had left its mark for posterity in the cement of antialien legislation.

In the shock of sudden violence, Congress had sponsored for the first time since 1798 the exclusion and deportation of aliens whose views it deemed inimical to the general peace

and security of the country. But Czolgosz, like the conspirators at Sarajevo, was only the immediate cause. The crises
of the 1880's and 1890's had developed a deep distrust of
foreigners, and this nativism lying latent during the good
times of McKinley responded quickly to the fears awakened
by his death. How irrational and useless this response had
been. It hardly seemed possible that the disordered and
fanatical assassin would be touched by general legislation of
this kind. The idea that radicalism was a child of foreign
birth, however, might well prove to be a narcotic to which
legislators would become addicted in the future.

In the immediately succeeding years, this seemed doubtful.
The general sense of social and economic well-being was
quick to reassert itself in the vigorous times of Theodore
Roosevelt. The literacy test now faced much stronger opposition, progressivism had little quarrel with foreigners, and
immigrants seemed welcome again. Nativism was in obvious
decline.[76]

Before its reappearance, a new radical organization, the
Industrial Workers of the World, rose to challenge the status
quo. Would the country react to the Wobblies as it had to
the threat of anarchism? The immigrant as scapegoat had
symbolized the irrational nature of that earlier retaliation.
What pattern would the members of the I.W.W. evoke?
Would they frighten a perplexed and hostile nation into laws
and practices that extended the policy of 1903 or turned it
into new and more effective channels?

II

The I.W.W. Challenge

1905–1915

"Our duty," the speaker told an excited gathering of New York City workers, "is to compile the category of crimes perpetrated by the capitalist class." The hulking figure on the platform talked with the quiet but intense conviction that made him at one with his audience. Two hundred and seven miners had died that January night in 1912 from a mine explosion in Bryceville, Tennessee. Such events were "murder with the connivance or deliberate negligence of the capitalist class," which considered "human life cheaper than safety devices." [1]

If this crude, provocative language seemed to invert traditional morality, it was because the man and the crowd did not look at life through the plate glass window of a fashionable club. The man was William D. Haywood, the dynamic leader of the class-conscious, revolutionary Industrial Workers of the World, an organization which was at that very moment leading some thirty thousand unskilled textile workers to unexpected victory in a strike against the American Woolen Company at Lawrence, Massachusetts. [2]

The listeners were part of the unorganized and exploited wage-earning class, of whom thirty-five thousand could expect to die annually in industrial accidents. Ignored by the

American Federation of Labor, the unskilled felt the reality of the class struggle as no others could. Their strikes for improvement of conditions almost inevitably became "revolutions against industrial oppression." [3] And they could understand a labor leader who denounced the wage system as worse than slavery, who called the government a tool of the industrial empire, who placed the courts on the side of the capitalists, and who named the law as a thing to be despised.[4]

As it absorbed the optimism of Haywood that night, the audience might easily have sensed the proximity of the utopian society. The victory at Lawrence was to make the I.W.W. famous in a year full of organizing and propaganda successes. Socialist strength rising more like a flood than a tide looked as if it would permanently inundate industrial America. Perhaps it was time to stop compiling the crimes of capitalism and get on with the execution. No one could have foreseen that this 1912 meeting was solemnizing the senescence rather than the ripe maturity of these two movements. At the time each seemed destined for a brilliant future.[5]

By the second decade of the twentieth century, many people had become convinced that progressive reform was not solving the complex problems of American capitalism. Machine technology and large-scale corporate enterprise continued to develop injustices toward great portions of the population, subjected to severe maladjustments in the economy. The actualities of life in America were still ugly and convincing. Two per cent of the population owned 60 per cent of the wealth, while 65 per cent of the people were left to divide some 5 per cent among themselves. So tenuous was labor's position that even the most highly skilled worker with all his A.F. of L. gains had no reserves for unforeseen misfortunes. One third to one half of the population lived at a near-starvation level. Not only did a large majority of the industrial army fail to receive a fair share of the national wealth and income or the opportunity to earn a living, but it found itself as well unable to receive justice "in the creation, adjudication, and administration of the law." [6]

By transforming the old worker-master relation, machine production had also created the displaced persons of technology, a friendless, helpless, and easily replaceable horde. These refugees became the indentured servants of capitalism, bound either to the company town or to the migratory harvest. No labor union interrupted the dreary security of their poverty or the endless fatigue of their toil, for the A.F. of L. concerned itself with the aristocratic fringe of skill.

That such evils remained a part of American life after ten years of progressive reform was an indication of the nature of that movement. It had been staffed by those middle-class professional men, small capitalists, independent farmers, and white-collar workers who had become conscious of their own precarious position. They saw the growth of tenant farming, the increasing domination of the trust, and the monopoly of money by two New York banking syndicates as the barricades of a plutocratic America across the old avenues of opportunity. Nor could these problems be attacked so long as the corrupt alliance between business and politics existed and government on all levels granted special privileges to wealth. The muckraking movement had made the middle class increasingly aware of this situation by advertising the cold statistics of corporate expansion and political graft in the dramatic propaganda of exposés. By helping to destroy the reverential acceptance of the old truths of classic capitalism, the muckrakers had thus developed a middle-class outlook that was more and more sympathetic to change.[7]

Yet this search for the essence of the good society during the relaxed first decade of the twentieth century had been both cautious and conservative, led by a skilled elite of the A.F. of L. and by the progressive movement. Each of these groups accepted the basic institutions of capitalism and private property while limiting its attack to various inequalities and privileges within this framework. Each sought the restoration of status (in one case of opportunity, in the other of security) that had been destroyed by monopoly capitalism.[8] Middle- and upper-class progressives had been anxious to restore the economic opportunities and responsible politics that they thought characterized the earlier age of democratic individualism. With their white collars buttoned on firmly, progressives had marched "as swift as respectable reform could hurry, away from conservatism."[9] Since they largely represented the spectrum of society on the right side of the tracks, they fought to harness irresponsible power more nearly to the general welfare, not to destroy the power itself.

There were, however, groups willing to challenge the basic principles of a capitalist community. The age of reform was also the "golden age of American socialism."[10] A large and heterogeneous assortment of critics found a home, albeit often a temporary one, within the Socialist party. They agreed that mere tinkering with the machinery was not enough. Many of these communicants were not true believers in Marxism. What attracted them was much less socialism's "cold, rational analysis of society" than its "moral indignation at poverty and the evangelical promise of a better world."[11] These were the early days of the faith, however, and diversity was tolerated for the sake of success. Socialism had not yet had its Reformation. In 1912 it constituted the left-wing element of reform whose right was held by the progressives. A similar situation prevailed in labor where the I.W.W. played the revolutionary foil to Gompers' steadfast moderation.[12]

In the age of reform, the promise of speedy and fundamental change was more alluring for many people than the achievement of tedious and limited progress. It was in this context that the I.W.W. recruited the outcasts of Gompers' craft clubhouse and welded them into an organization that uniquely combined the practice of industrial unionism with the preaching of revolutionary ideals. The Wobblies shot across the firmament of reform brilliantly and erratically. During a brief but memorable solidarity, they followed their program with a militant and daring disregard for the conventional mores. The Wobblies were also searching for the good society, but with an intensity and recklessness that frightened and angered the world around them.

The I.W.W. made its move, moreover, at the very time when progressive reform was developing new anxieties in American life. By 1910 the promise of further change frightened the conservative right, while the failure to reconstruct society more thoroughly embittered the radical left. The widespread restlessness that had nurtured nativism in the past seemed ready to do so again. To send conservatives and reformers into "hysterical recoil" in this atmosphere would not be difficult. The Wobblies thus evoked a further pattern of suppression during the tense twilight of Wilsonian progressivism.[13]

II

Organized at Chicago in June 1905, the I.W.W. hoped to create a labor-union equivalent of the Socialist party. This founding convention had been "like a meeting of *Meistersingers*, [with] almost every major radical voice in America . . . represented." [14] Chairman William D. Haywood pictured the meeting as the "Continental Congress of the working class," whose purpose would be to place that group "in possession of the economic power, the means of life, in control of the machinery of production and distribution, without regard to capitalist masters." [15] The I.W.W. preamble restated these objectives in more emphatically extravagant terms: "The working class and the employing class have nothing in common. There can be no peace so long as hunger and want are found among millions of working people and the few, who make up the employing class, have all the good things of life . . . Between these two classes a struggle must go on until the workers of the world organize as a class, take possession of the earth and the machinery of production, and abolish the wage system . . . It is the historic mission of the working class to do away with capitalism." [16]

The preamble set the tone, but not the extent, of the rebellious Wobbly propaganda. The I.W.W. framed its opposition to capitalism in vivid, inflammatory Marxist prose that threatened "to use any and all tactics" to overthrow the existing economic system.[17] I.W.W.'s refused to consider the question of right or wrong when that problem was phrased by capitalists: the worker was right from his point of view, wrong from theirs. That was not the point. The point was: who was going to control the machines, and for whose benefit? [18]

Since the ultimate aim of the labor movement was the destruction of capitalism, the I.W.W. rejected the trade agreement or union contract that made a general strike impossible and recognized that "the bosses" had some rights.[19] The organization also discarded the A.F. of L. theory of the "identity of interest" between labor and capital as being theoretically absurd and practically suicidal.[20] No union should make agreements to cooperate with the enemy. In a class struggle, constant revolutionary agitation by striking was to prepare the way for the final overthrow.[21]

In the achievement of this day-to-day crippling of capitalism, the I.W.W. approved of any "militant 'direct action' it had the power to enforce." [22] "Direct action" in its broad meaning included any acts of the working class at the site of employment calculated to force concessions from the boss. Peaceful strikes and picketing were mild forms of such activity. The general strike, slowdowns in production, sabotage, and theoretically, at the right moment, revolution itself, were alternative weapons.[23]

The field in which the I.W.W. operated demanded direct

action rather than conciliation, for industrial and migratory workers could not "follow the same diplomatic and slow procedure" as a skilled craft union,[24] which had its skill and financial reserves. The Wobbly, ever fearful of strikebreakers and bankruptcy, needed swift and forceful action to win. In addition he usually faced an employer equally prepared to use any and all tactics to break the strike. The I.W.W. suggested that force and violence would meet force and violence.

Behind the bold façade of its revolutionary rhetoric, the I.W.W. carried on its "pork-chop unionism," the tight-lipped, deadly earnest desire for concrete gains. When the Industrial Relations Commission asked Haywood why he had fought for the unskilled poor, the one-eyed ex-miner replied, "I talked for the necessities of life, food, clothing, shelter, and amusement." He added, "We can talk of Utopia afterwards; the greatest need is employment." [25] At the first convention Haywood had promised, "We are going down in the gutter to get at the mass of workers and bring them up to a decent plane of living." [26] The I.W.W. hoped to provide it by organizing the unskilled worker into "one big union," industry by industry.

That program, set in its Marxist framework, would have sufficed to stereotype the Wobblies as radical and un-American. But the I.W.W. did not stop there. As if impelled to be "an organization which derided all . . . [the] fond moralities," it rejected the church and the flag as the dishonest tools of the exploiting class.[27] The "long-haired preachers" that offered "pie in the sky when you die" betrayed the workers' fight against the capitalists by inculcating a slavish acceptance of the status quo.[28]

The Wobblies had a flag, a red one, and they urged the workers to "live and die . . . beneath the scarlet standard high." [29] What could patriotism mean to them? "Of all the idiotic and perverted ideas accepted by the workers from that class who live upon their misery, patriotism is the worst," the I.W.W. declared. In a mockingly caustic analysis, the organization alleged that "a patriotic working stiff is the nearest approach to an effect without a cause that is today known to science." The emotional responses of modern nationalism were not always evoked in the day-to-day conditioning of unskilled workers. A Wobbly editor suggested why: "Love of country? They have no country. Love of flag? None floats for them. Love of birthplace? No one loves the slums. Love of the spot where they were reared? Not when it is a mill and necessity cries ever 'move on'. Love of mother tongue? They know but the slave driver's jargon whose every word spells wearisome toil followed by enforced idleness." [30]

As if to make its alienation from the community complete, the organization never replaced the extremism of youth with the conservatism of middle age. Rightly or wrongly, most unions adjusted to the presence of a restraining and unfriendly middle class by abandoning the violent methods of industrial combat and softening the invective of class war. Recognizing that the "public" was committed to the ideology of labor's enemies, most unions felt the need to go slowly, to refrain from any hint of violence, and to bargain cautiously, respectfully, and tactfully with their employers. An admission of weakness, this tactic embodied a chameleon wisdom that sought survival by changing with the "social topography." [31] The I.W.W. never made this reconciliation. It stubbornly and defiantly maintained its original revolutionary zeal. This eventually made the Wobblies the easiest and most noticeable scapegoat for the antilabor and antiradical passions of the country.

A series of schisms also furthered the commitment to a class-conscious, rebellious unionism. From 1905 through 1908 the cold blasts of internal dissension kept burning off the doctrinal disagreements until the I.W.W. emerged pure and hard, but unable to bend. In the process, the so-called "proletarian rabble" or "bummery" of the West became the dominant element. Since the unskilled migratory Westerners favored direct economic pressure, the I.W.W. became more and more hostile to politics of any kind, including Socialist politics. In 1908, the Wobblies prohibited all political action; the "overall brigade" had triumphed, and thereafter its philosophy of anarcho-syndicalism characterized I.W.W. policy.[32]

Spread over the vastness of the territory west of the Mississippi, the I.W.W. had become less a stable union than a revolutionary cadre whose ranks swelled and diminished with the spectacular crises of periodic class war. Composed primarily of the migratory logger, construction worker, miner, and harvest hand of the West, the Wobblies also became on occasion a temporary shelter for the unskilled factory worker of the East. As a home for the "neglected and lonely hobo worker," the local I.W.W. halls and "jungles" were often the only refuge in a hostile or disinterested community.[33]

Regardless of its major function, the I.W.W. became the militant champion of the disreputable and derelict elements of society. It sent them confident and unawed into towns, employment halls, and work camps, where before they had been irresolute and submissive. This refusal to be cowed galled employers and their subservient politicians more than anything else. The wage slave had become a man, and, although there were never many converts, those few could make a noise like a million.

Beginning in 1909, a series of victorious free-speech controversies gave the I.W.W. the reputation of unbeatable militancy. Since the organization's founding in 1905, its precarious, schismatic career had been buried on the back pages of contemporary history. It had been lucky to survive. In the free-speech fights, the I.W.W. fought the propertied classes and civil authorities to a standstill and won. With the Bill of Rights supporting the Wobblies, there seemed to be no legal way to silence them. As one old farmer was reported to have complained, "You can't kill 'em; the law protects 'em." [34]

The free-speech fight swept the revolutionary propaganda

of the I.W.W. to the doorstep of the American home, and confronted the average citizen with a choice between law and order and his enraged emotions. But locking the speaker up in this instance simply called forth a succession of soapbox orators who jammed the city jails until town fathers were ready to give in.[35]

While the Wobblies won the right to free speech, in the long run they lost, for "the net effect on the public mind was that the violence was chiefly on the part of the I.W.W. or directly incited by them." [36] From Spokane in 1909 to San Diego in 1912, through Washington, Montana, South Dakota, Minnesota, Wisconsin, Pennsylvania, Massachusetts, Missouri, and Colorado, the I.W.W. inoculated otherwise peaceful communities with the virus of repression. Wobbly defense of the First Amendment had somehow become subversive and seditious, while the nonviolent resistance of I.W.W. speakers left Americans scared and perplexed. Citizens felt themselves being dragged into the deep water of anarchy by an uncontrollable current of protest.[37]

In 1912 the Wobblies had again terrified conservative and respectable elements by their dramatic strike at the Lawrence textile mills in Massachusetts. The unorganized and unskilled workers there revealed the potential of mass action under revolutionary leadership. Passive solidarity defeated the overt force of the employer. In addition the I.W.W. leaders united their ranks with the cohesive language of extremism. "General strike," "boycott," and "sabatoge" were the lyrics of a new and disturbing song.[38]

To most citizens the I.W.W. battle at Lawrence challenged "the fundamental idea of law and order" and threatened the "whole current morality as to the sacredness of property and even of life." [39] For the first time the whole country became acquainted with a rebel frame of mind that had already suggested itself in the free-speech fights. Lawrence made the nation familiar with "direct-action" tactics based on the

I.W.W. rejection of the ethics of capitalism. The Wobblies frankly stated that they would no longer accept the bourgeois canons of conduct that were exploiting them. When it qualified the sacredness of property by proposing its destruction, the I.W.W. claimed that this was a tactic to enforce respect for the sacredness of the workers' lives and natural rights. The "sabotage" of machines by employees was as "right" as the constant "sabotage" of individuals by employers. "Big Bill" Haywood remembered the hypocrisy of Colorado mineowners who could "wreck a whole population . . . [then raise] a maudlin cry because a mill had been destroyed." [40] In their concern for human rights over property rights, the I.W.W. spoke in the language of Lincoln. A nervous middle class translated it as a vocabulary of violence that would destroy American business.[41]

By 1912 the free-speech activities and the Lawrence strike had made the I.W.W. a potent psychological force conditioning the behavior of numerous groups. The development of this nationwide reputation paralleled the geographic spread and growing intensity of nativism. Americans were thus becoming much less willing to tolerate any challenge to social homogeneity and national unity at the very time when Wobbly agitators and strikers were making radicalism an effective threat to both. The anti-Catholic fundamentalism of rural areas, the growth of restriction sentiment in the West and South, and the more racist attitudes of the population at large were representative of the same hypernationalism. It was an emotion that the I.W.W. could relieve in either of two ways.[42]

On the one hand, the Wobblies greatly stimulated the drive to Americanize the immigrant. The New England textile strikes aroused the North American Civic League to the existence of a "threatened conflagration" and "incendiary movements" among foreign-born workers. The Americanizers hoped to counteract radical agitators by "a program of in-

culcation and education . . . along behavior patterns more
in keeping with what they believed to be the 'real' American
way of life." [43]

On the other hand, the I.W.W. advances stepped up demands for repression. There were many not willing to trust
in or await the effects of counterpropaganda. The inflation of
the Wobblies' reputation meant an age of easy political and
social profits for those willing to attack them. Since the
I.W.W. stood to the left of the entire reform movement,
making even the socialists seem conservative in comparison,
few friends were willing to defend the rights of such outcasts.

The damnation of the I.W.W. began in the presidential
election year of 1912, a memorable season for the reformer,
radical or otherwise. The Wobblies themselves were never
stronger. The Socialists achieved their greatest size and influence, while Roosevelt and Wilson, the two major candidates, competed for the progressive inheritance. It did not
seem to be a time for proscription, especially one coming
from the party of Eugene Debs.[44]

III

In 1912 the Socialist party convention agreed to subsidize
the travels of its delegates in Pullman palace cars. This desire
for capitalist comforts reflected the degree to which the party
had become middle-class and reformist.[45] One might expect
Socialist delegates who rode in Pullman berths to attack the
extremism of the I.W.W. and shrink back from its emphasis
on working-class action. The I.W.W.'s were still riding to
their conventions in boxcars. Perhaps this measures how far
apart these two organizations had moved since 1905.

The I.W.W. alienation of Socialist affections was com-
pounded of several elements. The increasingly influential
conservative right wing had fought to broaden the appeal of
socialism. After 1910 it successfully diluted the working-class
base of the party with converts from the "small middle class."

Morris Hillquit's report *The Propaganda of Socialism* stressed that "the ultimate aims of the movement far transcend the interests of any one class in society, and its social ideal is so lofty that it may well attract large numbers of men and women from other classes." [46] The elections of 1910 seemed to confirm the right-wing opportunistic approach of practical politics. The victorious candidates had won with reform votes and were themselves ministers, lawyers, editors — the conservative professional segment of socialism. By 1912 they had so altered the complexion of the party that "large numbers of reform voters had joined the organization and large numbers of radical working men had left it." [47]

As the Socialist party moved right, the I.W.W. and its militant fellow travelers in socialism became more uncompromisingly extreme. The Wobblies seemed to be taking their own propaganda seriously. They were making "sabotage" and "direct action" the core of a program that emphasized the supremacy of revolutionary aims and the efficacy of class economic pressure. The I.W.W. of Lawrence and free speech made socialism look "respectable — even reactionary — by comparison." In addition there was the question of politics. Socialists seriously assumed "that when the I.W.W. in 1908 'repudiated political action' it really declared war on the Socialist Party." [48]

Both the right and left wings of socialism saw the 1912 convention as the decisive test, but before the meeting, an unexpected confession of criminal violence by two well-known labor leaders favored the chances of the conservative faction. John and James McNamara, officials of the A.F. of L. Structural Iron Workers, admitted dynamiting the *Los Angeles Times* building as the culmination of their union's war with the Erectors' Association. This confession startled and confused a labor and radical world convinced that the arrest and indictment of the McNamaras had been another capitalist plot. The trade unions and Socialists had so identified themselves with the McNamaras that their guilt was indistinguishable in the public mind. The desperate efforts to get back from the end of this limb was in part responsible for the furious assault on the left wingers. The crucifixion of the I.W.W. might atone for the sins of the McNamaras. Ironically the Wobblies were victimized by the violence of the American Federation of Labor.[49]

The Socialist party convention of May 1912 met in an atmosphere made tense by the determination of left and right wings to capture control. Early radical victories on the endorsement of industrial unionism and the selection of a chairman awoke the conservatives to the necessity of a decisive blow against the extremists. Article II, section 6, drafted as an amendment to the Socialist constitution by the reform faction, was designed to drive the radicals from the party. It stated in unequivocable terms: "Any member of the party who opposes political action or advocates crime, sabotage or other methods of violence as a weapon of the working class to aid in its emancipation shall be expelled from membership in the party." [50]

The conservatives were clearly after Haywood, then a member of the national executive committee of the party, and all those who agreed with the revolutionary tactics of the I.W.W. There was to be no negotiation on this issue. Victor Berger claimed that I.W.W. articles were "as anarchistic as anything that John Most has ever written." Then he added: "In the past we often had to fight against Utopianism and fanaticism, now it is anarchism again that is eating away at the vitals of our party. . . . The I.W.W. can go to hell." [51] Even Debs came out flatly against sabotage and direct action. "If I had the force . . . I would use it," he said, but Debs thought that the working class of America lacked the "class psychology" and the need for creating such force.[52]

Haywood and the Wobblies were equally intractable. The I.W.W. leader refused to qualify his support of direct-action tactics. "No Socialist can be a law abiding citizen," he wrote, for in no way and at no time could a "fighting organization" take itself out of the class struggle. "When we come together and are of a common mind, and the purpose of our minds is to overthrow the capitalist system, we become conspirators then against the United States government," Haywood insisted.[53] Although he felt that the solidarity of all labor should replace dynamiting as the weapon of force, the I.W.W.'s militant spokesman would never criticize individuals who waged war against the capitalists. Even they were justified by the class struggle and by the criminal actions of the capitalists against the working people. The war was on and all was fair.[54]

With mutual contempt and recriminations the two factions then parted. The convention approved the antisabotage clause by a vote of 191 to 90. In February 1913 a national referendum recalled William D. Haywood from the national executive committee of the party, while in May of that year a determined endeavor to repeal section 6 failed, 43 to 16.[55]

The separation benefited neither defendant nor plaintiff. The tonic of respectability did not restore vigor to a declining socialism. The aging movement waited expectantly for the advertised results, but the middle-class rejuvenation did not appear. The withering away of socialism was, of course, the product of numerous forces — the loss of populist support, the defection of many to progressivism, the European war — but the purge of the militant left wing by means of the sabotage clause was a crippling catharsis. In this respect heresy hunting backfired because it expelled and alienated radicals without attracting the protest vote of the practicalminded reformers. On the other hand, the I.W.W. was now cast as a rootless delinquent cut off from association with the more moderate elements of protest, its revolutionary ardor disintegrating into fruitless fanaticism.[56]

The ritual of self-purification also left a more tragic legacy.

The Socialists were the first group to create an index of permissible belief and action within the framework of discontent. The Socialist antisabotage clause was the ideological forerunner of the criminal syndicalism laws and the deportation statutes aimed at dissident members of the community.[57] It was not surprising, moreover, that the more conservative and moderate elements of society should rush in where the Socialists had not feared to tread. When political necessity or public hysteria required it, Progressives, Republicans, and Democrats were equally eager proponents of a repressive antiradicalism.

IV

The resurgent vitality of the I.W.W. in 1912 was also reflected in the pre-election maneuvers of California Republicans. Smarting under the Progressive domination of state politics and anxious for William Howard Taft to defeat Theodore Roosevelt and Wilson in November, they planned to convert the collateral of anti-Wobbly bitterness into the cold cash of Republican votes. If the President would only institute some federal action against the organization, his supporters felt certain he could carry California.[58] The state seemed ready for repression. Fear of the "Yellow Peril" both at home and abroad and frustration with the failures of Far Eastern imperialism gave the citizens of the West Coast insecurities beyond those affecting other sections of the country.[59] More important, the memory of the Wobblies was still fearfully fresh in California. Their activity, in fact, had been a politician's dream, for a revival beginning on February 1, 1912, had survived until late the following summer. September and October now remained for Taft's countermeasures. The strategy seemed faultless, since the thrust of revolutionary agitation had propelled California's citizens far along the road of irrational behavior.

The peculiarly hysterical reaction on the West Coast

stemmed from the nature of I.W.W. organizing techniques. The class-conscious program of the Wobblies, added to the migratory character of their recruits, impelled the organization to seek converts in the middle-class cities rather than the rural slums. During the slack winter period, "harvest stiffs" concentrated in urban areas; these were also the major assembly zones for the markets of casual day labor. Since the I.W.W. was less concerned with the promotion of union benefits than with the incitement of a rebellious solidarity, its major emphasis was the education of migratory workers during the seasonal layoffs. The winter propaganda drive was the prelude to the coming summer strike. Wobblies were thus forced to carry on their agitation within the walls of the enemy, a fifth column of economic treason that the cities saw no reason to tolerate.[60]

During 1910 and 1911 conservative forces determined to resist the annual fall and winter campaigns of the I.W.W. They chose one of the most important citadels of agricultural labor in California, Fresno, the nerve center of the San Joaquin Valley. There the public authorities sought to close the I.W.W. hall, suppress street speaking, and prevent the distribution of literature. In the free-speech fight from October 1910 until March 1911 "strong measures of suppression were employed," but the Wobblies won a limited victory and "gained for the organization a status and importance among agricultural laborers far beyond its numerical significance." [61]

A year later the Wobblies achieved much more costly and significant recognition at San Diego, where they attracted nationwide attention in a nine-month battle for free speech, the longest such contest on record. The dispute blazed up in December 1911, when city merchants induced the council to prohibit street speaking. As usual, the I.W.W. called up the shock battalions of its floating reserves and flooded the city jails. In response, a citizens' vigilante committee sought to prevent by force the entrance of Wobblies and suspected

Wobblies into the city. The lawlessness even included as victims those liberals who fought for the Bill of Rights. So inflamed was respectable opinion that the San Diego *Tribune* could write of the I.W.W.'s in March 1912: "Hanging is too good for them and they would be much better dead, for they are absolutely useless in the human economy." The paper suggested that "they are the waste material of creation and should be drained off into the sewer of oblivion, there to rot in cold obstruction like any other excrement." [62] Such words were the clues to reality. "Overcrowding," "rotten food," "illness," "brutality," characterized the confinement of Wobblies; beatings, kidnapings, deportations, and death were the lot of those apprehended by the committee. And still the Wobblies came and eventually won. [63]

The local community suffered from the even-handed objectivity of the state government perhaps as much as it did from the I.W.W. invasion. Special Commissioner Harris Weinstock, sent by the Progressive Governor Hiram Johnson to investigate the charges of brutality, corroborated the cruel and illegal actions of the vigilantes. In his report Weinstock confessed that "it was hard for him to believe that he was not sojourning in Russia, conducting his investigation there instead of in this alleged 'land of the free and home of the brave.'" [64] The subsequent indictment of leading vigilantes (they were never brought to trial) symbolized the humiliating defeat that Johnson's Progressive administration had delivered to the local forces of reaction. Having lost locally, these forces now shifted ground.

The Republican old guard of California sensed an opportunity to eliminate the I.W.W. and at the same time to have the national administration benefit politically from the public disgust over Johnson's mild-mannered policy toward the Wobblies. Sugar capitalist John D. Spreckels, a long-time investor in San Diego real estate and utilities, and Los Angeles newspaper editor Harrison Gray Otis, an arch con-

servative and uncompromisingly antilabor Republican, sponsored a citizens' committee of five hundred to seek the
redress of their grievances. In the late summer of 1912, this
group sent a representative east to confer personally with
President Taft.[65] In the hyperbole suggestive of imminent
disaster, the committee warned Washington that some ten
thousand I.W.W.'s and anarchists were organizing to create
a new government in the southern California region. The
United States attorney at Los Angeles placed the authority
of his office behind the anti-Wobbly proposals. Castigating
the Weinstock report as rabidly partisan in favor of the
I.W.W., he requested a federal indictment against the organization for conspiring to overthrow the government of
the United States and to invade Mexico.[66]

William Howard Taft seemed convinced that the threat
was genuine and that "that corner of the country is a basis
for most of the anarchists and industrial world workers, and
for all the lawless flotsam and jetsam that proximity to the
Mexican border thrusts into those two cities of San Diego
and Los Angeles . . . We ought to take decided action," Taft
urged his Attorney General, because "the State Government
is under an utterly unscrupulous boss, who does not hesitate
. . . to do [business] with these people and cultivate their
good will." Therefore, it was most decidedly "our business to
go in and show the strong hand of the United States in a
marked way so that they shall understand that we are on the
job." [67]

The inflammatory material sent east by the Californians,
however, turned out to be more smoke than fire. A scrupu-
lously careful examination by the Department of Justice
failed to reveal sufficient evidence to indict I.W.W. leaders
for conspiracy to overthrow the government of the United
States by force, to oppose its authority by force, or by force
to prevent the execution of any of its laws. No prosecution
was possible under section 6 of the Penal Code, which pro-

hibited seditious conspiracy.[68] Nor could federal troops be dispatched to preserve the state against domestic violence under Article IV, section 4, of the Constitution, except on the request of the governor or the legislature of the state.[69] There was no deportation law aimed at Wobbly aliens as yet, and the antianarchist provisions were limited to those immigrants who had been in the country less than three years. The Justice Department simply saw no way to "show the strong hand of the United States," as Taft desired.[70]

The I.W.W. was obviously a problem for local or state authorities. Had there been any evidence of violence against life, government, or property, or of conspiracies to attempt such action, the state could have indicted the Wobblies under its own general criminal statutes, as it did the vigilantes.[71]

In their unsuccessful appeal the California Republicans exemplified the character of future antiradical behavior. Theirs was the first of many attempts to have the national administration relieve a situation that local authorities could not or would not meet. Nothing so infuriated and dismayed certain businessmen and law enforcement officials as their inability to prosecute labor agitators. Lacking any evidence of criminal activity and unable to indict men simply because they refused to work, threatened strikes, or joined organizations hostile to capitalism, the exponents of repression envisioned the federal government as a *deus ex machina* for their difficulties with radicals. Until World War I, however, Washington was equally embarrassed by the lack of laws suitable for the prosecution of dissident members of the community.

The federal investigation of radicals in 1912, as in the years that followed, was the result of political pressure on the administration at Washington. The impetus for indicting or otherwise harassing groups like the I.W.W. came from the segments of society that were being antagonized by the economic program or philosophy of the organization. Thus the government was called upon to initiate prosecutions, not to punish obvious violations of law, but to satisfy the political appetites of friends of the administration.

v

Before the Republicans again came to power in Washington, the I.W.W.'s had been largely eliminated. In the intervening eight years, the pressure to suppress radicals won out over the indifference and impotence once expressed at the federal level. The government did find a way, and a new atmosphere of action was to permeate the search for the effective tools. While the appeals for aid did not change dramatically, the circumstances did. With nativism propelling a powerful restriction movement, World War I stimulating nationalism, and global revolutionary disorder creating anew the horror of social unrest, the forces speaking for tolerance and civil liberties were silenced or shattered.

The shift came first in California. There the Progressive administration of Hiram Johnson took a second look at the Wobblies it had befriended at San Diego and quickly abandoned its former objectivity. By 1915, it was demanding the destruction of the I.W.W. At first glance, California's progressive antipathy of 1915 seems contradictory to the tolerance of 1912; yet in reality there had been no fundamental change in the Progressive mentality. It was one thing to defend the civil liberties of free-speech fighters who were the victims of illegal and vicious mob action. It was another thing entirely to accept the continuous violent action of I.W.W.'s at the point of production as they fought back against the forceful repression of California fruit growers, ranchers, and farmers. A humane feeling for the "underdog as an individual" under attack paralleled enmity for the underdog as a competing social class.[72] The clue to 1915 may be found in the progressive attitude toward labor unions and radicals, and in the paths that both the I.W.W. and the progressives followed after 1912.

The progressives' bias against labor unions was exceeded only by their deep-seated fear of class-conscious radicalism. They were committed to adjusting and cleaning the political machinery, enhancing the position of the independent propertied class, and restoring a harmonious individualism. Given that frame of reference, the average progressive distrusted organized economic power by both corporation and trade union. He disliked even more the Marxist, with his relish of the class struggle and his hatred of the middle class. Finally, the I.W.W. rejection of the ethics and moral code of the capitalist system shocked the Progressive, who always imagined himself to be an ethically superior person, morally justified in his actions. Compared with conservative Republicans, progressives were more aware of the economic basis of ideologies and more inclined to investigate and correct the worst abuses of modern capitalism. But they also turned with greater fury on the radicals, whose "social pangs" would not be eased by this moderate reform.[73]

Between 1912 and 1915, California progressivism tempered much of its reform fervor and became less tolerant of organized labor in general. After 1913 it lost its legislative vitality and tended to become indistinguishable in political and economic outlook from its Republican counterpart.[74]

The Wobblies meanwhile had moved out of the cities and on to the farms of California. The free-speech fights had given the I.W.W. the prestige and publicity indispensable to any serious operation among the migrant workers. From 1912 on, its economic activities steadily expanded. This I.W.W. intrusion into the life of the California "bindle-stiff" occurred in an already explosive economic atmosphere.[75]

For years dreadful living accommodations, "insecure and intermittent employment," low wages, and unbearable working conditions had been the seasonal rewards of agricultural labor. Yet the abject recipients of this treatment had made no real protest for decades. The situation changed after 1912. "Severe depression and industrial unemployment had driven into casual farm labor a class of people unaccustomed to the conditions which it imposed." Their strikes were "the emotional result of the nervous impact of the exceedingly irritating and intolerable conditions" upon a group still free from the apathy of long-endured exploitation.[76] The most sensational and significant of these strikes occurred in August 1913 on a hop ranch in Wheatland, California.

The Wheatland riot was "a purely spontaneous uprising . . . a psychological protest against factory conditions of hop picking" that had been instituted by E. B. Durst, owner of the ranch. Durst had deliberately attracted a labor surplus by misleading advertisements in order to beat down wages and impose his own terms for working conditions. In addition he provided little or no housing, no sanitation, no garbage disposal, and insufficient drinking water. He controlled the purchase of food through his own store. Some three thousand pople of twenty-seven different nationalities found these terms so repugnant that they went out on strike. A mass meeting organized by the I.W.W. turned into a riot when fired upon by a deputy sheriff. Several public officials and workers died, and the state seized the two I.W.W. organizers as the persons responsible for the tragedy.[77]

This migratory disaster forced the progressives into decisions that exposed their fundamental philosophy. Their punitive and remedial measures after Wheatland clearly indicated the balance between repression and reform that a progressive might be expected to achieve in situations of labor conflict. Governor Johnson's initial move was the dispatch of National Guard troops "to overawe any labor demonstration and to protect private property." [78] He thus placed the state squarely behind the California fruit interests. At the same time the California Commission on Immigration and Housing began an extensive investigation of the living and working conditions of the migratory workers. Under the leadership of chairman Simon J. Lubin, the commission worked hard to turn the suggestions of its investigator, Professor Carleton H. Parker, into concrete improvements.[79] But it did not let the matter rest there.

In the shocked aftermath of Wheatland, Durst, and other California fruit ranchers had formed the Farmers' Protective League to see that strikes and riots should never again threaten the gathering of a ripened crop. Since the fruit grower was "seasonally confronted with the necessity of harvesting his crop within a matter of hours or see it spoil . . . [he] needed amenable and low cost labor for a few days of the year, which he then wanted to disappear quietly until the next harvest." The league was thus specifically an antiunion organization, and broadly an antilabor lobby. It fought against "pro-labor legislation of the type that many progressives had proposed." And the Farmers' Protective League had as its ally in this antiunion program the progressive Commission on Immigration and Housing. Quite obviously the I.W.W. was the major threat to the existence of "amenable and low cost labor." [80]

The Wobblies were militantly active after the riot at the Durst ranch, aroused not only by the possibility of organizing the agricultural workers but by the desire for revenge as well. The two organizers, convicted of second-degree murder on superficial evidence, were serving life sentences. The I.W.W. considered this another capitalist plot, threatened a general strike to secure their release, and distributed large quantities of "stickers and circulars, with a picture of a hunched black cat showing its claws, the emblem of sabotage." [81] In 1914 the Hop Pickers Defense Committee estimated that "owing to the action of the I.W.W. the hop crop is 24,000 bales short." [82] In 1915 the I.W.W. dropped its picket line of the hop fields, but told its members to rely on "their own individual action to make every kick count." In this fight to release the organizers convicted after Wheatland, the Wobblies felt that "it is no use appealing to the master's sense of justice for he has not got any, the only thing left is action on the pocketbook, he has got a considerable dose of this but it seems he wants more." [83] There is no doubt that the I.W.W. was fighting the California farmers and fruit growers with every weapon at its disposal. If Wobblies were to be blacklisted, mobbed, and illegally imprisoned, they would in turn recruit I.W.W. members by force, if necessary, to attain job control, they would slow down on the job, they would use direct action and sabotage, and they would start sudden and disastrous strikes. By 1917 the I.W.W. estimated that the Wheatland riot convictions had cost the California bosses $10,000,000 a year, while the authorities themselves set the total figure as $15–20,000,000 dollars since 1914.[84] As long as the I.W.W. operated, the Farmers' Protective League could assume that labor would not "be amenable".

While the California Commission on Immigration and Housing was endeavoring to improve conditions for the migratory workers, the league at first tried to eliminate the I.W.W. by itself. Durst and his associates created their own police force of private gunmen and detectives as a protection against the I.W.W. at a cost averaging over $10,000 a year for individual growers. [85] By the end of 1915 they had still not successfully controlled the I.W.W. menace, and they realized that it was "not going to be an easy matter to rid the Coast of these operators." [86] Anxious to shift or eliminate the financial burden of their antilabor policy, league members favored action by the federal government, "strong state co-operation" with it, and "a publicity campaign to enlist the assistance of all good citizens." This affidavit formed the bulk of the material sent east to the Department of Justice by the Commission on Immigration and Housing.[87] On October 5, 1915, the high-level support desired by the large agricultural interest became a reality.

Under the leadership of Governor Hiram Johnson, the chief executives of California, Oregon, Washington, and Utah urged the Wilson administration to investigate the I.W.W. immediately for possible federal prosecution. Working confidentially through their progressive ally in the Cabinet, Secretary of the Interior Franklin K. Lane, the four governors reported:

> California, Oregon, Washington and Utah are experiencing abnormal disorder and incendiarism. These experiences are coincident with threats made by I.W.W. leaders in their talks and publications, and are in harmony with doctrines preached in their publications. Local or state apprehension of ring leaders impracticable, as their field of activity is interstate . . . Through federal machinery covering the whole territory involved, the national government might get at the bottom of this movement . . . Exigencies of the situation demand absolute secrecy.[88]

When informed of the situation by Lane and Attorney General Gregory, Woodrow Wilson wholeheartedly endorsed "this inquiry which seems to mean so much to the whole section which it concerns." [89] The Department of Justice thereupon dispatched a special agent to uncover the interstate conspiracy and to bring the ringleaders to federal justice.

Working closely with the Commission on Immigration and Housing and using the evidence it had amassed after two years of investigation, the federal agent was unable to discover any violations of the nation's criminal laws. His report, far less sensational than the implications in the governors' message, buried the I.W.W. issue for the Department of Justice until the wartime Espionage and Selective Service laws gave the department jurisdiction to destroy local radical movements. The investigator found the I.W.W. an organization composed "chiefly of panhandlers, without homes, mostly foreigners, the discontented and unemployed, who are not anxious to work." There were perhaps some four thousands members in California and Washington.[90] To the Farmers' Protective League and the progressives it was a disappointing verdict in response to a promising indictment. They had hoped for much more.

These disillusioned proponents of federal suppression might well have concluded the government would never be moved far from the Bill of Rights. A flourishing radical organization blatantly challenging the status quo had brought down upon itself the combined enmity of socialists, progressives, and conservatives. The I.W.W. should have been put down in 1912. In the years that followed it did not become more dangerous or extreme, nor did its opponents become more cognizant of its doctrines or less anxious to destroy it. Yet the passions that came into being at that time were not then relieved by the official remedies of national action, and a red scare passed into history with federal policies unchanged.

If such was the case, there were those who vowed to make up for the deficiencies of federal power. The point was: Could they marshal support in Congress for additions to the criminal or deportation laws? Much would depend on the mood of the country, of course, and the degree to which legislators were willing to support traditional freedoms and tolerate dissent.

The pattern of future repression thus became keyed to a congressional struggle waged in an atmosphere first of increasing nativism and then of war crisis. This four-year battle once again focused on the immigrant and produced new and more effective deportation legislation to destroy the supposed alien foundation of the radical superstructure. While the legislators debated, federal judges in the Pacific Northwest found in the naturalization law an antialien program with which to oppose the forces of radicalism. This

judicial attack reflected the well-known ability of local repression to move ahead of congressional policy-making.

Delayed by unforeseen and unrelated circumstances, the
bill to exclude and expel I.W.W.'s took some four years to
pass after its introduction in 1912. The radical-deportation
crusade awaited its place in history. In 1917 the war and this
improved alien legislation coincided to furnish the opponents
of the I.W.W. with weapons of which they had long been
dreaming.

III

Naturalization and a New Law

1912–1917

In 1891 Richard Sauer, a law-abiding, industrious German immigrant living in Texas, petitioned to become a citizen of the United States. During his examination by Judge Paschal of the district court, Sauer admitted that he was "a socialist, and a firm believer in the doctrines of socialism." This startled the judge, who told the immigrant that "the principles of socialism are directly at war with and antagonistic to the principles of the constitution of the United States, and absolutely inconsistent with his being 'well disposed to the good order and happiness' of the people and government of this country." Socialist ideas, Judge Paschal emphasized, were "un-American, impracticable, and dangerous in the extreme to society as organized throughout the civilized world, and particularly in this free country." The court thereupon denied Sauer's application for citizenship. In the judge's opinion the time had come "when the safety and perpetuity of our free institutions and of constitutional government in this land . . . demand that those who apply for the privilege, honor, and distinction of becoming American citizens should be free from doctrines which are not only subversive of constitutional government and our free institutions, but of organized society itself." [1] At the same time the court admitted aliens who were "ignorant . . . unable to read or write . . . and who cannot explain the principle of the Constitution" as long as they had been "thoroughly law abiding and industrious . . . of good moral character." [2] A little learning seemed a dangerous thing.

While not typical of his day, Judge Paschal's decision prophetically anticipated the later concept of ideological ineligibility. Nativist apprehensions had already made suspect divergencies in race, color, and in the nationality of immigrants. Increasingly disliked as racial groups, aliens were to find that their thought processes and intellectual associations became additional barriers to naturalization. Disregarding the entrenched conservatism of the mass of alien arrivals, the newer nativism singled out the foreign-born as the most likely subversives and security risks. By 1950 the cold war and demands of national security would make citizenship much more difficult to obtain and easier to lose for the immigrant with radical views.[3] The conscious withholding of citizenship from these aliens also kept them deportable. The Bureau of Naturalization outlined this strategy in 1922: "As long as the advocates of these malignant and un-American doctrines remain aliens, they may be deported and their gospels may be overthrown at their inception, but once they succeed in obtaining their citizenship, this method of purging our country becomes more difficult, if not impossible." [4]

After 1900, the courts took on the increasingly difficult function of determining what beliefs were malignant and un-American. The I.W.W. played an important role in the evolution of a naturalization standard for radicals. The 1912 Wobbly revival focused the courts' attention on the alien members seeking naturalization. The judges were forced to decide whether loyalty to the organization was compatible with good citizenship. Their decisions were the only consistent prewar attack on the I.W.W. by the federal government. The refusal to naturalize drove members out of the I.W.W., and it also maintained the alien status of those who stayed in.

Originally the naturalization laws contained no clauses against radicals as such. Under the power of the Constitution "to establish a uniform Rule of Naturalization," Congress had passed the Act of 1790.[5] This law sanctioned the the naturalization of "any alien, being a free white person" who was of good moral character, who swore to support the Constitution, and who had resided in the country for two years.[6] The succeeding Act of 1795, as amended by the Act of 1802, remained the basic naturalization legislation until 1906. It increased the required residence from two to five years, provided for a declaration of intention, and demanded proof of attachment to the principles of the Constitution as well as good moral character.[7]

Before the twentieth century only the Naturalization Act of 1798 specifically attacked foreigners as potential subversives. In line with their general antialien policy, the Federalists raised the residence requirement from five to fourteen years, claiming that it took "at least this long to transform rebels and incendiaries into respectable, peace-loving American citizens." As Theodore Sedgwick of Massachusetts suggested, the United States should "admit none but reputable citizens, such only were fit for the society into which they were blended." Under the preceding liberal naturalization laws, the Federalists claimed, the country already had accepted too many "treasonable ingrates." [8]

The aberration of 1798, however, proved to be temporary. There is no indication that judges generally denied naturalization to aliens with extreme political and economic beliefs. Until 1903 such immigrants might have been disqualified for lack of attachment to the principles of the Constitution, but, with a few exceptions, the courts did not so construe the law. As long as an immigrant was law-abiding, industrious, and of good moral character, he had no trouble. In fact even these requirements were not always met, for the "notorious ease with which naturalization could be acquired, [and] the wholesale issue and sale of fraudulent certificates" were also characteristics of nineteenth-century practice.[9] Americans generally heeded President Buchanan's injunction to "protect the rights of our naturalized citizens everywhere to the same extent as though they had drawn their first breath in this country." Not until after the turn of the century did they disregard his plea to "recognize no distinction between our native and naturalized citizens." [10]

The country again manifested its concern with the radical opinions of alien applicants after the assassination of McKinley in 1901. Previously Congress had ignored the suggestions of several Presidents. Cleveland urged that citizenship be conferred with "scrupulous care," while Benjamin Harrison had favored the investigation of an alien's moral character to make sure that he felt a "good disposition toward our government." Harrison did not want "avowed enemies of social order" to become citizens of or even to reside in the United States.[11] It was not until the antianarchist aftermath of Czolgosz's attack, however, that Congress took action. It now not only passed an exclusion and deportation law, but prohibited as well the naturalization of anyone who disbelieved in or was opposed to organized government, favored the removal of public officials by assassination, or joined organizations that held these ideas.[12]

The 1903 legislation, therefore, created a criterion of thought and conduct for naturalized citizens that was unknown to native-born Americans. In addition it established a pattern of disqualification based upon beliefs and associations only. Congress established increasingly greater liabilities for the naturalized alien "with respect to enjoyment of certain fundamental freedoms," until he was to be classified by many witnesses before the 1952 President's commission on immigration and naturalization as a "second class citizen." [13]

Soon after the statutory requirements for radicals were

created, the government entirely reformed the administration of naturalization laws to eliminate the historically loose and fraudulent acquisition of citizenship. In 1905 the abuses had become so gross that Theodore Roosevelt appointed a special commission to tighten up the system; the Naturalization Act of 1906 incorporated its findings. Thus the government added a new seriousness and integrity to a now uniform system at the same time as it brought the radicals under its special scrutiny.[14]

Several provisions in the statute of 1906 held special meaning for alien radicals. An applicant for citizenship had to state that he was "not a disbeliever in or opposed to organized government or a member of or affiliated with any organization or body of persons teaching disbelief in or opposed to organized government," and to swear that he was not an anarchist.[15] The petitioner also had to declare his support of the Constitution and show that for five years preceding "he has *behaved* as a man of good moral character attached to principles of the Constitution of the United States, and well disposed to the good order and happiness of the same." [16] Two credible witnesses who were citizens had to testify that the alien had so acted during the five-year period.[17] But the law was silent on the meaning of these clauses, and to whom they were to apply. It left the decision of such questions to the naturalization examiners and to the courts, which did not take long to formulate answers when they faced the petitions of I.W.W. aliens.

In this oblique assault on the organization, the precedents were set in the Pacific Northwest. An I.W.W. alien applying for citizenship in that region after 1912 found himself the victim of the organization's nationwide and local reputation. To federal officials, the I.W.W. meant more than rumors of distant violence in San Diego or rebellious mass action in Lawrence. The northwestern administrators had suffered through the Portland strike of 1907 in the timber mills, the free-speech victory at Spokane in 1909, and an almost constant succession of strikes and free-speech contests thereafter.[18] Seattle, the district headquarters of the naturalization service, witnessed "a generation of I.W.W. trouble" from 1912 on.[19]

Regardless of his own beliefs and actions, therefore, the I.W.W. alien was held responsible for the exaggerated phrase-mongering and the revolutionary strike tactics of the organization or any of its members. Many men joined the I.W.W. with little knowledge of its program, some for the concrete gains that organization might win for them, others without an awareness that the economic program of the I.W.W. implied any hostility to the Constitution, government, or laws of the land. In addition, it would hardly seem that an individual assumed responsibility for the actions of any and all other members or for any statements that might be made in the future simply by joining an organization.

During 1912 and 1913 federal officials in the Northwest specifically defined the I.W.W. as a group that taught disbelief in and opposition to organized government. The judges and examiners relied on various quotations from I.W.W. propaganda to prove his point. "Might is right," "No man is great enough or good enough to rule another," "The I.W.W. is creating its own ideas of morality and ethical conduct," were some of the statements cited to show the anarchistic nature of the I.W.W. The organization's preamble and Wobbly contempt for government interference during strikes were also used as examples of opposition to organized government. Having so characterized the I.W.W., the courts then barred all of its alien members from naturalization under the law of 1906.[20]

Even the most temporary or tenuous association with the I.W.W. served to disqualify applicants. As little as two months' membership in the organization sufficed to prove that petitioners were not attached to the principles of the

Constitution. While they may well have joined for the legitimate purpose of improving their wages, hours, or working conditions, aliens arrested during I.W.W. strikes were refused citizenship. Pro-I.W.W. activity, regardless of membership, constituted grounds for disqualification. An alien who had been a member of the I.W.W. at any time during the five years preceding his application but who was no longer a Wobbly could not become naturalized. The courts considered that such individuals had not behaved for five years as men attached to the principles of the Constitution and well disposed to the good order and happiness of the United States. They were allowed to file new declarations of intention, however, and could become citizens by living another five years free from I.W.W. associations. The Naturalization Bureau objected to aliens who had attended I.W.W. meetings and admitted they knew the character of the organization, but the courts admitted such persons when people of standing and prominence in the community appeared as witnesses on their behalf.[21]

The character of the two citizens who testified about the petitioner's behavior often became crucial in the proceedings. According to the law only the credibility of the witness had to be established. But what established credibility? Witnesses were regularly interrogated concerning their own social, economic, and political beliefs. Apparently examiners believed that the credibility of deponents improved as they became conservative and conformist in their thinking.[22] Petitioners who were not members of the I.W.W. themselves who chose citizen I.W.W. as witnesses were denied citizenship. The courts declared that I.W.W.'s were not competent to testify, since they were not attached to the principles of the Constitution, and therefore were not credible. Government officials rejected the testimony of individuals having even the most indirect I.W.W. affiliation, such as marriage to a person sympathetic to the organization.[23] Nor was this attitude typical of the Pacific Northwest alone, for Alaska, Minnesota, and Wisconsin reasoned along these same lines.[24] Behind this judicial hesitation lay the strong and perhaps honest conviction of the times that loyalty to the working class precluded loyalty to the state. According to the judges no divided allegiances could be tolerated. Devotion to the I.W.W. was on its face inconsistent with attachment to the United States.

If such worries seemed to indicate an awareness of the socioeconomic climate in America, the judiciary on the whole acted as though it were dealing with life in a vacuum. There was no understanding of why men joined the I.W.W., no realization that it was often "a bond of groping fellowship" in which membership "by no means implies belief in or understanding of its philosophy." [25] The courts seemed unaware of the conditions that drove migratory harvesters and lumber workers into the arms of the Wobblies, the only union that fought for their rights. This ignorance certainly victimized the radical petitioner. In addition he had to suffer examination and judgment by men whose blindness to the facts of economic life was matched by their adherence to a particular economic philosophy. This became especially important when the issue was the interpretation of such phrases in the law as "attachment to the principles of the Constitution."

Federal officials who were responsible for naturalization were unable to develop a legal sophistication superior to their antiradical bias, for they confused the economic and the constitutional theories of alien applicants. Opposition to the economic system was taken to be opposition to the government or the form of government, so closely were the two identified in the popular mind. A congressional investigating committee had the following exchange with John Speed Smith, chief naturalization examiner at Seattle:

Q. Did you get the impression that he [the alien] meant simply that property should be owned by the government, and the fruits of it distributed among the people?

A. Yes sir; I may say that I did get that impression.

Q. That is the impression that you got and that is what you would believe to be opposition to the principles of the Constitution, is it?

A. I do not regard that as in keeping with the form of government that we have.

Q. Are those two things synonomous in your mind, that is, is one who believes in radically changing the provisions of the Constitution not attached to the *principles* of the Constitution?

A. Yes sir, looks to me like it.[26]

The courts also based attachment to the Constitution on economic theory. One judge found an alien unfit for citizenship because "he is a socialist . . . advocating a propaganda for radical changes in the institutions of the country." The jurist concluded, "Those who believe in and propagate crude theories hostile to the Constitution are barred . . . [since their] propaganda is to create turmoil and to end in chaos." [27]

To its credit, the Department of Justice at Washington considered such actions "a grave error," and attempted for the first time to create a criterion of legal radicalism in naturalization cases.[28] It emphasized that the law required attention to behavior rather than to belief, and that belief could disqualify an applicant only if it concerned disbelief in or opposition to organized government, namely, anarchism.[29] The Attorney General clearly distinguished attachment to the principles of the Constitution from attachment to all of its provisions. Advocacy of any modification at all in the form of government or the economic system was permissible if the changes were to be brought about by the ballot and other constitutional means. Resort to force was, of course, a different matter.[30] Finally, the desire to substitute communal for private ownership of property was not proof of a lack of attachment to the Constitution.[31]

While such directives from Washington might affect the outcome of a specific case, there is no indication that they permanently reformed the administrative behavior of local bureaucrats in radical cases. Those officials continued to withhold citizenship from aliens whose "crude theories" sanctioned "radical changes." [32]

Although the government tried and failed to make the naturalization of alien I.W.W.'s consistent and according to law, it never endeavored to create among the different branches and agencies of government a uniform conception of that organization's character. The Naturalization Bureau and some courts treated the I.W.W. as anarchistic, yet the I.W.W. really had nothing in common with the anarchists. It opposed a government dominated by capitalists, not government as such. It hated despotism and autocracy, political or economic, but it sought to fashion the industrial union as "the administrative unit in the future industrial democracy." [33] The preamble and the constitution of the I.W.W. did not advocate the use of force or the violation of any law in furthering the abolition of the wage system and capitalism. J. Edgar Hoover, who, for the purpose of deportation, made the most searching analysis of the I.W.W., wrote, "I believe that the allegation that this organization is anarchistic can neither be sustained in point of law nor fact." [34] The Immigration Bureau never used the anarchist deportation law against members of the I.W.W., nor did congressmen who opposed the Wobblies ever suggest that they might be expelled as anarchists. In fact the lawmakers realized the necessity of amending the 1903 legislation with clauses aimed specifically at the I.W.W. The Department of Labor also ruled that the organization was not anarchistic. [35]

I.W.W. aliens were thus the first martyrs to the new nativism, which fostered ideological standards of fitness. The immigrant seeking admission to, continued residence in, or naturalization by the United States was no longer dependent upon simple objective tests. Instead, he found his future dependent upon the subjective and variable interpretations of laws dealing with opinions and beliefs. One man's faith was another man's bias, and the indefinite nature of the provisions against radicals made a government by men, not law, almost inevitable.

The naturalization process clearly revealed the dangers inherent in this trend. In 1912 local judges and examiners had formulated a definition of the I.W.W. that was clearly at odds with the facts and with the judgment of other government officials. For the purposes of naturalization Wobblies were anarchists; in exclusion and deportation cases they were not. These contradictions were never resolved. Within the citizenship process radical aliens faced the unforseeable results that accompanied the application of vague standards by unsympathetic judges.

The naturalization officials, examiners, and judges were a part of that varied number who sought the suppression of the I.W.W. before World War I, and they successfully translated their antipathy into effective action. Denial of citizenship to some of the Wobblies would maintain an alien reservoir of deportable radicals and drive others out of the organization. Despite its limited success, however, the naturalization process was an indirect and negative approach to the radical menace. Public officials were not satisfied with the occasional and fortuitous character of the federal attack. Still believing in the alien nature of radicalism, Congress now determined to destroy the I.W.W. by rewriting the deportation law — a decision that grew out of the alarming Wobbly advances of 1912 and the parallel resurgence of nativist anxieties.

II

After the Lawrence strike and the free-speech fights, Congress began to prepare a new immigration law. The pro-

posal to deport any alien "advocating or teaching the unlawful destruction of property" was aimed specifically at
the I.W.W.[36] This antiradical provision did not, however,
stand by itself; it was attached to general legislation containing the controversial literacy test. Special-interest lobbying against the test by big business and immigrant blocs,
political evasion of the issue during the election years of
1912, 1914, and 1916, and presidential vetoes of the literacy
test in 1913 and 1915 delayed passage of the act until early
1917. In spite of the rising antiforeign hysteria, therefore, a
plucky opposition fought the restriction movement to a
standstill until overwhelmed by the nationalist fervors of
the crisis with Germany.[37] While there was much less of a
struggle over the antiradical clauses, congressional debate
revealed some strongly held sentiments against too sweeping
a break with previous tradition. On the other hand, the four-
year postponement afforded enemies of the I.W.W. further
opportunities to write into law more thoroughly repressive
stipulations. The combined impact of these fortuitous events
was, then, a mixed one: the deportation explosion was delayed, but the ultimate concussion was increased.

The literacy test and the antiradical clauses also shared
a common intellectual paternity in the then widely accepted
interpretation of the new immigrants from southern and
eastern Europe. Not only were they supposedly less literate
than the earlier arrivals from northern and western Europe,
but they also were presumably more likely to bring with
them erroneous ideas. Racist thinkers had been publicizing
the degenerate characteristics of the new immigrants ever
since the 1890's. These aliens were "beaten men from beaten
races," thoroughly unfit in the struggle for survival, representative of the very worst and lowest elements in the population, and devoid of the intelligence, initiative, vigor, and
ability of the aliens of the old stock.[38] Representative Albert
Johnson, a West Coast foe of the I.W.W. and the crusading

chairman of the House Immigration Committee, typified in his analysis the distortion then current in congressional debates. The new immigrants, he found, possessed "inherited misconceptions respecting the relationships of the governing power to the governed. Unlike Americans, these aliens had not "descended from generations of free men bred to a knowledge of the principles and practices of self-government." [39]

The feeling about the new immigrants made it easier to justify a much harsher exclusion and deportation policy. Between 1912 and 1917 Congress abandoned the conviction that radicalism could be a home-grown phenomenon and cut down the procedural safeguards protecting aliens and radicals. Congress, in other words, tried to eliminate discontent by repressing speech and belief with methods alien to democratic judicial traditions. One does not have to favor the destruction of property to criticize this point of view. There were alternatives. The lawmakers could have attacked the problem by legislation to remove the social and economic conditions that made the I.W.W. doctrines attractive. Congress could also have protected the unskilled industrial and migratory workers from exploitation. Failing to do this, it might have spelled out additions to the Penal Code to punish clearly proven actions of destruction of property. The legislators could have called for a nationwide crackdown and increased federal police action against property destruction. If they were determined to use the techniques of deportation, however, they might still have singled out only *behavior* rather than punishing advocacy — that is, deeds rather than ideas. And Congress could have insisted as well that all individuals rounded up under the new legislation have all the procedural safeguards accorded to any accused criminal in the courts of the United States. Instead, the federal lawmakers struck at the symptoms of discontent expressed in the free speech of alien radicals.

Shutting its eyes to the evidence of shocking industrial conditions uncovered by various investigating commissions, Congress keyed its solution of domestic unrest to the mistaken theory that described current radicalism as a foreign import of the new immigration. Therefore, it sought not only the expulsion of the alien agitator but also the exclusion of his ignorant, misguided follower. The agitator and the illiterate complemented each other, for, as one representative said, "The more illiterate of the aliens once here quickly absorb the teachings" of the radical leader.[40] The sponsor of the 1917 law, Congressman John L. Burnett, felt that the literacy test and the antiradical provisions would surely eliminate domestic discontent. In a dramatic characterization he recalled for his colleagues the I.W.W. strike at Lawrence: "The educated blackhander led the long procession and stirred them to frenzy and to crime, but behind him was the horde of illiterates with a bomb in one hand and a banner in the other on which was inscribed 'No God, No Law, No Master.'"[41] With such rhetoric was the conservative mythology of radical behavior to be stereotyped in the law of the land.

Within the framework created by this hostility to the new immigration, there was considerable debate over the I.W.W. clause in the new deportation law. During the four years of discussion, prolonged by presidential vetoes, an increasing hysteria toward radicalism appeared, accompanied by the determination to expel dissident aliens no matter how long they had lived in the United States. The public conscience was also on display, for Congress wrestled with a definition of radicalism that might conform with America's traditional role as the haven for the world's disaffected. Thus the ideology of suppression was clearly hammered out on the anvil of that four-year debate.

Although Congressman John E. Raker of California had introduced the new antiradical amendment in order to deport members of the I.W.W., some representatives suspected that it might do more than that. A few congressmen feared its application against conservative labor unions; others worried lest the militant suffragettes be excluded and deported from America; and still others wondered whether leaders of unsuccessful revolutions abroad could still find refuge in the United States. Only one member framed his objections as a defense of the right to unlimited free speech. Congressman Augustus Gardner's lonely appeal that "men ought to be permitted to preach any doctrine which to them seems good" evoked no sympathetic response, and the House easily rejected his proposal to strike Raker's amendment from the bill.[42]

Granted that the clause defined a specific illegal propaganda, it was still vague enough to be adaptable to legitimate labor disturbances. The history of the trade-union movement in the United States up to that time indicated a pattern of forceful strikebreaking followed by inevitable violence. There was little reason to expect a sudden termination of this struggle. Under the provocation of bitterly contested strikes or endlessly wretched working conditions, men could speak in protest with excitement and passion. In such circumstances, there was bound to be some dangerous speech. Would Congress give the Immigration Bureau broad powers to decide whether the advocacy of unlawful property destruction in these situations was cause for deportation? [43] Socialist Congressman Meyer London from New York's lower east side and Democratic Representative Adolph J. Sabath from Illinois anticipated that employers would use the immigration law to remove strike leaders and to avoid court trials and judicial methods. They pointed out that the clause was superflous, since advocating or teaching the destruction of property was already a crime for which an offending alien could be deported.[44] The majority of congressmen, however, ignored such suggestions.

The proposal to exclude and deport those advocates and teachers of the unlawful destruction of property also ran into unexpected opposition from the friends of the militant suffragette. In Congressman James Manahan of Minnesota women found an ally who understood their tactics. He did not want the government to attack those suffragettes who advocated property damage simply as a propaganda device in the fight for the vote. Such advocacy on their part, he claimed, was far different from the offense of "unrestrained anarchy" and should not be linked with it in the immigration law. If the "sabotage" provision became law, Manahan believed it would exclude from admission to the United States "some of the best women of England." Militants of such high quality should be reformed, not penalized, by their adopted country, he suggested.[45]

The proponents of the clause remained unconvinced. There seemed to be no reason to excuse such assaults upon the sanctity of property merely because they stemmed from well-bred female propagandists. Burnett of Alabama, who led the fight for immigration revision, hoped that militant suffragettes "who, on the other side, burn churches, blow up buildings, and destroy mail boxes" would be excluded. He was certain that American women would not favor the use of "anarchy, bloodshed, and murder" to obtain the ballot. And there the matter was dropped.[46]

Devotion to America's revolutionary ideals and to its historic career as an asylum for Europe's oppressed clashed with the equally intense distaste for domestic radicalism. If the "immigration law is an index of the extent of our acceptance of the principle that tyranny is forever abhorrent and that its victims should always find asylum in the land of the free," would the "sabotage" clause deny this principle?[47] Did a law prohibiting the advocacy and teaching of the unlawful destruction of property extend to the radical leaders of European revolutions who resisted the despotism of the old world by unlawful and destructive violence?

The debate revealed that a lingering respect for political radicalism abroad still flickered. Senator Ellison D. Smith of South Carolina insisted that the sabotage clause should not operate so as "to run the risk of denying asylum to those patriots who in resisting oppression have incidentally done violence to property." Other senators agreed that in the struggle for political liberty the destruction of property was a natural instrument "which men must apply to secure what they consider to be their rights." [48] An imperturbable and self-satisfied friendship for the European radical of the lost cause warmed the Senate Chamber. It seemed right that "those who resist force with force" should be welcome in America.[49]

Equally clear was the careful distinction that officials made between foreign revolutionary movements political in character and revolutionary tactics in pursuit of economic reform at home. Suddenly the destruction of property lost its magic appeal and utility and became — "sabotage." As one whose state had seen the I.W.W. at work, Senator James D. Phelan of California made a distinction between political and economic radicalism. "Where property is destroyed as a means for obtaining some industrial end," he stated, "I do not think it should be encouraged." The Senator concluded that "the destruction of property is not the way to settle difficulties or even to get a hearing." [50] Those who advocated the destruction of property in the United States had no grand design, it was said, such as animated people who suffered from intolerable oppression. On the contrary, those agitators "from their own preconceived ideas simply desire to destroy property for the purpose of destruction, or because they do not like a particular individual." [51]

Following President Taft's veto of the first bill in 1913, Congress passed the general immigration bill a second time in 1915 without resolving the dilemma implicit in the sabotage clause. Friend and enemy alike faced exclusion and deportation, for the immigration inspectors had no authority to exercise discretion. In the application of the law, they could not possibly distinguish between the leaders of "broad revolutionary movements" and the "criminals" who advocated the destruction of property for industrial ends.[52]

Opponents of the provisions dealing with property destruction, therefore, carried their fight to President Wilson in hope of a veto. A group of well-known public figures had arranged a conference with Wilson in January 1915 to discuss the pros and cons of the literacy test. At that same meeting Oswald Garrison Villard, editor of the liberal weekly *The Nation*, and the ex-muckraker Socialist Charles Edward Russell forcefully denounced the idea of singling out those who advocated the unlawful destruction of property. Villard described this as a "new and important departure in our national policy." Recalling the Boston Tea Party, he reminded the President of the many historical occasions when "advocating and teaching the unlawful destruction of property have led men and women to come to freedom, to democracy, and to a better common life." The country, Villard and Russell warned, should not sit in judgement on foreigners whose resort to force had expressed the popular will.[53]

Their suggestions must have appealed to the liberal idealism of the presidential political philosopher. Although Wilson's veto of the immigration bill dwelt largely on the well-publicized literacy test, he found another clause equally unjustifiable. In words reminiscent of Villard's the President also rejected the act because it "seeks to all but close entirely the gates of asylum which have always been open to those who could find no where else the right and opportunity of constitutional agitation for what they conceived to be the natural inalienable rights of man." Wilson would not deport radical labor agitators at the risk of forever excluding the hunted political exile.[54]

His veto by no means ended the matter, for Congress was determined not to let solicitude for foreign revolutionaries stand in the way of its suppression of the I.W.W. In the end it found a simple enough solution. Recognizing the force of Wilson's objection, the legislators agreed to meet it with a simple amendment. If the country was to remain an asylum for the political radical, Congress would exempt from the operation of the property-destruction clause all those that had been "convicted, or . . . admit the commission, or advocate or teach the commission, of an offense purely political." [55] Despite the toleration of such individuals in the 1917 immigration act, the nation had again moved toward a policy based on fear rather than faith in people. The once generous admission of immigrants regardless of what they believed, joined, or advocated was anachronistic in the security-conscious twentieth century. As the immigration laws became substantively narrow, former procedural safeguards also disappeared.

It had been traditional policy to limit the time during which deportations could be effected for violations of the immigration law. The act of 1907, for example, restricted deportations for all classes of cases to a period within three years after entry. The country thus recognized the essential hardship involved in uprooting aliens once they had settled permanently in the United States. It also accepted its responsibility for what an alien might become because of conditions in his adopted home. In 1910, however, Congress abandoned these protective limitations for one class of persons. Madams, prostitutes, procurers, or anyone in any way connected with this profession were made deportable at any time after entry regardless of how long they had lived in the country.[56]

The time limit was to be removed for other groups as well.

During the early debates on the sabotage and anarchist aspects of the new law, Congress had favored the retention of a brief and definite probation. The lawmakers felt that the country should be able to reform such radicals as might slip past the border guards within three years or accept the consequences. Congressman James Manahan believed that "deportation is a confession that we cannot handle the person deported." One of the bitterest enemies of the I.W.W., Representative Albert Johnson of Washington, favored a five-year limitation; if in that time the nation could not pry the aliens loose from their beliefs, "we will just have to fight it out with them." The antiradical Burnett, who sponsored the law, assumed that ideas and beliefs acquired by an alien after a five-year residence were necessarily the product of his American experience.[57]

In 1914 the House had emphatically supported this point of view. Congressman J. Hampton Moore of Philadelphia was convinced that no honest, hard-working foreigner would become a radical because of domestic conditions. He therefore introduced an amendment to require the deportation of alien anarchists and advocates of property destruction at any time, no matter how long their residence. The representatives rejected his proposal. Within two years, however, the ideas of Congressman Moore had triumphed. After Wilson's first veto, the rewritten bill dropped all time limits on the expulsion of alien radicals. In agreement with Moore that an American made dissident was "a far fetched proposition," the legislators in effect placed the alien with radical ideas and associations on indefinite probation. To avoid banishment the alien resident had to be a conformist or, at least, a silent critic of the system.[58]

The United States had repudiated a long tradition in immigration history when it shifted responsibility to the alien alone for what the country had made him. To the applause of his fellow congressmen, Representative James C. Slayden of Texas indicated the direction in which official thought was moving: "Now I would execute these anarchists if I could, and then I would deport them, so that the soil of our country might not be polluted by their presence even after the breath had gone out of their bodies. *I do not care what the time limit is.* I want to get rid of them by some route . . . or by execution by the hangman. It makes no difference to me so that we get rid of them." [59]

On February 5, 1917, when Congress overrode President Wilson's second veto of the literacy test provisions, a new immigration bill and a novel deportation policy became law. The antiradical clause of the act stated: "Any alien who at any time after entry shall be found advocating or teaching the unlawful destruction of property, or advocating or teaching anarchy or the overthrow by force or violence of the Government of the United States or of all forms of law or the assassination of public officials . . . shall, upon the warrent of the Secretary of Labor, be taken into custody and deported." [60]

Despite the broad and indefinite nature of these provisions and the termination of the time limit, not one congressional voice had warned the nation against the potential injustices and obstacles in the untested legislation. Instead officials had seized upon deportation as the quickest and most effective method of suppressing the propagation of dangerous ideas because of its very antithesis to due process. Congressmen did not want to determine the rights of anarchists and other radicals "by the long slow process of courts." As one representative said, "A long-delayed snail-paced" trial would only encourage radicals "to ply their trade instead of making an example of them." [61] If repression was the aim, then a noncriminal, administrative procedure was far more efficient and gave immigration officials great latitude in defining guilt. Yet Congress had been so busy drawing up clauses to eliminate the "blackhander" and his illiterate follower that there had been no discussion of what exactly did constitute guilt.

The legislature had given the enforcement agency no hint of its interpretation of the law. What, for example, was "advocacy"? Did it mean ranting soapbox agitation, suggestive innuendos in books and pamphlets, contentious conversations with friends, or confessions of belief wrung from a frightened foreigner by an insistent immigrant inspector? If an alien contributed funds to the I.W.W., which then used part of the money to publish its literature, was the alien "teaching" the doctrines of the organization? Would immigration officers apprehend newsboys who sold I.W.W. papers as advocates and teachers of the unlawful destruction of property? No one had thought about such problems, but the immigration officials were prepared to travel to the frontiers of relevancy in search of proscribed behavior. The commissioner general believed that Congress "also intended to reach the passive and insidious forms [of radical activity] . . . as the only assuredly effective means of curing the active forms; in other words intended to reach the word as well as the deed, and in some respects, *to reach the underlying thought as well.*" [62] Since men have not yet devised a scientific process for arriving at the convictions of the human mind, this policy meant the adoption of a standard of constructive intent for that of overt acts. The immigration inspectors were apparently ready to become America's first thought police.

The implications of the new policy remained as undefined as the law's terminology. By eliminating the time limit on deportations, Congress might well have opened the door to blackmail and encouraged the spies and informers already thickly infiltrated into the labor movement by the private detective agencies. The legislature had unconsciously handed the Immigration Bureau an imposible task. Even with the categories clearly outlined, the service lacked the men, ability, and time to uncover "the passive and insidious forms" of radicalism. And the inspectors, unable to do the job carefully and justly, operated under the pressure of local antiradical vindictiveness and hysteria. The justice, wisdom, and expediency of attempting to legislate a state of mind out of existence had not entered into the calculations of the Sixty-fourth Congress.

A complacent optimism in the executive branch matched the confident carelessness of the legislature. The Secretary of Labor's annual report left no doubts of the effective and meritorious steps forward that had been taken. The immigration law, it stated, was now "much stricter, much clearer, and much more inclusive." The report predicted the dawn of a new era, because, it declared, the act is "couched in such language and arranged with such care that those charged with its enforcement are enabled to temper justice with mercy without doing violence to their conscience, and at the same time the results intended are attained." [63] Unhappily the law did not turn out to be the Magna Charta of the alien deportee.

III

By 1917 the United States had created a crazy quilt antiradical pattern, as unthinking a patchwork as the fear that motivated it. Originating with the antianarchist legislation after McKinley's assassination, federal policy had once again narrowed the field of permissible belief and action and committed itself to the theory of deporting unrest. In addition the country had continually increased the time limits within which it could deport aliens who became radicals. Apart from these trends official policy seemed to be attempting several different things.

First, the government established certain categories of radicals whom it excluded from entry into the country. Belief in or advocacy and teaching of certain proscribed doctrines and membership or affiliation with any organization teaching such ideas served to disqualify such aliens. On the chance that these individuals might still gain admission, however, the law provided for their deportation if caught within five years of entry. Belief, advocacy, and membership were all penalized for aliens attempting to enter as radicals and for aliens that did so enter and were discovered within five years.

In the second place, the law created classes of aliens that were deportable after a legal entry. In other words, immigrants who became radicals after living in the United States could be expelled at any time if they advocated or taught proscribed ideas. It must be noted that the government did not prohibit belief or membership for such aliens as yet, although it was soon to do so.

Finally, an alien radical who had somehow survived both exclusion and deportation fell into the third category of those to whom the government denied naturalization either for belief or for membership.

In 1917 there were still two weaknesses in the rules from the official point of view: the five-year limitation on the deportation of aliens who were radicals at time of entry, and the restricted expulsion of later converts to those who taught and advocated their principles. Deportation at any time because of past or present belief, advocacy, or membership would effectively eliminate these loopholes. Before the antiradical crusade of World War I came to an end, they had disappeared.

The prewar arsenal of repression, so clearly antialien in character, had not, however, been tested in battle by 1917. With the exception of the naturalization program, federal activity had not passed beyond the blueprint stage. Extreme as these plans were, they had affected relatively few people. Had it not been for the war, the antiradical legislation might have merely symbolized for future generations the vague terrors of the past.

On the other hand the war and postwar floods of suppression were considerably dependent on the prewar erosion of rights and safeguards. The vague terminology of deportation legislation, the removal of time limits, the withering away of due process in immigration procedure, the bureaucratic ignorance of radical ideology, and the administrative mind conditioned by its dealings with defenseless undesirables characterized governmental practices by 1917. There were other warning signals as well, such as the tendency of local groups to call for federal aid and their willingness to substitute administrative for judicial process in radical cases. A business community unsympathetic if not openly hostile to the conservative unionism of the A.F. of L. had shown itself anxious to use the I.W.W. as its antilabor scapegoat. Twice before the economic opponents of the I.W.W. had unsuccessfully sought the resolution of their labor troubles at Washington. Given an I.W.W. revival and the appropriate legal techniques, a progressive national administration could not be expected to ignore additional proposals of this character.

By all odds the federal government should have met an I.W.W. resurgence by an attack on its alien segment. Years of debate and preparation suggested that deportation would be the punishment for ideological misconduct. History was ready to concoct this result from the raw materials of the past; yet history has a way of making eleventh-hour renunciations of such strict determinism. Before the federal government could turn to deportation, the United States had entered World War I. The antiradical crusade then took on an entirely new character and tempo.

IV

Military Repression

1917–1921

Iɴ this mad chaos of bloodshed and slaughter that has engulfed the world," the general executive board of the I.W.W. said in 1916, "we reaffirm with unfaltering determination the unalterable opposition of the Industrial Workers of the World and its membership to all wars, and the participation therein of the membership." [1] Such emphatic pacifism was not uncommon in America at that time. Although many progressives and reformers were ardent nationalists and expansionists, nevertheless, from the start of the European conflict the economic interpretation of war had provided other liberal-minded Americans with a rationale for peace. [2] The Socialist party's official position re-enforced the wavering line of pacifism. Its dogmatically antiwar Marxism attributed the conflict above all to "the capitalist system." [3] In 1915 the party urged the American worker to resist not war alone but any and all policies that promoted it. [4]

The I.W.W. could add little but color to the antiwar ideology created by progressive reformers and socialists before 1917. "We will resent with all the power at our command," the organization warned, "any attempt . . . to compel us — the disinherited, to participate in a war that can only bring in its wake death and untold misery, privation and suffering to millions of workers, and only serve to further rivet the chains of slavery on our necks, and render still more secure the power of the few to control the destinies of the many." [5]

The Wobblies considered themselves as exempt from military service as the Quakers or any religious sect that opposed war, and I.W.W. members apparently were ready to resist conscription. In February 1917 the *Industrial Worker* threatened, "Capitalists of America, we will fight against you, not for you!" [6] And after the declaration of war, the same paper expressed the I.W.W. attitude more poetically:

> I love my flag, I do, I do,
> Which floats upon the breeze,
> I also love my arms and legs,
> And neck, and nose and knees.
> One little shell might spoil them all
> Or give them such a twist,
> They would be of no use to me;
>   I guess I won't enlist.
>
> I love my country, yes, I do
> I hope her folks do well.
> Without our arms, and legs and things,
> I think we'd look like hell.
> Young men with faces half shot off
> Are unfit to be kissed,
> I've read in books it spoils their looks,
>   I guess I won't enlist. [7]

As America drifted into war, the reformers, the socialists, and the Wobblies accommodated themselves to the new militarism. The majority of progressives were prowar. For them the horror of fighting and its domestic consequences fell before the idealism of Wilson, their own infatuation with national honor, and the promise of international reform. [8] The Socialist party gave its principles to Marx and the majority of its leadership to Wilson. On April 7, 1917, the St. Louis declaration of the emergency convention branded the conflict as a struggle among "predatory capitalists" and urged Socialists to oppose the war by any means from individual resistance to a class conscious "mass action." Yet the Socialist leaders, outside of Debs, Hillquit, and Berger, supported Wilson and the American intervention.[9]

Although the I.W.W. considered the war a purely imperialistic-capitalistic struggle, and although its leaders remained antiwar, it sought an equivocation that might spare it from governmental attack. As a result the leadership left the questions of registration and conscription to individual decision, but warned its members that opposition to the draft would only lose workers who were needed for organizational activity.[10]

Tactics and expediency in the struggle with America's capitalists were thus impelling forces behind the I.W.W.'s cautious policy. "The only cure for militarism," said the editor of the Seattle *Industrial Worker*, "is industrial anti-capitalism. We can't beat the boss by yelping at him. We must organize in industry before we will have the power to stop war."[11] Anticipating the use that the capitalists would make of the war issue, the I.W.W. cautioned its members not to destroy their power by a senseless anticonscription stand. Above all, the I.W.W. feared entanglement in the courts, for it was felt that "you cannot fight the masters with the legal weapons they have built for their own protection."[12] Organization was the key to all other issues.[13]

Registration by eligible I.W.W.'s ran as high as 95 per cent in some localities, and in general most draft-age Wobblies filled out their forms. Some individuals, of course, acted on their own personal responsibility, agitated against the draft, and refused to register, but there were only two noticeable antidraft movements. In Rockford, Illinois, some hundred men — I.W.W.'s, Socialists, and unattached pacifists, a large number of them Scandanavian aliens — decided to resist the draft. Among the Finns on the Minnesota iron range, there was also a concerted violation of the conscription law. These instances, however, were related to nativity and national hatred (the Finnish antipathy to the American ally, Russia) rather than to ideology. According to its chief counsel, the I.W.W. did not defend the slackers who turned up within the organization nor take notice of appeals for anticonscription strikes. Quite clearly it was concentrating on industrial action. By toning down or ignoring its antimilitaristic and antigovernmental background, the I.W.W. sought a last-minute reprieve from official repression. It even expurgated some of the more extreme and obvious propaganda of sabotage and direct action. The effort was to prove fruitless and irrelevant, for the I.W.W. was convicted in large part for what it had been in the past.[14]

In the wartime hysteria of 1917, Americans were in no mood to accept reasonable interpretations of the inflammatory and incendiary prose by which the I.W.W. had lived. Identified by past actions and former writings, Wobblies could never divest themselves of these connotations and took the full brunt of damnation by association. At the same time the I.W.W. made certain such ammunition would be used. Its relentless industrial program destroyed whatever benefits might have accrued from toning down sabotage and anti-militarism. By emphasizing the continuing war with the master class and by refusing to abandon the right to strike, the I.W.W. retained the very concepts that were to ensure its suppression. Nor were their strike plans only utopian dreams. In 1917 the apparent success of the I.W.W.'s dramatic organizing campaign was a frightening reality in several sections of the United States.

II

The I.W.W. comeback had been foreshadowed as early as 1915. The chartering of the Agricultural Workers Organization (the A.W.O. no. 400) in that year pulled the I.W.W. off the edge of oblivion. In decline from the climactic heights of 1912, the Wobblies had a pitiful membership backed by a penniless treasury. Within two years the A.W.O. had sent organizers into the lumber, oil, mining, and construction industries of the West, reviving a defunct unionism in those areas and serving as "the financial mainstay of the whole I.W.W." [15]

The A.W.O.'s success in the middle western wheat belt was the foundation upon which it built its own as well as the I.W.W.'s new power and authority. The harvest fields were ripe for a union campaign, since the mechanized, seasonal operations had destroyed the personal relationship of farmer and hired hand and created a class of casual laborers alien to and hated by the rural population.[16] With every member a potential organizer, the I.W.W. operated under cover, avoided free-speech fights, and converted losing strikes on the job into slowdowns in production. Stuart Jamieson concluded that "by the practice of such methods the A.W.O. became entrenched in the wheat belt and, in a period of relative labor shortage and rising wages, it secured wage increases and better working conditions." [17]

Measured by the loathing and fear it evoked, the I.W.W. was doing an effective organizing job. Against the strikes and union activity he had never seen before, the farmer responded with vigilante committees, illegal arrests, and deportations. Grant Wood's America thus witnessed so much class warfare that the local press reported "a reign of terror" in the summer of 1916 and a feeling of helplessness that "all methods of handling the situation have proven unavailing." [18] The year 1917 promised an even worse harvest for the farmer. His hysterical fear of the Wobblies was inflamed by supposedly reliable newspaper sources predicting the future destruction of the crop. Reports of I.W.W. incendiarism and sabotage were widespread, exaggerated, and thoroughly believable to an excited populace.[19]

Other industries equally crucial to a successful war effort faced the revived determination of I.W.W. organizers. The seventy-mile-long Mesabi iron range in northern Minnesota saw some seven to eight thousand immigrant miners walk out spontaneously in June 1916. Only the I.W.W. answered their appeal for help. Fighting a subsidiary of United States Steel with its private police force, organized citizens' committees, and subservient local officials, the Wobblies lost the strike but maintained a constant agitation thereafter.[20]

Beginning in the fall of 1916, the I.W.W. initiated a vigorous campaign to organize Arizona's four metal-producing districts, which supplied 28 per cent of the nation's copper.[21] In June and July of 1917 the conservative International Union of Mine, Mill, and Smelter Workers and several A.F. of L. unions joined the small Wobbly force in a general walkout. They were protesting in common the refusal of the copper companies to adjust or arbitrate grievances, the failure of wages to match the wartime price rise in copper, and the industry's discrimination against union activity and union employees.[22]

Denouncing the strike as German-inspired, the corporations refused to bargain, stocked up arms and ammunition, and used illegal violence against I.W.W.'s to adjust their labor difficulties. Although the strikers had been peaceful and orderly, local businessmen under corporation leadership conspired to remove all labor agitators and troublemakers from the mining towns of Jerome and Bisbee, Arizona. On July 10 the citizens of Jerome shipped sixty-seven I.W.W.'s in cattle cars to the California border. Two days later Bisbee had its roundup, loading twelve hundred I.W.W.'s, suspected I.W.W.'s, pro-I.W.W. townspeople, and others on a twenty-seven-car train that ended up in the desert near Hermanas, New Mexico. Taken in charge by federal military authorities, the Bisbee refugees remained under army guard in a stockade that was not completely emptied until the end of September.[23]

While their organizers were infesting the wheat fields, the

Mesabi iron range, and the mines of the Southwest, the I.W.W. also attacked at Butte, Montana the largest single copper-producing district in the United States. This town had not always had the poisonous labor relations of class warfare. For a generation before 1914 the Western Federation of Miners and the copper companies had maintained an industrial peace undisturbed by any serious strike. But in 1914 the Western Federation lost all control in Butte, and thereafter three organizations struggled for power: the conservative WFM group, now named the International Union of Mine, Mill, and Smelter Workers; the I.W.W.; and the local and equally radical Metal Mine Workers Union. Among them they had organized only 10 per cent of the miners, for Butte had become an open-shop town.[24]

The copper companies dramatically reversed their labor policies when the Western Federation no longer commanded the allegiance of the majority of miners. Under the leadership of the Anaconda Copper Company, they were determined to drive radicalism from the mining camps. Abandoning the closed shop and the trade agreement, the corporations introduced the "rustling card," an identification used as a blacklist against union advocates and labor agitators. Mutual suspicion and ill-will replaced the harmonious relations of the early period. Mine guards, military protection, and labor espionage characterized industrial relations at Butte after 1914.[25]

The Speculator mine disaster, suffocating and burning to death 164 workers in June 1917, touched off a series of strikes that plagued Butte throughout the war. The miners walked out in order to improve bad underground conditions, eliminate the rustling card, and obtain wage benefits in line with Butte's cost of living increase, one of the nation's highest. The I.W.W. simply cast the agitation into a more radical framework.[26]

As in Arizona, the corporations and their allies refused to

treat the 1917 strike as a legitimate labor dispute. Despite its orderly nature, the work stoppage became stereotyped by its opponents as lawless anarchy destroying Montana's industries. The newspapers published distorted accounts of the strike, magnified the role of the I.W.W., and assigned to it events that never took place.[27] To the Wilson administration at Washington went reports that "matters in Montana are in a very critical condition," and that only immediate federal action could "make secure the lives and property of the people."[28] Yet the evidence revealed no lawlessness, but only, as the senator from Montana admitted upon investigation, "a lot of intriguing and seditious talk."[29]

The final and perhaps decisive factor impelling the Wilson administration toward some forceful repression of the I.W.W. was the lumber strike of 1917 in the Pacific Northwest, the Wobblies' "first and last real display of power" in that region.[30] Here, as in other areas, the wartime manifestations of labor unrest were the almost inevitable outcome of an industrial development that for one reason or another had disregarded or neglected its working force. Historically the lumber operator had been a speculator rapidly liquidating his stumpage rather than carefully exploiting it. This in turn had led to a "sawdust-pile, ghost-shack town" form of development.[31] In addition, there were both seasonal and intra-seasonal shutdowns due to climatic conditions. The "lumberjacks," "blanket stiffs," or "river pigs," all terms of contempt, were migratory, often workless, usually womanless, and generally the luckless beneficiaries of the "roughest and crudest" living and working conditions.[32] The average lumberjack had spent his life in filthy, crowded, vermin-infested camps, and had worked long hours for low pay in "an atmosphere of distrust and suspicion."[33]

The industry had uncompromisingly opposed every attempt by the lumberjacks to organize. The migratory and temporary nature of the work together with the determination of the employers to concede nothing had successfully smothered the union movement before the war. The operators, as one government forester observed, "held the whip hand for a long time." The harvest they reaped was of their own making.[34]

In the summer of 1916 a violent conflict developed at the open-shop mill town of Everett, Washington. Following an unsuccessful strike by A.F. of L. shingle weavers, I.W.W. organizers tried their hand at agitation. Volunteer vigilantes of Everett's Commercial Club arrested, clubbed, and deported I.W.W.'s who flooded into the town. Not to be denied, and in the tradition of their free-speech fights, the Wobblies set sail some three hundred strong from Seattle in two chartered boats. On November 5, 1916, this expeditionary force failed to breach Everett's Maginot line — several hundred armed citizens waiting at dockside. In the ensuing battle five Wobblies and two vigilantes died; thirty-one Wobblies and nineteen citizens were wounded.[35] The aftermath of the massacre equally embittered the contending forces. The state held seventy-four I.W.W.'s for first-degree murder, but released them when the first defendant won his acquittal. For the people of the Northwest "The Everett conflict . . . helped to fix the image of an internal enemy in an embattled society." [36]

To the I.W.W.'s, Everett was the harbinger of further success in the woods. Soon after the close of the Everett trial and approximately concurrent with the United States declaration of war, an active propaganda for the eight-hour day spread through the lumber industry. In addition, the workers requested higher wages and greatly improved living conditions in the camps. Although wartime price increases made these demands financially feasible, the lumber operators determined to make a fight to the finish with labor.[37]

The I.W.W. was the major beneficiary of this obvious intractability. The lumberjacks, faced with counterpressures from employers refusing concessions and from a radical element demanding changes, joined the radicals. In many areas 90 to 95 per cent of the men in the woods became members of the I.W.W. For the most part they joined it in order to make an effective protest rather than to forward its revolutionary aims.[38]

Beginning in June 1917 the timber strike brought lumber production to a virtual standstill during the summer. If continued this would have seriously threatened the vital airplane, cantonment, and shipbuilding programs of the federal government. An alarming shortage in boxes also promised to tie up the Northwest's fruit harvest.[39]

The operators, meanwhile, had taken two kinds of action: local defensive measures and appeals to the national administration. Refusing to bargain as long as the I.W.W. was a factor in the strike, the employers formed the Lumbermen's Protective League. Members agreed to support the ten-hour day or forfeit a heavy fine. Retail-dealer boycotts of eight-hour lumber supported this plan.[40] The operators also tried to keep all I.W.W. lumberjacks out of the woods, first, by blacklisting them with a rustling card system, and second, by urging the government Forest Service to secure its fire fighters only through company agencies. The Forest Service refused to so ally itself, and striking I.W.W.'s formed the majority of the generally excellent crews used that year.[41]

The proposals that poured into Washington were many and varied. Defining the I.W.W.'s as public enemies, sealing all railroad boxcars to prevent their movement, building an internment camp for "local malcontents," and punishing any curtailment of production were some of the ideas that reflected the Northwest's growing desire to suppress the I.W.W. without making concessions to it.[42]

The war had thus affected the course of repression in several ways. In the first place, a strike could now be described not only as a legitimate labor struggle but also as seditious interference in war production. The Wilson administration disliked all interruptions of war production caused by labor disputes, but it did not handle them all in the same way. The federal government tolerated strikes by the recognized union movement and dealt with the issues involved by mediation, conciliation, and concession. There were, in fact, hundreds of wartime A.F. of L. walkouts. The government understood the need for keeping labor behind the war effort and in a reasonable frame of mind. There was no such sympathetic flexibility, however, for the labor radicals. I.W.W. strikes were outside the realm of mediation, and because of the organization's earlier antigovernment and antiwar propaganda, the Wilson administration found it easy to consider all I.W.W. strikes illegitimate. In the second place, the Wobblies' militant and dramatic surge in the lumber, mining, and agricultural centers of the West had established the organization as a menace to numerous communities producing essential war materials. Thus, the apparent necessity and agitation for the repression of labor radicals coincided with their increasing demands for concessions.

Finally, an atmosphere of war hysteria colored all decisions from the local to the national level. One hundred per cent Americanism, with its demand for conformity and distaste for dissent, savagely resented any threat to national unity, especially of a class and radical nature. Nativist anxieties increased this tension. Such an irrational and emotional atmosphere encouraged patriots, businessmen, and politicians to indoctrinate official Washington with exaggerated accounts of a treasonable I.W.W. conspiracy. Convinced of its own helplessness in the face of Wobbly solidarity, each locality hoped that the federal government would resolve an intolerable industrial crisis.[43]

Despite these appeals, the question of federal suppression remained up in the air. The speed, extent, and character of any crackdown would depend, of course, on the attitudes of

Wilson's officials and their ability to find new techniques or to utilize prewar precedents appropriate to the task. The Department of Justice was at first unable to find any federal law under which it move. During June, July, and August, the Attorney General promised to continue the investigations by federal agents, but he reminded state officials that domestic tranquillity was their responsibility.[44] This, of course, satisfied no one. Those who wanted immediate action, therefore, turned to the Immigration Bureau for help. It was assumed that labor relations would improve if the country deported its alien agitators.[45]

III

Local officials and businessmen had no reason to expect either delay or confusion in eliminating I.W.W. radicalism. The Immigration Act of 1917, aimed specifically at the Wobblies, would most certainly be an efficient instrument for this purpose. Ex-Governor John Lind of Minnesota, an influential member of the state's public safety commission, was a representative spokesman of the West. He urged the local immigration inspectors to arrest all I.W.W. alien agitators on the iron range.[46] Estimating that two thirds of the organizers and delegates were alien, the former governor predicted that deportation would be simpler and cheaper than a federal criminal trial and much more "wholesome." The threat of expulsion, he felt, had a much greater deterrent impact than any jail sentence.[47]

Local proponents of suppression did not demand a full-scale attack on the alien membership, but rather a carefully selected purge of a few agitators accompanied by a well-publicized but fictitious threat to deport all alien members. Wrongly convinced that the I.W.W.'s were largely foreign-born, their enemies hoped to eliminate the leadership and scare the rank and file. Deportations were thus to be numerous enough to frighten the labor force but not so numerous

as to cripple it. The last things the lumber and mining interests desired during a wartime labor scarcity were mass
arrests that might injure production. In addition, any large-
scale depletion of workers would tend to strengthen the bargaining position of organized labor. The workers must be
kept on the job — but brainwashed from their radical beliefs and divorced from their support of radical organizations.
With its alien component gone, the I.W.W. was confidently
expected to collapse from lack of financial support.[48]

Prosecuting attorneys and employers also looked upon deportation as the most flexible and discretionary weapon available for their attack upon radical labor agitators. Proof of
individual guilt was the great stumbling block in labor disturbances. The failure of Idaho to secure convictions under
its criminal syndicalism law was a further indication of the
dilemma.[49] In addition, the judicial process with its "discussion of the rules of evidence or immaterial technicalities"
handicapped the prosecution and was notoriously slow.[50]
Any act left to the administrative interpretation and enforcement of local inspectors could easily surmount the one
puzzling obstacle — lack of legal evidence of guilt under
local, state, or federal law. Deportation legislation, so many
believed, was ideally designed to reflect such variables as
wartime labor scarcity, seasonal shift in employment, a sudden influx of radicals, or politically inspired hysteria.

Immigration Bureau officials at Washington were seismo-
graphic recorders of the antiradical tremors in the West,
being much more sensitive to local pressures and much more
the captive audience of hysteria than the superior authorities in the Department of Labor. By July 25, 1917, the commissioner general and his chief law officer had accepted the
pro-German stereotype of the I.W.W. and were urging the
Department to adopt "a vigorous policy." Admitting that the
roundup of I.W.W. aliens might be "a very expensive and

onerous undertaking," the bureau felt justified in "taking every possible step in the direction of putting an end to the propaganda."[51]

Secretary of Labor William B. Wilson's caution momentarily quarantined this enthusiasm for large-scale arrests. Wilson, a former member of the United Mine Workers and sympathetic to the underdog, was too liberal and humane to prejudge the Wobbly "working stiff." Before applying the 1917 law, the Secretary ordered a thorough investigation of the I.W.W. constitution, preamble, and literature. Did the organization advocate and teach the unlawful destruction of property; what did "advocacy" and "teach" mean; and did mere membership bring an individual under the law?[52]

The legal experts on the Immigration Bureau staff gathered scant solace from their survey of I.W.W. literature. Apparently the Wobblies as an organization had stayed within the law. From the excerpts gathered by immigration inspectors and Department of Justice agents, the lawyers found that the I.W.W. writings *"hinted at"* resistance to organized government and its representatives, but "contain nothing in direct advocacy of anarchism, active opposition to organized government, or the destruction of property, public or private." Although the bureau's investigators discovered some direct advocacy of "the turning out of worthless products at the factories, the impeding of factory output . . . and the practice of 'sabotage,' " they dejectedly announced that the meaning of that word was "not altogether clear or well defined."[53]

Failing to discover evidence in the organization's own statements, bureau lawyers suggested proving their cases with newspaper accounts and reports of public and business officials about I.W.W. activities. Then membership plus advocacy of organization principles would constitute cause for arrest.[54] But Secretary Wilson, then traveling westward to investigate labor conditions on the coast, deferred a final decision on the I.W.W. and approved in the interim an extremely limited application of the 1917 law.[55]

The Secretary insisted that inspectors thoroughly substantiate personal guilt before requesting a warrant of arrest. Warrants would issue only after an exhaustive inquiry into the alien's beliefs, teachings, and actions.[56] This interpretation of the law stunned the local offices of the bureau, for it created a standard of guilt as exacting as that in judicial proceedings.[57] Immigration officials might well have wondered how they could implicate aliens in their individual capacity. In the understaffed, overworked Immigration Bureau, local inspectors covered huge territories. Wilson's policy demanded an all but impossible surveillance of innumerable migratory agitators, part of a decentralized leadership too numerous to trail. If state and local law enforcement agencies could not detect any individual violations of the law, what could a few immigration inspectors do? [58]

The dilemma was an almost hopeless one. If the Department of Labor insisted on individual guilt, then it created a standard the bureau could not achieve. If it lowered the standards, then the door was wide open to the wholesale deportation of I.W.W.'s regardless of individual guilt or innocence, and superpatriots or overenthusiastic inspectors might easily get out of hand. For the moment, the department was unwilling to sanction the administrative discretion demanded by the lower echelon. Secretary Wilson refused to approve an exploration beyond the well-mapped terrain of personal guilt.

This unexpected impasse between Washington and its officials in the field was characteristic of the wartime crusade against radicals. Time and again federal policies that seemed headed in one direction suddenly shifted course. Wilson's limiting criterion of individual guilt was not to last out the year. Under local pressure for deportation drives, immigration inspectors would begin to violate widely the standards established by the Secretary of Labor. A new immigration law would also establish guilt by association. Yet these were slow in coming, too slow to satisfy the West. During the immediate crisis in the summer of 1917, the Immigration Bureau was obviously not eliminating the I.W.W., and so communities threatened by Wobbly strikes sought other solutions.

The drive to suppress labor radicals thereupon developed two additional and unforeseen phases: use of federal troops under the wartime emergency, and judicial prosecutions by the federal government, also under cover of the war. All three — troops, trials, and deportations — ran more or less simultaneously, but the deportation crusade always remained the favorite weapon. And to it the government returned when the war emergency had passed.

IV

During July and August of 1917, businessmen and public officials of the West called in troops to eliminate the radical threat. At the very moment when the Wobblies seemed to be winning the lumber strike of 1917, the timber interests employed the federal army as their strikebreakers. The participation of federal troops in local strikes was unusual, unconstitutional, and linked to the war emergency. Not since the violent labor disturbances of 1877 and 1894 had federal troops guaranteed labor peace. In fact, for many years states had quelled domestic unrest either with injunctions or with a national guard that had grown in efficiency and power. When the Wilson administration called the National Guard into federal service as the war crisis neared, however, the states found themselves lacking an effective force in the face of mounting labor unrest and radical activity.[59] If troops were to be used, they would have to be federal troops.

Under the Constitution (Article IV, section 4) and the

laws which give it effect (sections 5297, 5298, and 5300 of the Revised Statutes), the army may suppress disturbances on its own initiative only when they contravene federal laws, and may put down insurrections against state authority only when the legislature or the governor certifies the state's exhaustion of all local remedies and its inability to meet the emergency.[60] Even then the President must first issue a proclamation for the rebels to disperse peacefully within a stated time. Should they fail to do so, federal forces are sent into action. In addition, by the act of 1878 federal troops may not be used as a *posse comitatus* to federal law officers. Previous to the passage of that act federal marshals had often called on the army in making arrests. Needless to say, state and local officials had never had the legal authority to use federal troops as a *posse comitatus*.[61] How then were troops to be justifiably committed in the lumber and mining strikes of 1917?

The situation in the West hardly involved open insurrection or lawlessness. Prosecuting attorneys in Montana and Washington and special agents of the Bureau of Investigation testified to the peacefulness of the strikes and the lack of violence and intimidation by the I.W.W.[62] Almost all the appeals for help lacked evidence of actual violence and concentrated instead on the possibilities of future destruction and imminent catastrophes — the great fear being that of I.W.W. job control.[63]

Government action, however, was not to be based on the realities that investigators reported or on the world as it was, but on a deliberately created public hysteria against the I.W.W. in the press, in petitions to Congress, and in manipulated mob violence on the local level.[64] Here was an unreasoning anxiety that demanded the suppression of the Wobblies and the restoration of the community's sense of security. Behind this pressure were the bankers, businessmen, lumber operators, and farmers who desired to break the I.W.W.

strikes with nonmembers and to force the I.W.W. out of the harvest and fruit fields. All these groups anticipated possible resistance and considered troops essential to the maintenance of order. New theories sanctified the new procedures that met this need.[65]

War Department authorizations to local army officers in March, April, and May of 1917 that they should "sternly repress acts committed with seditious intent" and should protect "public utilities" essential to the war provided criteria vague and flexible enough to cover intervention in industrial disputes.[66] In addition, army officers could arrest I.W.W.'s who committed acts of violence or "similar acts . . . in pursuance of prearranged plans contemplating violence," under the theory that such acts were disloyal.[67] Although President Wilson approved this course of action, he urged Secretary of War Newton D. Baker to warn army commanders to distinguish carefully between "ordinary offenses against the law and against public order" and "acts committed under the provocation of the present excitement and with seditious or disloyal intent.[68] This, of course, was exactly the fine line that the military was unable to draw.

The administration told commanding generals to deal directly with local officials and businessmen in suppressing sedition and safeguarding "public utilities." This authority was in turn delegated to the platoon level, so that lieutenants and their men were available to county sheriffs and district attorneys.[69] The army had become an illegal *posse comitatus* not only for federal authorities but for local and state officials as well. Neglecting the need for the President's proclamation or a declaration of martial law, the military assumed jurisdiction where the civil courts were functioning and where peaceable strikes were in progress. One way of preventing anticipated labor violence was to jail the laborer. Although Secretary of Labor William B. Wilson doubted the wisdom of such a policy, and the Department of Justice observed its illegal features, the War Department approved its execution.[70]

The pattern was similar throughout the West. In Montana, troops raided I.W.W. headquarters in Flathead County and held I.W.W. leaders and members "in confinement in the city jail in Whitefish for a period of several weeks without filing any charges against them." [71] The men finally won their release through habeas corpus proceedings. Elsewhere in the state soldiers patrolled the towns initiating a system of forced labor for Wobblies.

In Washington the army raided I.W.W. halls, broke up camp meetings, searched freights for migrant workers, arrested delegates and organizers, and jailed dozens of I.W.W.'s.[72] It held and questioned them on their memberships and social and economic views. The military released only those who were "willing to work without agitating strikes" and those who the army felt confident would not be "a menace to the best interests of industry." [73]

While a few Wobblies were legally detainable as slackers or unregistered alien enemies, over 90 per cent could have effected their freedom on habeas corpus. This was the inevitable result of a policy calling for arrests in anticipation of lawlessness. To meet this contingency, army officers, public officials, and local councils of defense agreed on the following plan: "Persons arrested by the troops will be turned over to the sheriffs to hold, subject to release by the officer in command. The civil authorities, federal and state, will take charge of such as may be legally held by them. The others will be subject to the order of the military commander so that if petitions for habeas corpus are presented, return can be made that the prisoners are held by military power." [74] The proponents of this veiled and illicit martial law were confident that the state courts would not interfere with such a procedure during a war emergency. When I.W.W.'s protested their confinement by the military power the courts, as expected, denied the writs of habeas corpus.[75]

The authorities justified the illegal detentions on the grounds that the Wobblies needed to be "protected against injury." Admitting that I.W.W.'s might dislike the arrangement, the United States attorney at Spokane insisted, "It is best for them, too, because the people are of such a frame of mind that any slight disturbance on the part of the I.W.W.'s might cause most serious results." In one county, for example, a citizen army of fourteen hundred was supposedly armed and ready "to inflict serious, perhaps, fatal injury" to any Wobblies.[76] Protective custody has often been the historical justification for the exercise of arbitrary power. The army preferred to preserve law and order by imprisoning an unpopular minority rather than by controlling the community violence directed against it. This breach of the peace theory "makes a man criminal simply because his neighbors have no self-control and cannot refrain from violence." [77]

The uninterrupted intervention of the army in the northwestern lumber strike eventually produced an equally extreme reaction on the part of the I.W.W. Seeing no end to martial law and not caring to be "protected against injury," the I.W.W. planned a regional general strike for August 20 to force the release of all "class-war prisoners," whether unjustly held by military authority or legally detained as draft evaders and alien enemies.[78]

The general strike threat was the final pretext for the military roundup of I.W.W.'s during that summer's disorders. Predicting the inevitable loss of the wheat and fruit crops if the I.W.W. agitators remained at large, state officials certified their helplessness and urged immediate military action. On August 19 troops shut down the Spokane headquarters of the I.W.W., arresting the strike leader and some twenty-five members, and holding them under military guard in the county jail. While the army prohibited "large and unusual congregations on the street," federal and state prosecutors and military representatives questioned the arrested men. The government detained anyone deemed to be "an agitator," "active in the movement," or "in any way a leader"; the others were released. The army congratulated itself on having "effectively saved the situation," while state officials agreed that "the use of troops at Spokane had a very salutary effect." [79]

While the summer of 1917 witnessed the only large-scale military intervention in labor disputes involving radicals, federal troops occupied the Arizona and Montana copper camps until 1920 and 1921 in order to combat the I.W.W. "menace." Just as in the lumber strike, the War Department authorized its subordinate officers to communicate with state officials and to "take such action as the situation demands." [80] The power granted to local commanders extended far beyond the specific strike and locality that had evoked it into a general grant of authority "applicable to any similar situation arising in your department." [81]

Although the federal government insisted that its troops should play an absolutely neutral role in any labor-capital dispute, there was no such fine impartiality in practice. Ostensibly the army had instructions simply "to preserve law and order and protect life and property." [82] Yet the very presence of troops had a repressive effect on the striking miners. The military could hardly act as a neutral bystander during a strike whose success depended on picketing to block the introduction of scabs and strikebreakers into the plant or mine. Soldiers protected those who wanted to work from intimidation, physical or otherwise, of the strikers. Without the thorough and continuously effective interruption of production, a strike had only a slim chance of achieving its aims. In the Arizona copper camps, the army used its forces "to disperse crowds" at mine entrances, "to prevent gatherings of large numbers of idle people for the purpose of intimidation of mine employees," to break up "seditious meetings blocking public streets," to guard mine and mill property, to forbid public meetings, and to patrol troublesome sections of the community.[83] At the beginning of the war the government justified this action by classifying the copper companies as major utilities to whom it owed federal protection. Later on it brought the copper areas under the Sabotage Act of April 1918. The mines then became "war premises," their output "war materials," and their processing and distributing plants "war utilities." At this point the army gave its commanders "authority to disperse or arrest persons unlawfully assembled at or near any 'war premises' for the purpose of intimidating, alarming, disturbing, or injuring persons lawfully employed thereon, or molesting or destroying property thereat." [84]

Other signs also indicated the degree to which the army took the view of the mine management in its dispute with labor. Local businessmen and police officials, company superintendents, and the "better elements" always gave army officers their orientation to industrial conditions. Military intelligence agents operating under cover accepted the reports of the private dectectives paid by the corporations. The troops themselves were quartered in barracks erected and owned by the mining companies, a practice that gave workers the idea that federal troops were guests of the management. The War Department believed that such billeting was "plainly necessary and entirely practicable," since the corporations had requested the guards for the protection of company property. (One can imagine the government housing troops in I.W.W. halls.) Army officers could also accept the management stereotype of Arizona's Governor Hunt as "socialistic" and possibly disloyal because of his sympathy with the miners.[85]

The military undoubtedly fulfilled its purpose. Not only did troops preserve law and order and prevent bloodshed; they also guaranteed the peaceful production of copper during the war. Soon after its arrival in July 1917, the army could report that "increasing numbers [of strikers] are returning [to work] daily depending wholly on protection of troops." [86] Army officers were convinced that the soldiers alone stood in the way of the I.W.W.'s supposed attempts to agitate, create unrest, impair mine output, and destroy property, while businessmen testified to the "undoubtedly . . . splendid moral effect" that the presence of the troops had had.[87]

Labor conditions at the end of the war were not stable enough to justify the withdrawal of the army detachments. At least the state officials and copper companies did not think so. They expected that lower wages following falling copper prices would produce unrest. Despite the protest of mine owners and of Arizona's Governor Campbell, the army removed its units, first from the Bisbee area in the fall of 1919, then from Ajo, Globe, Ray, Miami, and Jerome in early 1920. The commanding general felt that conditions by then were "normal" and that it was time to discover whether or not "civil authorities are able to control the laborers at those places." [88]

While the federal forces in Arizona adopted a police role that was mildly and, to some degree, unconsciously anti-labor, their counterparts in Butte, Montana, became at times the vigorous and open ally of the Anaconda Copper Company's drive against radicals. The lynching of Wobbly organizer Frank Little in August 1917 had been the excuse for the troops to restore law and order. They remained until January 8, 1921. During that period the army made several illegal excursions as a *posse comitatus* for the search and seizure of suspected labor radicals. The cooperation of the military with the officials and gunmen of the copper company was perhaps a natural growth of the peculiar situation in Butte.[89]

Both the United States attorney's office and the district court adamantly refused to succumb to the wartime hysteria and the antiradicalism then widespread in Butte as in the country at large. District Attorney Burton K. Wheeler and Special Agent E. W. Byrn were rigorously neutral in their calm enforcement of the federal laws. For this they won the enmity of local officials and businessmen. The latter referred to Wheeler as derelict and disloyal, and accused him of being in sympathy with the I.W.W.[90] Federal Judge George Bourquin made an even worse impression on eager patriots and copper executives. Highly esteemed legally and an appointee of President Taft, Judge Bourquin had a deep regard for the legal rights and civil liberties of individuals, including radicals. He interpreted the provisions of the Espionage and Selective Service laws strictly, and was out of sympathy with the excessive sentences typical of their enforcement. In addition, his son was a partner in the Butte law firm that defended Wobblies and aided the Non-Partisan League. So-called decent citizens, the local military intelligence, and the Anaconda crowd characterized Bourquin as "a Wobbly and pro-German sympathizer." [91]

Law enforcement in Butte was obviously not keeping pace with the excited apprehensions and insistent demands of its influential citizens. They therefore turned to the military for the satisfaction of their antiradical desires. The chairman of the Butte council of defense warned the army, "The minute the military here stop detaining men for seditious acts we have got to take it into our own hands and have a mob, and we don't want to start that. I can get a mob up here in twenty-four hours and hang half a dozen men." W. A. Clark of the Clark mining interests spoke for his fellow businessmen when he predicted that riots and bloodshed would follow the withdrawal of troops. "I don't believe in lynching or violence of that kind," Clark professed, "*unless it is necessary.*" It did not become necessary because the soldiers from the time of their arrival in August honored every request the council of defense made to them to protect the mines or the town itself. The president of the chamber of commerce reported that, as long as troops were on the scene, "every businessman . . . feels perfectly safe." [92]

Several incidents during 1918 illustrated how close and customary this cooperation became between local authorities and federal troops. The first such instance occurred when part of Butte's Irish and radical population planned to stage a St. Patrick's Day parade on March 17, 1918. Prominent citizens, fearing that a public demonstration of this kind might result in riot, influenced the mayor and the council of defense to prohibit the parade. On the request of Montana's governor, the commanding general of that area told his troops at Butte to "cooperate fully" with the local authorities.[93] When some six thousand workers assembled in the town on the holiday afternoon, the soldiers cleared the streets, helped police make over a hundred arrests, and chased off the few who resisted "with bayonets or rifle butts." [94]

Upon hearing of this resort to federal military power, the judge advocate general's office advised the chief of staff that the governor of a state had absolutely no authority to give orders to a United States Army officer, nor had the officer any right to obey such instructions. The army leadership apparently did not heed the cautionary warnings of its legal branch. The director of the War Plans Division, then acting chief of staff, thought that the situation at Butte fell under paragraph 487 of Army Regulations. This paragraph approved action by local commanders without presidential orders in cases of "emergency so imminent as to render it dangerous to await instructions requested through the speediest means of communication." The acting chief of staff believed the Butte troops had "acted entirely within the law and . . . shown most commendable good sense." [95]

In September 1918 the military detachment, once more disguised as a local police, joined forces with the Anaconda Copper Company in a crackdown on the radical element. The

move coincided with the government's conviction of the
I.W.W. leadership at Chicago. Facing long sentences for
conspiracy to violate the war laws, the Wobblies decided to
call a general strike in the Northwest. Perhaps they hoped
to force the release of "class-war" prisoners; most likely the
move was just a symbol of protest. The miners as a whole,
however, were apathetic to a walkout for the release of
"class-war" convicts. Special Agent Byrn confidently predicted that the Wobblies would be able to pull out only a few
hundred of their own members. At the same time he called
attention to the miners' bitter underlying hatred of the
Anaconda Company and their resentment against local conditions. Such feelings, Byrn felt, could always generate
sympathetic mass protest out of sullen resignation, if the corporation took any overt antilabor act.[96]

Anaconda seemed intent on a showdown. Its detective informers were high in the ranks of the Butte I.W.W. In vio-
lently incendiary speeches these company provocateurs encouraged their cohorts to adopt a position that the government would define as seditious and disloyal. In other words,
the copper company was having its paid agents help
organize a wartime strike against itself as a ruse for the indictment and elimination of the local radical menace.[97]

Once the I.W.W. strike became a reality on September
13, 1918, the federal troops played the role in which they
had been cast by the leading citizens of Butte. The strike itself was an apparent failure, for the Wobblies had lined up
a pitiful five hundred men out of total force of some twenty
thousand. The Bureau of Investigation agent reported to his
chief, "Conditions quiet all day on thirteenth." [98] That night
the army, aided by Anaconda officials and gunmen and the
local police, raided the headquarters of the independent
Metal Mine Workers Union, the office and plant of the
radical *Butte Bulletin,* and the local I.W.W. hall. Without
warrant of any kind the soldiers illegally seized Wobbly and

non-Wobbly miners, searched the premises of the respective organizations, took quantities of literature, and held the Metal Mine Workers headquarters and the *Bulletin* office isolated under military guard. The forty arrested workers were booked "as held for Council of Defense." [99]

Despite the fact that their roundup added nearly five thousand miners to the feeble Wobbly walkout, the military authorities continued to press for forceful action over the protests of United States Attorney Wheeler and his staff. It had been customary for the military to maintain patrols "wherever necessary to best protect the workers in the mines from physical violence and intimidation by I.W.W.'s." In pursuance of this policy the soldiers often dispersed "gatherings of idle men" and, when they failed "to comply with orders to move on," the army arrested and detained them.[100] In the days following the strike, the Butte detachment arrested seventy-four men without any legal warrant, often by force, sometimes brutally. The great majority were charged with "sedition," accused of causing a "disturbance," or simply "held for investigation by the Department of Justice." All but one were released for lack of any evidence with which to prefer charges.[101]

The federal law-enforcement officials urged Washington to bring the troops under control. The Attorney General warned the Secretary of War that the function of the federal troops was the protection of specific mines and utilities against unauthorized entry or violence. Troops had no authority to raid, much less to raid without warrant. Without martial law, state and local officials remained responsible for protecting property and enforcing state and local law. The responsibility for the federal laws lay, of course, with the United States attorney, not with the army or the military intelligence office. These protests and the armistice in Europe terminated the army's lawless subservience to the local officials and management in Butte.[102]

The army's defense of its action was an interesting document, reflecting the attitude of the military mind to the Constitution. The War Department commander claimed that his subordinates had made "detentions not arrests in technical sense" and argued that there had been "no time to secure formal warrants or comply with legal technicalities." Unless the troops had the power to make these informal "detentions," General Morrison guaranteed that "mob violence would surely occur." While the War Department agreed that "some of the arrests . . . were not strictly in accordance with the law," it justified them because they "produced results, received the commendation of the worthy citizens . . . and enabled the mines to keep up their output of copper and manganese." In addition, such arrests became excusable when they occured during an emergency and did not stem from "personal animus." The War Department's concluding remarks on the incident best revealed its fundamental attitude. The local officer, the report stated, "arrested or detained no worthy citizen [and] no worthy citizens have complained of his treatment of them." [103]

Besides their occupation of the western copper camps and their intermittent participation in the raids and seizures of striking radicals, the armed forces also kept a watchful undercover eye on all radical activity among the civilian population. The military intelligence officers of the Western and Southern departments, for example, stationed their personnel in the mining and lumber centers to furnish reports on the I.W.W. This counterespionage included the placing of military intelligence operatives in I.W.W. ranks, mail supervision, and the gathering of confidential data from the files of private detective companies and corporations. A corps of investigators, both army and civilian, made numerous investigations and placed many suspected radicals under surveillance. In the Western Department alone the military intelligence division collected data and kept files on "thousands of I.W.W.-Bolsheviki." In several instances local intelligence officers went beyond the mere gathering of information and actively helped organize and carry out roundups of I.W.W.'s and other radicals.[104]

Surveillance, occupation, and suppression marked the wartime participation of the federal troops in the drive against subversive labor elements. By September 1920 the army had put down twenty-nine domestic disorders without resort to constitutional procedures.[105] At one time or another the Department of Justice and the War Department's own judge advocate's office both emphasized the illegal nature of these proceedings. Such censure apparently had no policy-making role in army circles. Neither a sense of shame nor a conviction of wrongdoing motivated the military's embrace of the Constitution in 1921. By then the states had rebuilt their National Guard units and the emergency had passed. Opportunities for federal intervention simply withered away. In December 1920 Secretary of War Newton D. Baker looked back upon the widespread wartime use of the armed forces as a local police and dismissed the relaxation of the constitutional practices as "necessary in the public interest." [106]

The federal troops served a double function. At the peak of the I.W.W. threat during the summer of 1917 they provided the control of radicalism and sense of action that hysterical citizens and communities demanded of their government. While other departments of the federal administration searched anxiously but slowly for some legal procedure suitable for the disruption of the Wobblies, the army moved decisively and quickly. The soldiers could also suppress any local disorder — be it in mine, lumber camp, or city — originating from I.W.W. agitation. Military occupation guaranteed law and order. It was realized, however, that no matter how successfully the troops suppressed radicalism, they were purely a *temporary* and a *local* expedient.

The western governors understood that their use of the army reached only "symptoms" and neither cured the problem nor got to its causes. They wanted not the "federal policing of an existing situation" but "federal prevention." [107] While it could stabilize local emergencies, the army was powerless to crush the I.W.W. leadership or to police the vast migratory areas of the plains harvest fields. What it did and did well was to safeguard the threatened industries and communities until the Departments of Justice and Labor evolved their plans for the overthrow of the I.W.W.

V

The Day in Court

1917–1920

DURING August 1917 Ralph Chaplin, editor of the official I.W.W. newspaper *Solidarity*, used to look out across the Chicago street at the undercover operatives watching the I.W.W. building. "We were already being shadowed night and day by federal and city 'gumshoes,'" Chaplin later recalled. Government "stool pigeons and spies" were also swelling the attendance at local Wobbly meetings.[1] Some sort of federal action seemed imminent. In the United States attorney's office in Chicago special assistants to the Attorney General were secretly preparing the government's indictment of the I.W.W. By August 21, the federal lawyers believed sufficient evidence existed for prosecution — although they admitted that much of this valuable material was still in the possession of the Wobblies.

Having reached the point where it no longer feared publicity about its intentions, the government then resolved openly to seize the remaining evidence. On September 5, 1917, Bureau of Investigation agents raided simultaneously the I.W.W. headquarters, locals, and residences throughout the nation. The federal detectives seized official and personal correspondence, organization minutes and financial records, and other materials such as stickers, buttons, cards, membership lists, leaflets, pamphlets, circulars, books, and office equipment. With the tons of paper gathered from some sixty-four I.W.W. headquarters, the Department of Justice had at last the wherewithal to take the Wobblies into court. This was a procedure that I.W.W.-infested localities had unsuccessfully advocated more than once since 1912. From 1917 to 1919 the legal prosecution of radicals now characterized their suppression.[2]

In these wartime trials the prosecution sought to prove that the I.W.W. was a vicious, treasonable, and criminal conspiracy to oppose by force the execution of the laws of the United States and to obstruct its prosecution of the war. Each case had two general types of counts in the indictment — the industrial and the war. In what was usually the first industrial count the government classified I.W.W. strikes as a seditious conspiracy (section 6 of the Criminal Code) to prevent forcefully the execution of certain specified legislation that provided for the production and transportation of war supplies. In the second industrial count several of the indictments charged a conspiracy, under section 19 of the Criminal Code, to injure, oppress, threaten, and intimidate by strikes and sabotage a large number of citizens [contractors, manufacturers, or raw-material producers] in the exercise of a "right or privilege secured to them by the Constitution and laws of the United States," in this case the right to execute certain wartime contracts without interference. In the Wichita indictment, instead of a charge under section 19, the United States attorney accused the I.W.W. of a conspiracy to violate the Food and Fuel Control Act by urging strikers to cut off or decrease the production and supply of foods, feeds, and fuel necessary to the armed forces. Stripped of legal verbiage, these counts stated that all I.W.W. strikes with or without force were unlawful conspiracies.[3]

In the war counts the federal government indicted the I.W.W. for conspiracies to obstruct the Selective Service Act and to violate the Espionage Act. The organization supposedly conspired to induce individuals to refuse to register or, if they were inducted, then to desert. The indictments also charged a plot to cause insubordination in the military forces and to hamper the recruitment and enlistment service.[4]

The "overt acts" proving conspiracies in both the industrial and war counts were mainly official statements, policy declarations, newspaper articles, and personal expressions of opinion in private and organization correspondence. Distribution of any of these also served to establish the conspiracy. Although "overt act" carries with it the connotation of an act of force and violence, in most cases the prosecution relied on the spoken and written word to convict the Wobblies. Only in the Sacramento case did the government introduce to any great extent testimony on actual acts of vandalism, property destruction, or forceful intimidation. In other words, the government built its case largely on I.W.W. expressions of opinion about capitalism, the class struggle, the master class, strikes, sabotage, militarism, war and conscription. Much of this material predated the outbreak of the war and the passage of the war legislation, but the courts allowed its introduction on the theory that it revealed the intent of the accused and their preparation to commit the conspiratorial acts.

Even though the Department of Justice always maintained that guilt was personal and that it indicted I.W.W.'s as individuals, the essence of the prosecution's case "was to prove that the organization itself was essentially a criminal conspiracy."[5] The government went all the way back to the founding of the I.W.W. in 1905 to show a general criminal and lawless nature and to indict the very philosophy of the organization. Federal prosecutors threw into the case every extreme statement ever made, every violent act ever threatened or carried out, whether or not by plan of the I.W.W. and regardless of the industrial or other circumstances. Using all these to prove conspiracy, the government then turned the case around to imply that members were guilty because they had joined an unlawful confederacy. The act of any one individual was, of course, chargeable against all the members of the conspiracy.[6]

Success or failure of the I.W.W. cases hinged in the last analysis on the question of intent. What was the intent of the I.W.W. in calling its wartime strikes? Labor disputes whose objective was better pay or improved working conditions were perfectly legal. On the other hand, if the purpose of the strikes was to impair the prosecution of the war, then they were unlawful. The United States attorneys had no doubts. To them the I.W.W. was "notoriously anti-patriotic, anti-war, and essentially criminal in its aims and purposes."[7] The Attorney General's office conducted the proceedings from the very start on the theory that there was not "any danger of doing any injustice to innocent citizens . . . [for] these offenders ought to be reached and punished whenever the bare chance of successfully doing so presents itself."[8]

In its interpretation of intent the government had simply turned the I.W.W. propaganda of the prewar years back upon itself. Wobblies and other radicals had long been neutral or antagonistic to war. They had, moreover, continually denounced the government as capitalistic. The administration now accepted this analysis and equated an attack on capitalism as hostility to a government at war. Through the judicial doctrines of constructive intent and indirect causation, the Department of Justice indicted radicals for their political and economic views and their labor agitation. Arguing that these opinions and strikes could indirectly hinder the raising of armies and the success of the war effort, and presuming from this conclusion that the radicals expressed them with this intent, the government sought to win favorable verdicts from wartime juries.

The juries turned out to be frightened, jingoistic, and vindictive, all in all thoroughly sympathetic to the government's aims. The federal district attorneys reported almost unanimously in the I.W.W. prosecutions that public sentiment was so inflamed against radicals that "if these cases are presented to the grand jury, indictments will necessarily follow, and, if indictments should be returned, convictions will be secured as a matter of course." [9] The government could, therefore, dictate the terms upon which it fought the radicals.

The Department of Justice was in effect eliminating mob violence against I.W.W.'s and other nonconformists by removing the enraged citizen from the mob and placing him in the jury box. While this followed the form, it lacked the essence of judicial procedure. As Joughin and Morgan suggested in their analysis of the Sacco-Vanzetti case, the jury system collapsed in such instances because the community was "unfit to deal with any issue involving its hysterical passions." [10] With the outcome predetermined, therefore, the important question is why and how the trials were initiated. What political and economic pressures lay behind the Wobbly convictions?

II

The I.W.W. prosecutions largely depended on business influence, community hysteria, and the eagerness or common-sense restraint of local federal attorneys. The Washington office of the Department of Justice indicted and tried only the first-string leaders at Chicago. The other cases reflected local needs and thus were not subject to national control or centralized direction. Attorney General Gregory advised his district attorneys to be guided by "questions of broad public policy as viewed in the light of conditions peculiar to your immediate territory." [11] It is very difficult to find any real administration policy in the I.W.W. cases. There was, however, a great deal of local autonomy, which is always so responsive to local crises and unrest.

During the summer of 1917 the Department of Justice's policy towards the I.W.W. passed gradually through several stages and culminated in the late September indictment of the organization's top leadership at Chicago. *U.S. v. W. D. Haywood, et al.*, the trial of some 166 Wobblies, was a war priority of extreme significance that the department called "the most important set of prosecutions with which the government has been concerned in many years." [12] At first, the Attorney General's office had believed I.W.W. wartime strikes to be a purely local or state concern.[13] As demands poured in for federal action, however, the government assumed charge of the I.W.W. problem.

Once more the lumber operators of the Northwest provided the initial impetus in the evolution of federal policy. Although the timber companies had blacklisted the I.W.W. in an attempt to break the strike, they realized that this policy created a further dilemma. Since the I.W.W. was steadily gaining adherents, the blacklist might eliminate from the woods some of the industry's best workers.[14] Prosecutions by the federal government seemed the most likely way of removing the I.W.W. and at the same time retaining the labor. Despite the lack of any concrete evidence in the reports forwarded to Washington, enough disturbing appeals had been made by July 1917 to convince the Justice Department of the need for some action.[15] Still not seeing how the I.W.W. could be prosecuted, the Attorney General decided upon a thorough investigation of the now suspect Wobblies.

On July 11 all special agents and district attorneys were put on the I.W.W. alert. Attorney General Gregory, believing the organization to be "a grave menace" and suspecting that it was financed "by some hostile organization," urged his investigators to uncover any and all "data which may be useful to the Department in determining what action may be taken under the various criminal statutes of the United States . . . or would be useful to state authorities."[16] Avenues of information into I.W.W. plans were thereafter open. The Bureau of Investigation had its agents infiltrate high leadership positions, and corporations were willing to make the reports of their private detective informers available to United States attorneys.[17] While the investigations proceeded, two important groups came forward with policy suggestions. One was the western governors, led by the California Commission on Immigration and Housing. This organization represented logging, mining, and agricultural interests. The other group, a midwestern-centered lobby under ex-Governor John Lind of the Minnesota Commission of Public Safety, was chiefly concerned with the I.W.W. threat to the 1917 harvest.

Initially formed in 1915 to deal with the I.W.W., the organization of western governors placed a comprehensive plan for solving the radical threat before President Wilson personally in July 1917. Alarmed by the I.W.W.'s successes in the summer's strikes and by its increasing agitation, they were further disturbed by the Bisbee deportations. The governors were particularly anxious that those methods of mob action should not be repeated, since "a policy of floating . . . [Wobblies] from one section to another" could only cause "serious internal disturbances."[18]

The western governors, rejecting federal troops and trials, urged the Wilson administration to adopt a far-reaching internment of I.W.W. members as a war measure. The first point in the proposed program stated:

That members of the I.W.W. against whom there is evidence of intrigue or activity, not merely to agitate for better conditions, but to commit acts of treason and treasonably to hinder the operation of industries, or the harvesting of crops necessary to the prosecution of the war, be not arrested after charges, but they be interned during the period of the war — preferably in camps at some distance from the place of apprehension. This plan would effectively mistify and frighten them; would avoid making heroes of them; and would deprive them of their best material for propaganda — besides, avoiding rash action by citizens.[19]

The plan did not indicate how the government would distinguish between honest and treasonable agitation, but the executive officer indicated that the West was after "the ring leaders." If they were apprehended, their followers would be only "scattered, ineffectual individuals."[20]

The governors justified the harsh and illegal nature of their program by reference to the procedures that had been followed up to that time. The I.W.W. threat had been solved so far by the mob action of vigilante committees or by the lawless raids and arrests of federal troops. "We firmly believe," the western executives stated, "that the action which we suggest is neither so drastic nor so summary as that which the Federal troops are being called upon to take and . . . surely there would be no more illegality involved than there was in the action of Arizona citizens." A quiet, effective, and preventive internment was to check the innate western tendency toward vigilantism — a type of law and order that could only create sympathy for I.W.W.'s or stir up reprisals.[21]

A federal internment vindicated itself on other grounds as well. The supposed I.W.W. conspiracy was inter-, not intrastate. Second, state and local authorities had rarely been able to discover Wobblies committing crimes. Third, when they did get taken into court, they used the prosecution to make folk heroes and martyrs of themselves. Finally, only the federal government could secure a press censorship that would eliminate the publicity upon which the radicals thrived.[22]

An optimistic, if not utopian, expectation was to atone for the internment features. The western program urged federal investigation and reform of conditions causing labor unrest. Through appeals to their patriotism, the Wilson administration could "request employers who are threatened with strikes to quietly remedy, during the period of the war, all conditions . . . that may give pretext for the usual I.W.W. agitation." If conditions were to be so satisfactory, labor agitators deserved to be put away. The governor's representative believed this section "saves the plan from condemnation as being too autocratic." [23]

After careful consideration the federal government rejected the western proposals and urged increasing state attention to I.W.W. activities. The Department of Justice advised the President that there was, of course, no legal authority for any internment. The only Wobblies detainable in camps were the few who were alien enemies. Still adhering to the concept of labor radicalism as a local problem, the federal government called for increased state vigilance and investigation, state suppression of I.W.W. publicity, state surveys of working conditions, state improvement of migratory and lumber camps, and effective state counterpropaganda against radicalism. The western executives unanimously accepted these proposals, but few took any steps to implement the suggestions.[24]

The Department of Justice had hardly turned its back on the internment thesis when it received and followed a much more judicial suggestion for the suppression of the I.W.W. Coming from the Minnesota Commission of Public Safety and the state's ex-Governor John Lind, this second proposal culminated in the Chicago indictment, the prototype for all I.W.W. trials. On July 26, 1917, the commission under Lind's direction had summoned Hinton G. Clabaugh, chief of the Chicago branch of the Bureau of Investigation, to Minneapolis for a conference on the I.W.W. situation. The threat seemed serious, even critical, and the Minnesota group feared that the Wobbly organization of agricultural laborers was near realization. In urgent tones Lind wired

Attorney General Gregory, "If this raid on labor is not stopped promptly, a large percentage of our crops will be wasted and lost and . . . the lumber industry will be paralyzed." [25] Because of the wartime labor shortage, Lind knew that the I.W.W. could not be attacked through its members in the field. In the plains area, moreover, where population was sparse and scattered, towns small, and industrial communities few, there was almost no way to control migratory agitators. With the commission and Bureau of Investigation files, Lind and Clabaugh claimed to have enough evidence to "proceed effectively against the head organization in Chicago and the agricultural organization here." They boasted that they could "extend the drive as much farther *as is deemed expedient.*" According to Lind the state commission could no longer check the I.W.W. by itself. Unless the federal government helped out, he predicted that Minnesota and its local towns would "take the law into their own hands." [26]

That the Minnesota conference had to supply to the Department of Justice the legal theory with which to proceed is indicative of the embryonic stage of official thinking in late July. The Attorney General's staff had as yet no idea of an indictment based upon the criminal conspiracy code and the war statutes. Once the state commission had suggested this and elucidated the possibilities in personal conferences, the government moved rapidly to put the plan into effect.[27]

Lind saw the fruition of his lobbying in the Chicago I.W.W. trial. In it the government indicted and tried the executive board, the general organizers, the editors, and the leaders of the lumber, mining, and agricultural subdivisions. More than any other single event, the Chicago case helped turn the I.W.W. from the aggresive, organizing menace it had been that summer into the defending and then ex-champion of the radical world. The Chicago prosecution also set the pattern for a series of local indictments that struck at the second- and third-string leadership of the I.W.W. Only one man in the United States could have called off these prosecutions — Woodrow Wilson himself.

A progressive political philosophy, an administrative routine, a sympathy for the A.F. of L., and a tremendous antipathy for those who were neutral or opposed to American participation in the World War were the deciding elements in Wilson's approval of the I.W.W. repressions. As a progressive, Woodrow Wilson had finished tinkering with the economy in 1916. His reforms had been neither fundamental nor radical. Instinctively and philosophically, the President detested the Marxist, anarchist, or class-war theories of society. To Wilson the I.W.W. was "a menace to organized society and the right conduct of industry." [28]

In the administrative areas that infringed on civil liberties, the President trusted his subordinate Cabinet officers and left them free to run their departments without his continual interference. Fairly sensitive to liberal protest, President Wilson from time to time brought individual cases to the attention of Attorneys General Gregory and Palmer or Postmaster General Burleson. Were they not pushing suppression too far? Could not some indictment be quashed? Upon an assurance that the respective prosecution was justifiable legally, essential to the public welfare, or vouched for by the United States attorney, the President would let the matter drop. He wrote Burleson, "I am willing to trust your judgment after I have once called your attention to a suggestion." [29] Wilson, therefore, was relying on the opinions of the prosecuting officials — individuals not notorious for their objectivity in cases they have prepared. This procedure seemed even more incongruous in wartime trials, when the question was so much one of expediency and broad public policy. If the juries would convict, how far should the government go? Only the President could decide. The responsibility could not be delegated.[30]

Wilson's identification with the labor philosophy of Samuel Gompers and the aims of the A.F. of L. also made him sympathetic to the elimination of labor radicals. The I.W.W. had long been the chief labor enemy on the conservative craft unions' most wanted list. Anxious to put organized labor squarely behind the war effort, Woodrow Wilson saw the I.W.W. prosecutions as one way of positively encouraging legitimate unionism.[31] The Department of Justice also helped the A.F. of L. eliminate radical suspects from its ranks by forwarding to Gompers' headquarters the I.W.W. membership lists seized in the government raids.[32]

Most important of all in forming Wilson's attitude was the I.W.W.'s equivocal position on the war. For the Wobblies to call the conflict a capitalistic Wall Street war was to imply that it was a hypocritical mockery; and to sneer at Wilson's humanitarianism was the greatest of all possible affronts to the President. To Wilson the right attitude on the war could even offset an otherwise radical personality. He noted that many Socialists who supported the war had a "genuine American feeling and in no sense represented the revolutionary temper such as Mr. Berger." [33] Although the President always accepted the need for public criticism of officials and programs, he characteristically defined the limits of acceptable discussion. The government could only tolerate criticisms that were "patriotic and intelligent." [34] No one ever had the slightest doubt that the impassioned I.W.W. oratory was well below that level.

Once Attorney General Gregory had defined the Chicago I.W.W. case as a war priority and described the Wobbly strikes and propaganda as antiwar, presidential intervention was not to be expected. None of the appeals to Wilson by the I.W.W., the National Civil Liberties Bureau, or their few influential friends made any impression.[35] Part of the failure stemmed from Wilson's preoccupation with foreign affairs and the direction of the war.[36] Much more important was the fact that Wilson's political and economic philosophy left him personally unmoved by the misfortunes of I.W.W.'s. As the Department of Justice stepped up its activity, the President added his encouragement. "Our interest," he told the western governors, "is no less keen and active than is yours." [37] Wilson wrote his Attorney General that "the I.W.W.'s . . . certainly are worthy of being suppressed." [38] The White House encyclical guaranteed there should be no turning back in the Chicago trial, and, thereafter, the contagion for indicting the Wobblies spread rapidly around the country

III

Demands for further prosecution of the I.W.W. did not cease when the government put the entire top leadership in the Cook County jail. While reassured, frightened localities doubted whether distant court proceedings had snuffed out all Wobbly life. In addition, local indictments answered economic and political pressures that demanded satisfaction. A public reputation might also be enhanced. It was, perhaps, inevitable that the Chicago show should become a road company, and so the I.W.W. was stamped out in most of its old stamping grounds.

When I.W.W. organizers increased their activity in the mid-continent oil fields during the fall of 1917, the oil interests sought their suppression. In October and November the Wobblies had started a determined agitation for the organization of all the oil workers. Thoroughly alarmed by the threat of a general strike, the oil companies resolved to eliminate this potential. They turned for aid to the federal attorneys whose districts embraced the mid-continent field, one at Tulsa, Oklahoma, and the other at Kansas City, Kansas. The results were strikingly different.

United States Attorney W. P. McGinnis at Tusla quietly rebuffed the corporate invitation for an anti-Wobbly roundup. Representatives of the oil industry had urged McGinnis "to take steps to have every I.W.W. or person suspected of being such arrested and interned during the period of the war." This Department of Justice official, however, unlike his Washington superiors, considered the I.W.W. agitation legitimate labor activity for increased wages, not in intent or otherwise a violation of the war statutes. McGinnis would not act unless the oilmen's committee could produce evidence of violation of federal law. He refused to arrest I.W.W.'s in anticipation of what they might do.[39]

In the eastern part of the oil field, situated in southern Kansas, a most dissimilar solution prevailed. Compared with the Oklahoma area the I.W.W., its agitation, and the calls for its suppression were all the same.[40] The United States attorney, on the other hand, had a broad view of the law. While there had been no strike, but only a concerted membership drive, the local Department of Justice office in conjunction with state authorities apprehended some one hundred Wobblies on November 17, 1917. United States Attorney Fred Robertson and his special agents also seized large quantities of supplies, literature, and correspondence.[41] The district attorney justified the arrests and the indictments "as a preventative matter to prevent *possible* violence in the oil region in southern Kansas." [42]

Once the Wobblies had been indicted (thirty-five were held for trial), they were forgotten "in the rush of business." [43] The local office concerned itself with other matters while the I.W.W.'s suffered imprisonment in the Sedgwick County jail, a medieval dungeon, overcrowded, unheated, filthy, vermin-infested, and, as an inspector of prisons eventually discovered, "not a fit habitation for an animal." [44]

After a year had passed, the Department of Justice forced Robertson to proceed with the action and insisted that, since an indictment had been returned, the case should be "vigorously prosecuted to a successful conclusion." [45] It took another year, however, before the United States attorney was able to frame an indictment that would stand up in court. In other words, the government held the I.W.W.'s as prisoners in the Sedgwick County jail for two years before bringing them to trial. Even the Department of Justice had to admit that such handling "looks pretty bad." [46] In late December 1919 a Kansas jury finally convicted the Wichita defendants under the usual wartime conspiracy charges.[47]

In California the I.W.W. indictments climaxed a three-year battle between the Wobblies and the fruit and ranching interests of the San Joaquin and Sacramento valleys. In a bitter, tense class war dating from the 1913 Wheatland riot, the California combat became a guerrilla harassment. Because of the migratory nature of the work, the concentrated violence typical of industrial disputes was missing. Instead, there were isolated, scattered attacks and reprisals. I.W.W.'s were jailed, mobbed, and tarred and feathered; in return, fruit trays were dumped and haystacks burned. Destruction of lives was answered by destruction of property. Underneath this conflict, however, lay the fundamental issue. Could the I.W.W.'s succeed in enforcing their scale of wages and hours in migratory harvesting?

During the summer of 1917 I.W.W. agitation and organizing activity assumed a new tempo in California as they did all over the West. Raisin, grape, and citrus growers and packers found it difficult to obtain enough workers to harvest and process the crops unless the employers met I.W.W. demands. In addition a new outbreak of incendiary fires around Fresno was blamed on the Wobblies. A statewide inflammatory newspaper campaign described I.W.W.'s as German agents. These developments successfully frightened susceptible citizens, who now began to demand governmental intervention.[48]

When federal agents raided the Fresno state headquarters on September 5, 1917, to gather evidence for the Chicago trial, they arrested, and later had indicted, eighteen I.W.W.'s found on the premises. Although the government had as yet little evidence of property destruction, the United States attorney felt certain of a conviction on charges similar to those in the Haywood case. Community feeling, he reported, was that intense.[49] A year later the government released five of the eighteen prisoners for lack of any evidence against them. They had simply been unfortunate enough to have been in the I.W.W. hall at the time of the raid. The other thirteen were then reindicted at Sacramento, where the Justice Department was attempting to relieve the antiradical neuroses of northern California.[50]

The Sacramento trial originated in an atmosphere of ruthless bias as dense and impenetrable as the fog that rolls in across the Bay area. As usual, atrocity stories about the I.W.W. had inflamed public opinion, but the northern California indictment had behind it certain additional features that were peculiarly San Franciso's own.

Ever since June 1916, when the chamber of commerce organized its law and order committee to win the open shop, San Francisco had been the scene of a bitter struggle between capital and labor.[51] The committee had seized upon the Preparedness Day bomb explosion and the resultant Mooney-Billings trial as a means of smearing and possibly destroying unionism in northern California.[52] Leading this attack behind the scenes were Frank C. Drew, attorney for the chamber of commerce, and Justice Frederick W. Henshaw of the state supreme court, "the ablest, the narrowest, and the bitterest representative of the old Southern Pacific machine." [53] Henshaw's front man was San Francisco's district attorney, Charles M. ("Legs")Fickert, the tool of the corrupt interests.[54]

In 1917 Fremont Older, crusading editor of the San Francisco *Bulletin*, had unearthed evidence that Justice Henshaw had accepted a large bribe to change his vote in the famous

Fair Will litigation (Henshaw's vote approved the breaking of the James G. Fair trust by the heirs). Older had allowed the justice to resign without exposure on condition he sever his connection with Fickert and stop trying to frame the principals in the Mooney case.[55] Unknown to Older, Justice Henshaw continued his associations with the district attorney, and in the summer of 1917 the two of them decided to go after the I.W.W. The justice then offered his services to the Department of Justice. Accepting Henshaw as a respectable, highly regarded state supreme court justice (as yet unexposed by Older), the government thus unwittingly allied itself with the most corrupt, reactionary enemies of labor and the I.W.W.[56]

The influence of the Henshaw-Fickert combine was to sensationalize the sinister nature of radicalism and create the image of a vast pro-German (later pro-Russian) conspiracy. Claiming a special knowledge of the I.W.W. "inner circle," and financing his own special investigation, Justice Henshaw worked closely with federal agents and continually promised new and startling disclosures.[57]

In the fall of 1917, meanwhile, San Francisco witnessed a series of events that served as prelude to the Sacramento I.W.W. indictments. Sickened by District Attorney Fickert's failure to clean up the red-light district, a respectable reform group had demanded the recall of the corrupt politician. Certain union elements and Mooney supporters gave this movement sizable and potentially successful proportions. Fickert hung on to the support of the "underworld element, professional politicians, and corporations." [58] On the night before the recall election a bomb exploded at the governor's mansion in Sacramento, a device whose origin and purpose was never satisfactorily explained.

The explosion could hardly have been more fortuitous for Fickert and the enemies of the I.W.W. In San Francisco some thirty thousand unexpected voters, mainly from the well-to-do residential areas, turned out for Fickert as the champion of law and order against radical anarchy. The district attorney thereby won an easy re-election.[59] In Sacramento the bomb touched off the roundup of over fifty I.W.W.'s, there being no faster fuse to antiradical action than unsolved dynamitings. Finding no crime with which to charge its suspects, Sacramento then called in the federal authorities.[60]

To the shocked surprise of the city and state officials, the local Department of Justice office advised Sacramento police to release all but three Wobblies for lack of evidence.[61] The progressive *Sacramento Bee* threatened that this dismissal would "force citizens to maintain order . . . through extralegal means." [62] The city commission, Governor William D. Stephens, and Senator Hiram Johnson urged the federal government to initiate another Chicago case.[63] A prosecution for "seditious talk" under the conspiracy and war statutes, the Californians asserted, was the only possible way of reaching the I.W.W. Within a short time this pressure was decisive.[64] "Any danger of lynching or shooting the I.W.W. members," the United States marshal reported, "has seemingly passed." [65]

Some time later the Sacramento and Fresno cases were consolidated in a blanket indictment against sixty-two of the more active defendants. The others, who had been awaiting trial for ten to twelve months, were released. The government tried the Sacramento prisoners during December 1918, and the jury found them all guilty on January 16, 1919. It took the jurors just one hour to bring in this verdict.[66]

During the preparation of the Sacramento trial, District Attorney Fickert and Justice Henshaw continued their active, behind-the-scenes investigations of Mooney and the I.W.W. Aided by a deputy marshal and a special agent, Fickert and Henshaw were largely responsible for developing the testimony of a renegade Wobbly who turned in-

former and became a professional prosecution witness in
I.W.W. cases.[67] Before the Sacramento case came to trial,
however, a high federal official exposed the operations of
the Fickert-Henshaw clique. John B. Densmore, investigating the Mooney conviction for the Department of Labor,
had secretly planted a dictaphone in District Attorney
Fickert's office. Publicizing conversations overheard during
September and October 1918, the report outlined in stark
detail the crude frame-ups capable of being concocted by
Fickert and his friends. I.W.W.'s and their liberal sympathizers maintained at the time that the association of Henshaw and Fickert in the Sacramento proceedings completely
discredited the government case.[68]

While this extremely unfortunate alliance added nothing
to the integrity or credibility of the prosecution, it could not
impair the kind of conspiracy case that was then typically
convicting I.W.W.'s. The government had ample amounts
of Wobbly propaganda about the war and the class struggle
with which to impress eager juries. The Department of Justice also threw into the Sacramento trial the evidence of
I.W.W. sabotage. Two ex-Wobblies, Elbert Coutts and John
Dymond, testified that twelve of their former associates
committed or conspired to commit incendiary destruction.
The tales of violence went all the way back to 1912. Coutts
and Dymond were themselves coconspirators and, by all
odds, disreputable witnesses. Yet the jury was willing to accept the prewar random incendiarism and destruction committed by a dozen so-called "sabcats" during California's
class war as the evidence of a wartime conspiracy of all the
defendants against the United States government, its officers, and laws.[69]

In the Omaha district United States Attorney T. S. Allen
held a group of I.W.W.'s for over a year and a half before
he eventually dropped the case for lack of evidence. On November 14, 1917, the Wobblies had assembled in the Ne-

braska city for an organization meeting. During this convention, which federal authorities admitted was held "in an orderly way," government agents arrested sixty-four I.W.W.'s. A complaint that followed the Chicago indictments was filed against them.[70]

The Department of Justice would not, however, allow Allen to bring his case to trial, for the government had decided to give priority to the Chicago prosecution. The official theory was that any dismissal, acquittal, or reversal by any judge, jury, or appellate court might seriously prejudice a successful conclusion at Chicago. In line with this policy the Department of Justice repeatedly ordered delays in the various regional cases at Omaha, Wichita, Fresno, and Sacramento. Thus the Wobblies lost their right to a speedy trial, and some, even of those ultimately convicted, spent more time awaiting prosecution than they did serving out their sentences.[71] The summer of 1918 had arrived before the Omaha office could seriously consider disposing of its I.W.W. defendants.

By then Allen had very little inclination to try the Wobblies. Of the sixty-four originally arrested in Omaha, thirty-six had already been released. Realizing how weak its case was, the local Department of Justice office had offered paroles to those who quit the I.W.W., and some three dozen had agreed to do so.[72] The prosecutor hoped to make another deal with the remaining Wobblies. If they would plead guilty and refrain from further agitation, he would have them sentenced to the time already served and let them go free. Besides getting the government out of an embarrassing situation, the proposal would have delivered additional tractable labor to the harvest fields at a time when it was most needed.[73] But the imprisoned I.W.W.'s, hard-core idealists embittered by long confinement, demanded full vindication from the court they despised — unconditional release or a trial.[74]

Although Washington suggested a dismissal of the case, United States Attorney Allen feared the local repercussions of any such concession of error. "Many well meaning citizens may be dissatisfied and disappointed," Allen wrote his superior, unless he achieved a verdict of guilty one way or another. In addition, the I.W.W.'s would interpret the dismissal as proof of their frame-up by the capitalists.[75] The Omaha office therefore resolved to prosecute.[76]

By the spring of 1919, a year and a half after the original arrest, Allen still felt unsure of his case. All but a handful of his defendants had been mere "itinerant members," none of them "vicious." After holding the trial in abeyance, the Omaha office eventually cancelled the prosecution, probably believing that public opinion had by then been satiated. Allen himself felt self-righteously content. Dismissal of the proceedings, he reported, would prove to the radicals that when the government did have a weak case, "it is ready to recognize that fact." [77]

In contrast to the other regions, the I.W.W.'s in northern Minnesota turned themselves over wholesale by a mass violation of the Selective Service Act. These Wobblies were mainly Finnish aliens. Their confusion over the United States alliance with Russia (the traditional Finnish enemy) and their ignorance about legal procedures probably lay behind their failure to register. For aliens, not subject to military service, registration was a mere technicality. Conscious or not, the Wobbly actions in this matter greatly faciliated their suppression and proved the I.W.W. leaders correct. They had warned their members not to give the bosses any legal excuses for breaking the movement and had advocated only action on the job. In the mining camps of the Mesabi and Cuyuna iron ranges, the Wobblies paid the penalty for neglecting this fundamentally sound advice.

Without the Department of Justice action, the summer of 1917 might have been as uncomfortable for the mining companies as earlier forecasts had predicted. The I.W.W. had won a bitterly-contested strike on the iron range during 1916. The Wobblies had maintained their solidarity against an array of gunmen, deputies, sheriffs, county attorneys, and judges employed by or sympathetic to corporations controlled by the steel trust.[78] In 1917 the I.W.W. again returned to agitate among the foreign-born miners. In this explosive situation, the draft law provided the easiest way to industrial peace.

Fully aware of the decision of many I.W.W. Finns not to register and of their efforts to call a strike in the iron range mines, United States Attorney Alfred Jaques arrested over two hundred of them during the summer of 1917. In his report to the Attorney General, Jaques wrote that he had considered it "a good idea to keep these I.W.W. aliens so busy in defending prosecutions for failure to register that they would not have time to plot against the industrial interests of Northern Minnesota." [79]

While Jaques's policy prevented a strike, it did not entirely satisfy the corporate interests. When the first group of defendants were tried in late July, ex-Governor Lind, speaking for the mining companies, petitioned the Department of Justice to be lenient. "Their work is needed in the mines," Lind wrote Attorney General Gregory.[80] Jaques, believing that the nonregistration was wilfully committed, insisted on the full measure of punishment. At the second set of trials in January 1918, however, the court deferred sentencing the Wobblies until July 1918, "in order that they might keep at work." The judge would determine the penalty at that time depending on their interim behavior — in other words, the degree to which they avoided I.W.W. strikes and agitation.[81]

In some areas district attorneys used indictments against radicals as a preventive weapon, often with little thought of ever bringing them to trial. In Utah, for example, the Salt Lake City office used the Espionage Act against three

I.W.W.'s who were calling for a general strike. The district attorney indicted the Wobblies to curtail agitation in the copper camps.[82] In Arizona the Phoenix office thought it advisable to indict "dangerous and undesirable" individuals who were prominent labor agitators.[83] The St. Louis office indicted Wobblies even when the federal prosecutor realized there were no grounds for proceeding. The action had had a "salutary effect." [84]

Because of the "acute" danger from Wobblies and socialists in the Northwest, the Seattle district attorney was also willing to indict radicals even when doubtful of a successful outcome. "The necessity was so urgent," he wrote, "that the arrest of these men was necessary as a disciplinary measure in any event." [85]

In all the wartime indictments and trials the Department of Justice carefully followed constitutional and legal processes. If due process is considered in its narrow procedural sense, then the government was a stickler for routine. Its complaints dutifully informed the defendants of the charges against them, its federal agents and lawyers spent long hours painfully assembling the evidence, and its prosecutors offered the defendants opportunity for demurrers, rebuttals, and appeals. The I.W.W. had its day in court. In retrospect one wonders how meaningful that day was. At the time, both prosecution and defense, with one exception, assumed that the decision could go either way. On the one hand the government disregarded the community hysteria and the public-opinion research of its own district attorneys. Acting as though it had to convince the jury that the Wobblies were a menace, the Justice Department threw into these cases its best legal talent. On the other hand, the I.W.W. forgot its own well-emphasized precept that the courts were the agents of the governing class. The Wobblies searched for the most skillful lawyers, created a general defense committee, and fought vigorously to prove their innocence. Only the Sacramento defendants were true to their former principles. Assuming they could not obtain justice in a wartime capitalistic court, they adopted a silent defense, a tight-lipped and contemptuous rebuke to what they thought was judicial make-believe.

The general enthusiasm for these meaningless charades must lie in some ingrained American devotion to procedural due process. The prosecution conceded and the defense demanded the observance of certain historical forms without understanding that, in and of themselves, these routines promised nothing. "No defendant," Joughin and Morgan have written, "should be asked to stand trial before a jury of the sort which offers as a best hope the chance of one or two judicial men, or the consolation that there is no unanimous predisposition to a fatal verdict." [86] There is a lot more to due process than simply walking in and out of a courtroom.

The trials also provided a sense of public reassurance. Like old-fashioned morality plays these dramas underlined the acceptable values and consigned offenders to limbo. The prosecutions, as one government official later pointed out, were "the product of clamor more than truth." [87] Their function was to still that clamor visibly in the colorful, well-publicized surroundings of the typical American court. The defendants accepted their roles in the performance because they hoped to counterindict the capitalist class by publicly dramatizing the exploited misery of the industrial and migratory workers. Should they fail to convert their audience, there might always be the satisfaction of martyrdom in a lost cause. However senseless the decision now appears, the I.W.W. did insist on making its defense. The atmosphere in which this was conducted may well be the most accurate measure of the real due process.

IV

From 1917 to 1919 the I.W.W. became a defense rather than a labor organization, and drained off its leadership, militancy, and finances in a fruitless resistance. At no time did the organization benefit from the presumption that an individual was innocent until proven guilty. "This is not an instance in which there is any danger of doing injustice to innocent citizens," the Department of Justice had said.[88] The country presumed the Wobblies guilty and acted upon that conviction.

The results were threefold. First, the I.W.W. had difficulty in maintaining and supporting an effective defense organization. In addition, that organization, when functioning efficiently, had great trouble making itself heard through the normal channels of communication. In the third place, when and if the defense group did get its story across, few people were willing to believe it, and even fewer were ready to act upon that belief.

Signs that radicals were becoming isolated had already appeared when the United States entered World War I. The failure of the National Labor Defense Council in 1917 pointed the way to the eventual total collapse of solidarity among liberal and labor exponents of civil liberties. Frank P. Walsh, labor lawyer and ex-chairman of the Industrial Relations Commission, tried to establish the council as one way of guaranteeing the working class a fair and adequately defended trial. Stimulated by the Mooney case and the I.W.W. Everett prosecution, the National Labor Defense Council never really became a substantial organization. From the beginning early in 1917 the council lacked funds and the support of organized labor. The A.F. of L. opposed any close cooperation, while Gompers scorned the council as an organization of "uplifters and reformers." The war and this hostility defeated the well-intentioned council.[89]

Prowar, conservative labor and prowar Socialists, meanwhile, formed the American Alliance for Labor and Democracy, under Gompers' leadership. In addition to putting labor behind the war, it hoped to separate the labor movement from its radical spokesmen. The natural outcome of these aims was the American Alliance's vigorous opposition to any efforts to defend the I.W.W.[90] When the government trials began, therefore, radicals had almost no peripheral resources upon which to draw except those of the National Civil Liberties Bureau.

The National Civil Liberties Bureau devoted itself to the preservation of the fundamental personal rights guaranteed by the Constitution. It developed from the more conservative American Union against Militarism. As wartime jingoism spread, the American Union found that the problem of pacifism was becoming almost wholly the problem of defending the civil liberties of pacifists. Roger Baldwin, the driving force within the American Union, thereupon submerged the lesser of the two issues, and organized the new bureau. Among the objectives he demanded for the people was "the right to talk and print everything they think about peace and . . . democracy," even if that might incidentally "seem to hinder the conduct of the war." [91] Since those who took Baldwin's objective seriously soon found themselves under attack, the bureau's major activity turned into the search for a fair trial. No one needed such legal aid more than the Wobblies. The fight to give them an adequate defense was Roger Baldwin's first conclusive defeat.[92]

The Civil Liberties Bureau found that old friends of the Constitution had not died, but that they had faded away for the duration. Upholding the Bill of Rights seemed to imply opposition to the war. Such staunch liberals and socialists as Louis Post, John Spargo, and William English Walling rejected association with possible pacifists or pro-Germans. Charles A. Beard thought the N.C.L.B. "more anti-war than pro-liberty." [93] Periodicals such as the *New Republic*, the *Outlook*, and the *Atlantic Monthly* refused to carry advertisements appealing for funds to defend the Espionage Act cases.[94] Jane Addams wrote Roger Baldwin that she could not sign a bureau appeal for funds. "I am," she said, "obliged

to walk very softly in regard to all things suspect." [95] Even
the Non-Partisan League refused to help the I.W.W. defense.
Next to the I.W.W. it had probably suffered most from mob-
bings and official persecution, and also had been smeared as
pro-German and deprived of its constitutional rights. These
common experiences bred sympathy but not support. Fearing that contributions to the I.W.W. would be misconstrued
by its enemies, the Non-Partisan League simply could not
afford to injure its own political cause. [96] As a result the
I.W.W. stood alone, for in such excited times no one dared
take a chance. [97]

The government, meanwhile, guaranteed that there should
be no change in this atmosphere. By a rigid administrative
censorship the Post Office Department withheld from the
I.W.W. some of the rights most fundamental to a fair trial. A
defense committee ordinarily has two major functions: to
publicize its case, and to raise money. Failure to do either
properly creates a vicious circle impairing the success of
both. To a national radical organization in modern times the
mails are absolutely vital in a propaganda effort of this sort.
The defense committee must be able to reach not only its
own far-flung membership but also the isolated strongholds
sympathetic to the civil liberties cause. The federal government interrupted this essential contact by its interception,
delayed delivery, and outright seizure of I.W.W. defense
mail. The Wobblies did not function effectively as a defense
organization until the end of the war and the termination of
the postal and express censorships.

The Post Office Department had four weapons with which
to attack I.W.W. literature. Under section 211 of the Criminal Code the department had the power to declare nonmailable any "indecent" material. By a 1911 amendment, the
term "indecent" had been broadened to include "matter . . .
tending to incite arson, murder, or assassination." Postmaster
General Burleson and his subordinates could also exclude

anything that violated the Espionage Act of 1917 or its successor, the Sedition Act of 1918. The 1917 law qualified for exclusion those statements that obstructed the recruitment or enlistment service or interfered with the successful operations of the armed forces. In the 1918 amendments Congress vastly broadened the offenses to include "disloyal, profane, scurrilous, or abusive language, or language intended to cause contempt, scorn, contumely or disrepute as regards the form of government of the United States; or the Constitution; or the flag," and "urging any curtailment of production of any things necessary to the prosecution of the war with intent to hinder its prosecution." The 1918 legislation also gave the Postmaster General authority to prevent the *delivery of all incoming mail* to any individual or organization that he believed had violated the law. Finally, section 481½ of the Postal Laws and Regulations gave the department further discretionary license. Once he had banned a single issue of a paper or magazine, the Postmaster General could revoke its second-class mailing privilege on the ground that it was "not regularly issued at stated intervals" according to the law. [98]

Early in 1917, well before the passage of the Espionage Act and long before the Chicago indictment, Post Office authorities began to suppress I.W.W. literature under section 211. According to the inspectors, the radical Wobbly propaganda tended to incite "arson, murder, or assassination." With the passage of the wartime legislation, several leading I.W.W. newspapers permanently lost their second-class mailing privilege. In addition, most issues of all newspapers and the great majority of bulletins, leaflets, and circulars were individually denied access to the mails for violation of either section 211 or the Espionage Act. [99]

When the government arrested the I.W.W. leaders, therefore, the Post Office had already classified as criminal the very ideas and principles for which the I.W.W. was to stand trial. The I.W.W. general defense committee devoted to the Wobbly ideals and seeking to prove them innocent could not, therefore, make use of the mails, at least not legally.

Postmaster General Burleson and his assistants created a modern-day Index of illegal radical ideas by secret administrative decisions unknown to the I.W.W. This policy made both reform and protest impossible for the affected organization. Yet both were necessary, for Post Office interpretation banned almost everything the I.W.W. was writing. Any of the following statements or illustrations, for example, sufficed to make Wobbly literature non-mailable: (1) solicitations and exhortations to strike; (2) the analysis in the I.W.W. preamble, "the employing class and the working class have nothing in common;" (3) adherence to the principles of industrial unionism; (4) any anticapitalist remarks; (5) cuts of the Wobbly black cat (symbol of sabotage); (6) cuts of an I.W.W. prisoner behind bars; (7) the motto "An injury to one is an injury to all;" (8) assertions of the impossibility of getting fair trials; (9) verbatim reports of the Chicago trial; and (10) calls to organize workers.

How damaging these decisions were may be judged from the fact that much of this nonmailable matter appeared on almost all I.W.W. literature. The cut of the I.W.W. prisoner behind bars was printed on every sheet of I.W.W. defense literature. Regardless of the innocence of the contents, therefore, every piece of defense stationary was nonmailable. Every membership book contained that part of the preamble stating that "the employing class and the working class have nothing in common." The I.W.W. could not legally send its membership books through the mails; it could not carry on the most basic function of a labor union.

Nor could it lawfully conduct a defense. Post Office censorship excluded requests for contributions to the defense of the Chicago prisoners; it even prohibited the blank contribution forms themselves. Since the indicted prisoners had been charged with obstructing the prosecution of the war, the department believed they should receive no financial aid. By allowing the contribution blanks to circulate, postal authorities felt they would be "aiding and assisting the I.W.W.'s to continue their nefarious work." Price lists and advertisements of I.W.W. literature that had earlier been secretly banned also made the organization propaganda nonmailable. The I.W.W. resolution *against* sabotage was refused admission to the mails because it contained the word "sabotage." What was worse, the offensive remark or illustration served to exclude not only the item in which it appeared but all items, however harmless, packaged with it.[100]

In their tortuous reasoning Post Office lawyers either loosely interpreted the statutes to condemn I.W.W. ideas or supplied meanings and intentions not expressed in the words themselves. For example, the department used the Espionage Act section that prohibited "interference with the President's plans for a successful termination of the war" to ban anything that kept alive labor discontent.[101] If Post Office experts found propaganda on its face legitimate, they could assume it held a hidden significance or represented a "disloyalty *unexpressed.*" [102] In barring an issue of the *Defense News Bulletin,* the examiner found it had "a somewhat more audible undertone of disloyalty, though it is hard to designate the particular matter in it which violates the law." [103] With a theory of guilt by innuendo, the department's imagination knew no bounds. Almost any statement was a revolutionary call to arms.[104]

In all these analyses the examining officials were condemning the literature simply because it was an I.W.W. attempt to tell the I.W.W. side of the story. Every once in a while this bias broke through. Various decisions barred material that was "intensely 'I.W.W.' in tone" or "published in the interests of the I.W.W. [and] . . . devoted to its defense." [105] "There is not anything in this issue that is actually illegal," one official reported. He believed, however, that "the influence of this paper is . . . so pernicious that no one could be resigned to its circulation." [106]

The government censors struck most dramatically and repeatedly at the Chicago operations of the I.W.W.'s headquarters and general defense committee. In their seizure of I.W.W. mail, the postal inspectors used illegal general search warrants often so vague as to be meaningless. An inspector could search for I.W.W. mail with a warrant "for 5,000 envelopes bearing U.S. stamps and indicating payment of proper postage thereon." [107] The postal officials also searched into and seized material not covered by the warrant on the excuse that these letters "appear . . . to be a part of the general scheme and propaganda of the I.W.W." [108] The loss of the letters, newspapers, appeals, and circulars that were declared nonmailable was, of course, a crippling blow to the defense.

The agonizingly slow clearance for mailable matter was perhaps even more disturbing. *Eight to twelve* months often passed before the department approved an item and instructed the local office to deliver it.[109] Perhaps the overburdened Post Office lawyers were also deliberately indifferent. Solicitor William H. Lamar told the Civil Liberties Bureau that the postal authorities "gave first attention to people whose loyalty to the government was unquestionable." [110] The Wobblies tried to circumvent this censorship. They divided up their mail and posted it in sealed packages from widely scattered points in Chicago and its suburbs.[111] Radicals' parcels went out in disguise, one, for example, calling its sender "The Christian Singing Society." [112]

When the I.W.W. tried the express companies, however, the government swiftly retaliated. Realizing that their own censorship would put pressure on other forms of transportation, federal authorities arranged with the express companies to refuse to carry excluded mail, and with papers and periodicals all subsequently published issues as well. Section 19 of the Trading with the Enemy Act had made this possible by outlawing any transportation of material nonmailable under the Espionage Act. In determining mailability, express companies often subjected parcels to the same serious delays that took place under postal surveillance.[113]

Although the government could also have stopped all incoming I.W.W. mail,[114] the Department of Justice felt that such unlimited censorship might make plausible the defense charges of federal interference with a fair trial.[115] The Attorney General added that a total denial of the mails might additionally have an "inhibitory effect upon the right of free public discussion." [116]

During the trials the Wilson administration saw to it that the I.W.W. defense remained a precarious beachhead exposed to heavy shelling from the superior federal positions. Government agents continued to raid and ransack for "evidence" I.W.W. offices, including those of the various defense committees.[117] Military intelligence operations carried on a similar harassment.[118] The California prosecutor indicted that area's defense committee leaders.[119] Elsewhere the government arrested active defense workers and broke up their meetings. The Immigration Bureau in the Northwest detained for deportation I.W.W. aliens who contributed to defense funds, sold defense literature, or served on defense organizations.[120]

The federal governoment also maintained propaganda favorable to its own stereotype of the I.W.W. as seditious and disloyal. Prosecuting attorneys so characterized the defendants in numerous public interviews and statements.[121] Department of Justice officials warned individuals against contributing to "so-called 'civil liberties' . . . 'popular council,' 'legal advice,' or anti-war organizations." The government hinted that these groups were federated in a disloyal conspiracy to impede the prosecution of the war.[122] All this was in addition to the state, local, and newspaper campaigns against the I.W.W.

The liberal collapse, Post Office censorship, and governmental intimidation left the I.W.W. with few financial reservoirs. Caroline Lowe, Wichita defense attorney and a longtime resident of the region, could not even finance the trial preliminaries. *"Money cannot be obtained here,"* she wrote. "We cannot get bond for the boys after it is reduced to $500. Think of it! The poison has done its work in the small towns and rural communities." [123] Friends who would have responded to her appeals three years earlier no longer contributed to radical causes, a change she found true throughout the Middle West.[124] In the northern Pacific states $500 bail was beyond the reach of most Wobbly prisoners. Such defense money as the area could raise had to go east to Chicago, for the general defense committee there was constantly short of funds. Outside of its own membership, the I.W.W. could only count on the support of a few wealthy angels in New York and Chicago and several of the more radical labor unions and city centrals. Wobblies themselves, however, supplied the bulk of the contributions.[125]

The indictments and trials effectively suppressed the I.W.W. For over two wartime years the federal government did not tolerate the Wobblies either as a labor or a defense organization. Some thousand or more arrests and some five hundred indictments proved that the Department of Justice had used the war statutes as promised — "vigorously and with dispatch." The "hysterical passions" of the federal juries predetermined the outcome of these trials. Verdicts covering days of testimony and dozens of defendants were sometimes announced within an hour. While some of the prisoners were little fish, the Wilson administration also netted the organization's top executives, organizers, editors, and poets, many of whom received sentences of ten or twenty years.

The defense struggle, of course, did not stop with the convictions. From 1919 to 1921 the I.W.W. expended more of its lessening energies in appeals to the appellate courts. Two of the three judges reversed the verdicts under the so-called industrial counts. All the courts, however, upheld the convictions for violations of the Selective Service and Espionage acts. It was under these counts that district judges had assigned the longest prison sentences. The fight to release these wartime "political prisoners," therefore, carried the defense work well into the 1920's.[126]

The national emergency had helped the government consumate two important drives against labor radicals. Federal troops were the first and temporary solution to Wobbly agitation. The military suppressed the symptoms as they arose on the local level. The courts provided a medium for a second and more thorough nationwide attack disrupting the I.W.W. leadership and disorganizing its economic program. These moves, however, were unexpected, intense, and short-lived. As techniques of repression they could not survive the war. Deportation, always the first love of those who desired to rid the country of "isms," was not forgotten. It supplied the means for the third and final drive against radicals — a stage culminating in the well-known Palmer raids of 1919 and 1920.

VI

A Winter in Seattle

1917–1918

O~N~ January 29, 1918, the Reverend Mark A. Matthews of Seattle's First Presbyterian Church decided that it was time to write Attorney General Gregory a long and alarming letter. Dr. Matthews had been worrying for some time about the Northwest's subversive disloyalty, which seemed to be spreading as fast as the infectious diseases against which he had waged some notable campaigns. Sin and sedition had been, in fact, the targets of Matthews' reforming zeal ever since he had come as a crusader to the frontier port.[1] In this first winter of the war, however, the situation appeared worse than usual. Emphasizing that the "Kerensky overthrow . . . [had been] largely planned, schemed, and executed in the city of Seattle," Dr. Matthews implied that the town had fallen into the hands of "the pro-German forces, the I.W.W. fiends, and the vice syndicate agents of this country." These elements controlled the juries and made a farce of all civil authority. To meet this menace, Matthews proposed amending the Espionage Act. "If the military authorities had concurrent jurisdiction when the civil authorities broke down," he suggested, "they could arrest these fiends, court martial and shoot them." [2] The patriotic parson thereafter entered a forceful and constant candidacy for his appointment as northwestern provost marshal general, with authority to shoot all violators of the law.[3]

While the Wilson administration had no intention of following the lawless advice of the minister-dictator, it listened to his analysis with considerable respect. Mark Matthews was not the first, the only, or the most influential voice to warn the government of Seattle's deteriorating conditions.[4] By early 1918 the President himself believed that "it is thoroughly worth our while to consider what, if anything, should and can be done about the influences proceeding from Seattle." Reading over the reports he had received, Woodrow Wilson wrote to Attorney General Gregory, "if true, they state a very grave situation."[5] The administration was thus quite aware that Seattle's long, intense bitterness between labor and capital had openly erupted and become an embarrassing impediment to the war effort. Federal authorities also realized that the I.W.W. was somehow involved in the region's hysteria. What the government did not know was that the Northwest was about to stage the first mass deportation roundups of radical aliens in American history. Nor could anyone at that time guess that this crusade would largely determine the pattern of future antiradical repressions. Many elements combined to generate in the booming port city policies that led to the red raids of 1919 and 1920.

By the fall of 1917, Seattle's respectable and conservative citizens believed themselves surrounded by lawlessness and radicalism. Mayor Hiram Gill and his city administration were reputed allies in a notorious bootlegging operation. The state of Washington's 1914 dry laws had created a corrupt framework for municipal politics based on illegal liquor and its associated evils. Seattle had been an "open town" in the past, and, in 1916, had apparently become one again. The shipment and distribution of liquor took place openly and under purchased police protection. In December 1916 the federal government indicted Mayor Gill, the chief of police, four policemen, the "dry squad," and the King County sheriff for conspiracy to ship intoxicating liquor in interstate commerce. The trial was closely contested and often hinged on the testimony of the bootleggers. The subsequent acquittal of all defendants left the reformers stunned but vindictive. They carried to Washington their picture of a corrupt and rotten police force, a dishonest mayor, and an immoral city administration. Perhaps the federal government could give Seattle a good wartime cleaning.[6]

Industrial conditions in the Northwest presented an even more appalling prospect than did the municipal misgovernment of Mayor Gill. The antilabor policies of many employers helped produce an equally extreme and vigorous labor movement in reaction. Seattle's central labor council, for example, was one of the most radical groups in organized labor, and Socialists, anarchists, and, for many years, Wobblies had made the Puget Sound city their regional headquarters. The *Seattle Union Record* often attacked the status quo in a biting, anticapitalistic tone. In turn the three leading conservative papers, the *Post-Intelligencer*, the *Times*, and the *Star* used a distorted sensationalism to manufacture and preserve public hysteria towards labor radicals. The three papers may have taken added pleasure in attacking the sponsors of their rival, the *Union Record*.[7]

The I.W.W.'s resurgence during the summer of 1917, therefore, was superimposed upon this long-nutured antagonisms between the worker and his boss. This Wobbly vitality was simply the last straw for many employers. Their intransigence during the lumber strike, their refusal to improve conditions, and their obstinate opposition to the eight-hour day symbolized their determination to smash the radical movement. Federal troops, of course, had helped the timber interests weather the summer; the peace of "martial law" had kept a precarious balance in favor of the operators. Department of Justice prosecutions had also disrupted Wobbly solidarity. But none of this activity touched Seattle, where once more the enemies of radicalism ran head on into the unusual Mayor Gill.

According to his opponents, Gill's administration had coddled I.W.W.'s and other radicals for several years, thus aggravating an already dangerous situation. Gill's impartiality during the Everett massacre and trial and his support of free speech, including that of I.W.W.'s., had won him this reputation. In addition, Wobbly defense counsel George F. Vanderveer served as the personal attorney of Gill and the bootleggers. It was an easy matter in those impassioned days to exaggerate such relations. One could believe that vice and the I.W.W. interlocked through Gill and Vanderveer in a vast conspiracy against good government and correct industrial practices. As the United States attorney discouragingly reported, the local administration was both "spineless and crooked." [8] The city's future looked black. Its best citizens saw nothing ahead but a closed shop and an open town.

Seattle's deterioration evoked repeated and insistent demands for federal aid from Dr. Matthews, federal, state, and local officials, and the region's businessmen. "An interment camp" for "local malcontents" and the arrest of all aliens guilty of "industrial unrest" were some of the suggestions that forced the Wilson administration to look upon Seattle as a "hotbed of unrest and of possible outbreak." [9] Yet federal support came too slowly for the city's more impetuous patriots. These citizens thereupon proceeded with their own plans to suppress sedition.

A semivigilante group in the guise of a patriotic league was Seattle's immediate answer to disloyal radicalism. After several loyalty meetings during the summer of 1917, the Spanish War veterans created and dominated the Minute Men of Seattle. Some two to three thousand strong, this organization represented in part the war hysteria then sweeping the country. Elsewhere the American Protective League performed the same function of searching out and exposing disloyal individuals and spies. The Minute Men, however, had further and peculiarly local responsibilities, assuming the authority to detain, question, and arrest suspected radicals. Operating under the guidance of local federal officials, the Minute Men also served large corporations,[10] which received confidential information about their radical employees and in turn gave the Minute Men financial support.[11] With a member on duty in every city district and hotel, this patriotic league became a front-line antiradical force. By the end of January 1918, the Minute Men claimed to have tracked down "the most rabid leaders and agitators among the I.W.W., and [to] have been instrumental in making several hundred investigations, and having caused many arrests."[12]

In addition to the local patriots, the military forces stationed in Seattle began the surveillance and apprehension of radicals. Both the army and navy had counterintelligence divisions with antiradical branches. Construing the ideologies of Wobblies, anarchists, and socialists as near-treasonable and German-inspired, the armed services believed that "negative" intelligence should protect the troops and the civilian population from such subversion. While the army G-2 division operated mainly undercover in the Seattle area, naval intelligence was much more overt. It interpreted its obligation to protect the harbor and docks as a general authority to search and seize members of the I.W.W. without any legal process whatsoever.[13]

The United States attorney's office in Seattle also felt impelled to teach the seditious elements a wartime lesson. Clay Allen had come to this decision because Mayor Gill's regime "temporized" with the radicals, and because large numbers of foreign-born workers were supposedly antiwar. The instrument of this policy was a tenuous indictment against Hulet M. Wells, socialist and former president of the central labor council, and three of his associates. The government accused them of conspiracy by force to delay the execution of the declaration of war against Germany by writing and distributing an anticonscription circular *prior to the passage* of either the selective service or espionage laws.[14] Although Allen doubted whether the indictment would stand, he considered that "the arrest of these men was necessary as a disciplinary measure in any event." [15]

This small-scale program provided sufficient reassurance to Seattle during the summer of 1917. It worked because the I.W.W. threat was directed not against the city but against the lumber camps and outlying communities, where federal troops had already disposed of the Wobbly menace. It was the end of this summertime control that precipitated Seattle's memorable red scare of the following winter.

Public officials and leading citizens looked upon the annual fall migration of hundreds of workers from lumber camps and harvest fields to the cities as a treacherous I.W.W. conspiracy to seize Seattle. During the slack winter season, the shortened workday and the heavy snows drastically reduced employment. For many years Seattle had absorbed from five to seven and at times up to thirteen thousand displaced workers.[16] In past seasons these migratory lumberjacks, harvest hands, and construction workers had been largely unorganized. They posed an unemployment problem, perhaps, but nothing more.

The 1917 lumber strike, however, drastically altered the customary picture. For the first and last time in its history, the I.W.W. had made a sudden, substantial, and dramatic increase in its membership. The Wobbly red card had become the widespread symbol of resistance to long-endured exploitation. To already nervous and frightened Seattle citizens, therefore, the 1917 migration cityward seemed more like a seditious invasion than the normal backwash of the rural proletariat. Hordes of I.W.W.'s were coming to take over Seattle. In reality the return of the Wobblies was only an expression of the itinerant laborer's desire for the "home, friendship, and . . . sense of belonging" afforded by the I.W.W. hall.[17] The I.W.W. member was searching for the rest and relaxation provided by a big city, even if only by its Skid Road. The big city's leaders did not see it that way, and their lawless panic accompanied the otherwise peaceful influx of the Wobbly unemployed.[18]

A wintertime dragnet against radical agitators also promised a more peaceful industrial scene in 1918 than the lumber industry had had the previous summer. Although the strike had been called off, there was still no permanent settlement, for the operators had so far stalemated federal mediation efforts. The I.W.W., like Brer Fox, lay low. Both sides expected a renewal of the conflict the following spring. Sentiment against employers was supposedly strong enough to turn the walkout into another general shutdown.[19] If the I.W.W. was to be scotched, the winter break seemed the time to do it. The men were idle, their labor was not needed, and their leaders were concentrated in one urban center.

Official estimates that the I.W.W. had grown steadily more dangerous provided a final justification for suppression. This was curious logic, for it assumed that membership became more radical simply because it grew. Yet Seattle was convinced that the nine thousand Wobblies who had arrived by the end of December 1917 were largely "recalcitrants and troublemakers." [20] It was obviously the time for action, and time also for the Wilson administration to get behind the city's antiradical crusade.

By late 1917 the federal government was ready to do this: an authoritative and sensational report had made Seattle's crisis all too apparent. Hugh Campbell Wallace, Democratic national committeeman from Washington and a friend of Woodrow Wilson's, had gone as an emissary of the administration to investigate industrial conditions, unrest, and loyalty in the Northwest. After spending December on the coast, Wallace told the President, "Sedition exists to a considerable extent and effective measures will have to be taken to crush it." Wilson's envoy also gave his unqualified support to an account of local conditions prepared by Colonel M. E. Saville, head of the military police at Camp Lewis, and approved by the commanding general of that post.[21]

Colonel Saville's interpretation reflected all the nativist anxieties that had beset Americans since the 1880's. Seattle, he found, was suffering from a bad attack of conspiracy brought on by an overdose of radical, Roman Catholic, and foreign influences. "The prevalent seditious conditions in the Northwest," he discovered, "are attributable to the fact that the radiating center, Seattle, has been governed by a Vice Ring." According to the colonel, the controlling forces in this intrigue were Mayor Gill, George W. Vanderveer, and the Seattle National Bank, described as "the Vatican's instrument in the West." The incongruous mixture of big time crime, high finance, radical labor, and western Catholicism also had as a final element the sinister German influence. The Russian consul in Seattle, acting through the I.W.W., was manipulating this gigantic plot against the war effort. The consul was "undoubtedly a German agent." [22] The colonel's summary analysis was that "a vice ring, a pro-German ring, and an I.W.W. ring with interests interwoven and backed by political, financial, and religious elements of great strength were in control in Seattle, and that city was the pivotal point of all I.W.W. activities in the Northwest." [23]

The Saville interpretation saw ominous danger everywhere. When George Vanderveer went east to organize the trial preliminaries, Saville warned, "The outlook is not good because Vandeveer [sic] is extending his base to Chicago and New York." The colonel turned the Russian consulate into a base linking the I.W.W. with "French, Italian, and Russian anarchists," and was so certain that the I.W.W. lawyers were "in direct touch with German agents," that he kept them under army surveillance.[24] To counteract Seattle radicalism Saville recommended that the government expel the Russian consul, reinvigorate the local Bureau of Investigation, and replace United States Attorney Allen with a competent and forceful prosecutor.[25]

Convinced that sedition was now serious in the Northwest, the Wilson administration took rapid steps. The Department of Justice picked Clarence L. Reames, United States attorney at Portland, Oregon, as its special assistant for all war-related cases in Seattle. Considered by his superiors to be "the ablest and best district attorney in the West," Reames had also familiarized himself with Seattle conditions as prosecutor in the earlier bootlegging case. Attorney General Gregory felt that Reames was well enough acquainted with the "wild-eyed theorists" of the Washington district to avoid being led "into any impossible situations." An "impossible situation," however, was already under way by the time Reames reached Seattle.[26]

The officials and citizens of that city were mired in an an anarchy of their own creation and frightened by their own lawless activities. They had adopted the vigilante road to law and order. Two popular methods symbolized this commitment: illegal arrests of I.W.W.'s on a large scale and the detention of Wobbly aliens by the Immigration Bureau in violation of Secretary of Labor Wilson's stated policy. Upon his arrival, Reames's first task turned out to be the curbing of official and conservative elements rather than of the radical and seditious ones.

By early 1918, the public's suppression of undesirable individuals had reached a wildly chaotic state. Reames recorded the incredible but not indescribable situation that confronted him. "When I reached Seattle," he wrote the Attorney General, "every public officer, federal, state, and municipal, including the members of the Fire Department, and all volunteer organizations exercised the privilege of unceremoniously arresting citizens, aliens, and alien enemies and throwing them unceremoniously into jail, where they were booked for investigation by the Department of Justice." [27] The Minute Men alone, for example, had processed "several hundred investigations" and made "many arrests." [28] Public officials and volunteer organizations were not the only active detectives. Reames also discovered that "citizens without any semblance of authority at all were arresting men for pro-German utterances and turning them over to the police department where they were being held under the broad charge 'Held for Federal authorities.'" [29] Some of the luckless victims of this patriotic lawlessness had spent months in jail even though there was nothing in the way of charges or evidence against them.[30]

Reames found the Seattle Office of Naval Intelligence more haphazard than most in its approach to the law. The O.N.I. had been making "indiscriminate arrests" without accusation, warrant, or proof of large numbers of Wobblies whom it found on the waterfront or on ships in Puget Sound.[31] From October 1, 1917, until April 1, 1918, when Reames forced the Navy temporarily to discontinue the practice, the O.N.I. made 129 arrests. It was no wonder that he complained that the naval intelligence officers "openly defy the law." [32] Of those arrested most won release within a few days, but some spent two to four weeks under illegal detention. Charges were eventually preferred against a sparse nine of the 129 prisoners.[33]

Bringing the lawless antiradicalism of all these citizens, public officials, and volunteer organizations under control was Reames's first and most perplexing problem. He had to solve it secretly. A public confession of government error would only have added further ammunition to the Wobbly stockpile of illegal persecution.[34] The solution had to be achieved diplomatically so as not to alienate the patriots whose support Reames needed. It also had to be found quickly in order to terminate the lawlessness for which the Department of Justice was being held responsible.

Reames succeeded to a great degree in realizing these objectives. The Seattle office of the Department of Justice terminated seizures without warrants and induced all organizations, official or otherwise, to make no arrests without its approval or that of the United States marshal. The Attorney General himself forcefully urged the Navy Department to familiarize its subordinate officers with the Constitution.[35] To avoid further troubles on the waterfront, Reames directed the marshal not to issue waterfront passes to any Wobblies. Since the pass regulations were aimed at the exclusion of alien enemies, there was no legal sanction for applying the rules against mere members of the I.W.W. Reames justified his arbitrary order on the ground that it prevented "a number of unwarranted and illegal arrests by State and municipal authorities." [36] All these actions were taken without publicity that might benefit the Industrial Workers of the World.

There were, of course, lapses that Reames could not control: the May arrest of two hundred Wobblies by the Seattle chief of police and the unlawful detention of thirty-nine I.W.W.'s by naval intelligence in August.[37] In addition, Reames had to remind the armed services "almost every day" not to arrest summarily mere members of the I.W.W.[38] For the most part, however, Reames had thoroughly centralized all antiradical activities in his own office and at the same time had won the support and admiration of Seattle's patriots. He had proved to be an effective law-enforcement officer, thereby succeeding where United States Attorney Allen had failed.[39] In retrospect it can be seen why.

Seattle's reputation for unchecked corruption and sedition paralleled the illegal detentions of scores of I.W.W. members. Under Allen's regime the local Department of Justice office made no effort to stop the public-spirited arrests by self-appointed volunteers. The fact that individuals like

Wobblies were arrested and imprisoned created strong public presumption that they were guilty and, what was more, dangerous. When Allen was forced to release I.W.W.'s for lack of any evidence, the citizens of Seattle became convinced that he was incapable of enforcing the laws against disloyalty and radicalism. Men like Dr. Matthews and Colonel Saville saw only that Wobblies were being set free, never that these radicals should not have been arrested at all. The press, meanwhile, played up the arrests in distorted and sensational front-page accounts but did not reveal the illegal and unauthorized nature of the detentions. The Department of Justice also concealed this reality, for the truth would only have substantiated the radical charges of lawlessness. Reames's prompt reassertion of federal authority in the arrest of radicals interrupted the vicious circle. He was skillful enough as an administrator and tactician to prohibit mob action and yet retain the confidence of the mob.[40]

Meanwhile, in addition to the illegal arrests of suspected subversives and pro-Germans, Seattle had also initiated a deportation crusade of I.W.W. members. While motivated by exactly the same fears and hopes, the Immigration Bureau's project was much grander in scope. In fact, the public officialdom of Seattle agreed that these deportations would effectively terminate the I.W.W. threat to the Northwest, and had them well under way when Reames arrived. Far from discouraging this procedure, he had nothing but admiration for it and steadfastly gave it his warm support and encouragement.

II

On January 14, 1918, a committee representing all federal officials in Seattle unanimously agreed that the deportation of alien I.W.W.'s would be the most adaptable and persuasive technique of repression. Chairman Henry M. White, the commissioner of immigration, and his associates realized that the Department of Justice could not prosecute I.W.W.'s in the courts, at least not to the extent desired. According to Commissioner White, the group rejected trials "because of the multiplicity of suits and because of the procedure, *in that every man must be proven guilty of a particular offense.*" [41] The Immigration Bureau at Seattle thereupon inaugurated a campaign to arrest all I.W.W. aliens who were "undesirable" or "pro-German in their activity." [42] While such criteria may have suited the needs of Seattle, they were hardly the offenses prohibited by the immigration laws, at least as then written. The Seattle office had just assumed the authority to redefine the deportion legislation.

Beginning in late 1917, the Immigration Bureau began to approve new standards of guilt and looser arrest procedures in cases involving I.W.W.'s and other radicals. Local inspectors now detained for deportation mere members of the I.W.W. under the theory that possession of I.W.W. literature or belief in it amounted to advocacy of illegal principles.[43] The Seattle office was convinced that the organization did teach the unlawful destruction of property, despite the contrary findings of the legal experts in Washington. These departures also violated Secretary Wilson's earlier insistence on substantial proof of individual guilt before a warrant of arrest would issue.[44] Regardless of departmental policy, the bureau was obviously going to carry on an independent existence of its own.

Seattle's autonomy was additionally facilitated by the widespread resort to telegraphic warrants of arrest, which ordinarily were to be used only in cases of extreme necessity.[45] Since the bureau conducted its telegraphic correspondence in code, the practice was peculiarly susceptible to abuse. Washington simply had to assume that the district office had the substantial supporting evidence for deportation that was required by the rules. Such emergency methods successfully screened local officials from review by head-

quarters during the initial stages of the deportation crusade.
While the Seattle crisis was the major motivation for the
adoption of these slipshod standards and procedures, the
contemporary political atmosphere and the Immigration
Bureau's attitude toward I.W.W.'s were also influential.
Bureau personnel were sensitive to the spirit of unrest and
revolution abroad in the world and to the alacrity with which
new ideas spread among discontented people. The bureau
could, therefore, justify arrests "in view of conditions then
prevailing." The commissioner general did not consider that
an alien spreading radical ideas (or accused of doing so)
"should be given the benefit of any serious doubt." [46]

The northwestern district's hostility and contempt for
I.W.W. aliens was made clear in a mimeographed brief inserted in all I.W.W. records. "The organization and its members should be handled without gloves," the bureau stated.
The inspectors believed that most I.W.W.'s were "yegs and
tramps, men . . . lying idle as long as they can get sufficient
to eat without working." A final summary characterized the
Wobblies as "the scum of the earth . . . a landless and lawless mob, who, having no property themselves, recognize no
rights or property . . . no law, and no authority save the
policeman's night stick or physical violence." [47]

With its mimeographed indictment of I.W.W.'s and its
new standards of guilt, the Seattle Office was ready to play
its assigned role as the port city's savior. Businessmen and
public officials had envisioned the deportation of some three
to five thousand alien I.W.W.'s in order to break the back-
bone of the organization and thwart the spring strike
threat.[48] The Immigration Bureau manfully undertook to
realize these estimates. Beginning in late January 1918 it
rounded up nearly a hundred aliens in the first two weeks
alone. It filled its own detention station and loaded to capacity every available county jail in western Washington.[49]

Success came easily because the inspectors used almost any

excuse for an arrest. The district office detained aliens "supposed to be . . . prominent and active member[s] of the I.W.W."[50] Aliens who looked like I.W.W.'s were held.[51] A good many others found themselves in jail as "members who have come from . . . points East . . . for the purpose of agitating and causing disturbances among the lumber workers."[52] The bureau fabricated other complaints arresting aliens as prominent organizers and delegates, distributors of I.W.W. literature, collectors of funds, and believers in the organization principles.[53] There was naturally no legal authority to detain anyone as a "believer," "collector," or "organizer" without proof of an individual overt act. In almost all these cases guilt under the 1917 law could not be substantiated at the time of arrest and was rarely developed later by the alien's self-incrimination. Most of the prisoners were not agitators; few were dedicated Wobblies; the majority had joined up during the previous summer's membership drive.[54]

The Seattle office also participated in deportation arrests explicitly initiated by employers in order to rid themselves of agitators and troublemakers. The lumber companies in one section of the Pacific Coast, for example, raised a thousand dollars a month from each mill owner for counter-radical surveillance.[55] A large lumber manufacturer might have an alien Wobbly picket arrested for deportation; a railroad detective would call on the Immigration Bureau to detain an I.W.W. organizer; or a corporation would discharge a suspected radical and turn him over to the inspectors. Reports that an alien was active as a troublemaker in a logging company sufficed for his arrest under the immigration law.[56] In none of these cases, however, was there sufficient prima facie evidence under the 1917 act to justify issuing a warrant. Arrest was, rather, a convenient method for the removal and detention of undesirables. Besides, there was always the chance that an alien might incriminate himself during the hearings.

Just as the antiradical crusade was beginning to count its victims in the hundreds, it developed a crushing liability — arrests were fast outrunning available space. Apparently no one had had the foresight to obtain the appropriations, the staff, or the quarters for such an ambitious program. Only the Department of Labor, presumably the Secretary himself, could authorize the lavish funds that would support further uninterrupted detentions. The Seattle bureau, therefore, had to familiarize its superiors with the deportation drive or abandon it. Faced with this disappointing dilemma, the Northwest made a forceful plea for Washington's essential patronage.

Commissioner White, the Minute Men, Dr. Matthews, Special Assistant Reames, and influential politicians and business leaders carried on a sustained fight for the acquisition or construction of an internment camp of ample proportions.[57] They were still thinking in terms of three to five thousand arrests. According to one prominent local attorney, "Every commercial institution and employer of labor in the lumber and shipbuilding district are vitally interested and behind the movement." [58] The county commissioner offered the Immigration Bureau a building that could hold fifteen hundred prisoners. At nearby Everett, a landowner made available his island as a free detention station.[59] In Washington, D.C., the commissioner general considered the situation of "sufficient gravity" to call for a conference with Secretary Wilson.[60]

In Seattle, meanwhile, the immigration officials anticipated a favorable department decision and went on arresting aliens during February. This policy led to further serious overcrowding of the detention station and a further deterioration of the living conditions there. To relieve the congestion, the Seattle bureau sent fifty-five I.W.W. aliens hundreds of miles east across the mountains to the county jails at Ellensburg, Yakima, and Walla Walla.[61] The prison facilities of the entire state were seemingly to be exhausted before the campaign came to a halt. As it turned out, however, Secretary of Labor Wilson's decision occurred long before the Northwest expended its remaining antiradical energies.

The department now reversed the policy of mass and indiscriminate detentions it had implicitly sanctioned by its rubber-stamp approval of the warrants of arrest. This reassertion of high-level control again revealed the strength of the accidental factors at work in the antiradical crusade. It seems doubtful that the department would have reviewed the actions of the bureau and stopped them, had it not been for the question of the internment stockade. This is understandable only in the light of war confusion, a lack of administrative coordination among overworked officials, and the ever-present bureaucratic propensity for making discretionary decisions.

Secretary Wilson's views had been and continued to be directly at variance with those of the Immigration Bureau and its inspectors. Wilson did not believe that I.W.W. membership signified "belief in or understanding of its philosophy" or any desire to further a criminal conspiracy. Having seen the lumber industry's wretched working and living conditions, the Secretary recognized that the high labor turnover and the homeless, migratory life had turned many of the timber workers into "disintegrating forces in society." [62]

Secretary Wilson, therefore, confirmed his previous decision to deport only those aliens who personally violated the immigration laws, for he had ruled that the I.W.W. constitution was lawful. He could not logically approve the further roundup of *mere members* of the organization under an immigration act that called for some proof of *individual guilt*. He would not make Wobblies liable for what their fellow members did or wrote that might or might not be legal. The Department of Labor spelled this theory out in specific instructions to Seattle:

First, that we will not arrest, detain or deport any alien simply for joining the I.W.W.

Second, that we will arrest and detain, until we can deport, any alien, whether member of the I.W.W. or not, who is found advocating or teaching the unlawful destruction of property or advocating or teaching anarchy or the overthrow by force or violence of the Government of the United States or of all forms of law, or the assassination of public officials, or who is any other manner subject to deportation under the immigration laws, even though he may not commit any overt act.

Third, if the quarters at the Seattle station are not ample to take care of all who may be arrested and detained for deportation under these instructions, the commissioner at Seattle will be authorized to secure additional quarters.[63]

The Secretary's policy shattered the Northwest's hopes for any large-scale roundups of alien I.W.W. members, and Seattle realized this all too well. Once more, and now almost desperately, it presented the case for guilt by membership.

In his plea for a free and easy attitude toward the 1917 law, Special Assistant Reames symbolized the region's long-standing antipathy for standards of personal guilt. Along with many others, Reames had told the Department of Justice how seditiously repugnant the I.W.W.'s were proving to be that winter. In reply, Attorney General Gregory ordered his assistant to "proceed by pointing out to local Immigration officials particular persons who have offended or who are expressing offensive convictions." [64] This, of course, was exactly what no one was able to do, and why Seattle had turned to the deportation process.[65] A policy compelling immigrant inspectors to obtain proof of some overt act or statement was an equally impractical, if not hopeless requirement. The new Department of Labor order also placed the burden upon the government to prove the concrete violation of the immigration laws.

If the Wilson administration countenanced the Secretary of Labor's theory, Reames saw only one forlorn alternative left. His office might be able to destroy the I.W.W. threat "through the slow, tedious and almost impossible method of court procedure." [66] He knew that, regardless of the evidence in individual cases, "juries are anxious to convict." [67] To try some five thousand alien members of the I.W.W. one by one, however, struck Reames as "a physical impossibility." The thought of the choked and stifled court records, the indicted men waiting months to stand trial, and the endless defense harangues and rebuttals was too appalling.[68] There was a much more sensible approach for the government to adopt.

What the federal officials at Seattle wanted in essence was the authority to arrest all alien Wobblies and the discretion to deport the bad ones. The local bureau would detain only the I.W.W.'s who believed in the teachings and principles of the organization and would quietly release the duped, the ignorant, and the genuinely contrite.[69] The burden of proof would now be on the alien to explain satisfactorily his I.W.W. membership. Reames justified this novel procedure on the grounds that a war emergency existed. The government, he believed, had the right to punish those aliens whose attachment to the I.W.W. proved their violation of the "*spirit* of the laws." [70]

Try as they might, the Seattle administrators could not commit the federal government to the dragnet roundup of aliens merely because they joined the I.W.W. Attorney General Gregory and President Wilson both supported the Secretary of Labor in his adamant refusal to sanction guilt by association. In the detention of alien enemies, in fact, the Department of Justice followed a similar policy (often violated in practice) of not interning anyone for mere membership.[71] The constantly overcrowded jails and the meager staff and appropriations were a re-enforcing deterrent to further mass arrests. Although the Seattle office grudgingly conceded the Secretary his over-all policy, it continued to equate membership with guilt in scattered cases during the war.

Powerful elements in the government had thus brought to

heel a deportation policy inspired by Seattle's wartime and nativist hysterias. What was tragic, however, was that this opposition was neither consistent nor continuous. If President Wilson and Attorney General Gregory supported a standard of individual guilt in deportation, they paid little heed to it in the court cases attacking the I.W.W. And Secretary Wilson's high-minded devotion to personal rights never became effective at the lower echelons of his command. While he intermittently interposed his will, his major concern remained with matters of labor, not immigration. Alien affairs continued to be the province, therefore, of an administrative bureau that was increasingly the spoiled child of its department. Headstrong, independent, and emotionally responsive to local attentions, the Immigration Bureau received its discipline ungraciously and at moments of self-induced crisis.

Despite the abortive ending of the antiradical crusade, the story of sedition in Seattle had its happy ending. The town itself calmed down. Special Assistant Reames ended the numerous arrests by unauthorized groups and citizens while impressing the patriots with the forcefulness of his office. From time to time state and local officials made summary detentions without proof for short imprisonments, but Reames felt they "amount to nothing." [72] By accepting the eight-hour day and beginning the reform of camp conditions, lumber operators eliminated much general discontent. Many an ex-Wobbly went off to join the government-sponsored Loyal Legion of Loggers and Lumbermen. To watch those not so inclined, the army intelligence organized a counterespionage system among soldier spruce workers.[73] Contrary to the ominous predictions of Dr. Matthews and other alarmists, Hiram Gill had been decisively defeated in the March election. Ole Hanson, the new mayor, was a Wilsonian progressive and a bitter foe of all radicalism. The Russian consul had been proved to be neither a German agent nor the brains behind the I.W.W.[74] With arrival of spring the migratory harvest hands and lumber workers once more left the cities behind and relatively deserted. Seattle could no longer claim to be the target of a seditious invasion; its hysteria subsided and with it the pressure for further arrests.

Nevertheless, nearly 150 imprisoned alien victims of the winter's roundup awaited the hearings that would determine their deportability. These pitiful remnants of a city's excitement, almost forgotten at the time, were soon to have an historical significance far beyond their numbers. The I.W.W.'s would have been released into obsucrity had it not been for the kind of hearings conducted by the Northwest's inspectors. Remaining in jail, these Wobblies evoked new legislation and policies that shaped the course of an administration and the lives of hundreds of radicals.

III

In the I.W.W. hearings the immigration inspectors added to traditional practices antiradical procedures that again conflicted with the well-elaborated policy of the Secretary of Labor. To begin with, inspectors approached the hearing schooled in the techniques of the preliminary hearing, interrogation without defense counsel, and self-incrimination. Training and experience with docile, resigned defendants had accustomed inspectors to convicting almost everyone, and so they expected neither protest nor defiance from arrested aliens. In addition, their background had never prepared them for the intellectual exercise of unraveling radical beliefs or determining doctrinal meanings.[75]

In the second place, a conscious antiradical bias was superimposed upon this earlier antialien prejudice. The records forwarded to Washington were filled with obiter dicta emphasizing the general worthlessness of I.W.W.'s. Inspectors made the temporary nature of timber and harvest work appear, for example, as symptomatic of an unreliable and useless person unable to hold a steady job.[76] The Wobbly was usually portrayed as a "worthless (typical) bum," "the usual roving type," or "a very (extremely) undesirable type." [77] Prejudged in the mimeographed brief as "the scum of the earth," the I.W.W. alien could expect little understanding from the inspector holding the hearing.

Finally, the northwestern district conducted the hearings as it had earlier conducted the arrests on an erroneous interpretation of the 1917 legislation, an exegesis in direct violation of Secretary Wilson's findings. The local bureau assumed that an individual's belief in I.W.W. principles or in quoted inflammatory excerpts sufficed to make him deportable. The officials were convinced that their mimeographed collection of Wobbly literature proved that the organization taught and advocated sabotage, and hence claimed that a true believer would undoubtedly assist in spreading the illegal propaganda to which he had committed himself. Under this reasoning, the inspectors easily made the jump from *belief* (lawful) to *advocacy* (unlawful). The Seattle officials also argued that an alien's support of the I.W.W. automatically helped to spread its doctrines. An individual could therefore "advocate" simply by paying his dues or contributing to a defense fund. The immigration authorities did not bother to search for evidence that the alien had ever advocated or taught the unlawful destruction of property in the accepted public and overt manner. Instead, they spent their time subjecting him to an ideological cross-examination. Beliefs, rather than actions, became all-important. The fact of membership alone placed the burden on the defendant to prove the innocence of his associations. In such circumstances, the hearings degenerated into doctrinal controversies between the orthodox official and the heretic alien. In such "theological" disputes, victory had a way of going to the inquisitor. Certainly none of the surroundings favored the alien.[78]

The interrogations took place in an atmosphere poisoned

by class antagonisms and individual enmities. The administrative inflexibility, patriotism, and dogmatic conservatism
of the inspectors received fresh affronts from the surly, defiant, evasive, or non-cooperative answers of I.W.W. aliens,
who were sensitive about their rights and contemptuous of
authority. Believing they had been unlawfully detained from
the beginning, I.W.W.'s did not become more conciliatory
with long imprisonment. The first hearings, after all, were
not held until two to four months after the arrest. With their
health deteriorating from the enforced idleness in overcrowded, unsanitary county jails, the aliens grew embittered
by the seemingly deliberate delays. The inspector and the
deportation process appeared to them to be simply one more
tool of capitalist oppression. By the time the hearing began
they were decidedly on edge.[79]

It was the worst possible setting for an investigation of individual beliefs. On one side sat the inspector, with his collection of damning quotations from I.W.W. literature. Hope-
fully awaiting an incriminating admission from the alien, he
impatiently and belligerently tried to force the defendant's
philosophy to the surface. The inspector did not want explan-
ations, qualifications, or dissertations on the chosen selec-
tions. He wanted a useful, unconditional admission. As one
of the examiners said, "I don't care how you answer, as long
as you answer yes or no." [80]

On the other side, the I.W.W. alien was in no mood to
comply; in some cases he was also too ignorant to do so.
Some of the Wobblies had never heard of or read the radical excerpts upon which they were asked to pass judgment.
If they had, they often refused to discuss them. Familiar with
Secretary Wilson's emphasis on an individual overt act and
coached by fellow aliens, many prisoners refrained from approving any of the selected excerpts. A conviction that belief
alone had no relevance to guilt gave I.W.W.'s a cynical and
sometimes humorous contempt for the whole proceedings.[81]

"Have I the right to believe?" one alien cried out in exasperation with the senselessness of it all. "I would like to find out if an alien has the right to believe." [82]

The immigration officials introduced every conceivable statement that might seem to sanction violence. Did the alien approve of "direct action," "sabotage," "the use of any and all tactics," or "an unceasing struggle against the private ownership and control of industry"? Did he agree that "all peace so long as the wage system lasts, is but an armed truce," and that "property has no rights that its creators are bound to respect"?

The I.W.W. answers came to be as stereotyped as the questions. No, the alien did not believe in the destruction of property. According to the Wobblies, whatever the inspector produced was simply the individual opinion of the author. As for "sabotage" and "direct action," the aliens denied that those words signified forceful or unlawful methods. With monotonous regularity the Wobblies defined "sabotage" as no more than a slowdown, a strike on the job, or "a bum day's work for a bum day's pay." If the government wanted a more intellectual interpretation, then sabotage was "the conscientious withdrawal of efficiency" by the wage slaves. "Direct action" meant economic coercion or resistance applied at the point of production to enforce working class demands. But never did I.W.W. aliens knowingly admit a belief in the unlawful destruction of property, or their advocacy and teaching of such principles. [83]

Failing to obtain the desired admissions, the Immigration Bureau shifted ground with the I.W.W. If the organization was putting a nonviolent interpretation upon its practices, then the inspectors would reclassify such peaceful tactics as dangerous and illegal. So the Seattle bureau made "the conscientious withdrawal of efficiency" a more frightening concept than "sabotage," for the tactic of withdrawal represented sabotage in its "most insidious form, the putting out of poor quality." Inspectors believed that an article's shoddy construction might cause it not only to fall apart in use (that is, to be destroyed) but also to endanger or snuff out human life itself. The Washington office accepted this farfetched reassessment; ideologically, the I.W.W. had no place to go.[84]

Turning legitimate conduct into forbidden behavior was an easy matter for the creative imaginations of the Seattle inspectors. Support of the Chicago I.W.W. defense, for example, became advocacy of the organization's doctrines, despite the fact that the trial was still under way and the accused presumably still innocent.[85] One Wobbly protested, "I believe in donating towards any man that is in trouble, helping to defend him." To this the immigration official characteristically replied, "You just contributed to the fund to defeat the law."[86]

Other parts of the hearing revealed how easily one man's free speech became another man's sedition. To the inspectors, belief in or advocacy of I.W.W. strikes was seditious; the idea that workers should share in profits was equated with disloyalty to the American form of government; and an alien's failure to acquire citizenship was termed a contemptuous insult to the country.[87]

The fundamental schism between the alien and his examiner reappeared in final form in the summaries and recommendations that the lower echelon forwarded to Washington. Instead of an expert analysis of evidence proving the alien's guilt, the inspectors passed on a mélange of unsubstantiated, irrelevant, and misleading data calculated to prejudice the defendant's case. This material often reappeared in bureau memoranda prepared as guides for departmental action.[88] It all suggested that immigration officials considered general undesirability rather than specific guilt a cause for deportation. Aliens were variously described as "a serious menace to the peace of this country"; "an agitator, and a trouble maker"; "a typical agitator, an I.W.W. and proud of it"; or "a fanatic, willing to go to any extreme." Inspectors also included such remarks as, "It is believed that he [the alien] is in entire sympathy with such doctrines." [89]

Besides applying the 1917 antiradical law in extreme and exaggerated ways and making full use of its broad and indefinite terms, the Immigration Bureau also sought to deport radicals under immigration legislation that had not been designed for their apprehension. One such valuable weapon was an old enactment against persons liable to become public charges (LPC). This vague complaint had been in steady service for deporting the chronically ill, paupers, and the mentally disturbed. The burden of proving that he had not been liable to become a public charge at the time of entry was the alien's all but impossible task. He would have to demonstrate conclusively that the characteristics or weaknesses causing his disability did not exist when he landed. One safeguard limited the application of the LPC charge to five years after entry. The courts, however, had defined entry as the *last* entry into the United States, regardless of how many years' residence the alien had established previously. Nor did it matter how short an absence had occurred, as long as the alien had crossed the border.[90]

With a new interpretation the LPC charge made deportable many an I.W.W. alien whom the government could not otherwise touch. Immigration officials in the Northwest extended LPC coverage to include any jail sentence for any cause at all. Beliefs then became important. An alien's radical thought could well be assumed to make him liable to short- (and long-) term imprisonments in those days. How could the alien prove that his propensity for joining subversive organizations or associating with radical causes did not innately exist at the time of entry? Many I.W.W.'s had already served time. It was safe to suppose that alien recruits would become public charges in the future, imprisoned as free speech advocates, vagrants, or troublemakers. The Immigration Bureau had thus classified the victims of lawless community hysteria as worthy of deportation.

The five-year limitation also proved something of a phantom for I.W.W.'s. Their migratory roamings often took them across the Canadian border for brief periods. A harvest worker followed the wheat belt north regardless of national lines. Lumberjacks might also trail logging operations across the border or shift north with fluctuations in timber operations. Although they might have lived in the United States for twenty or thirty years, such aliens were nevertheless subject to the LPC provision for five years after their last trip to Canada.

The standards for deportation in I.W.W. cases now became about as loose as any the bureau could devise. Unable to prove the advocacy or teaching of illegal doctrine, it could still order aliens with "radical views" expelled as LPC's.[91] Having the "appearance and attitude" of an I.W.W., even though the alien was not a member; arrest as a supposedly active Wobbly, despite proof that the alien had no such affiliations; and sympathetic association with anarchists, I.W.W.'s, and similar groups — any of these sufficed for the deportation of aliens as potential public charges.[92] Numerous other cases firmly established the bureau's policy of deporting aliens for radical views whenever it found they had entered within the previous five years.[93]

The Immigration Bureau, however, did not limit itself to radicalism as indicative of LPC. With ironic humor, bureau officials turned the Wobbly's helpless migratory search for work against him. According to the government, evidence of an "alien's unwillingness to settle down and work in one place" or of his "nomadic habits" supported an LPC accusation.[94] Inspectors seized upon another characteristic typical of harvest and lumber workers during the off-season: "living on a summer's earnings" or "a lack of funds" (although employed at the time of arrest) also meant that the alien might become a public charge.[95] Immigration officials could even predict an alien's future confinement from personal or physical peculiarities such as "an abnormal head which . . . indicates criminal propensities," "a predilection for agitation," and a tendency to "spread radical propaganda." [96]

The alien had almost no way of disproving such charges. The government did not have to indicate that beliefs or traits *would* bring the alien into conflict with the authorities, only that they were *liable* or had some *remote tendency* to do so. How could an individual guarantee that "his relation toward . . . revolutionary doctrines" or his "radical, socialistic ideas" [97] would not make him a public charge? One could perhaps demonstrate that pauperism, tuberculosis, or venereal disease set in from causes originating after entry, but ideas like lunacy defied such precise detection.

Such charges and hearings sufficed to keep imprisoned the vast majority of aliens rounded up during Seattle's winter crusade. All during the summer and fall of 1918 the government held this group in the county jails and detention stations of the Northwest. Although inspectors had held hearings, both the Bureau of Immigration and the Department of Labor had yet to decide upon a policy toward these radicals being held under the 1917 law.

The summer of 1918 was therefore a turning point. The decision that would be crucial to the later deportation crusade of 1919–20 was whether higher officials would approve the extreme interpretations of the Seattle inspectors or reassert the policies of Secretary Wilson. The government might reinforce emphasis on individual guilt and insist upon a strict definition of the law. On the other hand, it might also plunge headlong into the murky waters of guilt by association, by belief, and by any one of a dozen other actions that administrative officials might secretly define as advocacy. That this choice had to be made, and at that specific moment was, of course, Seattle's responsibility.

The antiradical hysteria of one city thus projected its purely local campaign onto a national scale. The alien Communists rounded up by A. Mitchell Palmer's 1920 raids had undoubtedly never heard of the Reverend Mark Matthews or
Commissioner Henry M. White, yet those two men symbolized a complex of fears and pressures that set off a chain of
events culminating in the so-called red scare. Seattle had
wanted only to be rid of its seditious elements — a little
neighborhood repression would have served the purpose. By
the winter of 1917–18, however, an unsettled lumber strike, a
vacillating United States attorney, a neutral city administration, and the annual appearance of large numbers of migratory workers set the stage for widespread lawlessness. This,
in turn, reinforced Seattle's impression of sedition running
wild. The Wilson administration could not remain aloof, and
so it ordered a special assistant to the scene. Bringing the
vigilante elements to heel, Clarence L. Reames then found a
full-fledged deportation crusade under way. He and others
supported these arrests as the final solution to the local crisis.
Immigration detentions blocked habeas corpus actions,
avoided the puzzling problem of proving individual guilt,
and by-passed the delays and technicalities of judicial process. Secretary Wilson halted this dramatic attack on the
mass base of subversion, but could not induce the release of
Wobblies already detained. The bureau's analysis of these
cases suggested to it how federal officials might more adequately control the spread of radicalism. The northwestern
deportation crusade, therefore, is remembered less for crippling the I.W.W. than for the significant lesson it taught the
administration at Washington.

VII

The Labyrinth of Deportation

1918–1919

Anthony Caminetti, commissioner of immigration had always had decidedly strong views about radicalism. An Italian-American from California, he seemed anxious to prove his own loyalty by an all-out attack on immigrants suspected of subversion. His conservative philosophy reflected his own alien background as well as the phobias of West Coast nativism. IIis chief law officer, A. Warner Parker, had equally decided opinions. The war emergency and the Russian Revolution had intensified their attitudes. Both men considered the situation during 1917 and 1918 grave; and the bureau they supervised had responded to the crisis by creating a special division to handle I.W.W. and similar cases. The activities of these aliens had been "so pronounced and extensive" that it had become necessary to review, correlate, and coordinate all anti-radical hearings. The immigration Bureau dispatched a special examiner to the Northwest to supervise the preparation of I.W.W. records in that area and it analyzed the mass of collected evidence in conference with a special agent of the Department of Justice.[1]

In spite of these preparations, Caminetti and Parker were unhappy. They were not doing enough, they felt, and were losing the antiradical struggle. Their inadequacy in the midst of such extensive nationwide crackdowns stemmed from the 1917 Immigration Act. The two high officials found this legislation increasingly inadequate, for it did not live up to their previous expectations. The immigration laws must somehow be made to reflect the expressed intent of Congress to stamp out the radical menace; there was no time to waste for conditions were no longer normal. "I am prepared," Caminetti told Parker, "to go to the fullest extent by [such] amendment to existing law and by [such] additions thereto, as will not only carry out the will of Congress on the subject as expressed in past legislation but also to meet new conditions presented in this emergency." [2]

While awaiting the passage of a more comprehensive anti-radical code, the Bureau of Immigration might also force upon the Department of Labor a really vigorous application of the 1917 act. "Amendment to existing law," as suggested by Caminetti, did not have to be only congressional revision. Administrative reinterpretation of vague and indefinite provisions was an equally valuable amending device. During the summer of 1918, therefore, the commissioner general and his aides sought both legislative and executive enrichment of their storehouse of weapons. They were going to deal with the I.W.W. in one way or another.

The Seattle experience convinced the Immigration Bureau that the test of individual guilt under the 1917 law was a requirement of proof that its inspectors could not in most cases produce. Fearing that radicals under detention would win their freedom, the bureau proposed to make them deportable by writing a new law and applying it ex post facto. "There are now pending before the Department," the bureau wrote the Senate Immigration Committee in July 1918, " a large number of cases of aliens who fall within the provisions of the [proposed 1918] bill and *with respect to the possibility of deporting whom under the terms of the existing law there is considerable doubt.*" The bureau stated that "the matter is regarded as one of great importance." [3]

The Immigration Act of October 1918, drafted and backed

by the Department of Justice and the Bureau of Immigration, frankly proposed to remove any existing special immunities that favored radical aliens. The government now wanted to reach both believers and members. Guilt by association and guilt by underlying thought were thus to become deportable offenses for the first time in the country's history. The proposed revisions also eliminated the former five-year limitation, beyond which the government might not ferret out and deport those who had held proscribed beliefs and memberships in radical organizations before coming to the United States.[4]

Under the 1918 legislation the country moved a further long step away from its tolerant turn-of-the-century policy. No congressional voices decried acceptance of the dangerous doctrine of guilt by association, and the bill swept through the House and Senate as rubber-stamped, wartime-emergency legislation.[5] While this bill contemplated the deportation of specific radicals, especially the Seattle I.W.W.'s, it was to have far-reaching and unintended consequences. The membership provision alone made possible the mass character of the red raids of 1919–20. In such a disguised and unpublicized way the country once again took an irreversible step.

While awaiting the passage of the 1918 legislation, the Bureau of Immigration began a secret reinterpretation of the law that lasted right through the later red scare. The standard of deportability changed in July, early November, late November, and December of 1918, and in February, March, and April of 1919. These redefinitions had one purpose: to make the ambiguous terminology of the immigration code fit the cases of I.W.W.'s and similar radicals then under detention; or to put it the other way around, to convert the inspectors' miscellaneous data covering beliefs and associations into proof of individual overt acts.

In July 1918, nearly three months before Congress extended the country's antiradical coverage, the bureau devised a policy that would have made the great majority of arrested I.W.W.'s deportable. In an apparent effort to separate inactive sheep from active goats, the bureau would now judge the guilt or innocence of I.W.W. aliens by their overall support of the organization and its official literature, even though the Secretary of Labor had found both lawful.[6] The plan envisioned the following procedure:

> Membership in the I.W.W. *together with evidence* of knowledge on the part of the alien as to the nature of the propaganda and aims of the organization, as contained in the official literature, sympathy with and approval of such propaganda and aims, financial support by purchasing such literature or through paying membership dues into the general fund of the organization, to which fund the expense of publishing such literature is charged, voluntary contributions to the general defense fund for the members of the I.W.W. now under arrest or indictment, or in prison, and active support by distributing literature or acting as a delegate or organizer, and soliciting membership, collecting and transmitting dues, etc., shall be considered good grounds for deportation on the charge of advocating and teaching the unlawful destruction of property.[7]

No Wobbly was so inactive as not to be covered by this secret and retroactive July program, which again explicitly reversed the earlier, well-publicized statements of Secretary Wilson.

The first verdicts under the July memorandum came in September 1918, some eight months after the I.W.W.'s had first been imprisoned. These confusing, inconsistent decrees illustrated how far the Immigration Bureau had traveled from the clear heights of overt acts into the foggy depths of impressionistic intent. Some twenty Wobblies, whose cooperative attitude had impressed the inspectors, received paroles because of their willingness to leave the I.W.W. After eight months in jail on no charge other than membership, their recantation was perhaps not so surprising.[8]

The bureau certified eighteen others, thirteen members and five organizers, for deportation as undesirable individuals who *seemed* to believe in and support the I.W.W.[9] But immigration officials were really only guessing at this; for they admitted more than once that the alien's "own evasive testimony is hardly sufficient to prove the charge." [10] The bureau was composing a picture of guilt out of three elements. First, the government *assumed* that job delegates and organizers automatically advocated illegal doctrines by collecting dues and dispersing literature. No proof was offered here.[11] Second, the bureau characterized as dangerous those aliens against whom it had haphazardly uncovered some evidence of activity on behalf of the organization, regardless of how routine or innocuous (or legal) that activity might be.[12] Third, inspectors intuitively tracked down guilt in the alien's personality as revealed during the hearing. The fact that a man was "surly," "left an unfavorable impression," appeared to be a "fanatic," or refused to testify or was "evasive" about his beliefs created presumption in official minds of loyal support to the I.W.W. Resigned, submissive, or cooperative witnesses, on the other hand, had a much better chance of being released as harmless or misguided followers.[13]

Just as it was beginning to enjoy its discretionary role, the Immigration Bureau saw its July procedure crumble under the impact of a federal court decision. This rude, and as it later turned out, only momentary, shock from the Spokane district caused the bureau to review its tactics once more, this time in accord with the views of Secretary Wilson.

Judge Frank H. Rudkin of the eastern district of Washington discarded the policy of guilt by association with a legal organization, and narrowly redefined the meaning of advocacy and teaching. The case in question was that of an alien who had spent nearly a year in jail awaiting the department's decision and had at last instituted habeas corpus proceedings to force the government's hand. The record contained no evidence that the defendant had personally advocated the unlawful destruction of property. Instead, the file contained the usual materials compiled by the northwestern inspectors: the disclosure of beliefs and the admission that the alien had solicited new members and contributed to the general fund of the I.W.W.[14] Judge Rudkin emphatically rebuked the bureau for the reasoning it had been following in such cases. "It seems to me," the judge declared, "that the legislation in question is directed against the personal acts and conduct of the individual alien, not against the acts or conduct of an organization of which he may be a member . . . . Indeed so far as the record discloses, the petitioner may never have uttered a word to an individual other than the inspector. From this conclusion there is no escape unless a person can advocate and teach by silence, and I am clearly of the opinion that such was not the sort of advocacy or teaching that Congress had in mind." [15]

Future governmental policy would naturally have to take account of this judicial decision. Increasing numbers of I.W.W. habeas corpus suits in the Northwest would bring it about. By November 11 a new standard was in effect. Aliens whom the government would have deported in September, October, and early November were now to be paroled or released.[16]

The new Rudkin-induced formula focused much more narrowly on evidence of personal overt acts than the July procedure, but it also searched even more deeply into the inner recesses of motives, intent, and attitudes. Proof that an alien had *personally distributed* sabotage-teaching literature, or evidence in "the record as a whole" that he was "carrying on the propaganda" of the I.W.W. now were necessary for deportation.[17]

To uncover undesirable Wobblies, the bureau divided the I.W.W. membership into three classes, which it admitted were "not always clearly defined or discernible":

(a) That of the man who is a thorough believer in the most radical doctrines pronounced by I.W.W. leaders and published in books distributed by the organization, and who is active in spreading that kind of propaganda both directly and indirectly; (b) That of the man who is ignorant, who has no real conception of the radical doctrines advocated by the order, who has become a member through ignorance, force of circumstances, or as a matter of self defense . . . and who has not knowingly taken any active part, either directly or indirectly, in advocating and teaching the unlawful destruction of property; (c) That of the man who is fairly intelligent, who believes in certain of the less radical tenets of the order, who has joined with a view to bettering his condition as a laborer, and who has engaged more or less in indirectly spreading the teachings contained in the books and pamphlets published and distributed by the organization by paying dues and making contributions, but whose real intention has been, not to spread the more radical doctrines, but simply to advance the cause of the common laboring man along lines . . . ordinarily regarded as legitimate when followed by labor unions.[18]

While the bureau's willingness to save the ignorant follower or honest-to-goodness union man from deportation was laudable (and much more consistent with the law), this discretion involved the clear renunciation of all measurable standards. Bureau administrators could hardly have chosen worse yardsticks by which to discover dangerous subversives. For example, the strategy of making the personal distribution of sabotage-teaching literature a major illegal activity was a test peculiarly designed to net not the leaders and staunch supporters but the so-called misguided, if not innocent, hangers-on who sold the song books, the newspapers, and the pamphlets for a few cents' commission. The designation of this new criterion, moreover, had been made confidentially, and after the arrest of numerous I.W.W.'s.

In addition, the government had no certain technique for weeding out the enthusiastic radicals "carrying on the propaganda." Advocacy and teaching as generally understood were clear: the alien could avoid them, and the government could prove them by well-defined evidence. The new secret standards left the fate of aliens to chance and prejudice. Everything depended on what a hostile and emotional inspector interpreted as the intent, belief, and personality of the I.W.W. defendant. The records that immigration officials had assembled during the summer of 1918 were singularly deficient in proof of individual activity. Some eight or nine months after the initial arrest, the government then decided it wanted evidence that the aliens had been "carrying on a propaganda." It was clearly impossible to reopen investigation and develop such facts, except by an alien's further self-incrimination. The Wobblies were by then in no mood for such confessions.

The November theory also flew in the face of all past anti-radical experience. No one in the Immigration Bureau had even been able to develop prima facie proof of an alien's overt advocacy of illegal principles. In spite of this well-known fact, the bureau apparently believed its subordinates capable of even more refined investigations. Before requesting future warrants of arrest, inspectors would have to distinguish between a thorough believer and an ignorant follower and separate both from the "fairly intelligent . . . whose real intention has been . . . to advance the cause of the common laboring man." This could not be done when most antiradical arrests had been and were to be made by raids or mass roundups in halls and on the streets, or at the instigation of interested parties. The policy's successful operation, in fact, depended on the separation of the three classes after the alien's arrest. But this was contrary to the bureau's own, though little honored, regulations. It meant that men could be held for months on the possibility of uncovering qualities of leadership and devotion at self-incriminating hearings.

The revised November theory had been in operation less than a month when the Immigration Bureau decided to use the membership provisions of the 1918 act against the remaining I.W.W. aliens detained at Seattle. Judge Rudkin's verdict at Spokane had given bureau officials a shock, for it had torn to shreds the government's theory that the 1917 law could be broadly construed. Convinced that the November procedure could really distinguish between the "active and dangerous" Wobblies and the innocuous and inactive members, the bureau did not want to lose deportable radicals just because some judge narrowly interpreted "advocacy and teaching" in the 1917 legislation.[19] A number of aliens had instituted habeas corpus suits before Judge Jeremiah Neterer in the western district of Washington. Fearing another unfavorable decision, the bureau accused these aliens of violating the 1918 rather than the 1917 legislation. If the hearings indicated that the alien might be a thoroughgoing I.W.W., he was rearrested as a *member* of an organization that advocated and taught the unlawful destruction of property. Immigration officials believed that the court would not disturb their judgment against the I.W.W., for the records did contain a smattering of evidence indicating the organization's support of "sabotage" and "direct action," whatever these were.[20]

Here again, however, the bureau was operating at cross-purposes with its superior officials. After the passage of the 1918 act, Secretary Wilson had reaffirmed his department's 1917 finding that the I.W.W.'s "organic documents . . . disclosed no lawless purpose."[21] Secretary Wilson never declared illegal either the constitution or the aims of the organization, and, as far as he was concerned, the government would not deport any alien for a mere membership in the I.W.W.[22] That should have made the 1918 legislation a dead letter in the I.W.W. cases — assuming that deportation policy operated logically, which it rarely did.

Contrary to governmental expectations, Judge Neterer upheld the broad interpretation of the 1917 law that the bureau had earlier adopted. He thereby restored the administration's right to deport any Wobbly whose record revealed support of the organization. Unlike Judge Rudkin in the eastern district of Washington, Neterer rejected the interpretation of advocacy based on the spoken word. "There are several ways by which a person may teach or advocate," he ruled. "It need not be from the public platform or through personal utterance to individuals or groups, but may be done as well through the public press, or through any means by which information may be disseminated, or, it may be done by the adoption of sentiment expressed, or arguments made by others which are distributed to others for their adoption and guidance." [23] Since the aliens in question had been accorded a "fair though summary hearing," and since the court could not say that "there is *no evidence* upon which to predicate the finding of the Commissioner General," the judge denied the writs.[24]

With its freedom to discriminate among I.W.W. cases so completely restored, the bureau now prepared to deport aliens still in custody. By this time, however, there were not many of them left. The bizarre results of the Rudkin decision had further reduced the number of radical aliens under detention. Some had won release by habeas corpus at Spokane. The revised November policy had directed the parole of many others in both the Spokane and Seattle districts. A large percentage of these might well have faced deportation had the Neterer interpretation come a month earlier.

What Wobblies then were still left? Some were mere members whose attitude or activity classified them as dangerous.[25] Others were delegates and organizers assumed to be prominent supporters of the organization.[26] Still others, a quarter of the total, were aliens who had refused to accept paroles conditioned on their leaving radicalism alone. In revenge for this stubborn refusal to accept the government's terms, immigration officials ordered them deported under the 1918 legislation.[27]

In early 1919 the Seattle office prepared to ship some forty Wobblies to Ellis Island as the climax of its year-long deportation crusade. Symbolic of the region's antiradical hysteria, this odd assortment of aliens also represented the consequences of a haphazard immigration policy. All three variables in the process, administrative, legislative, and judicial, had been continually in flux. The time, the place, the inspector's impression, the alien's reaction, the judge's interpretation, the bureau's mood, and the Labor Department's attention, singly and in combination, affected the final outcome. No sensible and consistent standards could survive such storms of ex post facto discretion.

This mass movement of aliens east also took a nearly forgotten antiradical drive out of its northwoods setting and focused nationwide attention upon it. I.W.W.'s who had lain inactive in back-country jails for over a year now helped to determine the final pattern that the postwar suppression would take; the Wobblies were an exciting curtain-raiser for the thrills of the red scare to follow.

II

In 1919 the Immigration Bureau, as well as the government, crossed an antiradical watershed and sped downstream into new and uncharted territory. Without knowing it, all concerned were taking a course that led directly toward the rapids of large-scale deportations. Behind this development lay the fact that postwar America produced simultaneously an increasing reliance on and resistance to the deportation of radicals.

A marked increase in unemployment, labor unrest, and radicalism accompanied the readjustment to a peacetime economy. The demobilized soldier joined his war-industry fellow worker in the ranks of the temporarily jobless. The high cost of living made their economic insecurity more painful and also cut into the earnings of the employed. Union labor, meanwhile, sought to retain its wartime gains in membership, to extend the area of collective bargaining, and to stave off any further wage decreases. Industry's open-

shop drive symbolized its resolution not to remove the grievances responsible for much of the agitation. The employer's
American Plan foresaw the destruction of, rather than any
concession to, labor's aims. As a result, the United States
witnessed "an eruption of mass strikes on a scale never before seen in American society." Over four million workers
walked out in protest before 1919 came to an end.[28]

At the same time, the image and example of the Russian
Revolution continued to horrify the right-wing segments of
society as much as it invigorated and encouraged the left.
The Bolshevik seizure of power hardened the intransigeance
of each group by the very real hopes and fears that it evoked.
Socialist affection for the Soviet experiment had already
turned into an illicit union that produced numerous Communist party offspring. The Communist and Communist
Labor parties and the Union of Russian Workers made the
radical movement appear as well organized and vital as it
had been in the heyday of the I.W.W. If the business world
had been disturbed by the anarchy and syndicalism of the
quieter prewar years, it was even more upset by the radicalism that accompanied the turbulent industrial relations of
1919.[29]

The class antagonisms aroused by readjustment and revolution played on emotions still keyed to the fanaticism of
war. There was "an unwillingness to surrender the psychic
gratifications the war had offered." The American people's
unbated evangelical fervor might now be satisfied by a proscription of the enemy within. The birth of the American
Legion and the unexpected survival of 100 per cent Americanism indicated the strength of nationalism and nativism in
the postwar world. And this popular clamor for total conformity found an appallingly sympathetic audience among
many federal officials.[30]

By the end of the war, the federal government had developed an independent interest in the problem of internal

security. The specific pressures of local capitalists, politicians, and patriots, which had once propelled the administration forward, no longer seemed necessary. The executive branch had clearly seized the initiative when the Immigration Bureau and the Justice Department had extended the deportation clauses in the 1918 legislation. In time they would plan the campaign that gave effect to this law. No one had to urge men like Solicitor William H. Lamar of the Post Office, Brigadier General Marlborough Churchill of Military Intelligence, Department of Justice attorneys Claude R. Porter and Francis P. Garvan, J. Edgar Hoover of the General Intelligence Division, or Anthony Caminetti and A. Warner Parker of the Immigration Bureau to go out and purge the country of its radical menace. As public servants these officials felt duty-bound to promote just such a crusade.[31]

Attorney General A. Mitchell Palmer, the prototype for all his subordinates, provided the best short summary of this new executive function. He approached the radical problem in terms of the economic theory of his day. Assuming that American capitalism was a boom-and-bust arrangement in which the government played a negative role, Palmer related the red menace to the inevitable future depression:

> The chief evil of the Red movement, both here and abroad, consists in the fact that it accomplishes a constant spread of a disease of evil thinking. The germs of this demoralizing sort behave very much as germs of any kind of disease do. While the body is in good condition and well nourished, the infection is fought off and neutralized, but if anything happens to lower the vitality of the body then the disease is apt to make very rapid ravage. So long as our country remains prosperous and we have abundance of employment for the masses at good pay, the condition is not alarming, so far as likelihood of revolutionary outbreaks is concerned, but given a condition of depression, bread lines, and the pressure of any wide-spread real want, then I think the "menace" would prove grave indeed.

The Attorney General believed that the government's job was "to rid the country of the Red agitators who are attempting to lay the foundation for just such trouble." [32] Under this concept, a limited government forbidden to relieve the miseries of capitalism had very positive functions in the realms of free speech.

The industrial turmoil, the traumatic aftermath of the Russian Revolution, the persistence of wartime nativism, and the aggressive initiative of federal administrators were undoubtedly important elements in the postwar red scare. They did not create it. They extended and accelerated an antiradical momentum that had been irregularly picking up speed ever since the turn of the century. The antianarchist and anti-I.W.W. immigration acts, the naturalization regulations, and the anti-Wobbly crusade were indications of the country's prewar hysteria. But the precedents and the contemporary atmosphere, however important, did not fully explain either when or how the roundups under Palmer came to be carried out. The final outcome of the I.W.W. deportation cases and the return of peacetime conditions offered further clues.

With the postwar cessation of prosecutions under the Espionage and Draft acts, the Department of Justice could no longer overthrow radical organizations in the courts. During the war the government, juries, and the federal judges had often construed radical agitation and strikes as antiwar propaganda and war-obstructive walkouts. After the armistice, however, government lawyers abandoned the Espionage Act against radicals because they felt it would have been somewhat farfetched to have indicted Communists and other "reds" for obstructing a war when the fighting was over. [33]

If radical agitation reached the seditious-conspiracy stage, the Justice Department could always punish it under section 6 of the Penal Code. The trouble was, of course, that American Bolshevists seldom got that far; their program was mainly a lot of revolutionary talk. In addition, the circuit courts of appeals in the Chicago and Wichita I.W.W. cases had interpreted section 6 most narrowly. According to these decisions, conspirators must contemplate the use of force directed against the federal government or its officers in their execution of the laws.[34]

Individual agitators who were not members of any organization or conspiracy were naturally exempt from the provisions of section 6. What the Attorney General wanted and failed to obtain from Congress was a peacetime sedition law. Until the federal legislature outlawed radical agitation as such, the Department of Justice could not suppress Bolsheviks through criminal proceedings.[35] The full fury of federal repression therefore descended down the one remaining channel of deportation. Freed from the restraining influence of wartime labor scarcity, the government was soon to initiate wholesale expulsions of radical aliens. As the Wilson administration was shifting from trials to deportations, the liberal and radical world was also coming back to life. This belated revival helped force the federal program into its final form.

A reawakened and re-enforced defense characterized the postwar drive against radicals. No one could have anticipated that this opposition would go hand in hand with increasingly excited demands for suppression. During hostilities left-wing solidarity had disappeared and many liberals in their prowar enthusiasm had abandoned radicals and civil liberties to the abuse of the army and the Justice Department. By 1919 the liberals were fighting back. Perhaps they were disillusioned with the war and Wilson; perhaps they had belatedly discovered the degree to which fundamental freedoms were threatened. With some conservative help, organized labor and liberal forces defeated the government's desire for a federal sedition bill, while a campaign to release America's "political" prisoners soon got under way. Criticism and protest would almost certainly be the postwar greeting to the deportation practices that had rolled along in such silent acquiescence.[36]

By the end of the war the I.W.W. was also in a much better position to resist the deportation of its members. Earlier, the organization had exhausted its best legal talent and most of its funds in the fruitless court battles at Chicago, Wichita, Omaha, and elsewhere. The Department of Justice raids and postal censorship had further incapacitated the Wobbly defense. All this was now over, and the I.W.W. began to supply legal and financial support to detained aliens.

At the conclusion of the Chicago trial, the Seattle steam roller ran into the irrepressible resistance of George F. Vanderveer, the I.W.W.'s top attorney. Before his arrival upon the scene, immigration inspectors had as usual gone their own way, forcing aliens to give most of their testimony without legal advice and doing everything to discourage resort to the courts.[37] With Vanderveer on the scene, Wobbly aliens had begun to sue out writs of habeas corpus, a move that had driven the government into the policy revisions of November and December 1918. How reluctantly and resentfully the Immigration Bureau accepted these new conditions may be judged from Vanderveer's recollections. The inspectors, he reported, had given him "no consideration whatever." Writing to Frank Walsh, Vanderveer outlined his treatment: "With only one exception, every immigration official has denied me access to both defendants and the records and has questioned my authority in a manner that no court has ever yet attempted, in all my practice of the law. Not only that, but they have frequently stated that their purpose was, if possible, to prevent the men from securing a hearing in court, notwithstanding that they have been restrained of their liberty and denied their legal rights, all the way from seven to seventeen months."[38] From the moment

Vanderveer began to put pressure on the government with habeas corpus suits until the red scare had passed, deportation procedures were under the withering scrutiny of talented defense lawyers. Nothing like it has ever happened before or since.

The resurging Wobbly defense and a rising tide of unrest in Seattle made bureau officials anxious to strike a counteracting blow. I.W.W. aliens had been giving the local office increasing trouble ever since the end of the war. Exasperated by the seemingly pointless and endless detentions, the Wobblies had rioted and initiated hunger strikes in the fall and winter of 1918.[39] At the same time, the days of docile self-incrimination had passed. Vanderveer and other I.W.W. lawyers coached the aliens to testify no further as to citizenship, activity, or membership.[40] Aliens also stopped distributing all books and pamphlets mentioning sabotage, leaving such jobs to citizen Wobblies.[41] One hundred and twenty habeas corpus suits had in addition decidedly embarrassed the Seattle office of the bureau by forcing it to concede the insubstantial nature of many of the cases. The I.W.W.'s released or on parole publicized the injustice of their detentions and agitated against the existing immigration procedures. In reply, the bureau hoped to reassert its authority by a dramatic public move involving the I.W.W.'s still in custody.[42]

The gloomy apparition of impending labor troubles made Seattle immigration officials even more receptive to deportations. Army intelligence had reported as early as October 1918 that the I.W.W. planned a general strike to force the release of "class-war" prisoners.[43] Although this never materialized, the formation of soldiers, sailors, and workingmen's councils accompanied demobilization and dislocation in the shipyards. A.F. of L. unions seemed to be growing more radical.[44] In late December, therefore, the local bureau pressed the Department of Labor to move the remaining

I.W.W. aliens east. According to Commissioner Henry White, this would help restore "normal industrial conditions . . . at Seattle." [45]

While the Immigration Bureau was completing these preparations, the crisis on the Pacific Coast took a sudden turn for the worse. On January 21, 1919, seventeen unions of the Seattle Metal Trades Council went out on strike over a lowered wage rate in the shipyards. It was an inopportune time for bargaining. The war was over, and the government wage board and the shipbuilders had no reason to make concessions. Faced with a losing proposition, the metal trades unions urged the central labor council to call a citywide walkout. It would be the first general strike in the nation's history. With many of the more conservative union leaders away at a Chicago meeting to free Tom Mooney, the council's radical members induced its 110 union affiliates to agree to a standstill at ten o'clock on the morning of February 6. [46]

Federal officials expected and prepared for an insurrection of unknown proportions. The United States attorney wired the Department of Justice: "Intention of strike is revolution led by extreme element openly advocating overthrow of Government." [47] Army undercover operatives in the unions kept watch on the situation while the War and Navy departments placed military, naval, and marine detachments at the disposal of the governor of Washington. [48] The local bureau's deep-seated belief in and fear of a possible revolutionary outbreak provided the final motivation for moving radical aliens out of Seattle.

On February 4, Commissioner White, now thoroughly alarmed, telegraphed the Immigration Bureau that the situation was "acute," and that it was "essential" to have the I.W.W. deportation party leave Seattle before the ten o'clock deadline on February 6. [49] Speed and decisiveness thus characterized the final moments of the long and tedious crusade. By the time of the general strike, the port city's deportable radicals were well on their way east. Thirty-six supposedly unrepentant and desperate Wobblies were on board the "Red Special," rushing toward Ellis Island and embarkation for Europe. Once again Seattle's fright had determined their destiny.

This transcontinental trip turned out to be as meaningless to the outcome of the general strike as it was meaningful for the eastern finale of the government's deportation drive. Exhibiting a peaceful aimlessness, the strike succumbed to a combination of labor disunity and governmental firmness within a few days.[50] On the other hand, the Red Special, now sensational front-page news, helped to create the atmosphere of mutual recrimination and misunderstanding that thereafter plagued relations between the government and its opposition.

The trip to New York created one alarmist headline after another. A thousand I.W.W.'s and their sympathizers met an eastbound train at Butte, Montana, a perennial radical stronghold. They hoped to free their alien fellow workers, but a car-to-car search proved futile. The Immigration Bureau had wisely routed its shipment on the other eastbound train which went through Helena, Montana. At Chicago, fifteen plain-clothesmen, on detail to the Red Special, conveyed an impression of the aliens' vicious nature. The government alerted every county sheriff and constable along the remaining route to New York to be ready for trouble. On the barge to Ellis Island several I.W.W.'s refused to sit in their assigned places. There followed a free-for-all between the Wobblies and the inspectors "in which clubs were used freely," and the aliens were quickly subdued. The army then sent a detachment of twenty soldiers to guard against further rioting on the trip across the harbor. At the embarkation point the Immigration Bureau held the I.W.W.'s incommunicado.[51]

According to the government these cases were closed, and

detention at Ellis Island was merely a stopover on the trip to Europe. Since the aliens had exhausted their lawful remedies in the Northwest and final decisions had been rendered, the bureau felt that no attorney had the right to take further action. "Due process of law has been observed . . . in every particular," the commissioner general reported. There were to be no investigations by New York lawyers in hopes of finding some element of injustice.[52]

The eastern defense group and its supporters, on the other hand, saw nothing but an administration's oppression of radicals and a deliberately callous evasion of their civil liberties. For the most part, the people who became involved in the I.W.W. defense were unfamiliar with immigration procedures. They treated deportation as a judicial process and demanded all the safeguards and adjudication associated with criminal proceedings. Year-long detentions; rumors of self-incrimination; stories of shoddy jail conditions; the guards, beatings, and troops of the Red Special; and, finally, the imprisonments in solitary confinement added up, so it seemed, to a flagrant denial of due process. Given the current antired hysteria, it was understandable that the defense should regard the government's policy not as part of the ill-treatment of all aliens inherent in the law but as the specific persecution of aliens because they were radicals. Unable to see their clients or the records, the New York lawyers sued out a mass writ of habeas corpus.[53] The I.W.W. cases from the Northwest thus provided the first real test of the relative strength of the government and the defense in the postwar environment.

III

An invigorated defense, aided by the influence of sympathetic New York liberals, forced the Department of Labor to reconsider most of the Wobbly cases. For the first time the poverty of due process in deportation practices became clear to groups that were well organized and had adequate publicity channels. Technically the government need have made no concessions, for the New York district court had rejected the writs of habeas corpus. The organization attorneys succeeded, however, in obtaining permission to inspect the records, interview the aliens, and reopen the cases before the department at Washington. After examining the evidence, I.W.W. lawyers dispatched a persuasive and detailed brief to Secretary William B. Wilson and Assistant Secretary Louis Post. This statement rehearsed the technical and tenuous basis for many of the arrests and set forth the numerous illogical shifts in official policy.[54] It is quite probable that Wilson and Post had never before realized the glaring inconsistencies and weaknesses in the records prepared by their subordinates. As a result of this unusual last-minute review, a substantial number of the Red Special Wobblies won their freedom, deportation standards underwent another revision, and the government evolved a unique arrangement for the future arrest of alien radicals.

The I.W.W. cases made excellent atrocity stories for radicals to tell one another, and seemed particularly designed to embarrass the administration. The number held for deportation had been increased to 38 enroute to New York. These were supposedly the hard core of agitators, the "active and dangerous" aliens that the bureau believed "not capable of reformation." [55] Out of the 150 or so Wobblies arrested in the Pacific Northwest, these were the ones most worthy of deportation. Or were they? The evidence of their undesirability was as faint as that of their guilt. The Immigration Bureau, moreover, had revealed its vindictive nature by ordering the expulsion of nine aliens who refused conditional paroles. Twenty-seven of the Wobblies had lived in the United States over five years; 18, over ten years; and seven, over twenty. Two thirds of them had already been imprisoned on the warrant charges for a year or more, until final decisions were reached. The defense also highlighted the misleading and inflammatory summaries of the inspectors, the denial of counsel until late in the hearings, the examination into beliefs based on isolated excerpts taken out of context, and the infringements of the First, Fifth, Sixth, and Eighth amendments. While many of these procedures were legal and in accord with well-established immigration practice, they neverless appeared unjust and arbitrary, especially to radicals sensitive about their rights.[56]

The Immigration Bureau fought just as hard to convince the Department of Labor that its canons of constructive intent were the best test of an alien's deportability. The government should presume every Wobbly guilty, the commissioner general suggested, "unless the alien shows . . . that his membership was due to ignorance of the real character of the organization and that he has been simply and altogether a passive member, taking no active part in matters pertaining thereto."[57] How far the bureau was prepared to go if the Department of Labor would back it up was indicated by its 1919 reasoning:

> The non-active member, or the one who is not an agitator may be more dangerous than those of the former [active] class. The line in the judgement of the Bureau, should not be drawn on the reputation of a member as an agitator or active member, so-called, but on the question whether or not he knows the purposes of the organization to which he belongs. If he does, his failure to be an agitator, or to be otherwise active, cuts no figure in arriving at the question of his guilt or innocence. The question, after all, is one of intent . . . . The Bureau believes that on these lines there should be full enforcement of the law . . . . The organization develops its power for evil with the growth of its membership — whether composed of agitators, active men, or those who aid and abet its objects and purposes in silence. The object of the law in including organizations within its purview was to prevent their establishment and growth, and if established, to cause their destruction.[58]

Bureau reasoning in the cases of the nine aliens who had refused conditional paroles indicated its increasing use of underlying thought rather than overt expression as a test of guilt. The immigration staff admitted that the evidence did not indicate "very much more than bare membership in the organization." To reject the government offer of parole, however, indicated the alien's defiant unwillingness to "demonstrate their desirability." There was not better sign of intent than this.[59]

The Department of Labor refused to delve into the shadowy, uncertain realms of intent. Instead of penalizing thought or guilty knowledge, the department reverted to the narrower concept of advocacy suggested by Judge Rudkin. The Immigration Bureau was thus brought back to the position adopted by Secretary Wilson in 1918 — namely, that an alien was guilty only if he advocated or taught the unlawful destruction of property by word of mouth or by the distribution of sabotage-teaching literature. The bureau's policy of arresting for membership alone was also overruled. In confidential instructions the Acting Secretary of Labor told immigration officials that the department "has never finally held that the Industrial Workers of the World is an anarchistic organization or one which advocates or teaches the unlawful destruction of property, *as such*." [60]

Following this theory, the government turned loose twelve Red Special aliens on March 14, 1919. Eight of them were Wobblies who had previously refused conditional paroles in the Northwest.[61] Three of the other four released were delegates and organizers of the I.W.W. The Immigration Bureau would have deported them on the grounds that their duties necessarily involved the distribution of illegal literature, but the Department of Labor refused to accept guilt by assumption. If the local inspectors did not investigate and produce evidence of "substantial activities" of an I.W.W. official, he was not to be deported. All in all, the government set free seven members and five officers.[62] Five other Wobblies had already accepted deportation upon arriving at Ellis Island.

Discouraged by the seemingly endless detention, they chose expulsion as the easy way out, despite the fact that the evidence against them showed little more than membership in the I.W.W.[63] Soon after the March 14 decision, the Labor Department released two more aliens whose records left doubt as to their personal advocacy.[64] The nineteen remaining aliens thereupon sued out writs of habeas corpus.

The initial district court reaction upheld the I.W.W. and set in motion further second thoughts among immigration officials. On April 10, 1919, Judge Augustus N. Hand found no evidence that alien Sam Nelson had advocated destructive sabotage. "The only thing that I can derive from the record," Judge Hand reported, "is that . . . [Nelson] believes that there is an irreconcilable conflict between employer and employee, and he believes the fruits and even instruments of production belong to the laborer." [65] In the bureau's eyes, however, Nelson was a "dangerous alien agitator . . . antagonistic toward American laws, ideals, and institutions." Since Nelson was an organizer, the bureau had decided that there was "no room for doubt" that he had distributed illegal literature.[66] Judge Hand would not accept this supposition unless the records contained some evidence of the literature itself, and this material was singularly lacking.

Hoping to avoid further adverse decisions, the bureau quickly released three other organizers whose cases seemed similar to that of Nelson. These aliens had spent from eight to fifteen months in jail without the bureau's ever having doubted their guilt or deportability. The shock of Judge Hand's verdict changed this relentless self-assurance. Immigration officials now found that "the cases are pretty near the border line . . . have been so regarded right along." [67] The bureau also believed that successful habeas corpus suits would damage its prestige in the remaining cases.[68]

In early June, Judge Hand's second series of verdicts confirmed the guilt of six of the seven aliens still contesting deportation. The district court's opinion exhibited the Olympian detachment considered proper in immigration cases. The judge would not overturn administrative orders based on any evidence at all or attack procedures that followed bureau regulations, no matter how unfair. Unlike the Nelson record, these files contained samples of I.W.W. literature that the aliens had distributed. According to Hand, the bureau could justifiably interpret the word "sabotage" to mean the unlawful destruction of property and could equate the possession and distribution of literature, using that word, or the holding of office involving such possession and distribution with advocating and teaching under the 1917 law.[69]

Judge Hand also construed the right to counsel as a bureau regulation, "and not a strict legal requirement." Aliens, therefore, could not expect legal representation throughout the entire proceedings. In Judge Hand's view, the bureau had satisfied due process by giving the I.W.W. lawyers some opportunity to answer government charges. The judge referred those who disliked such deportation legislation and procedures to federal lawmakers, for Congress, not the courts, had the power to deport aliens "for any cause it sees fit." [70]

While upholding a loose interpretation of advocacy, Judge Hand drew the line at mere belief in the principles of the I.W.W. He ordered the government to set free an alien whose record was totally barren of evidence indicating the utterance, circulation, or possession of illegal propaganda.[71] This and the other decisions reduced the number of I.W.W. deportables to ten, the last survivors of the northwestern roundups,[72] yet not even all of these few alien radicals were returned to their home countries.

Failure to prove an alien's citizenship and European opposition to the return of undesirable expatriates thwarted the expulsion of three out of the ten I.W.W.'s. As late as 1924, Russia, Armenia, Turkey, the Ukraine, and Austria refused to accept America's alien deportees.[73] The Immigration

Bureau usually released on bond the individuals it could not repatriate, but here it ran into the zealous antiradicalism of the Justice Department, which would not tolerate the agitation and organizational activity of aliens awaiting deportation, and insisted upon the reincarceration on high bail. Various district courts, however, repudiated this policy because it involved an "indefinite imprisonment." [74] The government program had ended in typical fashion — a smattering of deportations seasoned with a dash of administrative recrimination.

Those aliens whom the government actually expelled were, in fact, a small minority of the total arrested, and not necessarily the leaders of the I.W.W. The Seattle office itself could find no more than 28 Wobblies bad enough to be characterized as "active and dangerous." [75] The government deported only seven of them, never found four, and canceled the warrants of 11 others. Three aliens voluntarily accepted repatriation without contesting their cases, and three, although ordered deported, could not gain readmission to their native lands. [76] Under its fluctuating standards, the bureau could classify an alien as "active and dangerous" in December 1918 and release him as harmless in March 1919.

During the long anti-Wobbly crusade, the government arrested over 150 I.W.W.'s and eventually shipped back to Europe 27 members, delegates, and organizers. In September and October 1918, the Labor Department deported nine aliens, paroled 22 others, and lost six habeas corpus cases. [77] An additional 56 I.W.W.'s were released during November and December, while 36 deportees rode the Red Special east two months later. Out of this number, however, as has been seen, only 12 actually left the United States. [78] The total number of deportations could well have been fewer than 27. Many of those had simply been unfortunate enough to face the bureau in an avenging mood, miss an appeal to the department, or press their cases before the wrong judge at the wrong time.

The I.W.W. deportation drive should be remembered not so much for its contemporary injustices in the form of actual detentions and deportations as for its impact on future anti-radical policies. At the very beginning of the roundups, the government prepared a more inclusive immigration law. Apprehensive lest I.W.W. aliens slip through its fingers, the Immigration Bureau pushed through Congress the 1918 legislation making mere membership a deportable offense. Without this act, no large-scale arrests would have been possible in 1919 and 1920. The I.W.W. cases also taught immigration officials a painful administrative lesson. During the war the bureau had run roughshod over the alien radical. Final decisions in most of the wartime cases did not, however, occur at this opportune moment. An overburdened staff and the expectation of more favorable legislation carried the I.W.W. verdicts well into the postwar period. By then, an aroused left wing, an invigorated defense, and a returning concern for civil liberties on the part of the public prompted the reassertion of Secretary Wilson's standards and authority and brought about the release of two thirds of the aliens whom the government had been ready to deport. These radical victories forced a serious reappraisal of deportation policy and the evolution of a new plan in the capital. Failure and frustration with the I.W.W. thus triggered the antiradical explosions of the following year and largely determined their timing and characteristics.

VIII

The Red Raids

1919–1920

THE I.W.W. attack upon the prerogatives and procedures of the Immigration Bureau raised rather than lowered the enthusiasm of its officials for antiradical pursuits. Aware of its weaknesses and shortcomings, the bureau aimed to design a program exclusively for subversive aliens. If it could do so, 1919 would still be a most rewarding year.[1]

The bureau hoped that Congress would provide it with enough funds to activate an expert corps to concentrate entirely upon antiradical affairs. The I.W.W. fiasco had indicated the need for special knowledge in such work and had highlighted the inability of immigration inspectors to keep alien radicals under surveillance.[2] A few untrained subordinates had not been able to discover or to investigate aliens who held or expressed radical beliefs. The government also understood how difficult it would be to *prove* charges involving *individual* acts or thoughts. The northwestern officials had turned out to be extremely incompetent detectives and lawyers, and equally untrustworthy judges. As a result, the bureau's record in the radical cases had been far below its achievement in other areas. It had been able to deport only about one sixth of the arrested radicals, whereas in ordinary immigration work it deported over 90 per cent of those

detained. It seemed clear, as Labor Department Solicitor
John W. Abercrombie pointed out, that "men with a knowledge of law and an understanding of criminal habits must
handle these cases . . . and an inability to specialize . . .
amounts to a substantial abandonment of real results." [3]

Earlier congressional appropriations to the Department of
Justice for the investigation of anarchistic activities encouraged the bureau to believe that it would receive similar
largess. Under the immigration laws the Department of
Labor and its subordinate bureau had the sole authority to
arrest and deport aliens. If the Department of Justice was to
uncover dangerous radical aliens in large numbers, the Immigration Bureau would have to be able to process them as
fast as they were turned up. While the House Appropriations
Committee considered this point, the two departments
evolved their own plans for joint action. [4]

Wartime relations had created a fairly substantial basis
for such cooperation. Immigration inspectors had obligingly
instituted deportation proceedings at the request of federal
agents. [5] The Justice Department's alien enemy division had
worked closely with the Immigration Bureau on cases of
German and Austrian radicals who might be deportable. [6]
The two agencies had also prepared together the more inclusive 1918 legislation.

This intimate coordination continued after the armistice.
To guide Bureau of Investigation agents in their antiradical
operations, the Immigration Bureau distributed to them its
confidential circular outlining the evidence required for deportation in I.W.W. and anarchist cases. [7] From a practical
point of view, this division of labor made a great deal of
sense.

The Attorney General's men seemed much better qualified
for the job of discovering and apprehending alien members
of illegal organizations. The Bureau of Investigation had expanded its force during the war emergency, and by 1920

this staff was spending over half its time in antiradical activity.[8] The Justice Department's undercover informants had infiltrated the newly formed Communist groups and could keep aliens under surveillance and obtain proof of membership far more easily than immigration inspectors working from the outside. In the earlier crackdowns against the I.W.W., moreover, the government detectives had developed and perfected the techniques of the dragnet raid. They considered these simultaneous arrests the quickest and most effective means of seizing organization members and correspondence. It seemed perfectly logical, therefore, that the Immigration Bureau would share its future alien radical duties with the Department of Justice.[9]

The only trouble was that this arrangement had little, if any, legal basis. J. Edgar Hoover, head of the Justice Department's alien radical division, admitted that there was "no authority under the law permitting this Department to take any action in deportation proceedings relative to radical activities." [10] His division's appropriations were for the detection and prosecution of crimes against the United States, and deportation, of course, was not a criminal proceeding.[11] The *investigation* of anarchists, I.W.W.'s, and Communists could be justified only under some federal penal statute, such as the seditious-conspiracy section. The department had already stopped indicting radicals under the wartime legislation. In other words, federal agents had a legitimate right to find out whether so-called radical-rebel forces were contemplating overthrow of the government. Secretary of Labor Wilson assumed that the Immigration Bureau would receive those cases in which it was "impossible to secure evidence to justify prosecution under criminal or penal statutes and where the persons are aliens." [12] Instead of limiting itself to this lawful area, however, the Department of Justice concentrated on deportation affairs. Its investigations were directed not at the detection of federal crimes in which radical aliens might be incidentally turned up but solely toward the roundup of such aliens.

The Immigration Bureau was apparently familiar with the illegal course that Hoover's detectives had charted for themselves. In late July 1919, immigration officials received word of new instructions forwarded to all agents in the field to concentrate on alien radicalism.[13] Commissioner General Anthony Caminetti told the House Committee on Appropriations what these regulations meant. "A dragnet *inquiry* would be made," Caminetti reported, "and *search* instituted for *suspected* anarchists and *radicals of all kinds*." He believed that "many of the persons thus apprehended would undoubtedly be found to be aliens and . . . that such aliens should be turned over to the Immigration Service for deportation." He realized this would be no ordinary program. Normal immigration procedures in radical cases had so far produced the deportation of possibly one hundred aliens *annually*. According to Caminetti, the one "dragnet inquiry" proposed might turn up "*many hundreds* of such cases . . . for investigation under the immigration laws." [14]

Despite the bureau's pleas, the House Appropriations Committee refused to advance its funds in anticipation of probable widespread arrests. Instead, the committee adopted a wait-and-see attitude. If federal agents actually discovered hundreds of deportable radicals, legislators would gladly vote an increase in immigration appropriations. This did not mean that the bureau should discontinue its plans for joint action. The committee chairman specifically warned Caminetti that "the Department [of Labor] would not . . . be justified in withholding its co-operative effort in the proposed drive of the Department of Justice because of the possible effect upon the appropriations." [15]

Immigration officials had no intention of abandoning the planned offensive. The bureau's income might be low, but its spirits were high. By midsummer 1919 it had established "very pleasant relations" with J. Edgar Hoover's alien radical division.[16] Their common animus against the alien radical gave these two agencies a close and sympathetic understanding that interdepartmental activity often lacked. By the fall of 1919 the bureau was fully committed to, and eager for, the oncoming dragnet inquiry, and was ready to strike at the mass bases of radicalism in the ranks of the newly formed Union of Russian Workers, the Communist Labor party, and the Communist party.[17]

As they made their preparations that summer, Hoover's men and the immigration staff became increasingly troubled by a change in immigration procedures that they believed might severely and unnecessarily handicap their program. Under rule 22 of bureau regulations aliens had had the benefit of counsel at some time during the hearing, but rarely at the beginning.[18] When the "Red Special" cases came to court, the I.W.W. defense publicized its clients' denial of legal advice and made the Department of Labor and its subordinate bureau appear to be administrators who enjoyed the violation of fundamental rights.[19] This bothered Secretary Wilson. On March 13, 1919, the day before the first I.W.W. decisions, he had the bureau revise rule 22 in the interests of "good administration." [20] The regulations now allowed "attorneys employed by arrested aliens to participate in the conduct of hearings from their very commencement." [21]

Immigration officials predicted that the revised procedure would cause them real trouble, especially in radical cases. The typical apathetic, ignorant, and penniless immigrant rarely insisted on his legal rights, and regardless of rule 22, most proceedings went uncontested. With alien radicals, it was entirely different. The organization or its sympathizers usually supplied legal aid of high quality.[22] In addition, radicals were most sensitive to persecution and insistent upon their rights. Finally, self-incriminating confessions of beliefs or associations played an extraordinarily large role in proving the guilt of these aliens.[23] The bureau rightly feared the disruption of its well-oiled bureaucratic process if the new regulation remained unchanged.[24]

After three months of experience with the amended rule, Comissioner General Caminetti suggested a return to the traditional practice. The present regulation, he reported, "interferes materially with the prompt and efficient handling of cases." [25] Byron Uhl, assistant commissioner at Ellis Island, described what he and other career civil servants meant. When counsel was present from the beginning, Uhl reported, "the government is very greatly hampered in securing essential facts." Past experience had shown that without a lawyer in attendance criminals and radicals usually answered all questions "more or less frankly." Now that these aliens were getting legal advice, they refused to incriminate themselves.[26] Quite obviously the Immigration Bureau found it almost impossible to abandon the habits by which it had been raised.

The Department of Justice and Bureau of Investigation had no such emotional commitment to early training, yet they felt equally anxious lest the revised rule 22 thwart the methods they had adopted for securing evidence against radical aliens. The dragnet inquiry under the 1918 law aimed at rounding up members of the Union of Russian Workers, the Communist Labor party, and the Communist party on the theory that these organizations were illegal in themselves. Federal agents hoped to prove membership through seizure of membership cards and lists in raids and through secret testimony of planted informers. The informers were to point out members and leaders, give evidence about their party activities, and otherwise help establish grounds for deportation. The Department of Justice insisted, however, that its agents "will constantly keep in mind the necessity of preserving the cover of our confidential informants and in no case shall they rely upon the *testimony* of such cover informants during deportation proceedings." [27] This directive was understandable from the Justice Department's point of view. The organizations under attack had only recently been formed. The government felt that it would be foolish to lose its informers at the very outset of their counterespionage careers. It did not want to expose them because it did not want to destroy the value of their underground investigations. If detectives should fail to obtain membership lists and cards, then the government would have to get aliens to admit their associations. Self-incrimination, therefore, would be the necessary legal substantiation of the confidential evidence supplied by undercover operatives. It would be wise to keep lawyers out of the hearings as long as possible.

The Immigration Bureau also hoped to exploit but not reveal the informer-witness. In borderline cases where deportation seemed debatable, the bureau could secure additional information about aliens from the Department of Justice's undercover informants.[28] Since confidential information would not appear in the record, the alien would have no way of answering it. Weak, technical cases were to become substantial, deportable ones on the secret word of undercover informants. With their reliability unquestioned and their statements unchallenged, these agents would become the real arbiters of the immigration laws. Commissioner General Caminetti thought his plan was "the best kind of an arrangement which we can make." [29] Even this solution depended upon the acquisition of a scintilla of evidence for the official record. There had to be something on which to base the deportation warrant; if not a membership card or list, the admissions of the aliens themselves.

As defense lawyers became familiar with immigration procedures, however, aliens were growing increasingly aware of their rights. If this trend continued, confessions would be more and more difficult to obtain. Some I.W.W.'s in the Northwest had already refused to testify. George Vanderveer, the I.W.W's chief counsel, was determined to make this resistance much more widespread. In October 1919 he struck back at the Immigration Bureau's procedures with an article widely circulated in the radical press. Vanderveer's call to arms, entitled "Our Constitutional Rights, Notice to Aliens," was an immigrant declaration of independence that caused tremendous consternation at Washington.[30] If any number of aliens followed Vanderveer's advice, the deportation of radicals would become almost impossible.

Since the deportation hearings had turned into a farce, Vanderveer and other immigrants' lawyers had decided upon a common program. They had planned, it was announced, "a course of procedure which, however undignified it may appear will defeat the present autocratic methods of the Department of Labor and either drive them [sic] to more autocratic extremes, so outrageous that an indignant public sentiment will spontaneously condemn them, or, as is hoped, compel the Department to conduct its proceedings in accordance with the spirit of the law and with regard for the rights of the accused." [31]

Defense attorneys urged aliens to take a vow of silence, an act of indescribable heresy to immigration officials. Vanderveer had had enough of the theology of self-incrimination. "I accordingly advise all aliens who have ever been active in labor work," he wrote, "that whenever they are arrested and booked by any officer of the law, whether city, or federal, and no matter what the charge, they shall refuse to give their true names, their true ages, their citizenship, place of birth, or any information about the time and manner of their immigration to the United States, or their movements since landing; also that they shall refuse to give any information about their connection with any labor organization, and shall refuse to discuss its philosophy and tactics, or their own opinions regarding such matters, until they can secure the advice of a reliable attorney." [32]

Vanderveer accurately appraised the disastrous consequences of this policy for future immigration activity. His program, if closely followed, would make it impossible to secure evidence for deportation, or, if the proof was in hand, to expel. Most countries would not accept deportees without evidence of citizenship. Refusal to admit essential facts would subject aliens to abuse and vilification, but, the article reminded its readers, "these autocratic practices are unavoidable under any circumstances." [33]

The early-warning program of the radical defense worried and shocked the Immigration and Investigation bureaus. They were on the eve of a "dragnet inquiry" that would mean the arrest of "many hundreds" of aliens. The two offices had no ways of gauging in advance how widespread the refusal to testify would be. Other reports coming into Washington indicated that the defense alert was spreading. Commissioners of immigration at the big Montreal and Ellis Island stations wrote that attorneys representing radical organizations had even prepared detailed instructions to guide their alien members picked up on deportation charges.[34] The entire governmental program might well be stalemated. Without the frank admissions of alien defendants, undercover informants would be of little value. The Department of Justice would then be forced to uncover its agents to save the crusade.

In early November 1919 Bureau of Investigation agents put an end to the suspense by raiding the offices of the Union of Russian Workers and arresting some three hundred members.[35] The dragnet inquiry had begun; it would provide concrete answers to the problem of self-incrimination. The first returns looked bad for the government.

The November arrests revealed the real problems that the two bureaus faced. Frank Burke, director of the Bureau of Investigation, explained how difficult it had been for his agents to find enough evidence. "As the activities of aliens who are radically inclined are always most secretive in character," he reported, "it *quite often is next to impossible to prove actual membership* with the organization alleged to be anarchistic." This did not mean that the detectives had nothing to use in the way of evidence. Burke insisted that "in most of the cases the agents of this department have been reliably informed by confidential informants that the individuals in custody are members." Yet everyone had agreed on "the inadvisability of calling such confidential informants as witnesses" for fear of destroying their "usefulness as such informants." What course then was left? Quite naturally, it had become the immigration inspector's job "to make an effort to obtain from the subject a statement as to his affiliations." [36]

This was precisely the point at which Vanderveer's advice and the activity of radical defense attorneys made the government program break down. In the first haul under the new dragnet policy, aliens consistently refused to answer all questions "concerning their affiliations or their connections or activities." [37] The "Notice to Aliens," the invigorated defense by radical organizations, and the experience with the Union of Russian Workers were all that was needed to convince Commissioner General Caminetti and his assistants. With the contemplated raids against the Communist and Communist Labor parties in mind, both bureaus desired to eliminate the radical attorney from the early stages of the hearing. [38]

On December 30, 1919, three days before the mass arrests of the Palmer raids, the Department of Labor restored rule 22 to the form it had had prior to the charges in March. Aliens would again be represented by counsel only after the "government's interests" had been protected. [39] Secretary of Labor Wilson was absent at this time. The approval of the bureau's request had, therefore, been the responsibility of Acting Secretary John W. Abercrombie, who was also the department solicitor. It is impossible to say whether or not Wilson would have withheld his consent to the amendment. Zechariah Chafee, Jr., in *Free Speech in the United States*, suggests that Abercrombie was eager to help the Department of Justice make the raids a success. As solicitor, Abercrombie was, of course, an appointee of the Attorney General, but there is no way of knowing how much this might have influenced his decision.[40] The implication of a conspiracy behind Secretary Wilson's back cannot be proved or disproved. It is more plausible to suppose that Acting Secretary Abercrombie approved the rule 22 change in the belief that the bureau, having found the amended regulations ineffective, was simply returning to its former practice, long upheld by the courts.[41]

The bureau's victory on December 30 represented, therefore, a return to "business as usual" after a disturbing nine-month interval. Once again, Anthony Caminetti predicted, an alien could testify by "telling the truth in most instances as he saw it, *without being hampered by the advice of counsel*." The bureau had advised Abercrombie that his approval of the suggested change was "extremely desirable." [42]

The fear that aliens would refuse to testify and the need to protect confidential informants also helped determine the mass quality of the red raids. The 1918 Immigration Act made widespread and simultaneous arrests possible, but did not necessarily require all members to be picked up at one and the same time. But the chronically understaffed and poorly budgeted Immigration Bureau could not detain alien members one by one as it developed proof of their affiliations, because the Department of Justice refused to cooperate.[43] Since aliens might refuse to incriminate themselves, every effort must be made to prove actual membership. Attorney General A. Mitchell Palmer argued that "to obtain evidence . . . to prove the cases against the individual member, it was necessary to obtain the records of the organizations to which the members belong." In individual arrests there was no seizure of such documents, and after these arrests they were then destroyed or hidden. Success lay with the sudden and surprise attack, not with a long sniper's campaign.[44]

One further procedural safeguard was still to disappear, the alien's right to bail. If lawyers were to be prevented from seeing the aliens during the early stages of the hearing, so must the latter be restrained from going to their attorneys. J. Edgar Hoover hoped to use inflated bail requirements to detain aliens until they had confessed.[45] Although the Eighth Amendment stated that "excessive bail shall not be required," the Justice Department repeatedly urged the Secretary of Labor to set bail at a figure high enough to preclude the alien's release. Otherwise, defense counsel could post the bond, free his client, and prepare him for interrogation. The Hoover-Caminetti group hoped to prevent this, either by excessively high bail or no bail at all.[46] Hoover complained that to allow aliens out to see their lawyers "defeats the ends of justice" and made rule 22 "virtually of no value." [47]

The Justice and Immigration officials also believed that their attitude toward bail would help the deportation drive curtail the "insidious propaganda" of the radicals.[48] Releasing aliens pending a hearing, the Attorney General said, would "lead to a detrimental effect upon the welfare of the community." [49] If the purpose of the antiradical crusade was to suppress agitation, J. Edgar Hoover could not see the sense in letting confirmed radicals spread their propaganda while out on bail.[50] The Immigration Bureau agreed, and it argued that no alien was entitled to this constitutional right.[51]

By the end of 1919, the Investigation and Immigration bureaus believed that they had a near-perfect procedure. It included sudden and simultaneous dragnet raids, secret testimony of undercover informants, seizure of organization correspondence and lists as well as membership cards, cross-examination of aliens without the interference of defense lawyers, and detention of radicals in isolation under high bail or none at all. Government officials were planning to introduce a scientfic speed-up into the deportation process. Like a pig in a Chicago packing plant, the immigrant would be caught in a moving disassembly line, stripped of all his rights, and packaged for shipment overseas — all in one efficient and uninterrupted operation. American know-how was going to put an administrative procedure on a mass-production basis.

II

The large-scale roundups of January 1920 proved that J. Edgar Hoover and Anthony Caminetti had been so intent on developing an airtight technique that they had not thought about the consequences of their actions. More important, they had forgotten that they were not policy-makers but administrators whose decisions a superior might well disapprove. Besides, they had not taken into account the reaction of men in a democratic state concerned about traditional democratic freedoms. Only one man had suggested the probable outcome of a "dragnet inquiry." George F. Vanderveer had told his alien-radical audience that the government might one day be driven "to more autocratic extremes, so outrageous that an indignant public sentiment will spontaneously condemn them." [52] Hoover and Caminetti, however, did not think of their program as either autocratic or outrageous. They had simply carried traditional immigration practices to a logical conclusion and they expected good results.

On January 2 and 6, 1920, Department of Justice agents carried out their "dragnet inquiry" in a series of nationwide raids on the Communist and Communist Labor party organizations. The net was so wide and bureau detectives were so careless that some ten thousand persons were arrested including many citizens and many individuals not members of either party. Abuse of due process characterized the early stages of the drive.[53] This ill-treatment proceeded from the official decision to protect undercover informers. Indiscriminate arrests of the innocent with the guilty, unlawful searches and seizures by federal detectives, intimidating preliminary interrogations of aliens held incommunicado, high-handed levying of excessive bail, and denial of counsel were the government's response to stiffening alien radical resistance to deportation. On top of this prearranged persecution there were unintentional, perhaps unavoidable, wrongs. An administrative breakdown, resulting from different-sized staffs and appropriations, caused many aliens to be detained for varying periods without legal process. Because of Immigration Bureau congestion at the local and Washington offices, some warrants of arrest went out long after the raids, and others not at all.[54] However unplanned this bureaucratic chaos was, its outcome symbolized the theme of the raids. The Department of Justice concerned itself with the preservation of its informers rather than with the protection of the rights of alien defendants. Sworn and extorted confession became the substitute for due process.

These arbitrary extremes eventually proved to be their own undoing. Such a large-scale, well-publicized violation of fundamental rights was a poisonous procedure that produced many antidotes of protest. Both liberal and conservative lawyers denounced the revision of rule 22 and the crude dependence upon self-incrimination. The Inter-Church World Movement, composed of twenty-six Protestant denominations, investigated and decried the lawlessness of the Attorney General's subordinates. Federal judges and United States senators were among others who objected to the obvious injustice and inhumanity of the red raids. The most authoritative rebuttal was that of twelve lawyers and law-school professors, including Dean Roscoe Pound of the Harvard Law School. Their *Report upon the Illegal Practices of the United States Department of Justice* censured the department for several major infractions of the Bill of Rights. The lawyers' committee found federal agents guilty of using third-degree tortures, making illegal searches, seizures, and arrests, using *agents provocateurs*, and forcing aliens to incriminate themselves. The report also charged that Attorney General Palmer had abused his authority.[55]

As a result of the same public uproar, Secretary of Labor William B. Wilson and Assistant Secretary Louis F. Post finally came to a full realization of the intrigues of their subordinate immigration officials, repudiated them, and reimposed a departmental policy. Such control from the top was long overdue. In theory, the wayward Bureau of Immigration was only carying out the desires and decisions of the Secretary of Labor. It had no independent policy-making authority. In practice, the bureau had captured control of deportation, ignored the interpretations of Secretary Wilson, and turned the superior department officials into submissive rubber stamps.

The Department of Labor's program involved the restoration of due process in deportation, the imposition of control over the hearings, and a repudiation of the alliance with the Department of Justice. On January 26, 1920, Secretary Wilson revised the procedure in order to give the alien legal protection. Disregarding the Immigration Bureau's plea that granting lawyers "free access" to their alien clients "would be to make out of the whole proceedings one grand and prolonged farce," Wilson ruled that henceforth the alien should have counsel from the beginning of the hearing.[56] He also decided that the bureau must admit an alien to bail should the hearing be delayed and must not consider his refusal to testify grounds for denying bail.[57]

The bureau and the Department of Justice, wanting to continue the autocratic practices facilitating deportation, opposed these revisions.[58] They were fighting to uphold techniques that the government had always used against aliens and that the Supreme Court had unconditionally supported.[59] Hoover and Caminetti believed that the Department of Labor had unjustifiably abandoned tradition during an antiradical roundup.

The two men were even more disturbed by what happened next. After Secretary Wilson had finished with rule 22 and the question of bail, he and Post began an examination of the aliens' records. Once again they overturned the well-laid plans of the Department of Justice and won for themselves the enmity of Hoover and Attorney General Palmer. The bitter disagreement between the two agencies culminated in several congressional investigations and in a fruitless effort to impeach Assistant Secretary Post.

In deciding the hundreds of radical cases, the Department of Labor steadfastly refused to adopt the extreme views of Justice and Immigration officials. Hoover had prepared elaborate briefs proving that the Communist and Communist Labor parties both advocated the overthrow of the government by force and violence in their official organic documents, thus bringing their membership under the terms of the Immigration Act of 1918.[60] Hoover urged a literal application of the law to all members regardless of the alien's intent or the circumstances involved in his joining the organization.[61] In response, Secretary Wilson ruled against Hoover on the Communist Labor party, holding that it did not advocate illegal doctrines so as to make mere members guilty just because they belonged to the party. Assistant Secretary Post next refused to deport automatically every Communist party alien. Instead, Post differentiated between "conscious" and "unconscious" membership, and declined to deport those aliens whose transference from the Socialist to the Com-

munist party had been an automatic change without the
member's knowledge. He also refused to expel aliens who
were unfamiliar with the illegal doctrines, those whose cases
were based on self-incrimination without counsel, and all
others whose records of membership had been illegally
seized.[62]

As if all this had not thoroughly confounded the Department of Justice crusade, Post carried the rebuff still further.
His speedy decisions to avoid unjustified detentions provided
additional evidence of a new look in deportation affairs. A
quick release, however, was just what Hoover did not want.
He therefore begged Post to hold all aliens against whom
there was no proof on the chance that his men might possibly
uncover evidence "in other sections of the country" at some
future date.[63] The Department of Labor refused on grounds
of both expediency and principle to put hundreds of aliens
into a state of legal suspended animation. The Immigration
Bureau was already holding several thousand aliens at its
expense, for radical attorneys had sought to release on bond
only those deemed guilty of the charges. The bureau could
hardly afford to detain hundreds of other aliens for an indefinite period until Hoover had made his investigations and
submitted his briefs.[64] Nor would Post tolerate further unjustified postponements at the alien's expense.[65]

The Assistant Secretary of Labor also repudiated Hoover's
proposal for the conditional parole of undeportable aliens.[66]
An alien on parole might be much more reluctant to resume
his former radical ways. This procedure, however, disregarded the fact that an accused individual found innocent
of the charges has the right to receive speedy and unqualified release.

As one alien release followed another, the Labor and Justice departments found their earlier intimacy degenerating
into a bitter, vindictive relationship. The struggle between
the two agencies resolved itself into a contest between

Hoover, backed by Attorney General Palmer, and Post, supported by Secretary Wilson. Their deep administrative differences did not stay quietly within the official family. Instead, they swept out into the public arena of several congressional investigations.[67]

Basically, the line was drawn between those who emphasized results and the rights of the state and those who focused on due process and individual liberties. Both Wilson and Post were liberals. Post, in fact, had long been a proponent of Henry George's single tax. In contrast to Palmer's ambitions demands for 100 per cent conformity, Post valued the enlightenment principles of freedom and dissent. Post the reformer and Hoover the policeman also had little in common. Their differing attitude toward immigration procedures accentuated this division. In addition, the sudden reassertion of control by Post and Wilson was easily misunderstood as a perverse defense of radicals rather than as a concern with aliens as such.

The Department of Justice, having grown accustomed to Commissioner General Caminetti's agreeable cooperation, thought it strange that the Department of Labor should reverse its subordinate bureau of experts and the practices of years during an all-important crackdown. Why was Post so anxious to give radicals the due process that had never been a part of deportation? The reason, so Hoover and Palmer came to suspect, was Post's sympathy for the radical cause. Hoover, in fact, searched military intelligence files for evidence that critics of the Palmer raids had radical associations or beliefs, and had the voluminous I.W.W. correspondence at Chicago sifted for proof that Post was a tool of the Wobbly organization.[68]

Certain congressional investigators were equally doubtful of Post's Americanism and suspected the existence of a sinister conspiracy. W. A. Blackwood, leader of the Seattle Minute Men, examined I.W.W. files as an expert consultant for the House Immigration Committee. "There is an influence somewhere, or else a condition of mind that is unhealthy," he reported.[69] Members of the committee imagined that Post's actions stemmed from his sympathy for an "unsound and vicious" social philosophy and that he was helping "a conspiracy to subvert our government." [70]

The Department of Justice and its congressional supporters had accepted the theories and recommendations of the lower-echelon staff as legitimate and sound. According to this view, Assistant Secretary Post had overruled the lawful judgment of his Immigration Bureau. The illegality of the arrests, the burlesque of due process, and the failure to prove the charges were outside the vision of eyes narrowly focused on final results. Transfixed by the sight of radicals going free, the Department of Justice's supporters held Post responsible for the procedural reforms that had torpedoed the great crusade.

Palmer's congressional allies attempted to impeach the Assistant Secretary for obstructing the antiradical program. This indictment merely satisfied the appetite for personal revenge. When the Rules Committee investigation of Post collapsed, only one further course of action remained. Congress could again rewrite the immigration law in a more effective and extreme manner.[71]

Several factors contributed to this determination. First of all, there was the government's obvious failure in the I.W.W. cases. While many Wobblies had been called, few were chosen for deportation. The government was not yet ready to leave the I.W.W. alone, and Hoover hoped to make the deportation of its members automatic and mandatory.[72] Realizing that the bad publicity surrounding the Palmer raids had made the dragnet unpopular, Hoover still believed he could make periodic and selective arrests of I.W.W. agitators in groups of five hundred until the organization was thoroughly crippled.[73] Hoover therefore urged Congress to pass a more stringent immigration act.[74]

In the second place, the I.W.W. itself contributed to the writing of a new law. In late 1919 the organization had once more aroused all the old fears and given them nationwide currency. The incident itself was a meaningless massacre, an omen, perhaps, that the I.W.W., no longer vigorous or vital, would go down fighting. The Armistice Day parade of American Legionnaires at Centralia, Washington, turned into a pitched battle between the Wobblies and marching veterans, with casualties on both sides.[75] The affair revived demands for Congress to deport all alien members of the I.W.W.

Finally, the release of many aliens seized in the Palmer raids was a further inducement for Congress to close the supposed loopholes in the law. House Immigration Committee members wanted the Labor Department to match the enthusiasm of federal agents and immigration inspectors so that deportations would correspond to arrests. The idea was to return the initiative and discretion to the local authorities and make Washington a mere rubber stamp. Spelling out guilt by association in the most detailed fashion would thus eliminate Secretary Wilson's administrative latitude.[76]

By 1920 congressional thinking on the subject of immigration bore little resemblance to the relatively lenient attitudes of 1903. The country had already abandoned all time limits on deportation in radical cases, penalized belief as well as advocacy and teaching, and accepted the principle of guilt by association. Some members of Congress were now ready to go much further.

Immigration Committee Chairman Albert Johnson told an applauding House of Representatives that the country was sick of being told how to run the government by alien radicals. "Free press is ours, not theirs; free speech is ours, not theirs," he said, "and they have gone just as far as we can let them go toward running over our most precious rights." [77] The congressmen seemed agreed that the government should not be "too tender" when handling alien radicals. As one member of the lower house expressed it, the nation should "deal with these men who are bringing poison to the heart of society as if they were the worst of criminals." [78] This was the frame of reference of the men who hoped to devise a final, foolproof, antiradical code.

In the Immigration Act of June 1920, the United States for the first time punished aliens for simply possessing literature, for advising rather than advocating and teaching, for holding membership in groups and societies as well as organizations, and for showing sympathy and support (apart from membership) by financial contributions.[79] Congress declared that the "giving, loaning, or promising money or anything of value to be used for advising, advocating or teaching of any of the above doctrines shall constitute advising, teaching, or advocacy and shall constitute affiliation therewith." [80] These provisions were designed to reach not only all members (paying their dues) but also the alien sympathizer and the nonmember who supported the financial drives of such organizations as the I.W.W. The lawmakers assumed that this section would reach both the intellectual upper-income alien and the so-called "parlor bolshevist," who gave so enthusiastically to left-wing causes. The philosophy behind the act of June 1920 was to close the loopholes revealed by experience with the I.W.W. and to resolve all doubts against the alien. As broad as this law was, however, it was passed with one fundamental defect, which would destroy its usefulness as an anti-Wobbly weapon. Although the members of Congress were trying to make deportation of aliens mandatory, they did not specifically name the I.W.W. in the bill. The Secretary of Labor, therefore, could exercise his discretion. During debate on the bill, Representative William R. Green of Iowa, who was sympathetic to the purposes of the legislation, pointed out that Secretary Wilson, having ruled the organization's constitution and by-laws legal, would again find the I.W.W. outside the specifications of the act. Despite

Green's warning, the House unanimously passed the bill without change.[81]

As had been prophesied, the sweeping deportation act of 1920 played no role in the subsequent elimination of I.W.W.'s and other radicals. The Secretary of Labor refused to apply the law to Wobblies. In addition, the legislation was passed at a time when the official red scare was on the wane, at least for the federal government. After the outburst of the Palmer raids, deportation as a method of dealing with radicals fell into disrepute, and then disuse. Just as the Centralia riot was the last I.W.W. flurry of protest, so too the law of 1920 was the dying gasp of legislative antiradicalism. It would be another generation before the United States devised and used further techniques to deal with its subversive population.

III

The decline of deportation as a repressive weapon and the Bureau of Immigration's return to normalcy characterized the 1920's. In each case early 1920 witnessed a climax. It was the peak year in the number of radical aliens arrested and it was also a time when important procedural safeguards at last became part of the deportation process. Thereafter the deterioration set in. If the bureau let the radical alien pretty much alone during the Harding–Coolidge–Hoover decade, it was left free to reimpose the traditional autocratic practices it had created before the Palmer raids. The average immigrant inspector may well have breathed a sigh of relief at this turn of events.

By mid-1920 the expulsion of aliens for advocating, teaching, or believing in certain principles of anarchism and sabotage or for joining organizations based on these concepts was virtually at an end. Publicly the red scare no longer manifested itself in the dragnet roundups or mass prosecutions of radicals. The Department of Labor had, of course, been attempting to pull the Immigration Bureau away from the I.W.W. ever since 1919. There was no repetition of the north-western crusade under the membership provisions of the 1918 act. Secretary Wilson's insistence on proving some individual act or utterance drastically reduced the opportunities for arrest after 1919.[82] The public reaction to the Palmer raids, the second and more effective intervention of Wilson and Post, and the termination of the peculiarly delicate relations between the Justice and Immigration officials made further dragnet operations impossible. J. Edgar Hoover did not realize his plans for the periodic arrest of I.W.W. alien agitators. The act of 1920 could not re-establish by legislative fiat a program for which the top administrators had no appetite.

Other changes in American life reinforced the executive distaste for deportation. The industrial warfare of 1919–20 had ended in a victory for management. Its dictated peace left labor disarmed throughout the 1920's, too weak to challenge the open-shop boundaries of that decade. As a result, the corporate leadership saw less need to harass the immigrant worker, once again the most obvious source of a submissive labor supply. Some of the business leaders even recognized at last how wrong they had been in equating aliens with radical unrest. In most communities, therefore, there was much less public pressure for the removal of foreigners. Not that nativism had died; it had simply separated from antiradicalism and would thereafter reveal its spirit in crusades for racial purity and restriction.[83]

At the same time the states began to re-examine their own resources for combating radicalism. When the federal government had rebuffed appeals for help in the early postwar years, it re-enforced the trend toward local solutions. The states increasingly relied on the recently enacted criminal-syndicalism statutes. In New York, Illinois, California, Oregon, and Washington, juries hurriedly returned the convictions demanded by state prosecuting attorneys. Convinced of the radical threat to the status quo, these juries seemed as eager to convict potential revolutionaries as the patriotic wartime panels had been to sentence the pro-German and the disloyal.[84] With this readily available agency for the removal of radicals, local officials could forsake their earlier reliance on federal deportations.

In two areas, however, the state criminal-syndicalism laws proved inadequate. In the mining regions of Nevada and Montana, it was simply impossible to secure a convicting jury. Tenopah and Butte had working-class populations sympathetic to the radical cause and hostile to the dominating corporations. Nevada and Montana mining interests, therefore, continued to call upon the Department of Labor to deport alien agitators. Pressure for the old-style round-up thus lingered on, even though Secretary Wilson's policy, the changed industrial climate, and the criminal-syndicalism trials had extinguished this program elsewhere.

In the Tonopah Divide area of Nevada, mine operators feared that Wobbly agitation would impair a profitable post-war boom in silver production.[85] The employers felt that the Tonopah Vigilance League, which had helped keep the peace in the past, "might be awkward and cumbersome and not altogether law-abiding in its methods of handling a bunch of I.W.W.'s." [86] The criminal-syndicalism statute was useless. Prosecution would give the Wobblies a platform for propaganda and martyrdom, and there was little chance of selecting a jury friendly to the mining interests. The mineowners desired "some effective way of eliminating these men [I.W.W. organizers] quietly from the community." Arrests on deportation warrants, so it seemed, would get the agitators out of town "without limelight or publicity." [87] Senators Key Pittman and Charles B. Henderson of Nevada and ex-Governor Miller of Delaware, who had extensive business interests in Nevada, urged the Immigration Bureau to move against the I.W.W. They warned Anthony Caminetti that "the propaganda which is being carried on may result almost anytime in the commission of overt acts." [88] The bureau's investigations, however, turned up no deportable offenses.[89] There were renewed demands thereafter for Immigration Bureau action, but the bureau never found the grounds for stepping in.[90]

A similar call for deportations at Butte marked its final drive against local radicalism, a policy climaxing the long saga of industrial strife and violence after 1914. Before the Anaconda Company and the authorities turned to deportations, they had made use of blacklists, mob violence, *agents provocateurs*, private gunmen, federal indictments, and a fairly continuous military occupation. As in Nevada, however, it was not expedient to enforce the state's stringent criminal-syndicalism law; this copper colony of Anaconda was a community too identified with and dominated by the radical view. By the end of 1918 the wartime suppression had not only not eliminated the I.W.W., but had pushed the entire copper camp farther left. At this point the Immigration Bureau was asked to do its duty.

The new strategy coincided with the postwar readjustment in the copper industry. The cutback in production, the closing or part-time operation of many Butte mines, and the consequent unemployment increased the general unrest. When Anaconda reduced wages a dollar a day, the miners struck.[91] Although the military again raided union halls, seized striking I.W.W. miners, and protected those willing to work, the federal officers, the governor of Montana, and the copper company thought that the Department of Labor should expel "the radical disloyal element" and save a critical situation. The bureau decided to see whether it could help.[92]

The resulting confidential investigation proved that there was little the bureau either could or should do, and that it would be wisest "to let Butte settle their own difficulties."

Contrary to the sensational reports forwarded to Washington, Special Inspector Olaf L. Root and his assistants found neither destruction of property nor the advocacy and teaching of it by the I.W.W.'s. Supposed proof gathered from company gunmen and informers was not forthcoming. "We have no evidence," Inspector Root reported, "neither can the A.C.M. Company show any where the I.W.W. has done anything but try to reinstate their men to which the Big Interest is deaf." [93] Instead of supplying legitimate proof, the corporation attempted to corrupt the local office of the Immigration Bureau. The company hoped to restore to an influential position an ex-inspector, who was to be the willing accomplice of the A.C.M. group in "a resort to wholesale and unlawful deportations." In addition, Root discovered that Anaconda gunmen had been supplying fake affidavits charging aliens with advocating and committing the destruction of property. Company agents were ready, moreover, to provide inspectors with fake affidavits in the future "so as to railroad the aliens by the carloads." Admitting that Butte was an industrially sick community, the bureau investigator warned that "gunmen, soldiers, and deportation is [sic] no remedy for it." [94] Root's confidential report on the copper camp permanently terminated the plans for a grandiose alien roundup, and the Department of Labor adopted a hands-off policy.

The 1920's thus witnessed no repetition of the large-scale deportation drives of the war and early postwar years. The Nevada and Montana case histories indicated how cautious and restrained the Labor Department had become. As a result, the deportation of radicals after the red scare fell from a high of 446 in 1921 to a low of one in each of the three years from 1928 through 1930. [95]

While the bureau stayed away from antiradical crusades, it returned to its favorite procedures. The superficial cure imposed by Secretary Wilson and Assistant Secretary Post failed to alter the ingrained habits of the Immigration Bureau. Getting the Justice Department out of the business of deportation was a fairly simple job, part of the public outcry of 1920. Unfortunately, those in opposition to the Palmer raids seemed to think that they had won the fight when they terminated the excesses of the Attorney General and his detectives. No one followed up on the reform of the Immigration Bureau, which was a much more difficult task.

At the time, Secretary Wilson and his top assistant seemed to have achieved important changes in deportation procedure. The Department of Labor guaranteed the right to counsel from the beginning of the hearing, provided for reasonable bail, and refused to consider self-incriminations made without an opportunity to consult a lawyer.[96] Assistant Secretary Post directed the bureau not to issue telegraphic warrants unless it had in hand prima facie proof of the alien's guilt. He also insisted that the department would not tolerate arrests without a warrant, either formal or telegraphic.[97]

Of equal importance was the Labor Department's reassertion of full control over the deportation process. Post eliminated the memoranda that the bureau had been preparing in individual cases. In memorandum decisions bureau officials had assumed an illegal quasi-judicial authority and had frequently departed from policies established by the department. The bureau had come to think of its advisory summaries as having a binding effect on its superiors. Over the years this custom had imposed on the department a largely rubber-stamping role. Post now confined the bureau to its intended tasks, the mere administration of hearings and the transmission of records for departmental decision. A newly created board of review was to serve under the Secretary of Labor as an advisory council on immigration affairs.[98] It was hoped that all these reforms would bring due process, speedy justice, and a consistent and recognizable policy to the expulsion of aliens.

Instead, the Bureau of Immigration began a steady retreat towards the familiar oppressive methods of the past. The arrest procedure was the first to regress. Border stations protested almost immediately that they could not await warrants of arrest before detaining aliens. The bureau thereupon modified the earlier directive.[99] Interior stations also indicated that certain aliens, such as radicals, criminals, and prostitutes, would escape unless detained until the receipt of the arrest warrant.[100] By the end of the 1920's, the telegraphic warrant was once more in general use; two subordinate officers under the Secretary of Labor were passing upon some twenty thousand applications a year. The Immigration Bureau was in effect detaining the majority of aliens until the warrant of arrest had issued.[101]

The reform of rule 22 was almost equally unsuccessful. For four years after the Palmer raids, the bureau accorded aliens the right to counsel from the start of the proceedings. In February 1924, however, the Labor Department agreed to revise the old regulation that provided for legal aid "preferably at the beginning" of the hearing, but otherwise at the discretion of the inspector.[102]

The "preliminary examination" reappeared at about the same time. This was the self-incriminating interrogation with no lawyer that preceded the application for the warrant of arrest.[103] It was an irresistibly attractive technique to men whose administrative routine had escaped classification as a judicial or criminal process, and it had served for many years as the cornerstone of the deportation structure. By 1930 this procedure was so successful that 95 per cent of all cases led to recommendations for deportation.[104]

The board of review, established as an agency under the Secretary of Labor to check the Immigration Bureau, rather quickly became inert. During the 1920's, the board degenerated into a council that gave its perfunctory approval to the decisions of the local inspectors.[105] Through the telegraphic warrant, the preliminary examination, the revision of rule 22, and the irresolute role of the board of review, the Washington authorities abdicated control over much of the deportation process. They left the inspectors and commissioners free to follow once more the techniques and ideologies of the wartime crusades. Only this time, no one fought back.

In the 1920's, no organized groups protested against the alien's loss of civil rights. Deportation cases were striking the friendless and the poor, the isolated and the ignorant. Radicals who might have objected were left alone. The figures showing that only 15 per cent of the aliens arrested could raise bail or obtain counsel are indicative of their sorry condition and of their inability to resist. Of those ordered deported, only 2 per cent sought release on habeas corpus, and five sixths of these failed.[106] This was hardly the kind of defiant insistence on their rights that aliens such as I.W.W's had made to the Immigration Bureau.[107] After the dam of radical opposition had collapsed, aliens were once more swept away in a torrent of harsh and unfair procedures.

The disintegration of due process in immigration affairs showed that antiforeign enmities still gripped the country during the 1920's. It was a bad time to be a stranger, a status within which anyone not a white native-born Protestant of Anglo-Saxon ancestry might then fall. The Ku Klux Klan and anti-Semitism were part of the general atmosphere of hate that was directed more specifically against aliens. Economic discrimination toward the foreign-born once more became prominent on the state level. Finally, in 1924, the restriction movement achieved its long fought-for success in the national-origins legislation.[108] Nativism had indeed survived the red scare, although it was no longer closely associated with radicalism, the suppression of which remained of separate but equal concern to the men at Washington.

Repression no longer manifested itself in the dragnet roundups, the group prosecutions, and the mass deportations of radicals typical of the war and postwar years; but the federal government had not lost all interest in the problem. Convinced that the class war was a continuing threat to America, the Republican administrations of the 1920's remained on the alert and, in some areas, on the offensive. Some loose ends still needed attention, among them the alien enemies interned during the war and the radicals convicted under the Draft and Espionage acts. During the quiet normalcy of the next decade, the federal government turned to these remnants of the red scare, and in doing so, clearly indicated its distaste for rebellious ideologies. The concerted wartime attack was over, but fear and hatred of left-wing beliefs endured as an influence on official policy.

IX

Holding the Line during Normalcy

O<small>N</small> December 4, 1918, the afternoon meeting of the interdepartmental conference of bureaus concerned with the intelligence war work of the government had debated the obvious necessity of obtaining from Congress further restrictive immigration legislation. Those present believed that none of the laws already enacted could either expel or exclude "members of those classes that have come to be described roughly as *Bolsheviki*." [1] Somewhat later, Attorney General A. Mitchell Palmer publicly expressed the point of view of the conference. "We can insist with more emphasis than we have employed heretofore," he said, "that those who come to our shores shall come in the right spirit and with the right purpose." [2]

To accomplish this objective, the bureaus had originally drafted a bill so broad that it would have deported and excluded all "undesirable persons or persons inimical to the peace and welfare of the United States." The law as finally passed did not reach ahead to the future immigrant but it did provide for the immediate removal of all aliens who had clashed with the government during the war. It seemed obvious that these individuals had proved that they were "inimical to the peace and welfare of the United States." The Immigration Act of May 10, 1920, provided for the deportation of all radical enemy aliens convicted under the war statutes whom the Secretary of Labor certified as "undesirable residents of the United States."[3]

The formulation and enforcement of this legislation was only one of the ways in which the government translated its antiradical antipathy into effective action. The disposal of interned alien enemies, the War Department's secret program to suppress radical and revolutionary outbreaks, the Bureau of Investigation's close cooperation in state prosecutions, the Justice Department's and Pardon Office's opposition to the release of wartime political prisoners, the Immigration Bureau's policy on the naturalization and denaturalization of radicals, and the Labor Department's determination to deport alien violators of the Espionage and draft acts were symptomatic of a very keen, high-level desire to keep America free from any taint of subversion. There was much less federal activity than during the war, not because of a conviction that the class war had been won, but because the states had reasserted their authority over the discontented elements within their borders. National guard units and state criminal-syndicalism laws provided effective methods for combating radicals. In some respects, such as the inability to use the Espionage Act or to make dragnet roundups, the federal government simply did not have the same tools with which to operate. Nevertheless, wherever it could, the national administration clearly indicated its commitment to the antiradical crusade.

A real fear of the class war and a neurotic alarm that the government might strengthen the radical element dominated the official thinking of the time. Nowhere were these sentiments expressed more precisely and frankly than in the memoranda of Pardon Attorney James A. Finch opposing the amnesty drive. Proponents of this movement hoped that they could force the release of all those imprisoned under the Espionage and Selective Service acts. The amnesty group called such victims "political prisoners." It recalled that the war, with its passions and hysteria, was over; it sought a reconciliation by forgiveness; and it pointed to the historical precedent of Lincoln's Civil War amnesty proclamation. Finch had no use for this last argument. "At the time the proclamation was issued," he replied, "slavery was dead, the South defeated, and there was no possibility for further revolution." Now, by contrast "Bolshevism, anarchy, and lawless discontent are rampant and growing . . . not dead but just beginning to spread. To think of liberating these prisoners at this time, when it needs a firm hand to show such malcontents that this government is strong enough to hold and keep its prisoners is, to my mind," Finch suggested, "a matter which should be well considered." [4] According to this theory, the war had been only the opening phase in the revolution and the opposition of radicals to the war had been "only incidental to their main purpose and object." [5]

Time and again United States attorneys, federal judges, and the President himself opposed the release of radicals who might invigorate the left-wing movement. The government always claimed that it had moved against these individuals for threatening or obstructing the success of the United States in wartime. Yet the Wilson, Harding, and Coolidge administrations liberated radicals only when their recantation or a relaxation of the class war made their freedom innocuous. [6] In 1922 President Harding explained why he had rebuffed the amnesty drive of that year. "I felt it undesirable," he said, "to pardon men with I.W.W. tendencies in a time when the nation was greatly threatened by the existing industrial strikes." [7] Thus, the amnesty of political prisoners depended on strikes, unrest, and domestic radicalism rather than on the justice of the convictions or the adequacy of the punishment. The war was over, but the class war went on.

The 1920's, then, were really not so different from the preceding decade. The overt delirium had subsided and the techniques of repression had changed. On the other hand, the ideological framework was certainly the same; perhaps it had even become more uncompromisingly antiradical. Federal officials continued to believe that the best radicals were either dead or deported ones, that the threat from the left was as real as ever, and that it was the duty of public servants to control and isolate this menace.

II

The Department of Justice faced the postwar years with a rather disappointing arsenal. Soon after the armistice, the Attorney General stopped indicting and trying the leaders of radical organizations, even though patrioteering groups continued to urge prosecutions of Communists and other "reds." [8] Both A. Mitchell Palmer and Harry M. Daugherty would have been glad to proceed against these agitators, but the Department of Justice had failed to obtain from Congress the appropriate peacetime-sedition legislation; and the Espionage and Selective Service acts were no longer applicable. Without a new law, the Attorney General's men doubted whether they could convict radicals.[9]

The seditious-conspiracy clause, section 6 of the Criminal Code, did not promise much help. The courts had insisted that section 6 was to be strictly construed, meaning that the Justice Department must prove a conspiracy to use force against the federal government or its officers in their execution of the laws.[10] Bureau of Investigation reports had not yet established with any degree of certainty that the Communist conspiracy had reached this stage. In 1924 department lawyers still found that "the missing element is a specific and definite agreement, fortified by at least some detail, to overthrow the government." [11]

Numerous individuals and patriotic organizations pleaded unsuccessfully for indictments under section 5 of the Penal Code, otherwise known as the Logan Act. This law punished any communication between American citizens and foreign governments when that correspondence was contrary to the best interests of the United States. Since the Bureau of Investigation had evidence connecting American Communists to the Soviet government and since the Justice Department could probably prove the relationship to be detrimental to the United States, there seemed to be a good case under the Logan Act. And yet nothing was done. This choice opportunity to convict radicals ran headlong into the foreign-policy position dictated by those opposed to the Soviet revolution. Commitment to the nonrecognition of the Soviet Republic destroyed the chance of using the Logan Act. The Soviets did not legally qualify as a *de facto* government much less as a *de jure* one. Even if the Soviets had received a limited *de facto* recognition, Department of Justice officials doubted whether the Logan Act prohibited correspondence with such a regime. Anti-Soviet foreign policy in the 1920's thus indirectly favored the survival and growth of domestic communism.[12]

Unable to prosecute radicals under either section 5 or section 6, and lacking a general peacetime-sedition law, the Department of Justice made its antiradical investigators and information available to the states, to industry, and to the Bureau of Immigration.[13] The outcome of making them available to the bureau had, however, produced the unexpected result of intervention at the Cabinet level that prevented federal detectives from making further alien roundups. This one major setback did not discourage the Department of Justice, and it continued its antiradical and antilabor surveillance until 1924. In addition, the Bureau of Investigation during the Harding-Daugherty-Burns interlude became a secret police force actively engaged in political as well as industrial espionage. By the time President Coolidge took office, this had become a national scandal. Coolidge resolved to clean up the Justice Department and appointed as Attorney General Harlan Fiske Stone, who effected a complete reorganization of the Bureau of Investigation. Limiting it to the investigation of federal crimes, the new Attorney General terminated its antiradical division, its links with notorious private detective organizations, its dissemination of propaganda on the "red menace," its undercover espionage in radical and labor groups, its incitement of state prosecutions, and its unlawful searches, seizures, and wiretappings.[14]

Officially and temporarily, the red hunt had ended for the Department of Justice and its subordinate bureau. Attorney General Stone stated that "the Bureau of Investigation is not concerned with political or other opinions of individuals." J. Edgar Hoover, newly appointed reform chief of the bureau, echoed the department line. "The activities of Communists and other ultra-radicals have not up to the present time constituted a violation of the Federal Statutes," Hoover said, "and consequently, the Department of Justice, theoretically, has no right to investigate such activities as there has been no violation of the Federal laws." [15] Under Stone's direction, the department and the bureau returned to their proper functions in law enforcement. By 1925 all that remained of the department's energetic crusade were the lists of suspected radicals and the confidential material about them that the zealous detectives under Palmer and Daugherty had gathered. Although Attorney General Stone opposed the collection of information about the opinions and lawful conduct of radicals, he had no authority to destroy Justice Department records without an act of Congress.[16] These files remained an idle symbol of a past hysteria until the reactivation of the General Intelligence (antiradical) Division in 1939. Then, reversing the Bibilical injunction, the government could use them to pour old gossip into new dossiers.[17]

The army was also alert to and stimulated by the revolutionary turmoil in the postwar world. Federal troops had already served during the war as an antiradical *posse comitatus* in the North- and Southwest, without a declaration of martial law and without the constitutional requirement of the Presidential proclamation. After the armistice, the National Guard, drafted into federal service, had to be discharged. As a result, the states were still left without forces to quell domestic disturbances. Until such units could be reorganized, the War Department continued the relaxed wartime regulations that allowed local commanders to dispatch troops directly to the scene of trouble upon the request of the governor or legislature of a state.[18] From the summer of 1920 on, under the prodding of the federal government, however, the states re-established the National Guard. By October 1922, all but Nevada once more had a military force of their own.[19]

The Military Intelligence and War Plans divisions, the Morale Branch, and the General Staff all formulated programs to contain or weaken the radical movement. The morale section investigated the attitude of the soldiers toward radical ideas, watched for the spread of such propaganda in the camps, and planned a series of lectures on "patriotism, good government, [and] civics" to counteract any possible radical influence.[20]

Replies from army posts throughout the country indicated that the army had been successful in "the creation and confirmation of good ideals among the men." [21] The assistant director of the War Plans Division noted with pleasure that "active and comprehensive measures have been continuously carried out for over two years to prevent radical ideas from developing among troops." As a result, morale in the armed forces was "very satisfactory." [22]

The army's high-level planners recommended the formulation of a program for, and the training of officers in, the handling of "radical rebel groups" attempting the overthrow of the government. Conscious of the successful communist revolutions in Russia and Europe, the army feared that local "reds" might try to disrupt food distribution, capture local arms depots, and starve the populace into submission.[23] The Military Intelligence and War Plans divisions estimated that the danger was "not a transitory affair" but was likely "to be present as a permanent feature to be reckoned with." [24] The army prepared, therefore, a lengthy plan known as "War Plans White," to deal with both minor and major emergencies arising out of labor and radical unrest.[25]

The postwar situation had indeed focused the army's attention more than ever on the question of internal security. Strikes such as that of the bituminous coal miners in 1919 made the General Staff think in terms of strengthening the military forces, for they might well be the "last resort of the government" in such crises. Any plan devised to control the unrest would have to fulfill certain requirements: "Provide enough men to finish the job and to overawe the radical element by their numbers in the beginning; be able to crush completely minor insurrections in many parts of the country at the same time without great bloodshed; be able to handle any moderately large body of radicals that may have effected a junction; and be able to guard arsenals and sensitive points and to garrison affected districts until peace and quiet are completely restored." [26]

The military leadership also recognized that it had neglected training in antirevolutionary warfare in the past and that such courses should be required at the General Staff College. Because of the development of War Plans White, the college was already offering lectures on the political, psychological, economic, and military situations in the United States; preservation of public order and protection of life and property; vital areas, industry and agriculture; and transportation systems. Nevertheless, the War Plans Division felt that the General Staff College course did not yet sufficiently stress "the fact that the forces of unrest within our borders are an organized potential enemy." The War Plans Division recommended an additional lecture on War Plans

White and such other work as might be suitable "while the situation remains acute." [27]

However ready the army generals and the Justice Department prosecutors might be, they could hardly put their plans into effect without some new, bold move on the part of the radicals. Unless the Bureau of Investigation developed evidence of a conspiracy to use force and violence or the military saw a strike turn into an insurrection, each of them simply had to wait expectantly for the worst to happen. It never did. On the other hand, the federal government could certainly clean out the dregs left over from the unbridled repressions of World War I. Here were a group of radicals already under restraint and of proven hostility to the United States. The antiradical crusade during the 1920's then, was largely a postwar settlement. The federal government's vendetta against its wartime victims was a way of relieving its hostility toward contemporary radicals and of squaring accounts with them.

III

There were three major aspects of the government audit: release of interned alien enemies, amnesty for "political prisoners," and deportation of all aliens either interned or convicted during the war. The last-named program was symbolic of the government's attitude; the mandatory deportation of all offenders regardless of the individual case expressed the belief that any radicalism, however slight, unconscious, or ignorant, was evil.

Almost immediately after the armistice, the government had to decide upon a policy toward the interned alien enemy. The Wilson administration could not long delay, for the release of all internees was obligatory as soon as the United States signed the peace treaties with Germany and Austria.[28] This appalled the Department of Justice, which might thereby have been forced to set a large number of radical aliens loose to contribute to the unrest then so prevalent. During the 1919 steel strike, for example, the department breathed a sigh of relief that alien enemy radicals had been unable to join the strikers and "add fuel to the flames." [29] The government paroled or discharged completely only those I.W.W.'s and radicals who severed their organizational connections and "adopted a more reasonable attitude towards American institutions." [30] Yet there was no way of knowing how many aliens might be induced to renounce their former affiliations. The rest would have to be deported.

Therefore the expulsion of radical alien enemies was a matter of the highest priority. Not the obvious pro-German, not the corrupt or near-treasonable businessman who had traded with the enemy, not the plain, ordinary enemy criminal or saboteur, but the alien enemy agitator and member of a radical organization, drew the government's heaviest fire.[31] Federal officials also considered the "violent pro-Germans, suspected or known German spies or agents, and criminals" worth holding in custody and deporting. But they were counted less important and less dangerous to the welfare of the country than the radicals.[32]

To make the deportation of such aliens certain — they represented one fourth or more of those interned — the Department of Justice framed a bill under which it could expel any interned alien at any time after entry.[33] While they were about it, the Attorney General's experts also took care of those aliens serving sentences under one or more of the war statutes. The proposed law provided for the deportation of any alien who, after August 1, 1914, had been convicted of a violation of or a conspiracy to violate the Espionage, Sabotage, or Selective Service acts. The Secretary of Labor merely had to certify these aliens as "undesirable residents of the United States" to make them liable to arrest. The government, in other words, wanted to make certain wartime activities a deportable offense after the act.[34]

Pressure for this ex post facto legislation stemmed from the usual lack of evidence against the detained radicals. The records of enemy aliens contained almost no proof that the individual had ever advocated or taught illegal doctrines, and Secretary Wilson would not approve the deportation of I.W.W.'s under the membership provisions of the 1918 act. Only self-incrimination would have eased the task; no wonder the government desired to make the interment itself the deportable violation.[35]

The expulsion of those convicted under the war laws also seemed to require further legislation. At the time of the imprisonments under the Selective Service and Espionage acts, the government could deport any alien who committed a crime involving moral turpitude within *five* years of entry.[36] Whether or not a conviction under the wartime statutes was such a crime, however, was a highly debatable point.

What exactly does "moral turpitude" mean? One dictionary defines it thus: "Everything done contrary to justice, honesty, modesty or good morals is said to be done with turpitude." [37] Congress had apparently meant it to apply to the lawless behavior of the common crook and felon. Anxious to exclude or deport criminals, the legislators had not wanted the term to cover political crime, for the United States still prided itself on being an asylum for European political refugees.[38] The judiciary had upheld the use of the term "moral turpitude" against those "whose records . . . warrant the inference that they are depraved and will continue to belong to the criminal classes." [39] The Labor Department's solicitor had described a crime involving moral turpitude as one "activated by malice . . . so far contrary to the . . . moral sense of the community, that the offender is brought into public disgrace." Yet the solicitor had also said that an act of moral turpitude could not be "the outcome merely of natural passion, . . . of weakness of character, of mistaken principles, unaccompanied by a vicious motive or a corrupt mind." [40]

Were aliens who violated the Espionage and Draft acts guilty of a crime involving moral turpitude? Were they ordinary or political criminals? The I.W.W.'s had certainly committed acts contrary to the moral sense of the patriotic community, resulting in their public disgrace. On the other hand, it could be argued that the I.W.W conflict with the Wilson administration followed from devotion to "mistaken principles, unaccompanied by a vicious motive." Although the government steadfastly refused to admit the existence of "political prisoners" in the United States, its desire for the special legislation of May 1920 was an admission that radicals fell into just this category.[41]

Making the internment or conviction of aliens a deportable offense after the act had more than the injustice of the usual ex post facto law, for a large number of them had been confined solely as a result of wartime hysteria. Many internees had been mere members of the I.W.W.; others had been locked up for the most trivial support of, or sympathy toward, the organization.[42] Even those radicals certified as peaceful and law-abiding by the local United States attorney found themselves interned "for the moral effect on the community." [43] The federal government had even incarcerated the alien enemy I.W.W. victims of the Bisbee, Arizona, vigilante deportations.[44]

The justice of the wartime convictions was also open to doubt. In the conspiracy indictments against large groups of I.W.W.'s, the government had in effect equated membership with participation in the objectionable activities and pronouncements of the organization. The Justice Deparement later admitted confidentially that "the testimony is meager with regard to many of the defendants, the government relying largely upon the general atmosphere surrounding the prosecution and the fact that the defendants were I.W.W., rather than upon direct, positive testimony . . . [and] the conviction is sometimes based largely upon conjecture." [45]

The pardon attorney found "that in many instances there was no evidence whatever to show that the defendants had even done anything to violate the Selective Service Act or the Espionage Act." [46] Under these circumstances a law indiscriminately expelling any and all aliens convicted under the war statutes only added to the injustice of the original sentence. The government seemed less concerned with past objections to war than with past and present radical beliefs.

Although its adminsitration backers assigned the legislation affecting the interned alien enemies and political prisoners a high priority, they had difficulty in rushing it through the Senate. The idea, of course, had been to pass the bill before peace with the principal European powers made obligatory the release of all alien enemies.[47] The head of the House Committee on Immigration enthusiastically supported the legislation, but Thomas W. Hardwick, chairman of the similar Senate group, refused to introduce the measure because of its unwarranted peacetime extension of power to the executive branch.[48] Several senators from the Middle West also objected. They remembered that the United States had convicted certain Hindu aliens from India whose revolutionary agitation against England during the war had brought them under the terms of the Espionage Act. Motivated by anti-British antagonism, these senators feared that the new act would entail the deportation of the Hindu rebels back to the vengeance of Great Britain.[49] Although the Department of Justice had hoped, as one of its staff reported at the time, "to take advantage of the Bolsheviki excitement" of 1919 to speed the bill's passage in the Senate, the department was unable "to raise enough of a tidal wave . . . to overwhelm Hardwick, Reed, and the other recalcitrants." [50] Approved by the House on July 30, 1919, the act died in the Senate during the same session. The administration's plan for the expeditious expulsion of radical enemy aliens was somewhat behind schedule.[51]

While Congress debated and then failed to pass the deportation legislation during 1919, the Justice Department found itself forced to release some of the alien enemies in custody. Faced with the usual postwar appropriations slashes, the War Department had begun to close down the internment camps. As a result, the Attorney General reluctantly paroled and freed the less obnoxious prisoners, namely, "those who are merely pro-German."

In the hope that its antiradical bill would eventually pass, however, the Department of Justice continued to hold on to any individual with "political sentiments . . . so extreme as to make him a dangerous member of society." [52] At the same time the government admitted that of those radical aliens held almost none was "dangerous in a criminal sense." [53] Some radicals won their freedom, of course, if they were willing to recant former views and associations.[54]

The alien enemy problem had almost solved itself by the time Congress approved the desired legislation in May 1920. Many interned merchant seamen had sought and received voluntary repatriation at the conclusion of the war.[55] By November 1919 further repatriations and paroles reduced the number still held to 250, all of whom were radical rather than pro-German.[56] By April 1920, the Justice Department was face to face with the imminent closing of all the camps and was determined to release all prisoners for whom the Immigration Bureau had not already issued warrants of arrest.[57] Less than two months later, Congress passed the Immigration Act of May 10, 1920.[58] This at last made possible the deportation of any alien internee of which there were, by then, none left to deport.

It cannot be said that the government did not accomplish its objective of removing or reforming the radical enemy aliens simply because the 1920 law came too late to be used. Faced with a seemingly endless internment and the threat of eventual deportation because of their views, many aliens had chosen voluntary repatriation. The Justice Department's parole policy had also won converts to recantation. A few aliens had been deported under the immigration acts of 1917 and 1918. On the other hand, some of the internees who held out to the very end succeeded in defeating the government's plan and maintained their residence in the United States.[59]

However irrelevant it may have been in the expulsion of enemy aliens, the 1920 legislation could still facilitate the deportation of those convicted as critics or opponents of war and America's war program. The procedure seemed airtight. Using the conviction as prima facie evidence of an alien's undesirability, the Secretary of Labor would then make a finding that the individual was "an undesirable resident of the United States." To avoid deportation, the alien would have to demonstrate positively that he was "a safe person to remain in this country." [60] That the legislation turned out to be much less successful than its framers had imagined was due to its inconsistent and contradictory enforcement by the Department of Labor and its subordinate bureau. This was, of course, a procedure traditional in the expulsion of aliens. Even before the new legislation had been enacted, the first arrests of wartime prisoners foreshadowed the chaotic, confused course that the government was to follow in the future.

The Immigration Bureau began its postwar campaign by rounding up the aliens whose one-year sentences expired during 1918 and 1919 and charging them under the moral-turpitude provision of the existing law. The largest single group apprehended were the sixty-two Rockford, Illinois, Scandinavian and Lithuanian immigrants who had resisted the Selective Service Act out of ignorance of their draft status and opposition on principle to war and militarism. Most of them were anxious to remain in America.[61]

The defense and the government quite naturally differed on the definition of the crime. Accordingly to John Metzen, the aliens' attorney, the Selective Service Act was founded on "political expediency" and was entirely temporary in nature. Failing to register, therefore, was not an inherently base or depraved act.[62] The Immigration Bureau, supported by the Labor Department, found that the refusal to register "must be regarded as particularly vicious and grave when the attendant circumstances are taken into consideration."[63] During 1918 and 1919 the government deported thirty-seven aliens in the Rockford group for conviction of a crime involving moral turpitude.[64]

Then quite suddenly in the summer of 1920 the Department of Labor awoke to the fact that its own solicitor had previously ruled that a violation of the Selective Service Act definitely did not constitute a crime involving moral turpitude.[65] The new interpretation did not help the thirty-seven Scandinavians already expelled, nor would it now free the aliens still under arrest. The 1920 legislation could still be applied.[66]

Despite the intent of the congressional framers and the pleadings of the Immigration Bureau, the Labor Department refused to deport these aliens on the basis of the wartime conviction alone.[67] According to Louis Post, the government must base its finding of undesirability "upon evidence extraneous to that upon which conviction and imprisonment resulted:"[68] Under this system an individual could still refuse to testify without damaging his case. If the sentence itself resulted in a presumption of undesirability, then the alien's silence would operate against him, and this was what the bureau and the Department of Justice had desired and expected.

In a number of the remaining Rockford cases, the Department of Labor released aliens whose records lacked proof of undesirability apart from the conviction.[69] As a result, aliens escaped deportation in 1920 for an offense for which their cellmates had been expelled in 1918 and 1919. Other immigrants might also have avoided arrest had not the government's interpretation of the 1920 legislation again changed.

A New York district-court decision in January 1921 led the department to reverse itself and accept the violation of the Selective Service Act as prima facie proof of undesirability. The case in question concerned a Finnish I.W.W. who had failed to register. The judge upheld the deportation order based solely on this fact because the alien had not overcome the presumption of guilt raised by his conviction.[70]

After this decision, therefore, alien violators of the Selective Service Act could escape deportation only by proving their desirability. And the soundest test of this quality came more and more to be abandonment of radical ideas and associations. As a result, deportations for convictions under the Selective Service Act depended on the current fashionable interpretation plus the degree to which the alien was willing to recant. Decisions concerning the Espionage Act were equally irregular.

The Department of Labor and the Immigration Bureau seemed unable to decide whether or not an Espionage Act conviction was a crime involving moral turpitude. At first they were positive it did and approved deportation for such a violation.[71] Then the department solicitor ruled the exact opposite. In a case involving one of the most serious of all the wartime violations — a Sacramento I.W.W. leader — the solicitor found in favor of the immigrant. The official judgment took notice of the following features of the Espionage Act and convictions under it: the legislation's purpose was the government's self-preservation; the government punished violators of the act regardless of their motives; and "the law and violators of it . . . are not concerned with general personal morality." These considerations persuaded the solicitor that "personal baseness and depravity are not of the essence of a violation of that law." [72]

This decision, however, did not establish a departmental

line that subordinate officials faithfully followed in the future. While the alien whose case the solicitor had examined escaped deportation, the department continued to issue warrants of arrest on the ground that an Espionage Act conviction was a crime involving moral turpitude.[73] The officials responsible for the uniform enforcement of the immigration laws simply seemed oblivious of the rulings of the department's highest legal authority. Whatever the merits of the controversy, sound bureaucratic procedure dictated that the solicitor's opinion, once delivered, was decisive. Yet, the government put itself in the position of deporting one alien and freeing another for the commission of exactly similar offenses. Such behavior was both arbitrary and unjust.[74]

An analysis of the government's treatment of the I.W.W. aliens jointly indicted, tried, and sentenced at Sacramento demonstrates the appalling absence of uniformity. Whether the Labor Department used moral turpitude or the 1920 legislation as a basis, the aliens were equally deportable (or not) under the immigration laws. What the government did, however, was to pursue these defendants with a bewildering variety of charges or, in some instances, did not pursue them at all.

At least ten different policies dealt with the Sacramento immigrants. The Department of Labor charged two of the group with the commission of a crime involving moral turpitude. Canceling the warrant in one case in line with the solicitor's decision, the department upheld the expulsion decree in the other.[75] The alien whose charges were dropped escaped rearrest under the 1920 legislation, although the Immigration Bureau usually used this law in other such proceedings.[76] The bureau accused two aliens of advocating or teaching the unlawful destruction of property, one of whom had received a short sentence, while the second had been given a ten-year prison term. This count grew out of the part of the Sacramento indictment that claimed that the

I.W.W. had conspired to destroy property in California. Construing the Sacramento conviction as proof of the advocacy of such destruction, the department deported the relatively harmless alien. In the case of the long-term offender, the government made no use of the trial record and canceled the warrant for lack of evidence. Charging another ten-year prisoner with membership in the I.W.W., the bureau revoked the warrant when it became clear the Secretary of Labor would not approve deportations for mere membership in this organization. No arrest under the 1920 law followed for either of these aliens.[77] The department did, however, proceed against two Sacramento defendants solely on the basis of their wartime convictions. Soon after President Coolidge commuted their sentences in December 1923, the government deported one of them.[78] The other, too ill to travel, appealed to the Immigration Bureau's board of review for a stay in the deportation order. The request was granted. Later affidavits testifying to the alien's renunciation of all radical activities and associations led the department to take no further action.[79]

Finally, there were the two Wobbly aliens who had received sixty-day sentences for their part in the conspiracy. One, an ex-secretary of the San Francisco Latin local, failed in his pleas for leniency. Despite his thirteen-year residence in the United States, two American-born children, and his withdrawal from the I.W.W., the bureau ordered him deported for having distributed the organization's literature.[80] The other had pleaded guilty and become a government witness. The United States attorney at San Francisco urged the district immigration commissioner to drop the case because the alien had been a "very co-operative witness" and had promised never again to join the I.W.W. or any group like it.[81] Due to his change of heart and his promise to supply further information on I.W.W. plans, signs, and passwords, the department paroled the defendant and a year later canceled the warrant.[82] Immigration records also indicate that the government failed to arrest several other Sacramento aliens on any charges whatsoever.[83]

It would be difficult to duplicate the bizarre and diverse methods with which the United States proceeded against that Pacific Coast immigrant group convicted of a joint conspiracy to obstruct the war effort. At times there seemed to be either utter unfamiliarity with or total disregard of the law. At other times the government matched a harsh inflexibility with a willingness to forgive and forget. The one law, the 1920 legislation, under which the department could have deported all of the aliens, was hardly used at all. Theoretically, the Labor Department and the Immigration Bureau were only to administer the policies outlined by Congress. In practice, as in the expulsion of the Sacramento aliens, the department exercised the most extensive latitude in the application of the laws. It could utilize a specific act or not use it, accept an official interpretation of an ambiguous phrase or disregard it, and drop or carry through on a case as it saw fit. Upon this bureaucratic wheel of fortune an alien could never tell whether he would lose all or break the bank.

IV

However important the expulsion of these radical aliens may have been to the government, the deportation story alone does not reveal the degree to which the Justice Department, the Pardon Office, and the President shared in the formulation of the postwar antiradical policy. The attitude of the Democratic and Republican administrations stood forth most clearly in the struggle over the release of the political prisoners and in the deportation of the alien segment of this group. These two phases were closely interrelated. The Department of Labor could not expel the alien members until and unless they were released from Leavenworth. Whether the President offered the radicals a pardon or a commutation of the sentence was also a significant factor. The Immigration Bureau could not proceed against any prisoner who received a pardon that wiped the offense off the record as though it had never been committed.

The I.W.W. political prisoners convicted at Chicago, Wichita, and Sacramento again provide the most illustrative case history for a survey of federal policy. They were the largest single group at Leavenworth, the most vocal, the most insistent on their rights, the most devoted to their principles, the most detested by the government authorities, and the ones longest incarcerated after the war.

The Wilson administration set the tone which the Republicans followed in the twenties. Attorneys General Gregory and Palmer, advised by local prosecuting attorneys, district- and circuit-court judges, and the Pardon Office itself, opposed any general amnesty for the wartime defendants.[84] President Wilson abandoned his own predisposition to forgive because Gregory and Palmer convinced him that political prisoners were criminals who had turned against their country in a time of crisis.[85] Warren G. Harding considered political crime more a menace "to all we hold dear" than ordinary crime. "A general grant of amnesty to political prisoners," he stated, "is no more justified than a general grant of amnesty to yeggmen." [86]

In spite of their opposition to a general amnesty, Gregory and Palmer approved a careful case by case review of the wartime sentences under the Espionage Act. The Justice Department's War Emergency Division, which had originally prosecuted these opponents and critics of war, had jurisdiction over the postmortem. Under its chief, attorney John Lord O'Brian, this division reduced some sentences and commuted others to the time already served.[87] O'Brian's branch did not, however, review the I.W.W. cases, because these had been prosecuted by a special section. This put the government, as O'Brian suggested, in the position "of deliberately failing to review convictions under the Espionage Act simply because the defendants were members of the I.W.W." [88] But there were no further reviews; the Wobblies had missed their big opportunity.

In the years that followed, the government did its best to avoid liberating the I.W.W. contingent at Leavenworth. The federal authorities feared the effect of such a release on the general social and industrial situation, and doubted whether the Wobblies had been sufficiently punished. Department of Justice officials also hoped that confinement would have a corrective effect on the radical views of the defendants. "Most of the I.W.W. prisoners are still defiant," Pardon Attorney James A. Finch reported, "and have not as yet learned the needed lesson of citizenship, nor have they become amenable to constituted authority." [89] When the amnesty movement seemed to be gaining political strength and fairly widespread support in late 1921, President Harding and Attorney General Daugherty ordered the release of their main prisoner, Eugene Debs, in order to "stop the discussion which had a tendency to unsettle situations." [90] Daugherty explained that Debs's "release . . . [was] brought about before the movement in that direction had succeeded or gone too far." [91] The policy paid off, for immediately thereafter, one of the major forces behind the amnesty drive called off its campaign. The American Federation of Labor ceased its operations on behalf of political prisoners because it believed "a full measure of success had been achieved." [92] The I.W.W.'s remained at Leavenworth.

Under these circumstances it was not surprising that the aliens in the group turned to deportation to avoid what then looked like an interminable detention. First eighteen immigrants and then thirty-one agreed to accept expulsion if the government would give them a group amnesty or commutation of sentence within a reasonable time. [93] It would have been extremely simple for the United States then to have rid itself of what it considered to be wholly undesirable agitators. The Department of Labor accepted the proposal, but the Pardon Office believed that aliens should serve their full terms so that the immigrant would realize he faced the full penalty of the law for violating it.[94] After this failure, the solidarity of the aliens, like that of the whole I.W.W. group at Leavenworth, disappeared, and each of the prisoners tended to go his own separate way.

Faced with the discouraging discrimination against their release and embittered by the already lengthy confinement, citizens and aliens alike sought their salvation as their consciences dictated.[95] The petulant factionalism that replaced the once-cherished unity sprang as well from disagreements over the tactics and principles of the amnesty struggle.[96] The Department of Justice traditionally required individual applications for clemency from convicted prisoners, not only so that the latter might indicate their desire for release, but also so that they might present the arguments concerning the injustice of their sentences. Many Wobblies, however, had looked upon individual applications as an indirect admission of guilt, a renunciation of their beliefs and ideals, and a weapon that allowed the government to deal with them singly, although they had been convicted as a group. Numerous I.W.W.'s also disliked begging favors from a Justice Department that they believed had wrongly prosecuted them for the exercise of their free speech. Others felt that individual applications were a weaker procedure than group action. In this controversy, aliens divided along the same lines as their citizen cellmates: some made individual appeals for clemency; others refused to bargain with the government and proudly awaited a general amnesty.[97]

In December 1921 the Harding administration began offering selective commutations of sentence conditioned on immediate deportation. In this piecemeal manner, the government was able to deport a dozen aliens whose imprisonment no longer seemed justified but whose presence in the United States was objectionable to the authorities. The Harding administration thus skillfully avoided a general amnesty that might have implied some injustice or excessive severity in the original convictions but was still able to extort a deportation from those whose continued incarceration might have embarrassed the government. In addition, the policy further disrupted the solidarity of the Wobblies as one alien after another abandoned his fellow workers at Leavenworth.

In these commutations the government recognized that it had little or no evidence proving a violation of the Espionage Act, yet the remaining prisoners were now all serving time under that count alone.[98] The pardon attorney's records are filled with such phrases as "nothing specifically shown within period of indictment"; "very little against this man"; and "nothing shown under count 4." [99] Not all of those whom the department approached responded favorably. Some saw no reason why they should voluntarily expel themselves to avoid a longer imprisonment unwarranted by the evidence. In time they won a happier fate.[100]

While the government was still resisting any general amnesty for I.W.W.'s, a number of them with five-year sentences walked out of Leavenworth in early 1922 as free men. The Department of Labor immediately rearrested the aliens under the act of 1920.[101] Although they sued out writs of habeas corpus, the district judge rejected their pleas on the well-known ground that "Congress has the right to enact a law providing for the removal of any or all aliens at any time for any reason or for no reason." [102] In an appeal to the Supreme Court, Chief Justice Taft upheld the government on its right to use ex post facto legislation against aliens. Taft also agreed that the Secretary of Labor could justly find the I.W.W.'s "undesirable as residents" on the basis of their wartime conviction alone.[103] The aliens had only one opportunity

left to defeat deportation: a presidential pardon wiping out
the wartime conviction would make the aliens as legally
innocent as if they had never committed the crime. There
would thus be no evidence for deportation under the 1920
legislation. Determined to exhaust all possibilities, the immigrants applied for the pardon, and the Labor Department
agreed to postpone action pending the outcome of these applications.[104]

In early 1925 President Coolidge pardoned the four alien
petitioners because they had renounced their former views
and associations and because the government did not desire
to "agitate these matters anew." By 1925 the whole political-
prisoner controversy had been settled for over a year, for
Coolidge had unconditionally communted the sentences of
the last thirty Wobblies in December 1923. Attorney General Stone doubted whether it would be wise to try to deport
the four aliens in question or to reawaken the old hostilities
of the amnesty crusade. Besides, the aliens had quit the
I.W.W., had sworn to uphold the constitution, and had
promised to be law-abiding in the future. The imprisonment
and the threat of deportation had taken them a long way
from the defiant radical solidarity of the war years; it seemed
to the authorities that the aliens might even become good
citizens in time.[105]

Although citizens and aliens slowly dribbled out of Leavenworth as their sentences expired or as they accepted commutations for deportation, the process had not seriously de-
pleted the ranks of the prisoners by December 1922. At that
time there were still forty-nine I.W.W. inmates of the federal
penitentiary. The amnesty campaign had again revived after
the setback to it following the release of Eugene Debs. While
not as inclusive as before, the drive to release the remaining
political prisoners was led by Senators George Pepper and
William E. Borah and by the American Civil Liberties Union.
They flooded the Department of Justice with detailed re-

ports analyzing the insubstantial nature of the evidence and they played up for public support the free-speech aspects of the Espionage Act convictions.[106]

So far the government had refused to budge. The widespread strikes in 1922 had precluded any administration clemency lest a premature release of radicals encourage the nation's dissatisfied elements.[107] In addition, Pardon Attorney Finch had delayed any action by his refusal to consider I.W.W. cases as long as the amnesty fighters were picketing the White House.[108] On the other hand, as time wore on, the Pardon Office came to feel increasingly less sure of its case and more and more irritated by criticisms from "good citizens [of a] . . . high class type" who were advocating amnesty.[109]

As a result, the pardon attorney devised a new form of commutation in December 1922, a procedure designed to solve in one stroke the complicated situation of the political prisoners and to extricate the government from the controversy unscathed and above censure. Finch proposed that the Department of Justice offer the imprisoned Wobblies commutations conditioned upon their promise to be law-abiding in the future with a proviso that the President might return them to Leavenworth if they violated the agreement.[110] It was a plan based not on benevolence, justice, nor mercy, but on calculating expediency. It aimed to split the I.W.W. between those anxious for release on any terms and those insisting on unconditional clemency. The latter, believing themselves innocent of the charges, thought a promise to be law-abiding in the future implied they had not been so in the past. They also realized they would have to quit the I.W.W. to live up to the promise. A man could not be both a Wobbly and law-abiding in much of America in the 1920's. State criminal-syndicalism laws took care of that; and any labor organizer, I.W.W. or not, faced vagrancy, disturbing the peace, or similar trumped-up charges from the many hostile open-shop communities in which he might operate. To accept the government's terms would have meant a cessation of all labor activity, and many Wobblies would not agree to such a pledge.[111]

If the Leavenworth prisoners rejected the commutations, however, they would appear to have refused to be law-abiding, an attitude on which Finch expected the government could capitalize. In any event, the I.W.W.'s would lose. They would either all accept the commutations and thus abandon the organization, divide themselves by adopting different points of view, or ruin themselves with public opinion by acting defiantly above the law. According to the pardon attorney, the conditional commutation would also "silence the bunch of agitators including Borah and his followers" and put the administration in a favorable light.[112] After much soul-searching and bitter internal conflict, the I.W.W.'s made up their minds. On June 19, 1923, fifteen of the forty-nine, among them six aliens, agreed to be law-abiding in the future. The participation of the aliens created further legal confusion for all concerned.[113]

The point at issue was whether or not a conditional commutation precluded deportation. The Attorney General told the Department of Labor that, even though the commutations prescribed a law-abiding residency for compliance, this should have no effect on the aliens' liability under the immigration code.[114] The immigrants, on the other hand, insisted that they could not fulfill the provisions of the President's release if they were not in the United States. To deport them, they claimed, would be "an act of bad faith." [115] Refusing to testify or cooperate in the proceedings against them, five of the aliens sued out writs of habeas corpus.

The court battle revolved around the legal meaning of a conditional commutation. Was it or was it not a pardon? If it was, then the aliens were obviously not deportable. The defense contended that a release dependent upon the prisoner's acceptance of it or his future conduct was of necessity a pardon. A commutation merely substituted "a less for a greater punishment" and could be "imposed upon the convict without his acceptance and against his consent." Only a pardon could be conditional.[116]

Both the district and circuit courts rejected the argument that a conditional commutation was a pardon or that it could in any way block the deportation of aliens. Since deportation was not a punishment but a legislative prerogative, the courts held that "no commutation of sentence . . . can be held to prevent the operation of general law." Judge Learned Hand of the circuit court of appeals, however, dissented vigorously from his colleagues' interpretation.[117]

Judge Hand emphatically equated a conditional commutation with a pardon. A President could unilaterally alter a person's sentence only by shortening it; yet the terms imposed in this commutation specified a reimprisonment if the alien violated them. "To be released, to reestablish one's life in the world, and then to be retrapped is a vastly different matter from enduring at a stretch the pains of full execution," the judge concluded. If such a modification could not possibly be part of the presidential power to commute, then the aliens had definitely been tendered and had accepted a pardon. Hand also reasoned that the imposition of terms implied their fulfillment in the United States.[118]

In spite of judicial approval, the Department of Labor did not in the end expel the five aliens, but instead adopted a midway position, refusing either to deport them or to cancel the warrants. The immigrants thereafter dwelt in the twilight zone of a suspended sentence, always liable to be "retrapped" or deported if they again came into conflict with the law.[119]

Six months after the conditional commutations, the government in December 1923 released the last rebellious recalcitrants who had refused to bargain for their freedom. The effort to extract the promise to be law-abiding had been pretty much of a failure from the point of view of the numbers accepting. While the policy had undoubtedly alienated the Wobblies from each other and blackened their public reputation, it had not quieted the amnesty campaign. The Coolidge administration began to tire of the seemingly endless debate over the political prisoners from World War I. After all, these were the days of normalcy. The President, therefore, appointed a nonpartisan commission to investigate the problem and to recommend solutions for it. Bishop Charles H. Brent, General J. D. Harbord, and ex-Secretary of War Newton D. Baker found that there was little reason to perpetuate the I.W.W. imprisonment. Following their advice, President Coolidge commuted without any reservations the sentences of the remaining thirty unregenerated radicals on December 15, 1923. The amnesty controversy had finally ended, and, as usual, both sides claimed the victory.[120]

Throughout the long struggle over the political prisoners, pardons, commutations, and the cancelation of deportation warrants seemed to be closely correlated with an individual's defection from radical ranks. In answer to criticism of this procedure, the government officially disavowed any wish "to influence prisoners in reference to their views or beliefs upon any subject," [121] but the record indicated otherwise.[122]

Regardless of the evidence upon which the conviction had been based, the Departments of Justice and Labor separated the prisoners according to their attitude and tractability. Devotion to radical principles typed a man as a bad type, an agitator, or a person who had not yet learned his lesson.[123]

The lily-white purity in beliefs and associations that the government demanded and received from those seeking executive clemency and a stay of deportation was an ironic postscript to the wartime prosecutions. The government that had claimed to have indicted only those obstructing the war program and that had denied the existence of political prisoners now proceeded as though guilt sprang from radicalism. It was even more ironic that members of an organization devoted to solidarity and the principle of free speech should so generally have renounced the ideals and opinions for which they had sacrificed so much. At the end of the amnesty campaign the two opponents seemed to have accepted the logic of each other's arguments. On December 13, 1923, the pardon attorney admitted, "I am not satisfied that the defendants were actuated solely by their opposition to the government, but believe that they were actuated also very largely by the thought of improving labor conditions.[124] From the other side a leading Wobbly agitator reported, "My attitude is such that I can't subscribe to the doctrines of those who would have changes made, other than by direct political conformity." Recalling his long imprisonment, he concluded, "Sometimes it requires a great experience to see things in their true light and I can frankly say I had mine." [125]

v

In addition to reforming and deporting the undesirable remnants of the wartime crusade, the government also attempted to block the further naturalization of radicals and, if possible, to denaturalize still others. Successful in the blocking policy, the Republican administrations were unable to establish a precedent in the courts that would allow the Justice Department to convert citizen radicals back into aliens.

As its first line of defense, the government relied upon the Bureau of Naturalization, an agency eager to perform its task and aware of its responsibility. "As long as the advocates of these malignant and un-American doctrines remain aliens," the bureau asserted, "they may be deported and their gospels may be overthrown at their inception." [126] It was obviously a matter of identifying such people when they took out their first papers, yet the bureau's limited funds and staff made it wonder whether it could weed out all the radicals from the hundreds applying. According to Citizenship Director Raymond F. Crist, "socialistic organizations" were deliberately outrunning the investigative capacity of the government by flooding it with applicants. In response, the Division of Citizenship received reports from corporations about their alien employees' associations, memberships, and "character of thought." In the Northwest, the Loyal Legion of Loggers and Lumbermen fulfilled its Americanization program by denying membership or firing aliens who were not aspirants for naturalization, a candidacy closed, of course, to radicals.[127]

Both the bureau and the courts specifically denied naturalization to I.W.W.'s during the 1920's — an extension of the prewar policy.[128] The grounds were similar: namely, that an individual could not be both a member of the I.W.W. and attached to the principles of the Constitution at one and the same time. The I.W.W. did not advocate the forcible overthrow of the government, but did contemplate the elimination of its present political form and its replacement by a one-class industrial democracy achieved by direct action and the general strike against the capitalist class. Whether such activity necessarily involved an opposition to parts of the Constitution or laws stemming from them was a moot point. The courts believed it would, and that the I.W.W. could not, therefore, be in accord with the document itself.[129]

In its major denaturalization attempt, the government hoped not only to make one of the top I.W.W. agitators again deportable but also, and more importantly, to establish a precedent under which it might attack the privileged sanctuary of other naturalized radicals. A wartime case in which the Justice Department had successfully denaturalized an I.W.W. on the ground he had fraudulently procured his certificate encouraged the department to try its luck a second time. In the earlier decision, membership in the I.W.W. at the time of naturalization had been considered sufficient proof that the alien lied when claiming to be attached to the principles of the Constitution. According to the judge, the alien had deceived, misled, and perpetrated a fraud upon the court.[130]

The second case was not, however, so simple. The government had picked out James Rowan, founder and leader of the powerful (in 1917) Lumber Workers Union, who had received the maximum twenty-year sentence in the Chicago trial and the unconditional commutation of December 1923. Now the government hoped to prove that his naturalization had been a fraud; if successful, the Coolidge administration could move against nine other naturalized I.W.W.'s also convicted at Chicago. But all these cases were complicated by the fact that the aliens had acquired their citizenship before joining the I.W.W., including Rowan himself, who had been naturalized five years earlier.[131]

The legal theory of denaturalization did not favor the government in such instances. The courts consider the revocation of citizenship a serious matter in which "the burden is upon the government to prove by a preponderance of the evidence that the defendant obtained his naturalization wrongfully." The evidence itself must be "clear and convincing." [132] The fraud upon which the cancellation is based must exist either in the five-year probationary period preceding the final decree or at the time of naturalization itself. The government frequently does introduce, however, the subsequent activity of the defendant to infer his state of mind and his intent when he acquired citizenship. On the other hand, the government need not prove conscious deceit; a subconscious reservation is sufficient. Devotion to one's native country, for example, may remain unknown to the person himself until a crisis such as a war elicits old loyalties.[133] In Rowan's case, the Department of Justice sought to prove that high position in the I.W.W. and wartime conviction of disloyalty were facts from which the courts could legitimately infer a lack of attachment to the Constitution at the time of naturalization.[134]

Although the Spokane District Court upheld the government's contentions in early 1926, a year later Rowan won his appeal to the circuit court. The I.W.W. leader did not contest the facts in the case, but did convincingly demonstrate that none of them existed until he joined the I.W.W., five years after his naturalization. Rowan indicated the American and the economic basis of his radicalism. When he had received his naturalization certificate in 1907, he had known nothing of the exploitation in the lumber industry. Conditions there had led to his I.W.W. membership in 1912. Ten years after his naturalization, Rowan had stood trial for conspiracy to obstruct the war effort. He still believed, so he testified, in the American form of government and the principles upon which it was founded. The district court thought otherwise and stated that Rowan's lack of attachment to the Constitution in 1907 might reasonably be deduced from his actions five and ten years later. In reversing this decision the circuit-court majority decided the inference had been stretched too far. "To say that one who was not a member of such an organization in 1907, by merely joining the organization and remaining a member through 1917, must in 1907 have been opposed to organized government or been lacking in allegiance is far too conjectural," the court concluded, "nor do we think that the proven fact that ten years after 1907 Rowan was guilty of a violation of the Espionage Act is logically probative of his state of mind in 1907." [135]

Although the Departments of Justice and Labor were anxious to obtain a favorable precedent, they recognized the case was not a strong one.[136] There was no appeal, and the Rowan judgment has remained a limiting precedent in denaturalization affairs. While conduct indicating a mental reservation of allegiance has been sufficiently convincing to the courts as much as thirty years after naturalization, actions indicating a lack of attachment to the constitution must occur within five years to have probative value. In these cases the longer the time, the less willing the courts to accept the evidence.[137]

The unsuccessful denaturalization, the withholding of citizenship, the opposition to amnesty, and the deportation of alien enemies and wartime prisoners were the aftermath of an antiradical crusade born in the second decade of the twentieth century. The Department of Labor's capricious intepretations of the immigration laws and its willingness to be flexible when aliens recanted were part of this pattern. The Justice Department's amnesty program depended not on the sufficiency or fairness of the punishment but on the amount of social unrest, strikes, the supposed imminence of revolution, and the readiness of the prisoners to reorient their views. A grudging general commutation followed the official recognition that many men were serving terms on little or no evidence.

From 1923 on the American Civil Liberties Union fought for the restoration of radicals' civil rights by a general pardon. The times now seemed more propitious. With the victory of restriction in 1924 and the legendary prosperity of the succeeding years, nativist hysteria was on the wane. The renewed spirit of self-confidence, apparent in the breakup of the Ku Klux Klan and the decline of anti-Semitism, also inhibited the demands for repression. At the very peak of prosperity in 1929, the Pardon Office cautiously approved a pardon, feeling that it could cause "no particular harm." [138] Before President Hoover could act, the crash had initiated the great depression. In 1933, when the slump seemed to have reached rock-bottom, Pardon Attorney Finch was once more fearful of the encouragement such a pardon would provide to the radical movement. He felt that the lesson taught free-speech advocates by Espionage Act convictions should not be weakened by a general pardon. Looking at the number of hungry and unemployed men, Finch warned, "It is certain that we shall need the full force of such defensive measures, in all probability, in the not distant future." [139] But Franklin D. Roosevelt in his first year in office disregarded this advice and offered a Christmas pardon to all those convicted under the Draft and Espionage acts of World War I. Fifteen years after the prosecutions and during a much greater crisis, a New Deal administration was ready to close the wounds opened by the antiradical hysteria of its Democratic forebears.[140]

Epilogue

On May 24, 1954, a seven-to-two Supreme Court decision upholding the deportation of an ex-Communist indicated that the United States had continued down the narrow, intolerant road marked out in 1903. The nation's highest court had validated the constitutionality of the 1950 Internal Security Act when applied ex post facto to aliens who had been Communists at any time before its passage. Thus an alien who had been a member of a legal political party from 1944 until 1946 found himself deportable under an act passed four years after his rejection of the Communist faith. While the majority opinion recognized that the action in question "shock[s] the sense of fair play which is the essence of due process," the justices respected the power of Congress to handle alien affairs.[1]

Similar decisions in recent years have also acknowledged the "absolute" and "unqualified" right of Congress under its sovereign power to order the deportation of an alien for any reason or for no reason and at any time. Nor is the alien as yet protected by constitutional guarantees in deportation procedures.[2] The Immigration Bureau lapsed back into its historical practices soon after the Palmer raids; the reforms intended to quiet public criticism had largely been abandoned by 1924. As the President's Commission on Immigration reported in 1953, "The present hearing procedure . . . fails to conform to the now generally accepted standards for fair hearings."[3] Until the Supreme Court reverses the 1893 decision in *Fong Yue Ting v. U. S.*, it will continue to uphold deportation legislation and practice regardless of "how such policies may offend American traditions."⁴ The Court has referred critics of these undemocratic and unjust processes to the body that is responsible for them, Congress.

Congress has given no sign that it will reverse the trend toward sweeping antiradical and anti-ex-radical legislation. The New Deal interlude of the 1930's was a short and temporary respite that created a false optimism in the radical mind. World War II, the struggle with Russia, and the challenge of communism have aroused the old anxieties and tensions. The nation once again imagines that an enemy within may be destroying the American way of life. Hostility to "subversive" ideas that might weaken the state or disturb the peacefulness of social and economic relations has thus become characteristic of this era. It is a continuing affliction that can fester into a McCarthy-like inflammation at moments of crisis and that has made steady inroads in traditional freedoms. The Smith Act and the Alien Registration Act of 1940, the Internal Security Act of 1950, and the Immigration and Nationality Act of 1952 have made the radical-catching bills of the first two decades seem simple and harmless. Then the country punished individual advocacy or, at most, contemporary membership in illegal organizations. Present legislation penalizes conspiracy to advocate, *past* membership (no matter how far back), and membership, association, or affiliation with any organization required to register under the Subversive Activities Control Act of 1950. Bad as the practice was, a radical could once recant and save himself from deportation. Now he must face deportation unless his recantation involves five years' *active* opposition to a formerly held ideology. In the early 1900's the nation accepted its responsibility for domestically induced radicalism. Today it has made the radical or ex-radical everlastingly liable for what he once was or thought. It has reserved the right to create new classes of radicalism and to enlarge the index of dangerous ideas and associations for which an individual may find himself deportable in the future. In addition, Congress has chopped away at the protection formerly afforded by naturalization. Citizenship is much more difficult to obtain and much easier to lose for any radical or ex-radical. The country seems to have accepted the 1922 suggestion of the Bureau of Naturalization that "as long as the advocates of these malignant and un-American doctrines remain aliens, they may be deported and their gospels may be overthrown at their inception." [5]

In the security-conscious 1960's the rights of a large portion of the population — aliens, naturalized citizens, and native born radicals — have been sacrificed to the safety of the state. These groups are becoming the real displaced persons of the cold war, less free and less protected than the rest of us. There has been a steady progression toward a federal policy based on fear rather than on faith in people. Not only are we afraid of our own shadow, but we also would like to deport it. There are those who would raise the crisis issue involved in the cold war and the threat of subversion as a justification for present policies. Senator Thomas J. Walsh of Montana replied to such proponents of expediency during the antiradical hysteria after World War I, "It is only in such times [as the present] that the guarantees of the Constitution as to personal rights are of any practical value," he said. "In seasons of calm, no one thinks of denying them." [6]

The nation needs freedom of speech — including freedom of "dangerous" speech. Its economic and political rebels must be able to play their role as the militant critics of the status quo. By adopting a policy of official suppression, however, the federal government has denied its radicals this chance and in return has become the real loser. In 1912 an anti-Wobbly editor predicted the future course of events. The I.W.W., he wrote, are "the waste material of creation and should be drained off into the sewer of oblivion there to rot in cold obstruction like any other excrement." [7] The United States has followed the suggestion of the country editor for too long. Some day, one hopes, it will evolve a more generous, humane, and decent policy for the aliens and radicals of succeeding generations.

BIBLIOGRAPHICAL NOTE

NOTES

INDEX

Bibliographical Note

GENERAL RECORDS OF THE EXECUTIVE
DEPARTMENTS OF THE FEDERAL GOVERNMENT

The National Archives at Washington, D.C., contain an extensive and invaluable collection of relatively unexploited files that provide the raw materials for any study of official policy.

There are, however, some problems. Various departments have a time limitation that puts certain more recent files out of reach. The Justice Department, Pardon Attorney, and Immigration Bureau files, for example, were formerly closed as far back as forty years from the present, but in 1953 the Attorney General shortened this span to twenty-five years. The Adjutant General, Chief of Staff, and War Plans Division files also have a twenty-five year cutoff date. Also, a number of files are missing or have never been received at the National Archives. And some files are called back to departments for reference and thus may be temporarily unavailable.

Certain records, of course, were much more valuable than others for this investigation. The most important files were those of the Immigration and Naturalization Service, the Department of Justice, the Pardon Attorney Office, the Adjutant General, and the Post Office Department. Within this group the files were of two kinds: those concerned with general policy and those dealing with a specific individual case or problem.

RECORD GROUP 1: War Labor Policies Board, Correspondence of the Chairman and of the Executive Secretary, May 1917–February 1919.

This file covers the labor difficulties with which the War Labor Policies Board was concerned during World War I. There is not much in it dealing with the prosecution of labor radicals, since the board spent its time settling the problems of organized labor. Several folders were useful, however, in revealing the formation of policy to handle the unrest in the Arizona copper camps. The question of what to do with the I.W.W. in Arizona was part of this problem.

RECORD GROUP 16: General Records of the Department of Agriculture and Records of the Secretary of Agriculture.

The one item that contained some information on the labor and I.W.W. situation in the Northwest was a letter to the Secretary of

Agriculture from the chief forester enclosing a confidential report on spruce production. The Forest Service also produced some valuable analyses of the labor situation in the northwestern lumber camps. The Forest Service files are in Record Group 95, discussed below.

RECORD GROUP 28: General Records of the Post Office Department and Files of the Solicitor.

The Solicitor files contain much material on the suppression of radical pamphlets, periodicals, and newspapers during World War I. In general, each file number deals with a specific publication that the Post Office found offensive. The files spell out in frank interdepartmental memoranda the exact criteria by which the department excluded or temporarily withhheld matter from the mails. Numbers 47596 and 47596 A–H differ from the others in that they deal with the search-warrant proceedings against radical mail and the postal inspectors' reports about these seizures. The Solicitor files also have the correspondence between the Post Office Department and the other agencies of government concerned with the suppression of the radical movement. This record group is, in addition, a representative collection of the radical press, since each file has a sample of the material excluded.

RECORD GROUP 60: General Records of the Department of Justice.

The typical Department of Justice file gives a fairly complete history of the origin, development, prosecution, and conclusion of a federal criminal case. These files contain correspondence between the offices of United States attorneys and the appropriate divisions of the department at Washington. These exchanges are confidential and they represent most often either a summation of the local situation, with a request for advice, or a directive from headquarters as to the policy to follow. The files also include letters from interested and influential members of the community, Bureau of Investigation reports or paraphrases of them, decisions of the Attorney General, protest and refutations from the defense, district- and circuit-court opinions, correspondence with other departments and with the President or his administrative aides, reports of official conferences, correspondence with members of Congress, and newspaper clippings. In addition, a file may have a so-called enclosure — bulky material such as the court record that has been forwarded to Washington. When an important case or series of cases came along, the department usually created a general file covering over-all policy decisions, and then carried forward each individual prosecution under this same number with an additional subnumber.

One especially important file is the one I cite as DJ File Abraham Glasser. As war approached during the late nineteen thirties, the Attorney General had a detailed analysis made of how the federal government handled labor strikes during World War I, a study that would provide the department with precedents and guides for action should the United States once more become involved in war. As part of this project, Abraham Glasser, a Justice Department lawyer, prepared a lengthy report covering, among others, the Arizona copper strike, the northwestern lumber strike, and the unrest at Butte. These manuscripts are filed at the National Archives along with typewritten and photostated copies of the documents substantiating Glasser's work. Glasser was able to use military intelligence and Bureau of Investigation files that were closed, of course, to the author. Glasser's study is a well-written, dramatic, and apparently impartial account of the conflict between the government and the strikers.

RECORD GROUP 85: General Records of the Immigration and Naturalization Service.

In these files, important decisions are buried in individual case files rather than in general files dealing with a specific subject matter. The file on an individual alien consists of certain basic items: The request for the warrant of arrest, its authorization, transcripts of the preliminary and final hearings, the recommendations of the examining inspector and the district office, bureau memoranda on the case, the Department of Labor decision, and such appeals and reviews as may have occurred. The file may also include as evidence or rebuttal unsworn statements, hearsay, ex parte affidavits, personal letters, statements of informers, and unconfirmed opinions. The total record usually provides not only an objective account of why the arrests originated, that is, what forces besides the service itself wanted the alien detained, but also an unconscious delineation of the inspector's and bureau's own attitude in their reports and recommendations.

RECORD GROUP 94: General Records of the Adjutant General's Office.

Record Group 94 does not comprise all of the files of the army and the War Department. Record Groups 98 (records of United States Army commands), 107 (records of the office of the Secretary of War before 1921), and 165 (records of the General Staff, Chief of Staff, Military Intelligence, and War Plans Division) are important documentary sources. For the purposes of this investigation, however, Record Groups 94 and 165 provided the files relating to the preservation of public order. The single most valuable and important source in this area is the Adjutant General's decimal file 370.6. In this collection are the reports and correspondence dealing with the army's suppression of domestic lawlessness and disorder. It contains both the War Department directives and the operational reports of the commanders in the field, thus providing a high- and low-level account of the policy and practice in a specific disturbance. Supplementing this file are annual reports of the various regional-Department commanders, indicating what military intelligence was doing to combat and keep watch on the radical movement.

RECORD GROUP 95: General Records of the Forest Service.

The Forest Service files offer an objective source committed neither to the lumber barons nor to the I.W.W. strikers. It is historically fortunate that some foresters had a social consciousness sufficiently developed for them to appraise the timber industry's conditions and set them forth in their reports.

RECORD GROUP 174: General Records of the Department of Labor.

There is disappointingly little material in these files on the I.W.W. and the problems aroused by its strike activities during World War I. In fact, two files contain almost all of the relevant information: 20–77 and 20–473 and –473A. File 20–77 is a miscellaneous assortment that includes the remarkable internment proposals of the western governors presented to President Wilson by George L. Bell. Files 20–473 and –473A have many of the papers of President Wilson's mediation commission, whose investigations into the Arizona copper strike and the Northwest's lumber troubles produced some documents analyzing the causes of the unrest and the part played by the I.W.W. in the strikes.

RECORD GROUP 204: General Records of the Pardon Attorney's Office.

These files contain much valuable information on the operations of the Pardon Office and of the policies it followed in releasing the wartime offenders. There is an abundance of material although it is somewhat scattered among individual files and general files covering whole groups of radical prisoners. Three general serials dominate all the rest, namely, 39–240, and 39–241, and 39–242. Each file contains the memoranda of the Pardon Attorney, recommendations of the United States attorneys who prosecuted the cases, suggestions of the district judges who sentenced the defendants, briefs submitted by defense lawyers, pleas and proposals of various amnesty groups, requests of prisoners themselves, Bureau of Investigation reports on evidence against defendants, amnesty surveys, and letters from the Attorney General and the President outlining the policies to be followed. The government attitude, confidential at the time, is thus clearly and frankly spelled out.

MANUSCRIPT COLLECTIONS

The largest and most valuable manuscript collection was that of the American Civil Liberties Union, housed in the New York Public Library and at Princeton. Ever since its organization in 1917, the Civil Liberties Union has pasted into large scrapbooks its correspondence, minutes, conference records, exhibits, and newspaper clippings

on all the cases, appeals, and defense activity in which it has participated. By 1926 this collection had already reached three hundred volumes. While the volumes are arranged by year and by subject, in the
early volumes the correspondence is still somewhat scattered.

Of the private manuscript collections, that of lawyer Frank P.
Walsh, also in the New York Public Library, was the most important.
Walsh maintained a correspondence with numerous people in the labor
and radical movements, and with those interested in the wartime
preservation of civil liberties.

The other manuscript sources, housed in the Library of Congress,
are the Baker, Burleson, Gregory, Pinchot, and Wilson papers, which
contained some useful letters. The collections of President Wilson
and his Cabinet members did not add a great deal to the material in
the government files, however. Important attitudes and policy decisions were for the most part made clear in the official records. These
private papers provided corroboration and occasional further insight
into the motivation behind the antiradical policy.

OTHER SOURCES

Personal interview with Ralph Chaplin, Tacoma, Washington, April
1950.

SECONDARY SOURCES

(The histories discussed here are those that have contributed most
in background, insight, or further interpretation to the author's understanding of the subject.)

Immigration and the Alien in American Life

Both Oscar Handlin and John Higham have made discerning investigations of immigration and the alien's reception in America. Handlin's two studies, *The Uprooted: The Epic Story of the Great Migrations that Made the American People* (Boston, 1951), and *The American People in the Twentieth Century* (Cambridge, Mass., 1954), are
essential for an understanding of what the journey meant to the alien
and why he reacted as he did to his new and often hostile environment. The immigrants' deep-rooted conservative attitudes, sympatheti-
cally portrayed by Handlin, stand in sharp contrast to the erroneous
stereotypes developed by nativists and those in power. Higham's
study, *Strangers in the Land: Patterns of American Nativism, 1860–
1925* (New Brunswick, 1955), is a comprehensive history of nativism.

Kate Holladay Claghorn and Milton Konvitz accurately describe
the legal labyrinth that confuses so many aliens. Miss Claghorn's *The
Immigrant's Day in Court* (New York, 1923) covers the era of World
War I, while Konvitz's *Civil Rights in Immigration* (Ithaca, 1953)

places more emphasis on contemporary practices. Konvitz's point of view is that of the minority of the Supreme Court that has sought to give aliens the same constitutional rights as citizens.

Three specific analyses of immigrant deportation are: the official investigation of the late twenties summarized in Reuben Oppenheimer, *The Enforcement of the Deportation Laws of the United States: Report to the National Commission on Law Observance and Enforcement* (Washington, 1931); Jane Perry Clark, *Deportation of Aliens from the United States to Europe* (New York, 1931); and the exhaustive autopsy of bureaucratic practice in William Cabell Van Vleck, *The Administrative Control of Aliens: A Study in Administrative Law and Procedure* (New York, 1932). A good survey of denaturalization procedures is the Department of Justice's own *Denaturalization* (Washington, 1943). For the legislative history of immigration, the reader should consult Roy L. Garis, *Immigration Restriction* (New York, 1927), or Sidney Kansas, *U.S. Immigration: Exclusion and Deportation and Citizenship of the United States* (New York, 1940), which is more an encyclopedic collection than a monograph.

The I.W.W. and its Environment

The two standard histories of the I.W.W. are still Paul F. Brissenden, *The I.W.W.: A Study of American Syndicalism* (New York, 1920), and John S. Gambs, *The Decline of the I.W.W.* (New York, 1943). Each follows with scrupulous care the inner shifts of ideology and power that affected the I.W.W. These should be supplemented by William D. Haywood, *Bill Haywood's Book* (New York, 1929). Ralph Chaplin, *Wobbly: The Rough-and-Tumble Story of an American Radical* (Chicago, 1948), is the only account written by a close friend of Haywood. Chaplin left the I.W.W. after World War I, but his book still captures the flavor of the early protest and of the I.W.W.'s reaction to suppression. Lowell S. Hawley and Ralph Bushnell Potts, *Counsel for the Damned: A Biography of George Francis Vanderveer* (Philadelphia and New York, 1953), characterizes the fight for justice by the I.W.W.'s chief counsel. Men like Vanderveer, Clarence Darrow, Frank P. Walsh, and Fred Moore gave much to labor's cause in the courts — often unsuccessfully — and their story is a vital part of American legal history. The best expression of the Wobbly spirit still remains in the songs of protest in the little red songbook.

Studies of migratory labor are now becoming more common, but for the Wobblies' day only two are of real value. Carleton H. Parker, *The Casual Laborer and Other Essays* (New York, 1920), is a pioneering investigation of the psychological and economic problems that faced this exploited agricultural group. Stuart Jamieson, *Labor Unionism in American Agriculture*, Bureau of Labor Statistics, Bulletin no. 836 (Washington, 1945), is an equally original exploration that suggests how widespread and continuous the attempts at unionizing agriculture have been.

Since the I.W.W. faced not only the hostility of the conservative right but of the liberal middle and socialist left as well, an understanding of the peculiarly American nature of the latter two movements is important. George E. Mowry, *The California Progressives* (Berkeley, 1951), is a skillful analysis of the temperament and mentality of the middle-class reformer, especially when challenged by organized labor and migratory radicals. What Mowry suggests about the California response seems equally valid for the Wilson administration at the national level. The moderate drift of American socialism and its pragmatic search for political gain is well reported in Daniel Bell's essay, "The Background and Development of Marxian Socialism in the United States," in Donald Drew Egbert and Stow Persons, eds., *Socialism and American Life* (Princeton, 1952). This short summary can be supplemented with Ray Ginger, *The Bending Cross: A Biography of Eugene Victor Debs* (New Brunswick, 1949), and David J. Saposs, *Left Wing Unionism: A Study of Radical Policies and Tactics* (New York, 1926).

The Federal Government and the Radical

Despite the nation's great concern with internal security, this subject has not received any general treatment. Higham's work, of course, is relevant, since some nativist attacks on the suspected foreigner have involved the federal government. Zechariah Chafee, Jr., *Free Speech in the United States* (Cambridge, 1941) — a model analysis of the First Amendment — has material on the free speech of radicals and their punishment for exercising it. Dealing mainly with the period from 1920 until 1941, Chafee's work raises important questions about the justifiability of restraints that the government may impose on speech in the interest of national security. The reader should also examine G. Louis Joughin and Edmund M. Morgan, *The Legacy of Sacco and Vanzetti* (New York, 1948), which challenges the philosophy of trial by jury in cases where radicals are victims of community hysteria.

Two further histories focus on the role of the government's police arm: Max Lowenthal, *The Federal Bureau of Investigation* (New York, 1950), and Don Whitehead, *The F.B.I. Story: A Report to the People* (New York 1956). Each represents an opposing tradition of enforcement and detection. Lowenthal concentrates on the violations of due process, the expansion of surveillance, and the growth of a dangerous secret police authority. Much of his book covers the early period of F.B.I. history. Whitehead, on the other hand, records the achievements of federal agents, emphasizes the development of an expert criminal investigation body, and underscores the F.B.I.'s role in internal security. In Whitehead's book, the Palmer-Daugherty days are hurriedly dismissed. These two authors seem to be carrying on the long and still unsettled dispute between those who stress individual rights and those who insist on national results.

Specific outbreaks of antiradical hysteria have received some attention. Two good accounts of the suppression of the 1790's are John C. Miller, *Crisis in Freedom: The Alien and Sedition Acts* (Boston, 1951), and James Morton Smith, *Freedom's Fetters: The Alien and Sedition Laws and American Civil Liberties* (Ithaca, 1956). Federal intervention in the railroad strike of 1877 is briefly noted in Walter Millis, *Arms and Men: A Study in American Military History* (New York, 1956). The "red scare" of 1919–20 has been a frequent topic of both historical and polemical writers. The latest general treatment is Robert K. Murray, *Red Scare: A Study in National Hysteria* (Minneapolis, 1955). This history, depending almost entirely on published sources, is an excellent roundup of events, but gives little new analysis or understanding of their origin and development. Louis F. Post, *The Deportations Delirium of Nineteen-twenty* (Chicago, 1923), although inaccurate in places, is worth reading as the memoir of a high official who fought against the prevailing hysteria. The left presents its side in Robert W. Dunn, *The Palmer Raids* (New York, 1948), and the liberals their analysis in the National Popular Government League, *Report Upon the Illegal Practices of the Department of Justice* (Washington, 1920).

Notes

Abbreviations used in the Notes

ACLU   American Civil Liberties Union

AG   General Records of the Adjutant General's Office, Record Group 94

DJ   General Records of the Department of Justice, Record Group 60

DL   General Records of the Department of Labor, Record Group 174

IN   General Records of the Immigration and Naturalization Service, Record Group 85

PA   General Records of the Pardon Attorney's Office, Record Group 204

Introduction

1. *Whom We Shall Welcome*, Report of the President's Commission on Immigration and Naturalization (Washington, 1953), 281.

2. Robert K. Murray, *Red Scare: A Study in National Hysteria* (Minneapolis, 1955), 196–197, 212–217; Max Lowenthal, *The Federal Bureau of Investigation* (New York, 1950), 147ff.

3. J. Edgar Hoover to Frank Burke, Memorandum of February 21, 1920, DJ File 186701–14 between 82 and 83. Accounts of the malpractices involved in the raids may be found in Louis F. Post, *The Deportations Delirium of Nineteen-Twenty* (Chicago, 1923); Robert W. Dunn, ed., *The Palmer Raids* (New York, 1948); Constantine M. Panunzio, *The Deportation Cases of 1919–1920* (New York, 1921); Lowenthal, *Federal Bureau of Investigation*; Murray, *Red Scare*; National Popular Government League, *Report upon the Illegal Practices of the United States Department of Justice* (Washington, 1920); *Investigation Activities of the Department of Justice, 1919*, Senate Document 153, 66 Cong., 1 Sess. (1919); Senate Subcommittee of the Committee on the Judiciary, Hearings, *Charges of Illegal Practices of the Department of Justice*, 66 Cong., 3 Sess. (1921).

4. The most recent study of the 1919–20 red scare along these lines is Murray, *Red Scare.*

5. John Higham, *Strangers in the Land: Patterns of American Nativism, 1860–1925* (New Brunswick, 1955), 5–11.

6. *Ibid.*, 19.

7. *Ibid.*, 4, 38–41, 50–68, 76–79, 106–108, 158–192; Oscar Handlin, *The American People in the Twentieth Century* (Cambridge, Mass., 1954), 97–99, 144–146.

8. Higham, 38–105.

9. Handlin, *American People*, 60, 62, 69; Oscar Handlin, *The Uprooted: The Epic Story of the Great Migrations that Made the American People* (Boston, 1951), 108–112, 115–119, 192, 195–196, 204–205, 217–219.

10. Higham, 203.

Chapter I

The Immigrant as Scapegoat

1. *Fong Yue Ting v. U.S.*, 149 U.S. 698, 709; Milton R. Konvitz, *Civil Rights in Immigration* (Ithaca, 1953), 97–98.

2. *Fong Yue Ting v. U.S.*, 149 U.S. 698, 709.

3. F. H. Larned to Commissioner of Immigration, San Francisco, April 10, 1914, IN File 53244/1. See also *Japanese Immigrant Case*, 189 U.S. 86, 97.

4. Konvitz, 40–44, 97–98, 102; *Fong Yue Ting v. U.S.*, 149 U.S. 698.

5. *Fong Yue Ting v. U.S.*, 149 U.S. 698, 737, 740–741. Justice Brewer also quoted with approval James Madison, who said, "If a banishment of this sort [deportation] be not a punishment, and among the severest of punishments, it will be difficult to imagine a doom to which the name can be applied."

6. Quoted in Jane Perry Clark, *Deportation of Aliens from the United States to Europe* (New York, 1931), 48. Other justices have objected to the idea that deportation is not punishment. Chief Justice Fuller dissented in the Fong Yue Ting case. More recently Justices Black, Douglas, Murphy, and Rutledge have criticized or challenged the historic position of the court (Konvitz, 103–106).

7. E. J. Henning to Hon. Charles Nagel, July 30, 1923. IN File 54616/42.

8. William Cabell Van Vleck, *The Administrative Control of Aliens: A Study in Administrative Law and Procedure* (New York, 1932), 224.

9. Rule 22, subdiv. 3, of Immigration Bureau regulations, IN File 54549/622D; Van Vleck, 83.

10. IN File 53775/139, *passim*; Anthony Caminetti to the Assistant

Secretary, August 28, 1920, Alfred Hampton to Commissioners of Immigration, Seattle, El Paso, Montreal, September 30, 1920, and October 6, 1920, J. A. Flukey to Commissioner General, October 14, 1920, IN File 53244/1.

11. Rule 22, subdiv. 3, IN File 54549/622D. Author's emphasis.

12. Solicitor Charles Earl to A. Warner Parker, March 19, 1908, IN File 51924/30.

13. Oscar Straus and F. P. Sargent to all Commissioners of Immigration and Immigrant Inspectors in Charge, March 23, 1908, *ibid.*

14. Clark, 331–332; Van Vleck, 228; Reuben Oppenheimer, *The Enforcement of the Deportation Laws of the United States: Report to the National Commission on Law Observance and Enforcement* (Washington, 1931), 26–27.

15. F. H. Larned (Acting Commissioner General) to Inspector in Charge, St. Louis, July 31, 1908, IN File 53244/1.

16. Larned to Commissioner of Immigration, San Francisco, April 10, 1914, *ibid.*

17. *Japanese Immigrant Case*, 189 U.S. 86, 101. Author's emphasis. Much the same viewpoint was upheld in *Pearson v. Williams*, 202 U.S. 281.

18. William Williams to Commissioner General, May 21, 1910, IN File 53244/1. On the latter point the case of *U.S. v. Lee Huen*, 118 F. 442, 456, is relevant.

19. Anthony Caminetti to the Acting Secretary, July 24, 1919, IN File 54645/378; Oppenheimer, 43.

20. *Low Wah Suey v. Backus*, 225 U.S. 460, 471–472.

21. See the attitude expressed in Caminetti to Francis Garvan, July 27, 1919, IN File 54235/85C. Commissioner General Caminetti testified before a congressional committee that, if anything, the immigration hearings had been too fair (IN File 54549/662D). Examples may be found generally in almost any case history where the defense lawyer has challenged the procedure for lack of due process. See F. H. Larned to Inspector in Charge, Denver, May 17, 1914, IN File 53244/1B.

22. Williams to Commissioner General, May 21, 1910, IN File 53244/1.

23. Clark, 331–338, 361–386, 391, 422–423, 487–488; Konvitz, 107–109; Oppenheimer, 26–52, 59, 72, 80–92; Van Vleck, 83–89, 91–111, 172, 219–220, 224–228.

24. *U.S. ex rel. Iorio v. Day*, 34 F. 2d 920, 922.

25. Clark, 303–304, 377–382; Oppenheimer, 50–52, 86; this was true of the I.W.W. cases also until their defense became well organized.

26. Caminetti to Garvan, June 27, 1919, IN File 54235/85C.

27. Clark, 318.

28. The paragraphs on judicial review are based on a summary of Caminetti to Garvan, June 27, 1919, IN File 54235/85C; H. S. Ridgely to Solicitor General, Memorandum of November 23, 1920, DJ File 39–O–11x; Clark, 315–320; Van Vleck, 150–160, 171–173, 176, 180, 186, 193–197, 201–202, 208.

29. Clark, 487.

30. *Ibid.*, 41–54; Roy L. Garis, *Immigration Restriction: A Study of the Opposition to and Regulation of Immigration into the United States* (New York, 1927), 83–116.

31. Caminetti to Garvan, June 27, 1919, IN File 54235/85C.

32. Clark, 43–44, 51–53; Garis, 104, 107, 112, 134–135; Konvitz, 130–131.

33. Daniel Bell, "Marxian Socialism in the United States," in Donald Drew Egbert and Stow Persons, eds., *Socialism and American Life* (Princeton, 1952), I, 238–239; Eric F. Goldman, *Rendezvous with Destiny: A History of Modern Reform* (New York, 1952), 42.

34. Caminetti Memorandum of March 5, 1918, IN File 54235/36; Clark, 50–51; Sidney Fine, "Anarchism and the Assassination of Mc-Kinley," *American Historical Review*, LX (July 1955), 777–799.

35. Higham, *Strangers in the Land*, 7–8.

36. Quoted in Clark, 37. On the Alien Act and its twin, the Sedition Act, see also James M. Smith, *Freedom's Fetters: The Alien and Sedition Laws and American Civil Liberties* (Ithaca, 1956).

37. Quoted in John C. Miller, *Crisis in Freedom: The Alien and Sedition Acts* (Boston, 1951), 164; Konvitz, 96.

38. Quoted in Clark, 38.

39. *Ibid.*, 38–39; Konvitz, 95–96; Miller, 187–193.

40. Higham, 8.

41. Handlin, *American People*, 97–98; Higham, 30–105.

42. Selig Perlman, *A History of Trade Unionism in the United States* (New York, 1950), 81–105; Foster Rhea Dulles, *Labor in America, A History* (New York, 1949), 114–149, 166–183; Bell, 235, 238, 242.

43. Walter Millis, *Arms and Men: A Study in American Military History* (New York, 1956), 143–145.

44. Quoted in Higham, 31. See also Dulles, 115–116; and Higham, 30, 51.

45. Perlman, 81–105; Dulles, 114–149, 166–183; Bell, 235, 238, 242.

46. Quoted in Fine, 779.

47. Bell, 236–239; Fine, 779; David J. Saposs, *Left Wing Unionism: A Study of Radical Policies and Tactics* (New York, 1926), 13–14.

48. Bell, 238, 239; Fine, 777–799. See also IN Files 53423/338, /338A, 54182/2, /2A, 54235/20, /22, /33, /36, /36F, /36G, /39, /94–143, 54379/320–407, 54517/19, 54616/90, 54709 series, 54860/391–

582; DJ Files 186233–13, secs. I–III, 202600, secs. I–V, 202600–59, 203557; Post Office Department Solicitor's Files 46647, 46671, 46681, 46835.

49. The description is that of Henry David in his *History of the Haymarket Affair*, quoted in Fine, 779; see also Higham, 55.

50. Perlman, 81–105; Dulles, 114–149; 166–183; Bell, 235, 238, 242.

51. Bell, 238–239; Fine, 779–780; Dulles, 168.

52. Higham, 69, 78; Handlin, *American People*, 60, 62, 69; Handlin, *The Uprooted*, 108–112, 115–117, 195–196, 217–218, 289.

53. J. C. Burrows, "The Need of National Legislation against Anarchism," *North American Review*, CLXXIII (December 1901), 738–740.

54. *Congressional Record*, 53 Cong., 2 Sess. (1894), 6800, 8217, 8590–91, 8628.

55. S. 2314, secs. 1, 2, 3, *ibid.* 8557–58, 8590–91.

56. *Ibid.*, 8628, 8653–54; S. 209, *ibid.*, 54 Cong., 1 Sess. (1895), 22; S. 1051, *ibid.*, 55 Cong., 1 Sess. (1897), 118; Post, *Deportations Delirium*, 58–63.

57. Burrows, 727–728; Higham, 97.

58. Burrows, 742–744; *Congressional Record*, 53 Cong., 2 Sess. (1894), 8628.

59. Higham, 73–105, 108.

60. Fine, 780–781.

61. *Ibid.*, 781–787, 793–794, 798.

62. Index, *Congressional Record*, 57 Cong., 1 Sess. (1901), 21; Fine, 788, 790–791.

63. Quoted in Fine, 789–790.

64. Quoted in Garis, 102–103.

65. Fine, 790–793.

66. After 1893 each branch of Congress approved the literacy test a number of times. When the bill passed both houses in 1896, Cleveland vetoed the measure. Later, both Taft and Wilson vetoed legislation containing the literacy test. Congress had in Roosevelt a President who favored the measure, yet it framed no bill for him to approve. See Garis, 103, 123–124.

67. In one sense, this was not the first time that the United States excluded aliens because of their beliefs. The exclusion of polygamists antedated that of anarchists. The antipolygamy immigration legislation was certainly a restriction on ideas as well as on practice. However, the anarchists were the first to be restricted for beliefs and associations that supposedly made them a threat to the security and welfare of the country. The anarchists were the first radical group to come under official fire.

68. *United States Statutes at Large*, XXXIII, 1214, 1221; Anthony

Caminetti, Memorandum of March 5, 1918, IN File 54235/36; Garis, 104.

69. *Congressional Record*, 57 Cong., 2 Sess. (1902), 144. The senator mentioned specifically the government of the Moros of Sulu Island.

70. Solicitor Charles Earl, Memorandum of February 28, 1908, A. Warner Parker to the Secretary, March 17, 1908, IN File 51924/30; Clark, 50–51, 63–69; Garis, 107, 112, 114.

71. Kate Holladay Claghorn, *The Immigrant's Day in Court* (New York, 1923), 314.

72. Appendix, *Congressional Record*, 66 Cong., 2 Sess. (1920), 9280. The figures by year are: 1911, 0; 1912, 4; 1913, 4; 1914, 3; 1915, 1; 1916, 0; 1917, 0; 1918, 2.

73. Earl, Memorandum of February 28, 1908, Department Circular 163, March 3, 1908, IN File 51924/30.

74. Answers to Department Circular 163, n.d., *ibid.*; Handlin, *The Uprooted*, 109–110, 195–196, 217.

75. *Transmission through the Mails of Anarchistic Publications*, Senate Document 426, 60 Cong., 1 Sess. (1908).

76. Higham, 106–130.

Chapter II

The I.W.W. Challenge, 1905–1915

1. William D. Haywood, "Socialism, the Hope of the Working Class," *International Socialist Review*, XII (February 1912), 464.

2. Paul F. Brissenden, *The I.W.W.: A Study of American Syndicalism* (New York, 1920), 284, 286; Charles A. Madison, *American Labor Leaders: Personalities and Forces in the Labor Movement* (New York, 1950), 274.

3. *Final Report of the Commission on Industrial Relations* (Washington, 1915), 46, 89; Brissenden, 87, 155–168.

4. *Final Report and Testimony of the United States Commission on Industrial Relations*, 12 vols. (Washington, 1915), XI, 10573–74; William D. Haywood and Frank Bohn, *Industrial Socialism* (Chicago, 1911), 23, 34–35; *Proceedings of the First Convention of the Industrial Workers of the World, 1905* (Chicago, 1905), 579; Haywood, "Socialism," 467.

5. Bell, "Marxian Socialism," 267, 291; Brissenden, 283–293; Madison, *American Labor Leaders*, 275–276; Dulles, *Labor in America*, 215–219.

6. *Final Report, Commission on Industrial Relations*, 8–16, 23–76.

7. Eric F. Goldman, *Rendezvous with Destiny* (New York, 1952), 72–74, 171–176; Bell, 271.

8. Selig Perlman and Philip Taft, *History of Labor in the United*

States: Labor Movements (New York, 1935), 3–12; Goldman, 75–84.
9. Goldman, 162.
10. Bell, 267; Goldman, 73–74.
11. Bell, 269.
12. David A. Shannon, "The Socialist Party Before the First World War: An Analysis," *Mississippi Valley Historical Review*, XXXVIII (September 1951), 279–288; Bell, 267–302; Goldman, 73.
13. Madison, 264; Higham, *Strangers in the Land*, 176–177.
14. Bell, 278.
15. *Proceedings of the I.W.W., 1905*, 1.
16. Brissenden, 351–352; Vincent St. John, *The I.W.W.: Its History, Structure, and Methods* (Chicago, 1917), 4–5, 7–8. The original I.W.W. preamble was amended at the Fourth Convention in 1908, when those favoring political activity of some sort split with the proponents of economic direct action. The latter won and rewrote the preamble. The quotation follows the second, or amended, version.
17. St. John, 15.
18. *Final Report and Testimony, Commission on Industrial Relations*, XI, 10574, 10579; Haywood and Bohn, 22; St. John, 15.
19. *Final Report and Testimony, Commission on Industrial Relations*, XI, 10582; William D. Haywood, "The General Strike," *International Socialist Review*, XI (May 1911), 684; St. John, 15–16.
20. William D. Haywood, *Bill Haywood's Book* (New York, 1929), 231; *Final Report and Testimony, Commission on Industrial Relations*, XI, 10574; *Proceedings of the I.W.W., 1905*, 578–579.
21. Haywood, *Bill Haywood's Book*, 172; William D. Haywood, "An Appeal for Industrial Solidarity," *International Socialist Review*, XIV (March 1914), 544; William D. Haywood, "Lockouts in Great Britain," *International Socialist Review*, XI (January 1911), 415; *Proceedings of the I.W.W., 1905*, 577; *Final Report and Testimony, Commission on Industrial Relations*, XI, 10576, 10580; Mary E. Marcy, "The Battle for Bread at Lawrence," *International Socialist Review*, XII (March 1912), 539; Charles A. Madison, *Critics and Crusaders* (New York, 1947), 479.
22. St. John, 16.
23. Haywood, *Bill Haywood's Book*, 154; Haywood, "Socialism," 466, 469; William D. Haywood, "On the Paterson Picket Line," *International Socialist Review*, XIII (June 1913), 847; *Final Report and Testimony, Commission on Industrial Relations*, XI, 10575, 10579–80, 10592.
24. Louis Levine, "The Development of Syndicalism in America," *Political Science Quarterly*, XXVIII (September 1913), 472.
25. *Final Report and Testimony, Commission on Industrial Relations*, XI, 10598.
26. *Proceedings of the I.W.W., 1905*, 575–576.

27. Brissenden, 294.
28. Joe Hill, "The Preacher and the Slave," *I.W.W. Songs*, 14th ed. (Chicago, n.d.), 14.
29. James Connell, "The Red Flag," *I.W.W. Songs*, 2. Sentence order changed.
30. Mimeographed extract from *The Industrial Worker*, IN File 54379/76. Another I.W.W. analysis of patriotism went as follows: "You ask me why the I.W.W. is not patriotic to the United States. If you were a bum without a blanket; if you had left your wife and kids when you went west for a job, and had never located them since; if your job never kept you long enough in a place to qualify you to vote; if you slept in a lousy, sour bunk-house, and ate food just as rotten as they could give you and get by with it . . . if every person who represented law and order and the nation beat you up, railroaded you to jail, and the good Christian people cheered and told them to go to it, how the hell do you expect a man to be patriotic?" Quoted in Carleton H. Parker, *The Casual Laborer and Other Essays* (New York, 1920), 102.
31. Perlman and Taft, 169–207, 257.
32. Brissenden, 136–152, 213–242; Perlman and Taft, 253–254; Bell, 280; Ray Ginger, *The Bending Cross; A Biography of Eugene Victor Debs* (New Brunswick, 1949), 255–256.
33. In 1916 the I.W.W. made its last organized effort to become more than a western migratory group. From the new four-story headquarters building in Chicago, Haywood issued his famous call to get the Wobblies "out of the jungles and on to the job." The migratory "stiff" was to be a missionary to the eastern industrial worker. The movement to unionize Gary, Detroit, and other large centers failed. The western bummery was too anarchic for eastern conference-table work, and I.W.W. finances were inadequate for large-scale organizing. Finally World War I nipped the effort in the bud (interview with Ralph Chaplin, Tacoma, April 1950). See also Parker, 106.
34. Quoted in Roger N. Baldwin, "Free Speech Fights of the I.W.W.," in *Twenty-five Years of Industrial Unionism* (Chicago, 1930), 15; Brissenden, 181, 213, 261.
35. Baldwin, 14–15.
36. *Ibid.*
37. Brissenden, 262–265; Baldwin, 20.
38. Brissenden, 283–292; Perlman and Taft, 266–273.
39. Editorial, "After the Battle," *Survey*, XXVII (April 6, 1912), 1–2, quoted in Brissenden, 295.
40. Haywood, *Bill Haywood's Book*, 81.
41. Brissenden, 284, 286–292.
42. Higham, 164–172, 178–183.
43. Edward George Hartmann, *The Movement to Americanize the*

Immigrant (New York, 1948), 90–96, 267–270. Americanization is, of course, the other side of the coin of repression. The subject is not within the scope of this book but represents an interesting alternative that responded to similar conditions over approximately the same period.

44. Bell, 289, 291; Brissenden, 293; Goldman, 216; Ginger, 324.

45. Bell, 297. Bell has compared the evolution of travel allowances with the reformist direction of Socialism: 1904, delegates reimbursed for travel; 1908, sleeping-car fare paid; 1912, Pullman-car fare voted.

46. Quoted *ibid.*, 284.

47. Ginger, 308. The reform nature of socialism was disguised by what Bell calls "the cult of proletarian chauvinism." In this process the "repetitive litany of revolutionary rhetoric and phrase mongering" increased as the party drew away from its working class basis. "The practice of endowing all virtue in the man with the horny hands merely because he was a worker" paralleled the middle-class orientation of socialism. The oratory became more "bellicose and left" as the practice became more conservative and compromising (Bell, 294–297).

48. Levine, 505; Brissenden, 281, 293.

49. Perlman and Taft, 318–325; Ginger, 305–306.

50. Quoted in Brissenden, 280. Cf. Ginger, 309; Bell, 287.

51. Quoted in Brissenden, 281–282, and in Bell, 287.

52. Quoted in Bell, 288.

53. *Ibid.*

54. Editorial, *International Socialist Review*, XII (February 1912), 505; Haywood, "Socialism," 464; *Final Report and Testimony, Commission on Industrial Relations*, XI, 10581; Robert Rives Lamonte, "Socialist Respect for Capitalist Law," *International Socialist Review*, XII (February 1912), 501–502.

55. Brissenden, 280; Ginger, 309; Bell, 287–288, 290.

56. Bell, 291–292, 302, 308; Brissenden, 318–319, 332–333, 336–337.

57. Haywood, *Bill Haywood's Book*, 259. The rival Workers' International Industrial Union (the so-called Detroit I.W.W.) formed after the 1908 withdrawal of the Socialist Labor party by De Leon also adopted a manifesto on criminal syndicalism in 1915 (Brissenden, 254–255).

58. F. W. Estabrook to Charles D. Hilles, September 5, 1912, DJ File 150139, 1–20. Estabrook was on the executive committee of the Republican National Committee.

59. Higham, 171–173.

60. Stuart Jamieson, *Labor Unionism in American Agriculture*, Bureau of Labor Statistics, bulletin no. 836 (Washington, 1945), 59–60.

61. *Ibid.*; Brissenden, 265, 271.
62. Quoted in Brissenden, 266.
63. Baldwin, 17–18; Perlman and Taft, 240–242. On September 12, 1912, the I.W.W. once more was meeting freely.
64. Quoted in Brissenden, 266.
65. William Howard Taft to Attorney General George W. Wickersham, September 7, 1912, DJ File 150139–28.
66. DJ File 150139, 1–20, *passim.*
67. Taft to Wickersham, September 7, 1912, DJ File 150139–28.
68. Section 6 was originally section 5336 of the Revised Statutes and was passed in 1861. It states: "If two or more persons in any state or territory, or in any place subject to the jurisdiction of the United States, conspire to overthrow, put down, or to destroy by force the Government of the United States, or to levy war against them, or to oppose by force the authority thereof, or by force to prevent, hinder, or delay the execution of any law of the United States, or by force to seize, take, or possess any property of the United States contrary to the authority thereof; they shall be fined not more than five thousand dollars, or imprisoned not more than six years, or both."
69. Article IV, section 4, reads: "The United States shall guarantee to every State in this Union a Republican Form of Government, and shall protect each of them against Invasion; and on Application of the Legislature, or of the Executive (when the Legislature cannot be convened) against domestic Violence."
70. Assistant Attorney General William R. Harr to Wickersham, July 5, 1912, DJ File 150139–20.
71. Zechariah Chafee, Jr., *Free Speech in the United States* (Cambridge, Mass., 1941), 145–146.
72. George E. Mowry, *The California Progressives* (Berkeley, 1951), 143.
73. *Ibid.*, 55–56, 88–89, 92–98, 102, 299, 303.
74. *Ibid.*, 92–93, 143–157, 278, 295–296.
75. Jamieson, 60–61.
76. *Ibid.*, 61, 63.
77. *Ibid.*, 61–62; Perlman and Taft, 243–244.
78. Mowry, 199–201.
79. Jamieson, 63; Perlman and Taft, 244.
80. Mowry, 199–201.
81. Perlman and Taft, 244.
82. Headquarters Hop Pickers Defense Committee, *Bulletin*, September 22, 1914, in *Brief and Argument for Plaintiffs in Error, 9th Circuit Court of Appeals*, 38–39, PA File 39–241.
83. Charles L. Lambert to Richard Ford, June 6, 1915, *ibid.*
84. George Child to Lambert, August 4, 1915, Joseph C. Williams

to Phillip Gordet, November 26, 1916, Chris Luber to G. A. Roberts, February 9, 1917, Luber to H. C. Evans, February 12, 1917, *ibid.*, 40, 43, 51–52; Lambert to C. J. Bourg, August 5, 1916, *Industrial Worker*, May 1, 1917, in Report of the Pardon Attorney on C. L. Lambert, December 20, 1922, PA File 39–240; Report of Agent E. P. Morse, San Francisco, November 14, 1922, for November 1–14, 1922, in U.S. Attorney John T. Williams to Pardon Attorney James A. Finch, November 17, 1922, Senator George W. Pepper to Secretary to the President, June 5, 1923, Memorandum on Sacramento I.W.W. Cases, and Report of Agent Montgomery, San Francisco, March 12, 1923, for February 28 and March 1, 2, 3, 10, and 11, 1923, PA File 39–241; Report of Agent F. W. Kelly, San Francisco, December 13, 1919, for December 12, 1919, DJ File 206462–1. The government had a dictaphone planted in the jail where the I.W.W. defendants in the 1918 Sacramento case awaited trial. These dictaphone conversations fully substantiated the commission of acts of sabotage in the preceding years by a number of I.W.W.'s. It was almost impossible, however, to obtain evidence of such action.

85. Exhibits A through W, DJ File 150139–46.

86. J. H. Durst to George L. Bell, November 8, 1915, *ibid.*

87. Exhibits A through W, Durst to Bell, November 8, 1915, *ibid.*

88. Governors Johnson, Withycombe, Lister, and Spry to Franklin K. Lane, Confidential Telegram of October 5, 1915, DJ File 150139–48.

89. Lane to the President, Personal and Confidential Letter of October 6, 1915, Lane to the President, October 7, 1915, Woodrow Wilson to Attorney General, Personal and Confidential Letter of October 7, 1915, *ibid.*

90. Simon J. Lubin to T. B. [*sic*] Gregory, November 26, 1917, DJ File 150139–46; Report of Special Agent, December 7, 1915, in Assistant Attorney General William Wallace, Jr., to Hiram W. Johnson, Personal Letter of December 15, 1915, DJ File 150139–47.

Chapter III

Naturalization and a New Law, 1912–1917

1. *Ex parte Sauer*, 81 F. 355.

2. *In re Rodriguez*, 81 F. 237, 355.

3. *Whom We Shall Welcome*, Report of the President's Commission on Immigration and Naturalization (1953), 235–238; *The Immigration and Naturalization Systems of the United States*, Senate Report 1515, 81 Cong., 2 Sess. (1950), 695–696, 729–730, 769, 789–801. The color and racial bars went down in the following order: 1870, aliens of African nativity and persons of African descent; 1900, Hawaiians; 1917, Puerto Ricans; 1924, American Indians; 1927, inhabi-

tants of the Virgin Islands; 1940, races indigenous to North or South America; 1943, Chinese; 1946, people of India and the Philippines; 1952, no racial disqualifications. The two largest groups affected in 1952 were Japanese and Koreans. See also Konvitz, *Civil Rights*, 143–149.

4. Bureau of Naturalization, Radio Release no. II, October 16, 1922, DJ File 38–0, sec. 8.

5. U.S. Constitution, Art. I, sec. 8, cl. 4.

6. *Immigration and Naturalization Systems*, 675; John Palmer Gavit, *Americans by Choice* (New York, 1922), 73–74.

7. *Bureau of Immigration and Naturalization*, House Report 1789, 59 Cong., 1 Sess. (1905), 1–3; Gavit, 74–75. The act of 1795 was repealed by the act of 1798 but its basic provisions were re-enacted in the law of 1802. See also Sidney Kansas, *U.S. Immigration: Exclusion and Deportation and Citizenship of the United States of America* (Albany, 1940), 303.

8. Quoted in Miller, *Crisis in Freedom*, 47; and in Garis, *Immigration Restriction*, 29.

9. Solicitor to the Secretary of Commerce and Labor, June 6, 1912, DJ File 162150–10; Gavit, 75–83.

10. Quoted in Gavit, 78.

11. Quoted *ibid.*, 79–80.

12. *United States Statutes at Large*, XXXII, 1222; Garis, 108. Section 39 of the Immigration Act of 1903 prohibited the naturalization of those designated in section 38 for exclusion and deportation. An anarchist who survived for three years was, therefore, to be a perpetual noncitizen resident. He could neither be deported nor could he become naturalized, at least as long as he remained an anarchist. While there was no federal action before 1903, the supreme court of Baltimore apparently disqualified anarchist applicants as early as 1900. *Report to the President of the Commission on Naturalization*, House Document 46, 59 Cong., 1 Sess. (1905), app. C, 65–66.

13. Konvitz, 143; *Whom We Shall Welcome*, 236.

14. *Immigration and Naturalization Systems*, 675; *Bureau of Immigration and Naturalization*, 2–3; *Congressional Record*, 59 Cong., 1 Sess. (1905), 3640, 9807; Gavit, 80–83.

15. Sec. 4, subdiv. 2, par. 2, sec. 7, and sec. 27, Immigration Act of June 29, 1906, *United States Statutes at Large*, XXXIV, 597, 604.

16. Sec. 4, sub divs. 3, 4, *ibid.*, 597–598. Author's emphasis.

17. Sec. 4, subdiv. 4, *ibid.*, 598.

18. Brissenden, *I.W.W.*, 262.

19. Robert L. Tyler, "Rebels of the Woods and Fields: A Study of the I.W.W. in the Pacific Northwest" (unpublished Ph.D. dissertation, Department of History, University of Oregon, June 1953), 23, 34, 39, 47–49, 55.

20. Naturalization Examiner Henry B. Hazard to Chief Naturalization Examiner John Speed Smith, Report of June 28, 1913, IN File 53531/192A.

21. *Ibid.*

22. *In the Matter of the Impeachment of Cornelius H. Hanford, U.S. Circuit Judge, W. Dist. Washington,* House Report 1152, 62 Cong., 2 Sess. (1912), 142.

23. Hazard to Smith, Report of June 28, 1913, IN File 53531/192A.

24. IN Files 54379/114, /134, 54616/31, and 54709/473.

25. *Annual Report of the Secretary of Labor,* 1918, 20.

26. *Impeachment of Hanford,* 91, 93. Author's emphasis.

27. Decision of District Judge Hanford in *United States v. Leonard Olsson,* May 11, 1912, DJ File 162150-1.

28. Attorney General George W. Wickersham to U.S. Attorney, Seattle, June 3, 1912, DJ File 162150-2. See also Wickersham to Congressman William E. Humphrey, June 7, 1912, DJ File 162150-5.

29. Wickersham to U.S. Attorney W. G. McLaren, June 17, 1912, DJ File 162150-10.

30. Wickersham to Albert E. Joab, June 27, 1912, DJ File 162150-22; Wickersham to Humphrey, DJ File 162150-5.

31. Solicitor to Secretary of Commerce and Labor, June 6, 1912, DJ File 162150-10.

32. U.S. Attorney W. G. McLaren to the Attorney General, July 2, 1912, DJ File 162150-25½; U.S. Attorney B. W. Coiner to the Attorney General, October 1, 1913, DJ File 162150-33; U.S. Attorney Charles F. Riddell to the Attorney General, July 8, 1913, DJ File 162150-34.

33. Brissenden, 12.

34. J. Edgar Hoover to Frank Burke, February 21, 1920, DJ File 186701-14 between 82 and 83.

35. IN File 54235/85, *passim.*

36. Sec. 19, Immigration Act of February 5, 1917, *United States Statutes at Large,* XXXIX, 889; Anthony Caminetti to the Secretary of Labor, March 5, 1918, IN File 54235/36; *Congressional Record,* 64 Cong., 1 Sess. (1916), 4936-37; *ibid.,* 65 Cong., 2 Sess. (1918), 8117.

37. Higham, *Strangers in the Land,* 187-193, 202-204; Handlin, *American People,* 102-104. It was ironic that the large employers of labor, who detested radicalism and the I.W.W., were also opponents of the literacy test. They thus fought against the passage of an immigration bill that was designed to crush their radical opponents (Arthur S. Link, *Woodrow Wilson and The Progressive Era,* New York, 1954, 61). See also Garis, 123-125; Kansas, 10.

38. Higham, 66-67, 87-88, 137, 140-144, 172-173.

39. Albert Johnson's foreward in Garis, vii. Experience was later

to refute dogma. The I.W.W.'s arrested for deportation were overwhelmingly derived from the earlier migration; 70 per cent were Scandanavian, British, or Germanic, that is, of the "good" stock. Theory never had to withstand such factual assaults. The truth, however, was vaguely sensed in the Northwest's disillusionment after the war. People of that area talked disappointedly of how the Scandanavian immigrants who had joined the I.W.W. had not lived up to the high hopes envisioned for this stock. On attitudes toward the new immigration see Hartmann, *Movement to Americanize the Immigrant*, 14–23, and apps. A and B.

40. *Congressional Record*, 63 Cong., 3 Sess. (1915), 3028.

41. *Ibid.*, 64 Cong., 2 Sess. (1917), 2456. The arrival of the "educated blackhander" actually all but eliminated violence at Lawrence on the part of the workers and substituted passive resistance in the face of police, military, and civilian violence. What disturbed people was that the strikers were not respectably lawful or lawlessly riotous, both understandable, but instead peacefully anarchist. It was the I.W.W. inversion of ethics, not any reversion to bombs, that appalled America, but the debate was never cast in these terms. Cf. Brissenden, 286–288, 295.

42. *Congressional Record*, 64 Cong., 1 Sess. (1916), 4936; *ibid.*, 63 Cong., 2 Sess. (1914), 2895–96.

43. *Ibid.*, 63 Cong., 2 Sess. (1914), 2892.

44. *Ibid.*, 64 Cong., 1 Sess. (1916), 5166.

45. *Ibid.*, 63 Cong., 2 Sess. (1914), 2891–92; *ibid.*, 64 Cong., 1 Sess. (1916), 4936–37.

46. *Ibid.*, 64 Cong., 1 Sess. (1916), 4937. The southern white congressmen, including the indignant Burnett from Alabama, had apparently forgotten or preferred to ignore the degree to which the white citizens of their states used "anarchy, bloodshed, and murder" or the threat of them to deprive the Negro of his civil rights, his property, and his participation in the democratic process. Southern whites who condemned the alien anarchist used toward Negroes the very same tactics.

47. *Whom We Shall Welcome*, xii.

48. *Congressional Record*, 64 Cong., 2 Sess. (1916), 276, 313.

49. *Ibid.*, 64 Cong., 1 Sess. (1916), 4937.

50. *Ibid.*, 64 Cong., 2 Sess. (1916), 275.

51. *Ibid.*, 64 Cong., 1 Sess. (1916), 4936.

52. Ibid., 63 Cong., 2 Sess. (1914), 2892.

53. *Ibid.*, 63 Cong., 3 Sess. (1915), 3023–26.

54. *Ibid.*, 3068.

55. *Ibid.*, 64 Cong., 1 Sess., 1916, 4936. Author's emphasis. Congressman Gardner made the only objection. He felt that the militant suffragettes would still not be covered by the amendment.

56. Clark, *Deportation of Aliens*, 53; Garis, 112; *Whom We Shall Welcome*, 200.

57. *Congressional Record*, 63 Cong., 2 Sess. (1914), 2891–92, 2894. The House even doubted whether criminals should be deported, "because it is argued that those crimes may have been in consequence of conditions existing here" (*ibid.*, 2889).

58. *Ibid.*, 2890.

59. *Ibid.*, 2892. Author's emphasis.

60. Sec. 19, Immigration Act of February 5, 1917, *United States Statutes at Large*, XXXIX, 889; Clark, 55–56; Garis, 134–135; Kansas, 109–110.

61. *Congressional Record*, 64 Cong., 1 Sess. (1916), 5166–67.

62. Anthony Caminetti to the Secretary of Labor, Supplemental Memorandum of March 5, 1918, IN File 54235/36. Author's emphasis.

63. *Annual Report of the Secretary of Labor*, 1917, 126. It is interesting to compare this forecast with the retrospective observations of 1929. The *Annual Report* of that year said, "The immigration act of 1917 . . . is an impossible jumble, unintelligible, confusing and unreadable. Some of the paragraphs are so long, refer to so many subjects, and have so many provisos making exceptions as to what goes before that no human being can possibly know what they mean after reading them" (quoted in Clark, 54).

Chapter IV

Military Repression, 1917–1921

1. General Executive Board Statement on War, PA Files 39–240 and 41–628; John S. Gambs, *The Decline of the I.W.W.* (New York, 1932), 41–43. Sentence order changed.

2. Summaries of the progressive attitude toward war may be found in Goldman, *Rendezvous with Destiny*, 233–261, and in Link, *Woodrow Wilson and the Progressive Era*, 180–196.

3. Quoted in Bell, "Marxian Socialism," 313.

4. Ginger, *Bending Cross*, 329.

5. General Executive Board Statement on War, PA Files 39–240 and 41–638. See also the I.W.W. publication, *Pamphlet on War* (n.d.). According to *Solidarity*, April 21, 1917, "A slacker is not a slave who refuses to slit throats or get his hide perforated for the master class. A 'slacker' is one who is too cowardly or stupid to join with his fellow workers against the exploiters of Labor — one who neglects the interests of himself, his wife and family and of his class in order to make efficient profit or cannon fodder out of his worthless carcass."

6. *Industrial Worker*, February 10, 1917.

7. *Ibid.*, April 14, 1917.

8. Goldman, 243–253, 261.

9. Ginger, 341–343; Bell, 311–314.

10. American Civil Liberties Union Summary of Evidence against James Rowan, PA File 39–240 Bourg; Herbert Mahler to William D. Haywood, June 22, 1917, PA File 35–439 Mahler; Senator George W. Pepper, Memorandum of December 14, 1922, PA File 39–240; Don Sheridan to Harry Green, June 28, 1917, PA File 39–240 Sheridan; *Statement of Otto Christensen on the Chicago Case*, 25–26, PA File 39–240; Ralph Chaplin, *Wobbly: The Rough-and-Tumble Story of an American Radical* (Chicago, 1948), 206; PA File 41–638, *passim*.

11. J. A. MacDonald to S. R. Darnelly, April 12, 1917, PA File 39–240; *Solidarity*, May 5, 1917, and August 26, 1917.

12. MacDonald to Bert Kelley, May 25, 1917, PA File 39–240.

13. Herbert Mahler to Harry Lloyd, April 10, 1917; Mahler to Haywood, June 22, 1917, PA File 35–439 Mahler; MacDonald to Joseph P. Reagan, April 20, 1917, MacDonald to Kelley, May 25, 1917, MacDonald to Joseph Rawn, June 18, 1917, PA File 39–240; Don Sheridan to Harry Green, June 28, 1917, PA File, 39–240 Sheridan. Mahler wrote in June 1917 that had the I.W.W.'s not registered "the federals would likely have tried to prove conspiracy against registration by the I.W.W. and it might have caused us some trouble." This was exactly what happened later. Conspiracy against the draft was a major count in the indictments against the first-, second-, and third-string leadership.

14. Mahler to Haywood, June 22, 1917, PA File 35–439; Don Sheridan to Harry Green, June 28, 1917, PA File 39–240 Sheridan; U.S. Attorney Alfred Jacques to the Attorney General, January 15, 1918, DJ File 187415–35; Report of Lieutenant Colonel C. W. Thomas to the Inspector General, no date, AG File 085 I.W.W.; DJ File 186701–49, *passim; Transcript of the Wichita Trial (U.S. v. C. W. Anderson, et al.)*, 975–976, PA File 39–242; George W. Vanderveer to Frank P. Walsh, December 31, 1917, Walsh MSS.; *Solidarity*, June 16, 1917; Chaplin, 206.

15. Perlman and Taft, *Labor Movements*, 388; Brissenden, *I.W.W.*, 377, 340; Jamieson, *Labor Unionism in American Agriculture*, 399–401.

16. Paul S. Taylor, quoted in Jamieson, 399.

17. *Ibid.*, 401.

18. Brissenden, 338–339.

19. Jamieson, 402–403; Perlman and Taft, 387–388.

20. Gambs, 130–132; William D. Haywood to George P. West, September 6, 1916, DJ File 209264–Enclosures; IN Files 54182/2 and /2A, *passim*; Perlman and Taft, 388–390.

21. Enclosure regarding conference with I.W.W. leaders, Globe, Arizona, July 9, 1917, in U.S. Attorney Thomas Flynn to the Attorney

General, July 14, 1917 DJ File 186813–16; "Warren Copper District," in Arizona Copper Folder, DL File, Correspondence of War Labor Policies Board Chairman and Executive Secretary; Perlman and Taft, 398–399.

22. Meyer H. Fishbein, "The President's Mediation Commission and the Arizona Copper Strike, 1917," *Southwestern Social Science Quarterly*, XXX (December 1949), 176–177; Bureau of Investigation Report, April 24, 1918, DJ File 186813 following 59; Mediation Commission, "Summary of the Labor Situation in the Arizona Copper Districts," Arizona Copper Folder, DL File Correspondence of War Labor Policies Board.

23. Flynn to the Attorney General, July 14, 1917, DJ File 186813–16; Minutes of Governor's Conference with Citizen's Committee from Bisbee, July 23, 1917, in Flynn to the Attorney General, July 30, 1917, DJ File 186813–30; Industrial Peace League of Jerome to the President, August 28, 1917, DJ File 186813–45⅝; Congressman Joseph W. Fordney to T. W. Gregory, April 2, 1918, DJ File 186813–58½; Bureau of Investigation Report, April 24, 1918, DJ File 186813 following 59; Copy of Bill of Sale in Governor George Hunt to William C. Fitts, July 18, 1918, Fitts to Hunt, July 23, 1918, DJ File 186813-91; Fishbein, 177–79; Perlman and Taft, 399. Compare the beliefs of army officers of the Southern Department that German influence was behind the I.W.W. (AG Files 370.6 Arizona and 319.12 Southern Department), and the military intelligence reports cited in the manuscripts of Abraham Glasser dealing with the use of troops in the Arizona copper strike. These manuscripts are filed in the Justice Department section of the National Archives.

24. Commissioner of Conciliation Hywel Davies, "Survey of Copper Labor Conditions in Montana," July 3, 1918, DL File 33–1703, copy in DJ File Abraham Glasser.

25. *Ibid.*; Perlman and Taft, 401.

26. "Records of the President's Mediation Commission," DL File 20–473, *passim*; DL Files 33–438, –493, –574, –1730, copies in DJ File Abraham Glasser.

27. Report made by Agent E. W. Byrn, Jr., Butte, Montana, August 7, 1917, for August 4, 1917, Report made by Byrn, Butte, Montana, August 10, 1917, for August 8, 1917; U.S. Attorney Burton K. Wheeler to the Attorney General, August 21, 1917, DJ File 186701–27–15.

28. Senator Henry L. Myers to the Attorney General, August 3, 1917, C. H. McLeod, Kenneth Ross, Martin J. Hutchens, E. H. Polleys, J. O. Newcomb to Senator Myers, August 2, 1917, Copy of Telegram, DJ File 186701–27–1; Montana Bankers' Association to Woodrow Wilson, July 30, 1917, DJ File 186701–27–4; Myers to Fitts, August 10, 1917, DJ File 186701–27–8.

29. Myers to Fitts, August 10, 1917, DJ File 186701–27–8; Wheeler

to the Attorney General, August 1, 1917, DJ File 186701–54–1; Special Agent in Charge F. W. Kelly to Director William J. Flynn, Bureau of Investigation, January 14, 1921, DJ File 186701–54–11; Myers to the Attorney General, August 3, 1917, DJ File 186701–27–1.

30. Tyler, "Rebels of the Woods and Fields," 143.

31. District Forester F. A. Silcox, "Labor Unrest in the Lumber Industry — Northern Idaho and Western Montana," 1, DL File 20–473, copy in DJ File Abraham Glasser.

32. L. A. Nelson and Stanton Smith, "Confidential Report on Spruce Production in the Northwest, May 2, 1918," 45, in Chief Forester H. L. Graves to the Secretary of Agriculture, May 11, 1918, Department of Agriculture File, Correspondence of the Secretary of Agriculture, 1918.

33. Silcox, "Labor Unrest," 2; Similar descriptions of living and working conditions and the attitude of employers may also be found in M. H. Wolff, "Woods Labor Situation, Coeur d'Alene Region, Idaho," in Acting District Forester R. H. Rutledge by F. A. Fenn to Silcox, March 2, 1918, Forest Service Research Compilation Records, Nelson and Smith, "Confidential Report on Spruce Production in the Northwest", F. A. Fitzwater, Forest Supervisor, Sandpoint, Idaho, to District Forester, Missoula, Montana, November 17, 1917, R. P. Mc-Laughlin, Forest Supervisor, Kalispell, Montana, to District Forester, Missoula, Montana, November 20, 1917, Rosco Haines, Forest Supervisor, St. Maries, Idaho, to District Forester, Missoula, Montana, December 1, 1917, DL File 20–473, copies in DJ File Abraham Glasser; Valentine H. May, "History of the Lumber Industry on the Pacific Coast, Spring 1917 to August 1918," DL File 20–473.

34. F. A. Fitzwater to District Forester, November 17, 1917, DL File 20–473, copy in DJ File Abraham Glasser; see also Silcox, "Labor Unrest," 2; Wolff, "Woods Labor Situation," 18–23; May, "History of the Lumber Industry," 1; Tyler, 81; Perlman and Taft, 392–393.

35. Tyler, 56–71; Perlman and Taft, 390–392.

36. Tyler, 79.

37. May, "History of the Lumber Industry," 1–2; Silcox, "Labor Unrest," 2; Nelson and Smith, "Confidential Report on Spruce Production in the Northwest," 40–41; Wolff, "Woods Labor Situation." 1–16, 18–22; *Forest Service District One, Semi-Annual Report, May 1917, Missoula, Montana*, 7–9, Forest Service Records, Division of Operations, Reports District One, 1917.

38. May, "History of the Lumber Industry," 1; Tyler, 81–85; DL File 33–578, *passim*, copy in DJ File Abraham Glasser.

39. Congressman Burton L. French to the Attorney General, July 3, 1917, DJ File 186701–13–1; U.S. Attorney Francis A. Garrecht to the Attorney General, June 19, 1917, DJ File 186701–49–1; Western Red Cedar Association to Congressman Addison T. Smith, July 3,

1917, Copy of Telegram, DJ File 186701–49–4; U.S. Attorney Clay Allen to the Attorney General, July 6, 1917, DJ File 186701–49–6; Charles Warren to the Attorney General, July 26, 1917, DJ File 186701–38–5; Major Charles R. Sligh, Office of Chief Signal Officer, War Department, to Department of Justice, October 1, 1917, DJ File 186701–38–27; DL File 33–574, *passim*, copy in DJ File Abraham Glasser; Tyler, 86–88; Perlman and Taft, 394–395.

40. May, "History of the Lumber Industry," 2; Retail Dealers Protective Association Form Letter, October 8, 1917, DL File 33–574A, copy in DJ File Abraham Glasser; Perlman and Taft, 395.

41. Wolff, "Woods Labor Situation," 22–23, 33–34; Silcox, "Labor Unrest," 2–3; *Forest Service District One, Semi-Annual Report, November 1917*, 1–3, Forest Service Records, Division of Operations, Reports District One, 1917; Tyler, 93–94; Perlman and Taft, 394–395.

42. Report of Special Agent F. A. Watt, Spokane, May 31, 1917, for May 29, 1917, DJ File 186701–49–1; U.S. Attorney Clarence L. Reames to the Attorney General, July 26, 1917, DJ File 186701–38–18; Burton L. French to Attorney General Gregory, August 6, 1917, DJ File 186701–13–10; U.S. Attorney Clay Allen to the Attorney General, July 6, 1917, DJ File 186701–49–6; Spokane Chamber of Commerce to Senator Wesley L. Jones, June 30, 1917, DJ File 186701–49–2. See also DJ Files 186701–5, –13, –24, –27, –38, –49, *passim*; DL File 33–574, copy in DJ File Abraham Glasser.

43. Higham, *Strangers in the Land*, 195–197, 204–209, 218–219.

44. Gregory to Charles Warren, Memorandum of July 11, 1917, DJ File 186701–1; Warren to A. B. Bielaski, Memorandum of July 12, 1917, DJ File 186701 before 1; Gregory to all U.S. Attorneys, Circular of July 17, 1917, DJ File 186701–2; William C. Fitts to Senator Henry Myers, August 11, 1917, DJ File 186701–27–8; Gregory to Burton K. Wheeler, August 25, 1917, DJ File 186701–27–15; Gregory to Jones, July 5, 1917, DJ File 186701–49–2; Warren to Clay Allen, July 13, 1917; Warren to Carl Hayden, July 11, 1917, DJ File 186713–2.

45. Sheriff J. J. Campbell to U.S. Attorney J. H. McClear, June 29, 1917, McClear to the Attorney General, July 3, 1917, DJ File 186701–13–2; Alfred H. Henry to Jones, July 24, 1917, IN File 53531/192. Also DJ Files 186701–13, –27, –38, and –49, *passim*.

46. Inspector Brown McDonald to the Commissioner of Immigration, Montreal, July 18, 1917, IN File 54182/2A.

47. John Lind to Gregory, July 26, 1917, DJ File 186701–24–2.

48. Inspector W. J. McConnell to the Commissioner General, July 25, 1917, McConnell to William B. Wilson, August 10, 1917, Frank L. Moore, Prosecuting Attorney, Latah County, to McConnell, August 25, 1917, IN Files 53531/192 and /192A; John H. Sargent to the Commissioner General, August 11, 1917, IN File 54297/31; Congressman

Burton L. French to Gregory, August 6, 1917, DJ File 186701–13–9. Also DJ Files 186701–38–23, 186701–13, and 186701–49, and IN File 53531/192, *passim*. It is worth noting here that later mass round-ups of I.W.W.'s and Communists took place during a slack winter season and a period of postwar unemployment when labor was not scarce and industry was under no pressure to compromise.

49. McConnell to the Commissioner General, August 17, 1917, IN File 53531/192.

50. McConnell to William B. Wilson, August 10, 1917, *ibid.*; McConnell to the Commissioner of Immigration, Seattle, December 2, 1917, IN File 54235/43. There are also various expressions of public attitude in IN Files 53531/192, /192A, and 54235/43.

51. Anthony Caminetti to the Assistant Secretary of Labor, July 25, 1917, IN File 53531/192.

52. Louis F. Post to William B. Wilson, July 27, 1917, Caminetti to the Inspector in Charge, Chicago, August 8, 1917, *ibid.*

53. Caminetti to the Assistant Secretary, August 28, 1917, *ibid.* Author's emphasis.

54. *Ibid.*

55. *Annual Report of the Secretary of Labor*, 1918, 10–21. See also DL File 20/473, *passim*.

56. John Sargent to the Immigration Bureau, September 24, 1917, Caminetti to the Immigration Bureau, Seattle, September 27, 1917, IN File 53531/192A; A Warner Parker to the Commissioner of Immigration, Montreal, October 3, 1917, IN File 54182/2A.

57. McConnell to the Commissioner of Immigration, Seattle, October 3, 1917, IN File 54235/43. See also later complaints in DJ Files 186701–49 and 190159.

58. IN Files 53531/192, /192A, 54182/2A, 54235/43, and /85; also Tyler, 25

59. By section III of the National Defense Act of June 3, 1916.

60. Article IV, sec. 4, states: "The United States shall guarantee to every State in this Union a Republican Form of Government, and shall protect each of them against Invasion; and on Application of the Legislature, or of the Executive (when the Legislature cannot be convened) against domestic Violence."

61. "Supplement to Federal Aid in Domestic Disturbances," 22–23, Appendix F, 1–2, in Acting Judge Advocate General J. A. Hull to Adjutant General Robert C. Davis, September 26, 1922, AG File 370.6. It must be noted that, while under this constitutional limitation troops may not be *used* until the President's proclamation is published and violated, they may be *ordered to the scene* of the disorder for the moral effect of their presence. Nor do the legal procedures apply in cases of sudden and extreme cases of riot or disaster when commanding officers must take action without waiting for formal applications to the President (*ibid.*, 4, 18, and E. A. Kreger, Acting Judge Advocate

General to the Chief of Staff, January 6, 1921 [secret], 1–4, *ibid.*).

62. DJ Files 186701–27–14, –15, –17, and –20, and 186701–49–20.

63. U.S. Attorney Clay Allen to the Attorney General, July 6, 1917, DJ File 186701–49–6.

64. DJ Files 186701–22, –24, –27, –37, –38, –49, secs. I–III, 186813, secs. I and II, 195397, secs. I and II.

65. U.S. Attorney Francis A. Garrecht to the Attorney General, June 19, 1917, Report of Special Agent F. A. Watt, Spokane, May 31, 1917, for May 29, 1917, DJ File 186701–49–1; Spokane Chamber of Commerce to Senator Wesley L. Jones, June 30, 1917, DJ File 186701–49–2.

66. Adjutant General H. P. McCain to Commanding Generals, All Departments, March 21, 1917, AG File 2560557; AG File 2529745, *passim.*

67. General Bell, Commanding General, Western Department, to the Adjutant General, April 21, 1917, AG File 2581689, filed with AG File 2529745.

68. Newton D. Baker to Woodrow Wilson, March 28, 1917, Woodrow Wilson to Baker, March 28, 1917, Baker MSS.

69. Governor Ernest Lister to Baker, June 3, 1917, Adjutant General H. P. McCain to Commanding General, Western Department, July 3, 1917, AG File 370.6; Report of Lieutenant Colonel C. W. Thomas, Jr., to the Inspector General, AG File 085 I.W.W. (hereafter cited as Thomas Report); AG File 2529745, *passim*; DJ File 195397, *passim.*

70. William B. Wilson to Baker, May 31, 1917, AG File 2611874, filed with AG File 2529745; Thomas W. Gregory to U.S. Attorney Francis A. Garrecht, Spokane, July 24, 1917, DJ File 186701–49–13; Inspector General Chamberlain to Adjutant General, October 2, 1917, AG File 085 I.W.W.

71. County Attorney T. H. MacDonald to Gregory, August 21, 1917, DJ File 186701–27–14.

72. Sheriff Bert McManus, Chelan County, to Colonel C. E. Dentler, July 22, 1917, General Whitney to Dentler, July 18, 1917 (Exhibit B, Thomas Report), Captain H. M. Jones to Dentler, Portland, Oregon, July 14, 1917 (Exhibit C, Thomas Report), AG File 085 I.W.W.; Dentler to Major General H. Liggett, August 10, 1917, AG File 370.6 See also DJ File 189401.

73. Jones to Dentler, July 14, 1917 (Exhibit C, Thomas Report), and Thomas Report, *passim*, AG File 085 I.W.W.

74. U.S. Attorney Francis A. Garrecht to the Attorney General, July 14, 1917, DJ File 186701–49–10.

75. Thomas Report, *passim*, AG File 085 I.W.W.

76. Garrecht to the Attorney General, July 14, 1917, DJ File 186701–49–10.

77. Chafee, *Free Speech in the United States*, 151.

78. Thomas Report, 2–3.

79. Governor Ernest Lister to Dentler, August 22, 1917, Garrecht to Major Clement Wilkins, August 20, 1917 (Exhibit B, Thomas Report), and see Thomas Report, 5–6, AG File 085 I.W.W.

80. Adjutant General H. P. McCain to Commanding General, Southern Department, July 2 and 5, 1917, Major General James Parker to Adjutant General, August 19, 1917, AG File 370.6, in DJ File Abraham Glasser; Colonel George P. White to Commanding General, Southern Department, September 4 and 6, 1917, AG File 370.6.

81. McCain to Parker, July 15, 1917, AG File 370.6, in DJ File Abraham Glasser.

82. White to Commanding General, Southern Department, September 4, 1917, AG File 370.6; McCain to Commanding General, Southern Department, July 12, 1917, AG File 370.6, in DJ File Abraham Glasser.

83. White to Commanding General, Southern Department, September 4, 1917, AG File 370.6; U.S. Attorney Thomas Flynn to the Attorney General, July 14, 1917, DJ File 186813–16; Lieutenant J. E. Lewis, Commanding Officer, Ray, Arizona, to Commanding Officer, Arizona District, September 3, 1917, AG File 370.6, in DJ File Abraham Glasser.

84. McCain to Commanding General Southern Department, July 21, 1917, AG File 370.6; Major General Cabell to Adjutant General, September 26, 1918, Department Adjutant, Southern Department, to Commanding General, Arizona District, February 15, 1919, AG File 370.6, in DJ File Abraham Glasser.

85. Cabell to Commanding General, Southern Department, February 22, 1918, DJ File 186813 after –59; Governor George Hunt to Newton D. Baker, February 9, 1918, Acting Secretary of War Benedict Crowell to Hunt, March 5, 1918, AG File 370.6; Major General John W. Ruckman to Adjutant General, April 23, 1918, DJ File 186813-Enclosures; DJ File Abraham Glasser, *passim*.

86. Major General James Parker to Adjutant General, August 19, 1917, AG File 370.6, in DJ File Abraham Glasser. See also Governor Hunt to William B. Wilson, August 2, 1917, and William B. Wilson to Baker, August 30, 1917, Arizona Copper Folder, DL File, Correspondence of War Labor Policies Board Chairman and Executive Secretary.

87. Annual Report, Southern Department, 1917–18, AG File 319.12 Southern Department; Ruckman to Adjutant General, April 23, 1918, DJ File 186813 Enclosures; Captain E. N. Hardy to Cabell, February 19, 1918, Cabell to Commanding General, Southern Department, February 22, 1918, DJ File 186813 after 59.

88. Major General J. T. Dickman to Adjutant General, January 17

and 23, 1920, Intelligence Officer, Southern Department, to Director, Military Intelligence, November 20, 1919, quoted in DJ File Abraham Glasser; Brigadier General Henry Jervey to the Chief of Staff, January 23, 1920, Chief of Staff File 580, U.S. Guards, 120; Annual Report, Southern Department, 1919–20, AG File 319.12.

89. DJ Files 186701–27, 186701–54, 195397, and Abraham Glasser; AG File 370.6, Montana; Chief of Staff File 1000, Montana.

90. Report of Colonel Thomas J. Lewis, Inspector General, to Commanding General, Western Department, October 16, 1918, Appendices F and G, Chief of Staff File 1000, Montana (hereafter cited as Lewis Report). See also DJ Files 186701–27 and 195397, *passim*.

91. John Lord O'Brian to the Attorney General, February 27, 1918, and March 29, 1918, DJ File 189730–2 (9–19–1707); DJ File 27x56–1 between 4 and 5 and 16 and 17; DJ File 195397. The War Plans Division and the Military Intelligence thought that Judge Bourquin should be impeached (Colonel D. W. Ketcham to the Chief of Staff, May 1, 1918, Chief of Staff File 1000, Montana).

92. Statements of Eugene Carroll, A. R. Currie, and W. A. Clark, in Lewis Report, Chief of Staff File 1000, Montana. Author's emphasis.

93. Governor S. V. Stewart to Commanding General, Western Department, March 16, 1918, Colonel H. C. Benson to Commanding Officer, Butte, March 16, 1918, Major General Arthur Murray to Adjutant General, March 16, 1918, AG File 370.6

94. Captain Omar N. Bradley to Commanding General, Western Department, March 19, 1918, *ibid.*

95. Acting Judge Advocate General S. T. Ansell to the Chief of Staff, April 10 and 11, 1918, *ibid.;* Brigadier General Lytle Brown, Director, War Plans Division, Acting Chief of Staff to the Chief of Staff, May 6, 1918, Chief of Staff File 1000, Montana.

96. DJ File Abraham Glasser, *passim;* DJ Files 186838, 189738, and 195397.

97. The special agent of the Bureau of Investigation and United States Attorney Wheeler discovered and reported the existence of these company provocateurs. There is a possibility, which is impossible to corroborate, that these informers were also working for army intelligence (DJ Files Abraham Glasser, 186828, 189738, and 195397; *Helena Independent*, September 29, 1918).

98. E. W. Byrn to A. B. Bielaski, September 15, 1918, DJ File 195397–1.

99. *Ibid.* Also U.S. Attorney Wheeler to Thomas W. Gregory, September 16, 1918, DJ File 195397–2.

100. Lewis Report, Chief of Staff File 1000, Montana; John Lord O'Brien to Provost Marshal General E. H. Crowder, September 24, 1918, DJ File 195397–4.

101. Lewis Report, Chief of Staff File 1000, Montana; DJ Files 195397 and Abraham Glasser.

102. Gregory to the Secretary of War, October 23, 1918, DJ Files 195397-7, -8; also DJ File Abraham Glasser, *passim.*

103. Newton D. Baker to the Attorney General, October 14, 1918, DJ File 195397-7; Baker to the Attorney General, November 5, 1918, Chief of Staff File 1000, Montana. This letter was prepared but not sent, "in view of changed conditions due to armistice."

104. Report of the Department Intelligence Officer to Commanding General, Western Department, 1919, with Exhibits A and B, Report of the Assistant Chief of Staff for Millitary Intelligence to the Chief of Staff, Western Department, 1920, AG File 319.12 Western Department; Annual Reports, Southern Department, 1918, 1919, and 1920, AG File 319.12 Southern Department; DJ File Abraham Glasser; Gregory to the Secretary of War, October 23, 1918, DJ Files 195397-7, -8; DJ File 189891.

105. "Supplement to Federal Aid in Domestic Disturbances," 22, in Acting Judge Advocate General J. A. Hull to Adjutant General Robert C. Davis, September 26, 1922, AG File 370.6.

106. Baker to the Chief of Staff, December 2, 1920, *ibid.*

107. Report of George L. Bell, Executive Officer, California State Commission of Immigration and Housing, July 19, 1917, DL File 20/77.

Chapter V
The Day in Court, 1917–1920

1. Chaplin, *Wobbly*, 214–215. Not all this was federal surveillance. Volunteer patriots attended meetings and caused the arrests of suspected disloyal individuals. Because of a personnel shortage the Chicago office of the Bureau of Investigation had "a vast bulk of the work . . . done by volunteer agents and fourteen members of the Chicago Police Department." (Hinton G. Clabaugh to A. B. Bielaski, August 18, 1917, DJ File 186233–176.).

2. Oliver E. Pagan to William C. Fitts, August 6, 1917, DJ File 186233–72–23; Frank C. Dailey to the Attorney General, August 24, 1917, U.S. Attorney Clyne to Fitts, August 29, 1917, Thomas W. Gregory to Clyne, August 30, 1917, DJ File 188032, *passim; Transcript of the Wichita Trial*, 971, PA File 39–242; Chaplin, 220–228.

3. Indictments in *U.S. v. W.D. Haywood, et al., U.S. v. C. W. Anderson, et al.,* and *U.S. v. Edw. Anderson, et al.,* DJ Files 188032, 189152, 186701–57, and 188561, Enclosures.

4. *Ibid.*

5. Frank K. Nebeker, Memorandum of July 21, 1921, in Attorney General Harry M. Daugherty to Warren G. Harding, October 31, 1921, PA File 35–362, Box 53.

6. *U.S. v. W. D. Haywood, et al., U.S. v. C. W. Anderson, et al.,* and *U. S. v. Edw. Anderson, et al.,* DJ Files 188032, 189152, 186701–57, and 188561, Enclosures. Also PA Files 39–240, –241, and –242, *passim.*

7. Frank K. Nebeker to the Attorney General, December 4, 1917, DJ File 188032–81. See also William C. Fitts, "Statement of I.W.W. Aims," DJ File 188032–186½.

8. Assistant Attorney General to Frank C. Dailey, August 24, 1917, DJ File 186701–14–26.

9. U.S. Attorney Clarence Reames to the Attorney General, October 19, 1918, DJ File 186701–49–119; U.S. Attorney Robert O'Connor to the Attorney General, December 5, 1917, DJ File 188561–3. Also DJ Files 186701–28, –57, and 188561.

10. G. Louis Joughin and Edmund M. Morgan, *The Legacy of Sacco and Vanzetti* (New York, 1948), 204–205.

11. Gregory to Reames, October 4, 1918, DJ File 186701–49–112.

12. Fitts to U.S. Attorney Fred Robertson, January 21, 1918, DJ File 189152–18.

13. See Chapter IV at note 63.

14. R. H. Downman, Chairman, Lumber Committee, to W. S. Gifford, June 11, 1917, J. C. H. Reynolds, Secretary-Manager, Employers Association of the Inland Empire, to E. T. Allen, Western Forestry and Conservation Association, May 29, 1917, DJ File 186701–49x.

15. William Herron, Memorandum of June 12, 1917, *ibid.* See also Assistant Attorney General Samuel J. Graham to Clay Allen, July 7, 1917, DJ File 186233–107–2.

16. Gregory to Charles Warren, July 11, 1917, DJ File 186701–1; Gregory to all U.S. Attorneys, Circular Letter of July 17, 1917, DJ File 186701–2.

17. A. B. Bielaski to Charles Warren, April 1, 1917, DJ File 190470; Special Agent Ralph Izard, Milwaukee, to Bielaski, January 8, 1918, DJ File 188032, Special Confidential Section; U.S. Attorney Harry B. Tedrow to the Attorney General, October 22, 1917, DJ File 186701–5–26; U.S. Attorney Thomas Flynn to the Attorney General, August 1, 1917, DJ File 186813–34; U.S. Attorney W. P. McGinnis to the Attorney General, March 27, 1918, DJ File 186701–37–17; DJ File 188044, *passim.*

18. Governor Emmet Boyle (Nevada) to Woodrow Wilson, July 13, 1917, DJ File 186813–13. See also Governor Thomas E. Campbell (Arizona) to Woodrow Wilson, July 15, 1917, *ibid.*

19. Report of George L. Bell, July 19, 1917, DL File 20–77. See also Simon Lubin to Woodrow Wilson, March 29, 1918, Wilson MSS.

20. Supplementary Report of Bell, July 19, 1917, 7, DL File 20-77.

21. *Ibid.,* 5–7

22. *Ibid.*, 5–11. The report cited one example of an act for which the state governments could not obtain evidence. The I.W.W.'s were said to burn haystacks in California with phosphorous fireballs. After being thrown into combustible materials, these fireballs burst into flames spontaneously much later and long after the incendiary was far away.

23. Report of Bell, July 19, 1917, Supplementary Report of Bell, 11, DL File 20–77.

24. Lubin to Woodrow Wilson, March 29, 1918, Wilson to Lubin, April 12, 1918, Wilson MSS.; George L. Bell, "Additional Confidential Memorandum Regarding Western I.W.W. Situation," undated, Fragmentary Records of the President's Mediation Commission, DL File 20–473.

25. John Lind to Gregory (Telegram), July 26, 1917, DJ File 186701–24–1.

26. *Ibid.* Also Lind to the Attorney General, July 10, 1917, DJ File 186233–118–5. Author's emphasis.

27. Lind to Gregory (Letter), July 26, 1917, DJ File 186701–24–2; William C. Fitts to Lind, August 24, 1918, DJ File 188032–291. For other evidence of Lind's contribution see Oliver E. Pagan to Fitts, August 6, 1917, DJ File 186233–72–23; and Lind to Fitts, October 2, 1917, DJ File 188032–20; DJ Files 186701, –14, –24, and 188032, *passim.*

28. Woodrow Wilson to Roland Robbins (Keith Theater), August 26, 1919, Wilson MSS.

29. Wilson to Alfred S. Burleson, September 14, 1917, Burleson MSS. See also Wilson to Burleson, February 28, 1919, *ibid.*

30. Joseph P. Tumulty to George L. Bell, July 20, 1917, Woodrow Wilson to Gregory, October 1, 1918, and October 4, 1918, Wilson to Burleson, October 18, 1917 and October 30, 1917, Wilson to Herbert Croly, October 22, 1917, Wilson MSS.; DJ Files 185354, 186701–59, and 192980; Josephus Daniels, *The Wilson Era, 1917–1923* (Chapel Hall, 1946), 230–231. For the same policy in regard to the amnesty of the so-called political prisoners, see Wilson to Tumulty, June 28, 1919, and A. Mitchell Palmer to Wilson, July 30, 1919, Wilson MSS.; DJ Files 197009 and 197009–1.

31. Wilson to Samuel Gompers, August 31, 1917, Gompers to Wilson, August 10, 1917, Wilson MSS.; Wilson to Newton D. Baker, August 29, 1917, Baker to Wilson, September 1, 1917, Felix Frankfurter to Baker, Memorandum of September 4, 1917, Baker MSS.

32. Gregory to Gompers (Personal), December 7, 1917, DJ File 190470; A. B. Bielaski to Gregory, November 29, 1917, Bielaski to Gregory, December 6, 1917, Gregory to Bielaski, December 21, 1917, DJ File 186701 after 89; Ralph M. Easley to William C. Fitts, January 8, 1918, DJ File 188032–1–2.

33. Wilson to William Kent, July 17, 1917, Wilson MSS. See also Daniels, 37 and 364.

34. Wilson to Arthur Brisbane, April 25, 1917, Wilson MSS. Equally mystifying was the line Wilson drew between free speech and sedition. He accepted "the advocacy of political change, however fundamental," but condemned "passion and malevolence tending to incite crime and insurrection under guise of political evolution." Wilson never explained how juries were to differentiate the two in times of public excitement. The President also stated that "the seed of revolution is repression" (Quoted in Chafee, *Free Speech in the United States*, 188).

35. Roger N. Baldwin to Joseph P. Tumulty, January 31, 1918, Wilson MSS.; Baldwin to Baker, February 27, 1918, ACLU XXVII; Baldwin to Jane Addams, May 31, 1918, *ibid.*, LXXXVII; Baldwin, "The Fight for Civil Liberties during the War," *ibid.*, CVII; George F. Vanderveer to Baker, February 6, 1918, Vanderveer to Baldwin, February 6, 1918, *ibid.*, XXVII; Vanderveer to Frank P. Walsh, December 31, 1917, Walsh MSS.; E. F. Doree to Baldwin, January 31, 1918, ACLU, XXVII.

36. Colonel Edward House to Baldwin, February 17, 1918, and February 19, 1918, ACLU, XXVI.

37. Woodrow Wilson to Simon Lubin, April 12, 1918, Wilson MSS.

38. Woodrow Wilson to Thomas W. Gregory, April 13, 1918, DJ File 186701–227x.

39. U.S. Attorney W. P. McGinnis to the Attorney General, December 5, 1917, DJ File 186701–37–14.

40. S. B. Amidon to R. P. Stewart, September 25, 1919, DJ File 189152–135. See also DJ File 189152, *passim.*

41. U.S. Attorney Fred Robertson to the Attorney General, November 22, 1917, DJ File 189152–¼

42. Claude R. Porter to Gregory, September 7, 1918, DJ File 189152–36½. Also Fred Robertson to the Attorney General, December 11, 1917, DJ File 189152–1. Author's emphasis.

43. *Ibid.*

44. J. F. Fishman, Inspector of Prisons, to the Attorney General, April 5, 1919, DJ File 196609–4.

45. Porter to Gregory, September 7, 1918, DJ File 189152–36½.

46. Robert T. Scott to Assistant Attorney General R. P. Stewart, August 28, 1919, DJ File 189152 between 111 and 112. The district judge did not formally quash one indictment until a new grand jury had reindicted the defendants, who were, thus, always in custody. (Robertson to the Attorney General, June 12, 1919, DJ File 189152–104).

47. DJ File 189152, *passim*, and S. B. Amidon to A. Mitchell Palmer, December 19, 1919, DJ File 189152–162.

48. U.S. Attorney Robert O'Connor to the Attorney General, December 5, 1917, DJ File 188561–3; Report of Agent Edward P. Morse, San Francisco, November 14, 1922, for November 1–14, 1922, 5–6, in U.S. Attorney John T. Williams to James A. Finch, November 17, 1922, PA File 39–241 (hereafter cited as Morse Report).

49. O'Connor to the Attorney General, December 5, 1918, DJ File 188561–3.

50. O'Connor to the Attorney General, November 12, 1918, DJ File 188561–15.

51. Mowry, *California Progressives* 262; Fremont Older, *My Own Story* (New York, 1926), 333–338.

52. U.S. Attorney John W. Preston to the Attorney General, October 15, 1917, DJ File 185354–48½.

53. Quoted in Mowry, 253.

54. *Report of John B. Densmore*, House Document 157, 66 Cong., 1 Sess. (1919) Pt. 1, p. 10 (hereafter cited as *Densmore Report*). See also Walton Bean, *Boss Ruef's San Francisco* (Berkeley, 1952), 308.

55. Older, 197–204; Bean, 308.

56. *Densmore Report, passim;* U.S. Attorney John W. Preston to Thomas W. Gregory, August 23, 1917, Gregory to Preston, August 24, 1917, DJ File 186701–5–14; DJ File 188044, *passim*.

57. Frederick W. Henshaw to Preston, August 23, 1917, Preston to the Attorney General, August 29, 1917, DJ File 188044–1; DJ Files 186701–5, –57, 188032, and 188044, *passim*.

58. Special Agent Don Rathburn to Gregory, January 31, 1918, DJ File 185354–69.

59. *Ibid.*

60. Preston to the Attorney General, January 24, 1918, DJ File 186701–5–33; Governor William D. Stephens to Gregory, December 28, 1917, DJ File 186701–57–1; Senator Hiram W. Johnson to the Department of Justice, December 29, 1917, DJ File 186701–57–2.

61. Stephens to Gregory, December 28, 1917, DJ File 186701–57–1.

62. Quoted in Johnson to the Department of Justice, December 29, 1917, DJ File 186701–57–2. *Bee* editorials urged citizens to drown I.W.W.'s in the rivers if state and federal authorities did not provide sufficient protection against them. (*Sacramento Bee*, March 16, 1918).

63. Quoted in Johnson to Department of Justice, December 29, 1917, DJ File 186701–57–2; John W. Preston to the Attorney General, January 24, 1918, DJ File 186701–5–33.

64. *Ibid.* Also William Fitts to Preston, February 1, 1918, DJ File 186701–5–33; Fitts to Johnson, December 29, 1917, Gregory to Stephens, December 29, 1917, Stephens to Gregory, December 30, 1917, DJ File 186701–57–2–3 and –5. Fifty-five I.W.W.'s were indicted (Preston to the Attorney General, February 9, 1918, DJ File 186701–57–12).

65. U.S. Marshal J. B. Holohan to the Attorney General, January 5, 1918, DJ File 186701–57–12.

66. DJ File 186701–57, *passim*.

67. *Densmore Report*, 9–17, 21–25, 28, 32–43, 53–60, 64, 73, 75.

68. *Ibid.* Also DJ Files 186701–57, 186701–59, and 185354; PA File 39–241, *passim*.

69. John W. Preston to the Attorney General, February 9, 1918, DJ File 186701–57–25. The Department of Justice had evidence that it never used. It too had planted a dictaphone — in the Sacramento jail, where special agents monitored I.W.W. conversations that substantiated the Coutts-Dymond testimony. The government felt the latter's evidence amply covered the incidents and avoided the dictaphone material because of the Densmore publicity (Report of Special Agent F. W. Kelly, n.d., DJ File 186701–57–175x; Report of Kelly, San Francisco, December 13, 1919, for December 12, 1919, DJ File 206462–1.

70. U.S. Attorney T. S. Allen to the Attorney General, January 8, 1918, Allen to the Attorney General, June 28, 1918, DJ File 186701–28–3 and 7.

71. DJ Files 186701–17, –28, –57, 188032, 188561, and 189152, *passim*. In the Omaha case see William C. Fitts to Allen, January 12, 1918, and April 30, 1918, DJ File 186701–28–3 and –6.

72. Allen to the Attorney General, April 10, 1919, DJ File 186701–28–23.

73. Allen to the Attorney General, June 29, 1918, Fitts to Allen, July 3, 1918, DJ File 186701–28–7.

74. Allen to the Attorney General, August 9, 1918, DJ File 186701–28–8.

75. Allen to the Attorney General, September 7, 1918, DJ File 186701–28–12. Also Allen to the Attorney General, August 9, 1918, DJ File 186701–28–8.

76. Allen to the Attorney General, April 10, 1919, DJ File 186701–28–23.

77. *Ibid.*

78. Gambs, *Decline of the I.W.W.*, 130–132; William D. Haywood to George P. West, September 6, 1916, DJ File 209264–Enclosures.

79. U.S. Attorney Alfred Jaques to the Attorney General, January 15, 1918, DJ File 187415–35. See also DJ File 186233–118, *passim*.

80. John Lind to the Attorney General, July 10, 1917, DJ File 186233–118–5.

81. Jacques to the Attorney General, July 16, 1917, DJ File 186233–118–7; Jacques to the Attorney General, January 15, 1918, DJ File 187415–35.

82. Assistant U.S. Attorney, Salt Lake City, to the Attorney General, March 10, 1919, DJ File 187415–434.

83. Assistant U.S. Attorney John H. Langston to the Attorney

General, March 24, 1919, and March 25, 1919, DJ File 187415–482 and –486. The case against one agitator rested on his having said, "Why fight for democracy when there is none at home?" and "The opponents of labor were the ones behind conscription."

84. U.S. Attorney Charles P. Williams to the Attorney General, July 30, 1918, DJ File 9–16–12–2664–23.

85. U.S. Attorney Clay Allen to the Attorney General, June 27, 1917, DJ File 186233–107-2. This group of defendants charged that they had had an unfair trial because the jury had no individuals on it who believed in the principles of the accused. The district attorney agreed. The defendants were "dangerous socialists against every principle of the war policy of the administration," he wrote. "I would not permit a man entertaining such ideas to be upon the jury" (U.S. Attorney Clarence Reames to the Attorney General, May 10, 1918, DJ File 186233–107-18). See also C. B. Blethen, Editor, *Seattle Times,* to the Attorney General, November 12, 1919, DJ File 186701–74-1; U.S. Attorney Robert C. Saunders to the Attorney General, December 4, 1919, DJ File 186701–74-70; Decision of District Judge Jeremiah Neterer, DJ File 186701–74-90; Saunders to the Attorney General, March 8, 1920, DJ File 186701–74-95.

86. Joughin and Morgan, 219.

87. Alfred Bettman to Claude R. Porter, May 12, 1919, DJ File 188224 (reclassified as 9–19–1354).

88. See above, note 8.

89. Amos Pinchot to Edward C. Costigan, December 30, 1916, Helen Marot to Frank P. Walsh, January 1, 1917, Walsh to Helen Marot, February 27, 1917, Helen Marot to Walsh, March 5, 1917; Anton Johannsen to Walsh, March 10, 1917, and September 4, 1917, William P. Harvey to Walsh, September 17, 1917; Samuel Gompers to Theodore Johnson, May 24, 1917, in Harvey to A. M. Hoover, September 22, 1917, Walsh to Fay Lewis, December 28, 1917, Walsh MSS.

90. American Alliance for Labor and Democracy to Walsh, August 18, 1917, Walsh to George Creel, September 10, 1917, Statement of the American Alliance for Labor and Democracy, January 12, 1918, *ibid.*

91. Roger N. Baldwin to Philip Willett, August 22, 1917, ACLU, XXXV.

92. *Ibid.,* XXVII, XXVIII, XXXIV, and LXXXVII, *passim.*

93. Filed with Louis F. Post to Mary Ware Dennett, January 1, 1918, *ibid.,* III.

94. *Ibid.,* CVIII, *passim.*

95. Jane Addams to Baldwin, June 11, 1918, *ibid.,* LXXXVII. See also George F. Vanderveer to Baldwin, February 16, 1918, *ibid.,* XXVII.

96. Arthur LeSueur to Baldwin, June 25, 1918, *ibid.*, XXVIII.

97. Roger N. Baldwin, "The Fight for Civil Liberty during the War, October 1917 to January 1920," *ibid.*, CVII, *passim.*

98. Solicitor William H. Lamar to the Postmaster General, September 3, 1920, in Alfred S. Burleson to Woodrow Wilson, September 3, 1920, Wilson MSS; DJ File 9–12–388½, *passim*; Chafee, *Free Speech*, 38–42, 97–100.

99. Lamar to the Attorney General, January 8, 1918, William C. Fitts to the Attorney General, January 3. 1918, DJ File 9–12–388½; DJ Files 9–12–47, 9–12–203, 9–12–249, 9–12–277, 9–12–279, 9–12–292, 9–12–406, 9–12–464, 9–12–637, and 9–12–677. See also statement of Congressman James Byrnes on December 20, 1919, *Congressional Record*, 66 Cong., 2 Sess., 980–981.

100. Post Office Department Solicitor's Files 46637, 47417, 47457, 47490, 47573, 47596, 47596A–H, 49241, 50207, 50327, 50622, 50786, 50786A, 50811, 50818, 50961, 51107, 51302, 51328, and 51344 (hereafter cited as Solicitor).

101. See above, note 97. See also George Leonard, Memorandum of April 2, 1918, on *Defense News Bulletin*, Leonard, Memorandum of June 25, 1918, on *The Labor Scrap Book*, Solicitor File 50818; Leonard, Memorandum of July 23, 1918, on letter of Lee McLeland, Solicitor File 47596B. Another memorandum stated, "This paper is thus appealing to its readers to take part in the overthrow of the capitalist order, so-called, that is the present form of government" (Memorandum for The Solicitor, December 11, 1918, Solicitor File 46637).

102. Leonard to Lamar, May 6, 1918, Solicitor File 50818. Author's emphasis.

103. Memorandum (unsigned) of December 27, 1917, on *Defense News Bulletin*, Solicitor File 50327.

104. Leonard, Memorandum of July 12, 1918, on *Bulletin No. 14*, Solicitor File 47596B. See also Leonard, Memorandum of June 4, 1918, on *Bulletin No. 21*, Leonard, Memorandum of July 24, 1918, on *Bulletin No. 2*, Solicitor File 47490.

105. Memorandum of March 22, 1918, and January 17, 1919, on the *Labor Defender*, Solicitor File 50961.

106. Post Office Memorandum to the Assistant U.S. Attorney, May 29, 1918, *ibid.*

107. Inspector Albertie to the Inspector in Charge, August 28, 1918, Solicitor File 47596E.

108. Inspectors F. N. Davis and I. T. Miller to the Inspector in Charge, May 7, 1918, Solicitor File 47596A.

109. Solicitor Files 46637, 47417, 47457, 47490, 47573, 47596, 47596A–H, 49241, 50207, 50327, 50622, 50786, 50786A, 50811, 50818, 50961, 51107, 51302, 51328, and 51344.

110. Quoted in Roger N. Baldwin to the Directing Committee, National Civil Liberties Bureau, on October 17, 1917, visit to Washington, Pinchot MSS. See also Frank P. Walsh to Job Harrison, August 30, 1918, Walsh MSS.

111. Solicitor Files 47596, 50786A, and 50818, *passim*.

112. DJ File 9–12–677–1.

113. William C. Fitts to the Attorney General, January 3. 1918, DJ File 9–12–388½; A. B. Bielaski to All Employees, Bureau of Investigation, January 28, 1918, Solicitor File 49241; Bielaski to Fitts, March 11, 1918, DJ File 9–12–419. Also DJ Files 186701, 186701–14, 188032, 9–12–203, 9–12–272, 9–12–277, 9–12–278, 9–12–279, 9–12–292, 9–12–406, 9–12–420, 9–12–637; National Civil Liberties Bureau to President Wilson, September 23, 1918, DJ File 9–12–394–16. The procedure determining mailability went as follows: The Manager of the express company office asked the Committee on Express Transportation, it asked the Department of Justice, and the latter, in turn, requested an opinion from Solicitor Lamar. The information then passed back down the same hierarchy.

114. Quoted in National Civil Liberties Bureau to President Wilson, September 23, 1918, DJ File 9–12–394–16. On the purpose of the section see also DJ File 187415 before 72.

115. Inspectors Albertie and Davis to the Inspector in Charge, July 1, 1918, Fitts to the Solicitor of the Post Office Department, July 25, 1918, DJ File 188032–262.

116. Thomas W. Gregory to Woodrow Wilson, May 14, 1918, Wilson MSS.

117. Jack Law to Frank P. Walsh, December 18, 1917, Walsh to Roger N. Baldwin, December 26, 1917, Law to Walsh, December 28, 1917, L. S. Chumley to Walsh, December 29, 1917, Walsh MSS; Baldwin to A. B. Bielaski, January 19, 1918, Bielaski to Baldwin, January 22, 1918, Baldwin to Bielaski, January 30, 1918, Bielaski to Baldwin, February 18, 1918, ACLU, CVII; Baldwin to George Vanderveer, February 11 and 12, 1918, *ibid.*, XXVII; T. J. Howe to C. R. Porter, December 4, 1918, DJ File 189152–66. See also ACLU, LXXXVI, LXXXVII, and LXXXVIII, *passim*.

118. National Civil Liberties Bureau to President Wilson, September 23, 1918, DJ File 9–12–394–16; Assistant U.S. Attorney Isaac Blair Evans to the Attorney General, April 29, 1919, DJ File 186701–70–2.

119. Theodore Pollok, "Attack on Right of Defense and on Defense Members in Trial of I.W.W. at Sacramento, California," October 16, 1918, ACLU, LXXXVI; DJ Files 186701–57 and –59, *passim*.

120. National Civil Liberties Bureau to President Wilson, September 23, 1918, DJ File 9–12–394–16. The alien situation is discussed in a later chapter.

121. District Attorneys Clarence Reames in Seattle and Fred

Robertson in Wichita were two of the most active speakers, but the Sacramento case also suffered from this propaganda. See DJ Files 186701–49, 188032, 189152, 190159, and 190159–A; ACLU, LXXXVI, *passim*; Pollok, "Attack on Right of Defense."

122. Associated Press Dispatch, November 3, 1918, ACLU, XCV. See also the *New York World*, January 28, 1918, and the *New York Times*, June 18, 1919, for government-inspired propaganda against radicals.

123. Caroline A. Lowe to Roger N. Baldwin, July 24, 1919, ACLU, LXXXVI.

124. *Ibid.* See also Fred H. Moore to Baldwin, July 24, 1919, *ibid.*

125. "List of $500 and Over Contributions," ACLU, XXV; Alex Cohen to Frank P. Walsh, October 26, 1917, Walsh MSS.; Baldwin to Lillian D. Wald, April 23, 1918, Baldwin to Mrs. J. Sergeant Cram, June 11, 1918, Jack Law to Baldwin, June 25, 1918, E. S. Rose to Baldwin, March 16, 1918, ACLU, XXVII; L. S. Chumley to Amos Pinchot, May 3, 1918, Baldwin to Pinchot, July 2, 1918, Pinchot MSS.; Caroline A. Lowe to Baldwin, July 24, 1919, ACLU, LXXXVI.

126. DJ Files 186701–57, 188032, and 189152; PA Files 39–240, –241, and –242, *passim*.

Chapter VI
A Winter in Seattle, 1917–1918

1. Ezra P. Giboney and Agnes M. Potter, *Tall Pine of the Sierras: The Life of Mark A. Matthews*, (Grand Rapids, 1948), 31.

2. Dr. Mark A. Matthews to Thomas W. Gregory, January 29, 1918. DJ File 186701–49–52. Matthews was a Theodore Roosevelt in the cloth. Under his lapel he wore the badge of a special deputy sheriff and he carried a pearl-handled pistol. Like Roosevelt, Matthews also volunteered to raise and lead a regiment of troops in World War I. See Giboney and Potter, 29, 33.

3. Sepcial Assistant to the Attorney General Clarence L. Reames to Gregory, April 2, 1918, DJ File 190159–42.

4. Gregory to Matthews, February 6, 1918, DJ File 186701–49–52; W. Herron to the Attorney General, Memorandum of March 23, 1917, DJ File 12–140–32; Matthews to Gregory, July 31, 1917, DJ File 190470; DJ Files 186701–49, –61, 188032–Special Section, 190159, and 190159A, *passim*; IN File 54235/85, *passim*.

5. Woodrow Wilson to Gregory, January 10, 1918, DJ File 186701–61–1.

6. DJ File 12–140, *passim*; Lowell S. Hawley and Ralph Bushnell Potts, *Counsel for the Damned: A Biography of George Francis Vanderveer* (Philadelphia and New York, 1953), 156–170, 187–188; Giboney and Potter, 35–36.

7. DJ Files 186233–107, 186701–49, –61, and –74, *passim.* See also above, Chapter IV, Section II.

8. U.S. Attorney Clay Allen to the Attorney General, June 27, 1917, DJ File 186233–107–2. See also DJ Files 186701–49, 188032–Special Section, and 188032–1, *passim*; Hawley and Potts, 156–170, 187–188.

9. Gregory to Newton D. Baker, July 26, 1917, DJ File 186701–49–14. See also Matthews to Woodrow Wilson, July 25, 1917, Wilson MSS.; Matthews to Gregory, July 31, 1917, DJ File 190470; U.S. Attorney Clay Allen to the Attorney General, July 6, 1917, DJ File 186701–49–6; Allen to Attorney General, same date, DJ File 186701–49–5; Commissioner of Immigration Henry White to the Immigration Bureau, July 24, 1917, IN File 53531/192; John H. Sargent to the Commissioner General, August 11, 1917, IN File 54297/31; DJ File 186701–49; *passim*; Giboney and Potter, 35–36.

10. W. A. Blackwood to Senator Wesley L. Jones, January 30, 1918, DJ File 186701–49–51.

11. Allen to the Attorney General, November 20, 1917, DJ File 9–5–599–1.

12. Blackwood to Jones, January 30, 1918, DJ File 186701–49–51.

13. Report of the Department Intelligence Officer to the Commanding General, Western Department, 1919, with Exhibits A and B, AG File 319.12 Western Department; AG File 085 I.W.W., *passim*; Clarence L. Reames to the Attorney General, March 9, 1918, and April 8, 1918, DJ File 190159–23 and –44.

14. DJ File 186233–107, *passim.* Author's emphasis.

15. Allen to the Attorney General, June 27, 1917, DJ File 186233–107–2. The indictment stood, but the jury disagreed in the first trial. Wells and his associates were then convicted in a second trial.

16. Tyler, "Rebels of the Woods and Fields," 17–18.

17. *Ibid.*, 19–20.

18. DJ Files 186701–49, –61, 188032–Special Section, 189738, 190159, and 190159A; IN File 54235/85, *passim.*

19. A. B. Bielaski to William C. Fitts, January 25, 1918, DJ File 186701–49–48; Henry M. White to the Commissioner General, February 19, 1918, IN File 54235/85; DJ Files 189738–1 and –2; DL Files 20/473 and 33/574; DJ File Abraham Glasser.

20. Report of Colonel M. E. Saville to the Commanding General, 91st Division, Camp Lewis, March 30, 1918, DJ File 186701–49–88; DJ File 186701–49 and IN File 54235/85, *passim.*

21. Hugh Campbell Wallace to Woodrow Wilson, December 29, 1917, DJ File 186701–61–1; also appears in DJ File 188032–Special Section.

22. "Statement of Colonel M. E. Saville, U.S.A., regarding Seditious Activities in the Northwest, December 29, 1917," DJ Files 186701–61–1 and 188032–Special Section (hereafter cited as Saville

Statement). The evidence for the Russian counsul's pro-Germanism was fairly flimsy. It rested on his support of a separate peace, refusing passports to Russians favoring a continuation of the war, helping radicals reach Russia, and the Russian purchase of equipment from Germany rather than the Allies.

23. Report of Saville to the Commanding General, March 30, 1918, DJ File 186701–49–88.

24. Saville Statement; Report of Saville to the Commanding General, March 30, 1918, DJ File 186701–49–88.

25. Saville Statement.

26. Thomas W. Gregory to John Lord O'Brian, October 20, 1917, Gregory to Clarence L. Reames, January 12, 1918, DJ File 190470; Gregory to Clay Allen, February 8, 1918, DJ File 190159-2; Gregory to Reames, February 8, 1918, DJ File 190159-1.

27. Reames to Gregory, March 16, 1918, DJ File 190159-48.

28. W. A. Blackwood to Senator Wesley L. Jones, January 30, 1918, DJ File 186701–49–51.

29. Reames to the Attorney General, March 4, 1918, DJ File 190159–19.

30. DJ File 190159, *passim*.

31. Reames to the Attorney General, March 9, 1918, DJ File 190159–23.

32. Reames to the Attorney General, April 8, 1918, DJ File 190159–44; Reames to Gregory, April 23, 1918, DJ File 190159A–69.

33. Reames to the Attorney General, April 8, 1918, DJ File 190159–44.

34. Reames to the Attorney General, October 26, 1918, DJ File 193498-2. This letter gives a quick and excellent summary of the dispute between the Seattle office of the Department of Justice and the Office of Naval Intelligence. See also Reames to the Attorney General, November 23, 1918, DJ File 9–12–553–5.

35. DJ File 190159, *passim*.

36. Reames to the Attorney General, October 17, 1918, DJ File 9–16–13–82–64; Reames to the Attorney General, August 23, 1918, DJ File 9–16–13–82–58. In late 1918 the Department of Justice censured Reames for denying passes to mere members of the I.W.W., and the practice was abandoned (John Lord O'Brian to Reames October 11, 1918, and October 30, 1918, DJ File 9–16–13–82–56 and –64).

37. Reames to the Attorney General, May 3, 1918, DJ File 186701–49–90; Reames to the Attorney General, October 26, 1918, DJ File 193498-2.

38. Reames to the Attorney General, November 2, 1918; O'Brian to Reames, November 11, 1918, DJ File 9–12–553–2.

39. DJ Files 186701–49, 190159, 190159A, 193498, and 9–16–13–82; IN File 54235/85.

40. Reames to the Attorney General, February 27, 1918, DJ File 190159–14; Reames to Gregory, March 16, 1918 (Personal and Confidential), DJ File 190159–48.

41. Henry M. White to the Commissioner General, February 19, 1918, IN File 54235/85. Author's emphasis.

42. *Ibid.*

43. IN Files 54297/26, /31, 54235/54, and /92. See also Bureau Memorandum, December 17, 1917, IN File 54297/31. This position was later summed up in a mimeographed brief inserted in all I.W.W. records at Seattle ("Mimeographed Summary," 1, IN File 54379/76, and many other individual case files).

44. Anthony Caminetti to the Immigration Service, Seattle, September 27, 1917, IN File 53531/192A; A. Warner Parker to the Commissioner of Immigration, Montreal, October 3, 1917, IN File 54182/2A.

45. F. P. Sargent to all Commissioners of Immigration, March 23, 1908, Solicitor Charles Earl to A. Warner Parker, March 19, 1908, IN File 51924/30; Subdivision 3, Rule 22, IN File 54549/662D.

46. Anthony Caminetti to the Assistant Secretary, January 25, 1918, IN File 54235/36; IN Files 54235/20 and /85, *passim.*

47. "Mimeographed Summary," 6, IN File 54379/76.

48. DJ File 186701–49 and IN File 54235/85, *passim.*

49. Henry M. White to the Immigration Bureau, January 30, 1918, IN File 54235/85.

50. IN Files 54379/5–15.

51. Bureau Memorandum, November 20, 1918, IN File 54379/13.

52. Inspector T. M. Fisher to Commissioner of Immigration, Seattle, January 17, 1918, IN File 54379/44.

53. IN Files 54616/76, 54379/76, /173, /108, /109, and /414–425.

54. IN Files 54379/8–11, /13, /23–27, /29, /30, /32, /33, /35, /36–40, /42–46, /50, /51, /54–58, /63, /65, /69, and /70.

55. Inspector Lawler to the Commissioner of Immigration, Angel Island, May 20, 1918, IN File 53531/192B.

56. Inspector T. M. Fisher to the Commissioner of Immigration, Seattle, January 29, 1918, IN File 54379/101; IN Files 54235/92, 54517/16, /45, /50, /58, 54616/95, 54645/435, and 54861/371.

57. DJ File 186701–49 and IN File 54235/85, *passim.*

58. Clem J. Wittemore to Senator J. W. Beckham, February 14, 1918, IN File 54235/85.

59. Henry M. White to the Immigration Bureau, February 6, 1918, John H. Sargent to the Immigration Bureau, March 6, 1918, *ibid.*

60. Anthony Caminetti to the Assistant Secretary, February 1, 1918, *ibid.*

61. Clay Allen to the Attorney General, February 9, 1918, Allen to the Attorney General, February 13, 1918, DJ File 186701–49–54

and –58; John H. Sargent to the Immigration Bureau, March 6, 1918, IN File 54235/85.

62. *Annual Report of the Secretary of Labor*, 1918, 20.

63. William B. Wilson to the Assistant Secretary, February 28, 1918, IN File 54235/85.

64. Thomas W. Gregory to Clarence L. Reames, February 27, 1918, DJ File 186701–49–63.

65. Reames to the Attorney General, March 4, 1918, and March 23, 1918, DJ File 186701–49–76 and –81.

66. Reames to the Attorney General, April 15, 1918, DJ File 186701–49–83.

67. Reames to Gregory, March 16, 1918, DJ File 190159–49.

68. Reames to the Attorney General, April 15, 1918, DJ File 186701–49–83.

69. Reames to the Attorney General, March 23, 1918 DJ File 186701–49–81.

70. Reames to the Attorney General, March 4, 1918, and April 15, 1918, DJ File 186701–49–76 and –83. Author's emphasis.

71. Gregory to Josephus Daniels, March 16, 1918, DJ File 190159–25; Gregory to Reames, March 11, 1918, DJ File 186701–49–76; Reames to the Attorney General, April 15, 1918, DJ File 186701–49–83.

72. Reames to the Attorney General, April 15, 1918, DJ File 186701–49–83; DJ Files 190159 and 190159A, *passim*.

73. Report of Colonel M. E. Saville to the Commanding General, March 30, 1918, DJ File 186701–49–88.

74. Report of Agent Petrovitsky, January 13, 1918, for January 13, 1918, DJ File 188032 Enclosures; A. B. Bielaski to John Lord O'Brian, February 7, 1918, DJ File 186701–61–7.

75. Congressman Benjamin F. Welty in *Hearings before the Committee on Immigration and Naturalization*, July 16 and 17, 1919, 66 Cong., 1 Sess., IN File 54549/662D; Clark, *Deportation of Aliens*, 331–332, 363–376; Oppenheimer, *Enforcement of Deportation Laws*, 26–45; Van Vleck, *Administrative Control of Aliens*, 91, 98–103, 107–111, 219–228.

76. *Annual Report of the Secretary of Labor*, 1918, 20; Hawley and Potts, 46.

77. IN Files 54379/7, /19, /21, /30, /32, /38, /43, /62, /101, /122, /423, /425.

78. IN Files 54379/5–15, /20–33, /35–47, /49–71, /75–82, /85–94, /96, /97, /102, /103, /107–116, /122, /126, /173, /181, /184 (2 files), /193–203, /207, /235–241, /247–252, /414–425, /450, /451, /462, and /463.

79. IN Files 54379 series.

80. IN File 54379/415.

81. IN Files 54379 series
82. In File 54379/50.
83. IN Files 54379 series.
84. IN Files 54517/93 and 54709/28.
85. IN Files 54379/7, /18, /22, /32, /78, /89, /94, /97, /107, /173, /181, /194, /247, /415, /419, /450, and 54235/112.
86. IN File 54379/22.
87. IN Files 54517/45; 54379/241; Louis F. Post to the Commissioner General, March 17, 1920, IN File 54809/General, sec. 2; IN Files 54379/122 and 54616/14.
88. IN Files 54379/7, /33, /50, /65, /69, /186, and /421.
89. IN Files 54379/48, /91, /204, /415, /422, /424, and 54616/84.
90. Clark, 59, 75–76; Van Vleck, 113, 119; Anthony Caminetti to John Burke, Treasurer of the United States, January 10, 1919, IN File 54616/2.
91. Bureau Memoranda of September 28, 1918, and November 25, 1918, IN Files 54235/112 and 54379/417.
92. Bureau Memoranda of November 20, 1918, and February 19, 1918, IN Files 54379/13 and 54356/56; IN Files 54379/8 and /115.
93. IN Files 54235/39, /82, /112, 54379/13, /31, /33, /38, /61, /74, /75, /80, /93, /115, /186, 54616/15, /18, /34, /71, /73, /116, 54547/15, 54554/39, 54841/18, 54641/19, 54645/435.
94. Bureau Memoranda of November 22, 1918 and September 10, 1918, IN Files 54379/38 and 54379/42.
95. IN Files 54379/42 and /66.
96. IN Files 54379/66, 54235/43, and 54616/116.
97. IN Files 54379/38 and /75.

Chapter VII

The Labyrinth of Deportation, 1918–1919

1. Memorandum from Anthony Caminetti to the Secretary of Labor, May 13, 1918, IN File 54235/36A.
2. Anthony Caminetti to A. Warner Parker, March 23, 1918 IN File 54235/85.
3. John W. Abercrombie to Senator Thomas W. Hardwick, July 1, 1918, Abercrombie to Senator Albert Gore, September, 3, 1918, IN File 54235/36. Author's emphasis.
4. Caminetti to Parker, March 23, 1918, IN File 54235/85; Caminetti to John L. O'Brian, April 11, 1918, Thomas W. Gregory to the Secretary of Labor, February 23, 1918, Caminetti to the Secretary of Labor, March 5, 1918, IN File 54235/36; *Congressional Record*, 65 Cong., 2 Sess. (1918), 8109, 8117, 8938; Garis, *Immigration Restriction*, 138–140; Clark, *Deportation of Aliens*, 218–220.
5. Congressman John L. Burnett to William B. Wilson, May 29,

1918, Gregory to the Secretary of Labor, February 23, 1918, Caminetti to O'Brian, April 11, 1918, IN File 54235/36; *Congressional Record*, 65 Cong., 2 Sess. (1918), 8109. In his memoirs of the deportation crusade, Assistant Secretary of Labor Louis F. Post mistakenly described the enactment of the 1918 law. He believed that "the forest-region influences of the Pacific Northwest thrust through Congress the comprehensive law of 1918 . . . to compel the Secretary of Labor to deport aliens for mere membership in the I.W.W. without any proof of individual culpability." There is no evidence for this. Whatever pressure the Northwest exerted had exhausted itself in the winter crusade. While that region undoubtedly influenced the Immigration Bureau, it and the Department of Justice planned, rewrote, and had enacted the 1918 bill (see Post, *Deportations Delirium*, 65). Post's account shows the danger of accepting official memoirs uncritically, even when written as soon after the event as this one.

6. William B. Wilson to the Assistant Secretary, February 28, 1918, IN File 54235/85.

7. Memorandum of H. McClelland, July 26, 1918, IN File 54235/36A.

8. IN Files 54379/10, /20, /22, /26, /27, /29, /30, /32, /37, /39, /45, /46, /56, /58, /63, /65, /71, /77, /79, /102, and/250.

9. IN Files 54379/9, /33, /52, /62, /86, /90, /116, /196, /197, /199, /236, /237, /239–241, /249, 54235/112, and 54517/33.

10. Bureau Memorandum, September 20, 1918, IN File 54379/33.

11. IN Files 54379/196, /197, /199, and /240.

12. Bureau Memorandum, September 20, 1918, IN File 54379/241; IN Files 54379/52, /90, /236, and /239.

13. IN Files 54379 series.

14. Assistant U.S. Attorney Charles H. Leavy to the Attorney General, November 1, 1918, DJ File 196663–1; IN File 54379/237.

15. "Opinion of Judge Rudkin in the Matter of the Application of Carl Holm [*sic*] for a Writ of Habeas Corpus in the District Court of the United States for the Eastern District of Washington, Northern Division," DJ File 196663–1. Compare the exactly opposite decision by the New York southern district court the same month, Byron Uhl to the Commissioner General, November 9, 1918, IN File 54379/236.

16. IN File 54379/122.

17. John W. Abercrombie to the Attorney General, November 14, 1918, DJ File 196663–4; IN Files 54379/65, /89, and /423.

18. Anthony Caminetti to the Commissioner of Immigration, Seattle, November 14, 1918, IN File 54235/36B.

19. Caminetti to the Acting Secretary, December 2, 1918, *ibid.;* IN File 54379/76.

20. Caminetti to the Acting Secretary, December 2, 1918, IN File 54235/36B.

21. Post, 65; Caminetti to the Assistant Secretary, August 28, 1917, IN File 53531/192.

22. *Annual Report of the Secretary of Labor*, 1920, 76–77.

23. *Ex parte Bernat, Ex parte Dixon*, 225 F. 429, 432.

24. *Ibid.* Author's emphasis.

25. Members deported or ordered deported: IN Files 54379/33, /239, /241, /249, and 54547/15. Members paroled or released: IN Files 54379/7, /10, /15, /20, /21, /24–27, /29–32, are some examples. For a complete tally see note 78, below.

26. Organizers and delegates deported or ordered deported: IN Files 54379/54, /196, /197, /204, /236, /237, /240, /417, /451, 54517/16, and /68. Organizers and delegates paroled or released: IN Files 54379/14, /181, /184, /193, /194, /198, /226, /252, /450, 54408/22, 54517/33, 54616/31, /84, and 54860/912.

27. IN Files 54379/5, /23, /44, /50, /68, /76, /501, and two cases reported in 54235/85. A federal court later lashed out at the strange concept of conditional parole. In a Massachusetts case the judge declared, "He [the alien] is entitled to be deported, or to have his freedom." *Petition of Brooks*, 5 F. (2d), 238.

28. Bell, "Marxian Socialism," 329–330; Murray, *Red Scare*, 5–7, 67–68, 80, 105, 111–112, 117, 121–122.

29. Bell, 320–328, 334–41; Chafee, *Free Speech in the United States*, 219; Lowenthal, *Federal Bureau of Investigation*, 109-110; Murray, 36–37, 53, 84–85, 163.

30. Higham, *Strangers in the Land*, 222–227; Handlin, *American People*, 144–148.

31. IN Files 54235/36, /85, and 54809/General; DJ Files 186701–14, 195397, 202600, 203557, 205492, and 209264; Solicitor William H. Lamar to the Postmaster General, September 3, 1920, enclosure in Alfred S. Burleson to Woodrow Wilson, September 3, 1920, Wilson MSS.

32. A Mitchell Palmer to H. H. Hayhow, Tusculum College, February 18, 1920, DJ File 202600 between 439 and 444.

33. John Lord O'Brian to the Attorney General, November 20, 1918, DJ File 190470; O'Brian to U.S. Attorney Francis C. Caffey, January 8, 1919, DJ File 9-5-667-13; A Mitchell Palmer to U.S. Attorney Fred Robertson, June 12, 1919, DJ File 186701-17-9; DJ Files 189738 and 195397; *Investigation Activities of the Department of Justice, 1919*, Senate Document 153, 66 Cong. 1 Sess. (1919), 6–8.

34. Memorandum of Earl J. Davis to the Attorney General, June 10, 1924, DJ File 202600–2734. Cf. also Special Assistant to the Attorney General Clifford H. Byrnes, "Brief on Laws Having Possible Application to Communist Activities," DJ File 202600–2734 after 10; *U.S. v. W. D. Haywood, et al.*, 268 F. 795; *U.S. v. C.W. Anderson, et al.*, 273 F. 25.

35. DJ File 202600–59, *passim.*

36. Chafee, 169; Bell, 330–331; Higham, 230–233; DJ Files 197009, 197009–1, and 207406; PA Files 39–240, –241, and –242; PA Files, Boxes 49–52 and Box 54.

37. IN Files 54379 series.

38. George F. Vanderveer to Frank P. Walsh, November 6, 1918, Walsh MSS.

39. Immigration Prisoners, Everett County Jail, to Sheriff McCulloch, August 25, 1918, Henry M. White to the Commissioner General, December 28, 1918, White to the Immigration Bureau, January 11, 1919, IN File 54235/85.

40. IN Files 54379/226, /415, /501, 54517/68, and 54811/920.

41. IN File 54379/183; Inspector Baldwin, Butte, Montana, to the Inspector in Charge, November 7, 1919, IN File 54616/167.

42. White to the Commissioner General, December 28, 1918, IN File 54235/85.

43. Major F. S. Howes, U.S. Intelligence Office, Portland, Oregon, to Captain A. Bickford, Seattle, October 26, 1918, DJ File 186701–49 between 123 and 124.

44. White to the Commissioner General, December 28, 1918, IN File 54235/85; DJ File 198783, *passim.*

45. White to the Commissioner General, December 28, 1918, IN File 54235/85.

46. Hawley and Potts, *Counsel for the Damned,* 254–256.

47. U.S. Attorney Robert Saunders to the Attorney General, February 4, 1919, DJ File 198783–4.

48. General Peyton March, Chief of Staff, to Major General John F. Morrison, February 6, 1919, AG File 370.6.

49. Henry M. White to the Immigration Bureau, February 4, 1919, IN File 54379/134.

50. Hawley and Potts, 258–64; DJ File 198783, *passim.*

51. Memorandum of Inspector A. D. H. Jackson to the Commissioner General, February 13, 1919, IN File 54235/36C; Anthony Caminetti to the Commissioner of Immigration, Ellis Island, February 13, 1919, Byron Uhl to the Commissioner General, February 14, 1919 IN File 54235/36B.

52. Caminetti to the Commissioner of Immigration, Ellis Island, February 17, 1919, and February 13, 1919, IN Files 54235/36C and /36B.

53. *In re writ of habeas corpus sued out by Caroline A. Lowe on behalf of Christ L. Johnson, et al.,* U.S. District Court, Southern District of New York, February 13, 1919, IN File 54235/85A; "The Deportations," *The Survey,* XLI (February 22, 1919), 722–724.

54. *Ibid.;* Caminetti to the Commissioner of Immigration, Ellis Island, February 17, 1919, IN File 54235/36C; Caroline A. Lowe and

Charles Recht, *Brief on behalf of Deportees in the matter of the proposed Deportation of John Berg and others* in Caroline Lowe and Charles Recht to Caminetti, March 4, 1919, IN File 54235/85–Special Section.

55. Henry M. White to the Commissioner General, December 28, 1918, IN File 54235/85.

56. Lowe and Recht, *Brief.*

57. Caminetti to the Secretary, March 6, 1919, IN File 54235/85A.

58. *Ibid.*

59. Memorandum insertion in Caminetti to the Secretary, March 6, 1919, IN File 54235/85A.

60. John W. Abercrombie to all Commissioners of Immigration and Inspectors in Charge, March 14, 1919, IN Files 54235/36 and /85.

61. Supplemental Memorandum re James Lund, Caminetti to the Acting Secretary, March 14, 1919, IN File 54379/44; Caminetti to the Immigration Service. Ellis Island, March 15, 1919, IN File 54235/85A.

62. IN Files 54235/112, 54379/5, /23, /44, /50, /68, /76, /183, /185, 54517/93, and two cases (no files) reported in 54235/85 and /85A.

63. Byron Uhl to the Commissioner General, February 24, 1919, IN File 54235/85A; Bureau Memoranda of November 25, 1918, January 22, 1919, and February 4, 1919, IN Files 54379/417, 54517/68, and 54547/15.

64. IN Files 54235/102 and 54379/205.

65. Decision of Judge Augustus N. Hand, April 10, 1919, IN File 54379/204.

66. Bureau Memorandum, January 16, 1919, *ibid.*

67. Bureau Supplemental Memorandum, April 17, 1919, IN File 54379/82.

68. Two Bureau Memoranda of April 17, 1919, IN Files 54379/82 and /18. An additional three aliens escaped deportation at the same time, one proving citizenship, one going insane, and one escaping an LPC charge (IN Files 54379/86, /48, and /186).

69. *U.S. ex rel. E. E. McDonald, et al. v. F. C. Howe,* IN File 54379/501.

70. *Ibid.*

71. *Ibid.*

72. IN Files 54379/12, /101, /114, /134, /425, /491, /503, 54414/81, 54517/16, and /54.

73. IN Files 54379/12, /425, and 54517/16.

74. *U.S. ex rel. Martin de Wal v. Byron H. Uhl* IN File 54517/16; *U.S. ex rel. McGregor S. Ross v. Frederick A. Wallis,* DJ File 39–20–2. See also *Ex parte Matthews,* 277 F. 857, 858.

75. Anthony Caminetti to the Acting Secretary, December 2, 1918, IN File 54235/36B.

76. The seven deported: IN Files 54379/54, /114, /417, /491, /503, and /532 (two individuals); the four men never found: IN Files 54379/70, /126, /237, and 54235/43; the eleven released: IN Files 54379/18, /62, /76, /82, /86, /90, /183, /185, /249, 54235/112, and 54517/33; the three accepting repatriation: IN Files 54379/52, /64, and /116; the three ordered deported but not sailing: IN Files 54379/12, /425, and 54517/16.

77. Deported: IN Files 54554/39, 54379/9, /33, /196, /197, /199, /236, /240, and /241; habeas corpus: IN Files 54235/43, 54379/31, /70, /126, /237, and /239; paroled or warrent canceled: IN Files 54379/10, /20, /22, /26, /27 /29, /30, /32, /37, /39, /45, /46, /56, /58, /63, /65, /71, /77, /79, /102, /248, and /250.

78. Paroled or warrent canceled: IN Files 54379/7, /14, /15, /21, /24, /31, /38, /40, /41, /47, /55, /57, /60, /69, /78, /81, /85, /87–89, /91–94, /96, /97 (two cases), /101, /107–109, /115, /122, /173, /181, /184, /193–195, /198, /207, /238, /247, /252, /414, /418, /419, /422–424, /462, /463, 54408/22, 54517/45, /58, and 54709/39; "Red Special": IN Files 54235/102, /112, 54379/5, /12, /18, /23, /44, /48, /50, /54, /68, /76, /82, /86, /101, /114, /134 (2 cases), /183, /185, /186, /417, /425, /491, /501, /503, 54414/81, 54517/16, /33, /54, /68, /93, /54547/15 and three cases reported in 54235/36 and /85. The twenty-seven deportees were composed of nine in the September-October group, twelve in the "Red Special," and six others: IN Files 54379/2, /13, /451, /532 (two cases), and one case reported in Charles Recht, *American Deportation and Exclusion Laws* (New York, 1919), 32.

Chapter VIII
The Red Raids, 1919–1920

1. Anthony Caminetti to the Secretary of Labor, May 14, 1919, IN File 54568/General.

2. John W. Abercrombie to Senator Francis E. Warren, June 24, 1919, IN File 54568/General.

3. *Ibid.*

4. Lowenthal, *Federal Bureau of Investigation*, 84–85; Post, *Deportations Delirium*, 48–49; House Subcommittee of Committee on Appropriations, *Hearings, First Deficiency Appropriation Bill Fiscal Year 1920*, 66 Cong., 1 Sess. (1920), 457–458.

5. IN Files 54235/39 and 54235/82; above, Chapter VI.

6. DJ Files 186701–49 and 9–16–12, *passim;* IN Files 54379/36, /52, /61, /62, /64, /80, /90, /103, /113, /116, /248, /418, /422, /512, /514, /525, and 54517/50.

7. Alfred Hampton to W. E. Allen, March 20, 1919, IN File 54235/36C.

8. Lowenthal, 85.

9. William B. Wilson to A. Mitchell Palmer, June 10, 1919, IN File 54235/36C.

10. J. Edgar Hoover to Frank E. Burke, February 21, 1920, DJ File 186701–14 between 82 and 83. See also John W. Abercrombie to Senator Francis E. Warren, June 24, 1919, IN File 54568/General.

11. Post, 51–52.

12. Wilson to Palmer, June 10, 1919, IN File 54235/36C.

13. Bureau of Investigation Instructions, July 28, 1919, IN File 54670/A.

14. Memorandum of Conference with Hon. James W. Good, Chairman, Committee on Appropriations, House of Representatives, August 19, 1919, IN File 54568/General. Author's emphasis.

15. Ibid.

16. Hoover to Burke, February 21, 1920, DJ File 186701–14– between 82 and 83.

17. John Creighton to Anthony Caminetti, July 29, 1919, IN File 54670/A; Caminetti to Francis P. Garvan, July 27, 1919, IN File 54235/85C.

18. Rule 22, Subdivision 5, IN File 54645/378.

19. IN Files 54379 series, passim; George F. Vanderveer to Frank P. Walsh, November 6, 1918, Walsh MSS.; IN File 54235/85.

20. Caminetti to the Acting Secretary, March 13, 1919, IN File 54645/378; Post, 85.

21. Caminetti to the Acting Secretary, March 13, 1919, IN File 54645/378.

22. Max J. Kohler, Immigration and Aliens in the United States, (New York, 1936), 412–13.

23. Caminetti to the Secretary, May 14, 1919, IN File 54568/General.

24. Caminetti to the Acting Secretary, March 13, 1919, IN File 54645/378.

25. Caminetti to the Acting Secretary, July 24, 1919, ibid.

26. Byron Uhl to the Commissioner General, November 13, 1919, ibid.

27. Bureau of Investigation Instructions, July 28, 1919, IN File 54670/A. Author's emphasis.

28. Caminetti to Francis P. Garvan, June 27, 1919, IN File 54235/85C.

29. Ibid.

30. Report of Agent Frank D. Pelto, Duluth, November 2, 1919, for October 30, 1919, IN File 54235/36F.

31. George F. Vanderveer, "Our Constitutional Rights, Notice to Aliens," ibid.

32. Ibid.

33. Ibid.

34. John H. Clark to the Commissioner General, November 17, 1919, Byron Uhl to the Commissioner General, November 13, 1919, IN File 54645/378.

35. Lowenthal, 182; IN Files 54235/36F and 36G; DJ File 203557.

36. Frank Burke to Anthony Caminetti, November 19, 1919, IN File 54235/36F. Author's emphasis.

37. *Ibid.*

38. A. Mitchell Palmer to William B. Wilson, January 2, 1920, IN File 54809/General.

39. Caminetti to the Acting Secretary, December 30, 1919, IN File 54645/378.

40. Chafee, *Free Speech in the United States*, 209; Lowenthal, 210–213.

41. Caminetti to the Acting Secretary, December 30, 1919, IN File 54645/378; Post, 87.

42. Caminetti to the Acting Secretary, December 30, 1919, IN File 54645/378. Author's emphasis.

43. William B. Wilson to A. Mitchell Palmer, December 30, 1919, DJ File 205492–275; Palmer to Wilson, January 2, 1920, IN File 54809/General.

44. Palmer to Wilson, January 2, 1920, IN File 54809/General.

45. J. Edgar Hoover to Anthony Caminetti, January 22, 1920, IN File 54645/378.

46. A. Mitchell Palmer to William B. Wilson, January 2, 1920, IN File 54809/General; Hoover to Caminetti, January 22, 1920, DJ File 203557–74.

47. Hoover to Caminetti, January 22, 1920, IN File 54645/378.

48. Palmer to Wilson, January 2, 1920, IN File 54809/General; Hoover to Caminetti, March 16, 1920, DJ File 202600–190.

49. Palmer to Wilson, January 2, 1920, IN File 54809/General.

50. Hoover to Caminetti, March 16, 1920, DJ File 202600–190; DJ File 188032, *passim.*

51. House Committee on Immigration and Naturalization, *Hearings, Administration of Immigration Laws* 66 Cong., 2 Sess. (1920), 36–40.

52. Vanderveer, "Our Constitutional Rights," IN File 54235/36F.

53. Post, *Deportations Delirium;* National Popular Government League, *Report Upon the Illegal Practices of the United States Department of Justice* (Washington, 1926), Panunzio, *Deportation Cases of 1919–1920;* Lowenthal, *Federal Bureau of Investigation; Investigation Activities of the Department of Justice, 1919,* Senate Document 153, 66 Cong., 1 Sess. (1919); Senate Subcommittee of the Committee on the Judiciary, *Hearings, Charges of Illegal Practices of the Department of Justice,* 66 Cong., 3 Sess. (1921).

54. IN File 54809/General, *passim.*

55. Lowenthal, 147–266; Konvitz, *Civil Rights*, 122–123.

56. Caminetti to the Acting Secretary, January 10, 1920, IN File 54809/General, sec. 2.

57. William B. Wilson to Caminetti, January 26, 1920, IN File 54645/378.

58. Caminetti to the Acting Secretary, January 10, 1920, IN File 54809/General, Sec. 2.

59. *Ibid.* The Supreme Court decision was *Low Wah Suey v. Backus*, 225 U.S. 470.

60. Lowenthal, 117–118.

61. Hoover to Caminetti, March 16, 1920, DJ File 205492–582; Lowenthal, 177.

62. Post, 185; Lowenthal, 117–119, 174, 178–179.

63. Caminetti to Hoover, January 19, 1920, IN File 54809/General, Sec. 2; W. J. Peters to Caminetti, February 6, 1920, Hoover to Caminetti February 2, 1920, March 16, 1920, and April 6, 1920, IN File 54809/General.

64. Peters to Caminetti, February 6, 1920, IN File 54809/General.

65. Louis F. Post to Caminetti, May 24, 1920, In File 53244/1C.

66. Hoover to Caminetti, March 16, 1920, IN File 54809/General.

67. House Committee on Rules, *Hearings, Attorney General A. Mitchell Palmer on Charges Made against the Department of Justice by Louis F. Post and Others*, 66 Cong., 2 Sess. (1920); House Committee on Rules, *Hearings, Investigation of Administration of Louis F. Post, Assistant Secretary of Labor, in the Matter of Deportation of Aliens*, 66 Cong., 2 Sess. (1920); Senate Subcommittee of the Committee on the Judiciary, *Hearings, Charges of Illegal Practices of the Department of Justice*, 66 Cong. 3 Sess. (1921). There were also several investigations of the administration of the deportation laws by the House Committee on Immigration and Naturalization.

68. Hoover to General Marlborough Churchill, January 23, 1920, DJ File 205492–294; Hoover to Churchill, May 13, 1920, DJ File 202600–296; Thomas J. Howe to Hoover, January 21, 1920, DJ File 209264–Enclosures.

69. House Committee on Immigration and Naturalization Hearings, *Administration of Immigration Laws*, 66th Cong., 2d Sess. (March 30 and 31 and April 6, 1920), 86–87, 89. See also House Subcommittee of the Committee on Immigration and Naturalization, *Hearings, I.W.W. Deportation Cases*, 66 Cong., 2 Sess. (April 27–30, 1920), *passim*.

70. House Committee on Immigration and Naturalization, Hearings, *Administration of Immigration Laws*, 66 Cong., 2 Sess. (1920), 89–90, 92–93; *Congressional Record*, 66 Cong., 2 Sess. (1920), 5552, 6872–73.

71. House Committee on Rules, *Hearings, Investigation of Adminis-*

tration of Louis F. Post, Assistant Secretary of Labor, in the Matter of Deportation of Aliens, 66 Cong., 2 Sess. (1920), *passim;* Post, 238–239.

72. J. Edgar Hoover to Thomas J. Howe, December 11, 1919, DJ File 189152–157; Hoover to John T. Creighton, December 18, 1919, DJ File 202600–95; Hoover to Frank Burke, February 21, 1920, DJ File 186701–14 between 82 and 83; Hoover to Howe, March 1, 1920, DJ File 186701–17–25.

73. Hoover to Burke, February 21, 1920, DJ File 186701–14 between 82 and 83.

74. Hoover to George F. Lamb (Special Agent), June 10, 1920, DJ File 202600–59–47; Hoover to Frank R. Stone, June 7, 1920, DJ File 202600–59–42.

75. Tyler, "Rebels of the Woods and Fields," 144–81; Hawley and Potts, *Counsel for the Damned,* 283–284.

76. *Exclusion and Expulsion of Aliens of Anarchistic and Similar Classes,* House Report 504, 66 Cong., 2 Sess. (1919), 3, 7, 11.

77. *Congressional Record,* 66 Cong., 2 Sess. (1920), appendix.

78. *Ibid.,* 990–991, 994–995; 997–999, 1003; House Committee on Immigration and Naturalization, *Hearings, Administration of Immigration Laws,* 66 Cong., 2 Sess. (1920), 145–147.

79. Quoted in Clark, *Deportation of Aliens,* 65–66.

80. Quoted in *ibid.,* 219; Claghorn, *Immigrant's Day in Court,* 308–309.

81. *Congressional Record,* 66 Cong., 2 Sess. (1919), 1000–1001, 1003. The Attorney General had also found that the official documents of the I.W.W. skilfully avoided teaching either anarchy or sabotage (*Investigation Activities of the Department of Justice, 1919,* Senate Document 153, 66 Cong., 1 Sess. [1919], 33).

82. A Warner Parker, Memorandum of July 12, 1919, IN File 54568/General.

83. Higham, *Strangers in the Land,* 232–233.

84. Chafee, 165–166; Eldridge Foster Dowell, *History of Criminal Syndicalism Legislation in the United States* (Baltimore, 1939), *passim.*

85. Inspector A. P. Schell to the Commissioner General, June 3, 1919, IN File 54235/85B.

86. Arthur M. Allen, Special Agent, to the Commissioner of Immigration, San Francisco, April 5, 1919, IN File 54235/85B.

87. *Ibid.*

88. Caminetti to the Secretary, May 7, 1919, IN File 54235/85C.

89. Schell to the Commissioner General, June 3, 1919, IN File 54235/85B.

90. U.S. Attorney William Woodburn to the Attorney General, November 13, 1919, DJ File 186701–29–3; Senator Charles B. Hender-

son to A. Mitchell Palmer, January 17, 1920, DJ File 186701–29–4; C. R. Miller to Henderson, January 15, 1920, DJ File 186701–29–4.

91. DJ File Abraham Glasser; Olaf L. Root to the Commissioner General, April 4, 1919, IN File 54235/36C; *Ex parte Jackson*, DJ File 202600–67.

92. Inspector Charles K. Andrews to the Immigration Bureau, February 18, 1919, IN File 54235/85A; Root to the Commissioner General, April 4, 1919, IN File 54235/36C.

93. Root to the Commissioner General, April 4, 1919, IN File 54235/36C.

94. *Ibid.*

95. Clark, 255. The figures on radical deportation are as follows: 1918, 2; 1919, 37; 1920, 314; 1921, 446; 1922, 64; 1923, 13; 1924, 81; 1925, 22; 1926, 4; 1927, 9; 1928, 1; 1929, 1; 1930, 1. In comparison some representative figures for total deportations: 1919, 3068; 1920, 2762; 1921, 4517; 1922, 4345; 1923, 3661; 1924, 6409.

96. William B. Wilson to the Commissioner General, January 26, 1920, IN File 54645/378; Post, 185.

97. Anthony Caminetti to All Commissioners of Immigration and Inspectors in Charge, March 13, 1920, Caminetti to the Assistant Secretary, August 28, 1920, IN File 53244/1. The Immigration Bureau explained the laxness of the arrest procedure as follows: "This procedure has not been adhered to with any degree of strictness in the past, due, in some respects, to the fact that circumstances surrounding the cases of members of unlawful organizations whom it was desired to arrest *would not permit of investigation, in advance of arrest, of the individual members*" (Caminetti to All Commissioners of Immigration, March 13, 1920). Author's emphasis.

98. Louis F. Post to the Commissioner General, May 21, 1920, Commissioner General to Post, May 22, 1920, Post to the Commissioner General, May 24, 1920, IN File 53244/1C; *Annual Report of the Secretary of Labor*, 1920, 72–74; Post, 161–163, 196–197.

99. Alfred Hampton to the Commissioners of Immigration, Seattle, El Paso, and Montreal, September 30, 1920, IN File 53244/1.

100. J. A. Fluckey to the Commissioner General, October 14, 1920, IN File 53244/1.

101. Clark, 336; Kohler, 412–413; Oppenheimer, *Enforcement of Deportation Laws*, 30, 40–41; Van Vleck, *Administrative Control of Aliens*, 91.

102. Oppenheimer, 43.

103. Clark, 331–332, 361, 373; Oppenheimer, 26–27, 31–35, 80–83; Van Vleck, 91, 228.

104. Kohler, 412–413.

105. Clark, 377–381; Kohler, 412–413; Oppenheimer, 52. Kohler states that in 1930 ninety per cent of the inspectors' recommendations

were adopted by the board of review and were in turn approved by
the Assistant Secretary of Labor in charge of immigration affairs.

106. Kohler, 412–413.

107. The I.W.W. gave every Wobbly arrested in the Northwest the
opportunity to use the organization's legal staff and the majority of
the aliens sued out writs of habeas corpus. Towards the end, the
I.W.W's had publicity, some public sympathy, money, talented lawyers, and the benefit of an appeal to Washington. As a result, most
of them won their freedom.

108. Higham, 265–295, 300–330.

Chapter IX

Holding the Line during Normalcy

1. A. Warner Parker to the Commissioner General, December 5,
1918, DJ File 198438 before ½.

2. Address at Lafayette College, reported in the *Philadelphia Public Ledger*, October 17, 1919.

3. Parker to the Commissioner General, December 5, 1918, DJ File
198438 before ½; Commissioner General to the Assistant Secretary,
July 20, 1920, IN File 54379/255.

4. James A. Finch to the Attorney General, December 10, 1921,
PA File, Box 52. See also Finch to Solicitor General Biggs, May 29,
1933, PA File, Box 52, "War Violators" Folder. Finch was still concerned that a general pardon for those convicted under the wartime
acts would stimulate and encourage the radical movement of the
thirties.

5. Comments of Finch on Memorandum of Albert De Silver and
Morris Hillquit, May 19, 1921, PA File 39–240.

6. Dj File 186701–23–12; PA Files 39–240, –241, and –242, *passim*.
These files are the pardon attorney records covering the cases of the
Chicago, Sacramento, and Wichita I.W.W.'s See also U.S. Attorney
A. F. Williams to Finch, December 14, 1921, and S. B. Amidon to A.
Mitchell Palmer, October 2, 1920, PA File, Box 54, 35–360.

7. Warren G. Harding to John D. Ryan, September 26, 1922,
ACLU, CXCV.

8. DJ File 202600–2734, *passim*.

9. DJ File 202600–59, *passim;* John Lord O'Brian to the Attorney
General, November 20, 1918, DJ File 190470; O'Brian to U.S. Attor-
ney Francis G. Caffey, January 8, 1919, DJ File 9–5–667–13; A.
Mitchell Palmer to U.S. Attorney Fred Robertson, June 12, 1919,
DJ File 186701–17–9; Palmer to Congressman Andrew J. Volstead,
October 31, 1919, DJ File 202600–59–3; DJ Files 189738 and
195397; *Investigation Activities of the Department of Justice, 1919*,
Senate Document 153, 66 Cong., 1 Sess. (1919), 6–8.

10. *Baldwin v. Franks,* 120 U.S. 678; *U.S. v. W. D. Haywood, et al.,* 268 F. 795; *U.S. v. C. W. Anderson, et al.,* 273 F. 25; A. Mitchell Palmer to Frank L. Polk, February 1, 1920, DJ File 202600–59–27; DJ File 202600–2734–12; *Investigation Activities of the Department of Justice, 1919,* Senate Document 153, 66 Cong., 1 Sess. (1919), 7–8. The Spanish anarchist indictment was the El Ariete case. The government's position in this case was that propaganda was by then as much an instrument of force as "gas or liquid fire," and had already proven itself in Russia and Germany to be a powerful weapon by destroying morale.

11. Memorandum of Earl J. Davis to the Attorney General, June 10, 1924, DJ File 202600–2734. See also Special Assistant to the Attorney General Clifford H. Byrnes, "Brief on Laws Having Possible Application to Communist Activities," *ibid.* after 10.

12. Memorandum of Earl J. Davis to the Attorney General, June 10, 1924, *ibid.* See also DJ File 208767 on the question of whether Soviet Russia was or was not a *de facto* government.

13. Palmer to Joseph W. Fordney, September 9, 1919, DJ File 186701–3–1; Palmer to U.S. Attorney Moon, January 12, 1920, DJ File 205492–166; Robert P. Stewart to Peter C. Cannon, May 2, 1921, DJ File 9–12–734–51; Wilbert J. McBride to Harry M. Daugherty, January 7, 1924; Daugherty to McBride, January 16, 1924, DJ File 186701–3–13; Robert E. Tally to Daugherty, January 2, 1924, DJ File 202600–3–30; DJ File 186701–266, *passim.*

14. ACLU Memorandum, May 21, 1924, DJ File 202600–823–25; Report of Roger N. Baldwin on interview with Harlan Fiske Stone and J. Edgar Hoover, August 7, 1924; Report of Baldwin on interview with Hoover, October 17, 1924, ACLU, CCLXXII; Lowenthal, *Federal Bureau of Investigation,* 269–304; Don Whitehead, *The F.B.I. Story* (New York, 1956), 55–74.

15. Quoted in Lowenthal, 298–299.

16. Roger N. Baldwin, in Memorandum of August 7, 1924, ACLU, CCLXXII.

17. There is some evidence in the department files that the government continued to collect information about radicals. Although the General Intelligence Division was disbanded from 1924 until 1939, local offices apparently sent in reports on radical meetings, speakers, and organizations. The department, however, took no further action since there was no violation of federal law (DJ Files 202600–418, sec. VII, and 95–16–26). As late as September 1926, for example, the Chicago office had a special agent in charge of "red" activities (Inspector Weiss to the Commissioner General, September 16, 1926, IN File 54616/61).

18. Newton D. Baker to Governor Hugh M. Dorsey, November 7,

1919, Baker to the Chief of Staff, December 2, 1920, AG File 370.6; Colonel William Lassiter to the Chief of Staff, October 8, 1919, Chief of Staff File 1088, Omaha–6.

19. Acting Judge Advocate General J. A. Hull to the Adjutant General, October 31, 1922, AG File 370.6.

20. Confidential Memorandum, November 7, 1919, to all Morale Officers of Departments and Larger Camps from Colonel E. L. Munson, General Staff, Chief Morale Branch, Chief of Staff File 1010, Morale–47.

21. Memorandum of November 25, 1919, from Major General William G. Haan, Director War Plans Division, Acting Chief of Staff, to the Chief of Staff, Chief of Staff File 1010, Morale–47.

22. Memorandum of January 28, 1921, from Colonel Campbell King, Assistant Director War Plans Division, to the Director, Military Intelligence Division, Chief of Staff File 1010, Morale–69.

23. Brigadier General Marlborough Churchill, Director Military Intelligence Division, to the Director War Plans Division, October 27, 1919, War Plans Division File 1835 (hereafter cited as WPD). See also Churchill to Chief of Staff, November 18, 1918, Chief of Staff File 1150, Propaganda–33.

24. Memorandum of Major General William G. Haan, Director War Plans Division, April 23. 1920, WPD File 5215.

25. Adjutant General to Commanding Generals 3rd, 5th and 7th Corps Areas, September 27, 1920, AG File 381; Memorandum of Haan to the Chief of Staff, May 13, 1920, WPD File 5763.

26. Memorandum of Colonel E. D. Anderson, General Staff, Acting Director of Operations, to Chief of Staff, November 11, 1919, Chief of Staff File 580, U.S. Guards–117.

27. Memorandum from Colonel D. E. Aultman to the Commandant, General Staff College, May 5, 1920, WPD File 5215.

28. Thomas W. Gregory to Congressman John L. Burnett, January 9, 1919, DJ File 198438–1.

29. Memorandum of October 1, 1919, DJ File 9–16–12–1832. See also Clarence L. Reames to the Attorney General, April 1, 1919, DJ File 9–16–12–7519–175.

30. Special Assistant R. W. Sprague to the Attorney General, March 30, 1919, John Lord O'Brian to Sprague, April 5, 1919, DJ File 9–16–12–7519–87½.

31. A. Mitchel Palmer to William B. Wilson, May 14, 1919, DJ File 9–16–12–7519–269; Claude R. Porter to Congressman Benjamin F. Welty, June 30, 1919, Palmer to Senator LeBaron B. Colt, October 22, 1919, DJ File 198438–26 and –57; John Hanna to Francis P. Garvan, November 17, 1919, DJ File 9–16–12–7519 after 341.

32. Memorandum of John Hanna to the Secretary to the Attorney

General, July 15, 1919, Hanna to the Attorney General, July 28, 1919, Attorney General to Hanna, July 30, 1919, DJ File 9–16–12–7519–303 and –308½.

33. John M. Maguire to John Lord O'Brian, February 8, 1919, DJ File 198438 between 12 and 13.

34. A. Warner Parker to the Commissioner General, December 5, 1918, DJ File 198438 before ½; Commissioner General to the Assistant Secretary, July 20, 1920, IN File 54379/255; Clark, *Deportation of Aliens*, 216.

35. DJ Files 198438, 9–16–12–4297, and 9–16–12–7519, *passim;* IN File 54549/622A–D, *passim.*

36. Clark, 63–66.

37. *Bouvier's Law Dictionary* (Cleveland, 1934).

38. Clark, 162–163.

39. *U. S. ex rel. Mylius v. Uhl*, 210 F. 860.

40. Solicitor's Opinion, December 10, 1908, in re issuance of warrant of arrest for Francesco Pisasale, IN File 51924/27.

41. The files covering the question of amnesty deal with this rejection of the "political prisoner" concept (DJ Files 197009, Secs. I–III, and 197009–1, secs. I and II).

42. John Lord O'Brian to Clarence L. Reames, June 24, 1918, DJ File 186701–49–98; Reames to the Attorney General, June 30, 1918, DJ File 186701–49–101; Reames to the Attorney General, March 21, 1918, DJ File 190159–36. Reames to the Attorney General, March 9, 1918, and March 14, 1918, DJ File 190159–22 and –25; O'Brian to Miss Jessica E. Biers, September 28, 1918, DJ File 186701–59–22; U.S. Attorney John W. Preston to the Attorney General, July 31, 1918, DJ File 9–16–12–3720–6. The following individual case histories are relevant: DJ Files 9–16–12–414, 9–16–12–1548, 9–16–12–2691, 9–16–12–3004, 9–16–12–3218, 9–16–12–3331, 9–16–12–3623, 9–16–12–4001, 9–16–12–4769, and 9–16–12–4803; IN Files 54379/36, /61, /62, /90, /113, /512, /514, and 54616/95. IN File 54379/80 deals with a German who was arrested as an I.W.W. but proved himself not a Wobbly. He was interned nevertheless.

43. U. S. Attorney Francis A. Garrecht to the Attorney General, August 27, 1917, Memorandum, Charles Warren to the Attorney General, September 6, 1917, DJ File 9–16–12–414–6.

44. Secretary of War to the Attorney General, September 14, 1917, DJ File 186813–43. See also DJ File 205492–548½. The government did not intern alien enemies who were not I.W.W.'s nor did it arrest citizen Wobblies deported by the Bisbee league.

45. James A. Finch to the Attorney General, December 10, 1921, PA File, Box 52, "Records of the Pardon Attorney" folder. See also Harry M. Daugherty to Warren G. Harding, September 20, 1922, PA File 39–242.

46. Finch to J. T. Williams, September 7, 1922, PA File 39–241. See also Finch to the Attorney General, December 30, 1922, PA Files 39–240 and 38–478.

47. Thomas W. Gregory to Congressman John L. Burnett, January 9, 1919, DJ File 198438–1.

48. Burnett to Gregory, January 10, 1919, DJ File 198438–5; Thomas W. Hardwick to Gregory, January 27, 1919, DJ File 198438–10.

49. John Hanna to John T. Creighton, Memorandum of November 14, 1919, A. Mitchell Palmer to Hanna, June 11, 1919, Palmer to Robert M. La Follette, June 11, 1919, DJ Files 198438–61 and –64.

50. John M. Maguire to John Lord O'Brian, February 8, 1919, DJ File 198438 between 12 and 13.

51. *Congressional Record*, 66 Cong., 1 Sess. (1919), 3376; *New York Commercial*, July 31, 1919.

52. Acting Chief of the Bureau of Investigation to Agent James E. Finlay, Chattanooga, June 21, 1919, DJ File 9–16–12–7519 between 303 and 304.

53. John Hanna to the Secretary to the Attorney General, November 10, 1919, DJ File 198438–64.

54. A. Mitchell Palmer to Senator LeBaron B. Colt, October 22, 1919, DJ File 198438–57.

55. Statement for the press from Palmer, March 28, 1919, DJ File 9–16–12–7519–99.

56. *Ibid.*, Hanna to Francis P. Garvan, November 17, 1919, DJ File 9–16–12–7519 following 341; Hanna to Garvan, November 17, 1919, *ibid.*

57. Hanna to the Secretary of State, March 24, 1920, DJ File 9–16–12–7519–342.

58. *Congressional Record*, 66 Cong., 1 Sess. (1919), 3369, 3373, and 3376.

59. Inspector D. A. Plumly to Inspector in Charge W. R. Mansfield, Denver, August 12, 1919, and August 28, 1919, IN File 54235/85C. This lists the disposition of the cases of 129 radicals at Fort Douglas, Utah. In 36 instances the Immigration Bureau could not prove a violation of the 1918 law as interpreted by the Secretary of Labor. Sixty-two aliens had been repatriated or were seeking repatriation. Other cases were divided among paroles (6), releases (4), no records (7), pending (5), transferred (1), warrent of arrest refused (1), and unaccounted for (6). See also IN Files 54709/41, /43, /48, and /63.

60. A. Warner Parker to the Commissioner General, December 5, 1918, DJ File 198438 before ½; Thomas W. Gregory to John L. Burnett, January 15, 1919, DJ File 198438–5.

61. The Rockford cases: IN Files 54379/141, /144, /147–163,

/165–172, /174, /175, /177, /178, /254–256, /258–265, /267, /282–285, /288–290, /292–298, /306, 54389/88–90, and 54916/8.

62. Brief of John L. Metzen, May 23, 1918, IN File 54379/263.

63. Bureau Memorandum in re Charles Johnson, Jun 9, 1918, IN File 54379/155. See also Bureau Memorandum in re Sven Lindquist, May 6, 1918, IN File 54379/254.

64. Deported: IN Files 54379/141, /144, /147–153, /155, /158–163, /165, /166, /168, /171, /172, /174, /175, /177, /178, /254, /256, /258, /259, /262, /263, /290, /292, /295, and 54389/88–90; departed voluntarily: IN Files 54379/154, /170, and /265; in United States over five years and not chargeable: IN Files 54379/260, /282, /283, /289, /293, /294, /296, /297, and /306; citizen or naturalized: IN Files 54379/157 and /298.

65. Louis F. Post, Memorandum of May 22, 1920, IN File 54379/261; Post Memorandum of July 3, 1920, IN File 54379/156. Years later the Immigration Bureau board of review upheld this interpretation in the case of a Swedish alien deportee seeking readmission. The board stated, "The duty to register was one made solely by an Act of Congress for the purpose of obtaining men for the military service of the United States in the war which had then been declared. Failure to register, however grave the offense may be considered in view of the possible emergency existing, is not inherently an act of baseness, vileness, or depravity" (Board of Review Decision, June 6, 1936, IN File 54379/263).

66. Post, Memorandum of July 3, 1920, IN File 54379/156.

67. Anthony Caminetti to the Assistant Secretary, July 20, 1920, IN File 54379/255.

68. Post, Memorandum of July 3, 1920, IN File 54379/156; Assistant Commissioner General Alfred Hampton to all Commissioners of Immigration and Inspectors in Charge, August 18, 1920, IN File 53244/1B.

69. Alfred Hampton to the Inspector in Charge, Chicago, November 9, 1920, IN File 54379/255; IN Files 54379/267, /288, and 54916/8.

70. *U.S. ex rel. Suhonen v. Wallis*, January 13, 1921, IN File 54923/13.

71. Bureau Memorandum, June 3, 1919, IN File 54641/24. See also the following similar decisions: Bureau Memoranda of May 6, 1919, and June 28, 1919, IN Files 54408/17 and 54649/187.

72. The Solicitor to the Assistant Secretary, June 28, 1919, IN File 54641/24.

73. Louis F. Post, Memorandum of September 29, 1920, IN File 54641/24; Post, Memorandum of January 28, 1921, IN File 54616/42 (this covered 38 aliens); Bureau Memorandum, June 28, 1919, IN File 54649/187; E. J. Henning to Walter D. Nelles, November 26,

1921, Department Memorandum, February 25, 1922, IN File 54649/187.

74. State courts consistently ruled that convictions under the selective service, espionage, and similar laws involved moral turpitude. Three of these cases concerned a lawyer's disbarment. The Idaho Supreme Court stated, "If parties intend such wrong [avoiding registration] as when they conspire against the public interests . . . the act doubtless involves moral turpitude" (*In re Hofstede*, 173 P. 1087, 1088). The California high court ruled that obstruction of recruiting was "a base offense against his fellowmen and his country entirely regardless of statute prohibiting it . . . closely akin to . . . treason, than which . . . nothing could be more base" (*In re O'Connell*, 194 P. 1010, 1011–12). Compare *In re Kerl*, 188 P. 40, and *In re Wells*, 208 P. 25, 26–27.

75. IN Files 54649/187 and 54641/24.

76. IN File 54641/24; Post, Memorandum of July 3, 1920, IN File 54379/156.

77. IN Files 54379/176, 54616/36, and /146.

78. IN File 55119/48.

79. IN File 55119/121.

80. IN File 54379/524.

81. U.S. Attorney Robert Duncan to Edward White, Commissioner of Immigration, San Francisco, March 14, 1919, DJ File 186701–57–128.

82. IN File 54616/26. The promised information proved worthless.

83. After an exhaustive search in the National Archives, I found no sign that the bureau had moved against these immigrant defendants.

84. The government files containing a numerous correspondence on this subject of amnesty and commutation are DJ Files 197009, secs. I–III, and 197009–1, secs. I–II; PA Files 39–240–242.

85. Woodrow Wilson to Thomas W. Gregory, November 20, 1918, Gregory to Wilson, November 29, 1918, Gregory MSS.; Wilson to Norman Hapgood, December 2, 1918, Wilson to Joseph P. Tumulty, March, 26, 1919, Tumulty to Wilson, April 4, 1919, Wilson to Tumulty, June 28, 1919, Tumulty to Wilson, June 28, 1919, A. Mitchell Palmer to Wilson, July 30, 1919, Wilson to Palmer, August 1, 1919, and August 29, 1919, Wilson MSS.

86. Warren Harding, Omaha Campaign Speech, October 7, 1920, ACLU, CXCVII.

87. DJ Files 197009, secs. I–III, and 197009–1, secs. I and II.

88. John Lord O'Brian to the Attorney General, Memorandum of April 30, 1919, DJ File 186701, sec. I–71½.

89. James A. Finch to the Attorney General, December 10, 1921, PA File, Box 52, "Records of the Pardon Attorney" folder.

90. Harry M. Daugherty to Newcomb Carlton, January 10, 1922, PA File, Box 51, "Political Prisoners" folder 3.

91. Daugherty to Carlton, December 31, 1921, PA File, Box 51, "Political Prisoners" folder 3.

92. A.F. of L. Executive Council Report, 1922, American Civil Liberties Union to Samuel Gompers, June 16, 1922, ACLU, CXCVIII.

93. Otto Christensen to the Department of Labor, October 4, 1921, IN File 54616/38; Christensen to Daugherty, October 11, 1921, PA File, Box 51, "Political Prisoners" folder 3.

94. Roger N. Baldwin to Mary Gertrude Fendall, January 14, 1922, ACLU, CLXI; Baldwin to John W. Crim, April 19, 1922, *ibid.* CXCVII. See also Baldwin to Daugherty, February 27, 1922, and Daugherty to Baldwin, March 1, 1922, *ibid.*, CXCV.

95. Chaplin, *Wobbly*, 256–257, 312–313; American Civil Liberties Union, *The Truth About the I.W.W. Prisoners* (New York, 1922), 18. I.W.W.'s also split over the procedure to be adopted with regard to prison discipline.

96. For some of the personal descriptions of this bitter dissension and of the reasons for adopting opposing views see Chaplin, 256, 311–313, 322–323; *St. Louis Post-Dispatch*, June 27, 1923; Harry Feinberg to Roger N. Baldwin, April 10, 1923; James Rowan to Alex Daziers, September 30, 1923; Baldwin to J. T. Doran, December 18, 1923, Doran to Baldwin, December 22, 1923, ACLU, LXXII; John Pancner to Baldwin, October 8, 1922, Baldwin to Pancner, October 13, 1922, Archie Sinclair to the General Defense Committee, January 18, 1922, and February 16, 1922, *ibid.*, CXCVIII.

97. Undated Memorandum from Baldwin to the American Civil Liberties Union on his February 3, 1922, visit to Leavenworth, *ibid.*, CXCVI; Baldwin to the I.W.W.'s at Leavenworth, February 21, 1922, PA File, Box 51, "Political Prisoners" folder 3.

98. The evidence under the Espionage Act count consisted entirely of articles, pamphlets, and speeches printed, distributed, or spoken by the indicted Wobblies. They were being held, therefore, clearly for the expression of opinion (Charles Clyne to James A. Finch, December 12, 1922, PA File 38–487; Attorney General to Hon. C. Bascom Slemp, August 29, 1922, PA File, Box 51, "Political Prisoners" folder 3).

99. Report of the Pardon Attorney on the Chicago I.W.W. and Count 4, December 20, 1922, PA File 39–240; Finch to J. T. Williams, September 7, 1922, PA File 39–241; Finch to the Attorney General, November 28, 1922, PA File 39–240; Finch to the Attorney General, December 30, 1922, PA File 38–478; Harry M. Daugherty to Warren G. Harding, October 31, 1921, PA File 35–362, Box 53; Alexander Sidney Lanier to Woodrow Wilson, January 17, 1919, DJ File 188032–373; PA Files 35–362, 38–487, and 39–248.

100. Deported: IN Files 54297/18, 54235/39, /61, 54616/46, /48, /49, /52, /57–59, /145, /153; PA File, Box 49; Charles Clyne to Finch, December 12, 1922, PA File 38–487; ordered deported but died or unable acquire passport: IN Files 54616/45 and /148; Refused the conditions: IN Files 54616/43, /46, and /53.

101. IN Files 54616/38, /55, /56, /60, and /151.

102. Quoted in Inspector Howard Ebey to the Commissioner General, October 31, 1922, IN File 54616/38.

103. *Mahler, et al., v. Ebey*, 264 U.S. 32, 33.

104. IN File 54616/38 and PA File 41/638.

105. Attorney General Harlan Stone to Calvin Coolidge, January 9, 1925, PA File 41–638. See also PA File, Box 49.

106. The documents and appeals submitted by the proponents of amnesty appear throughout the following files: ACLU, LXXII, XCVIII, CLXI, CXCV, CXCVI, CXCVII, and CXCVIII; PA Files 39–240 and –241.

107. Warren G. Harding to Father John D. Ryan, September 6, 1922, ACLU, CXCV.

108. James A. Finch to Edith M. Chaplin, November 28, 1922, *ibid.*, CXCVIII.

109. Finch to the Attorney General, November 28, 1922, PA File 39–240.

110. *Ibid.*

111. As an example of what might happen, consider the case of the I.W.W. released on a conditional commutation who lectured in California for the release of his fellow class-war prisoners. The state arrested him under the criminal-syndicalism law as an active I.W.W. (Pierce C. Wetter to Finch, June 26, 1923, *ibid.*). Criminal-syndicalism convictions also served the deportations crusade. A mere member of the I.W.W. was, of course, not deportable. If convicted as a member of the I.W.W. under the syndicalism legislation, however, the Department of Labor deported him for committing a crime involving moral turpitude (Bureau Memorandum, November 16, 1921, IN File 54616/17). As so often happened, the department later reversed itself, holding that a criminal-syndicalism violation was not a deportable offense (Acting Commissioner Henry A. Maurer to the Commissioner General, May 13, 1922, IN File 54517/52).

112. Finch to the Attorney General, November 28, 1922, PA File 39–240.

113. IN Files 54616/39, /40, /42, /53, /145, and /150; PA File, Box 49.

114. E. J. Henning to the Attorney General, June 18, 1923; A. T. Seymour to Henning, July 20, 1923, PA File 39–240.

115. Henry H. Curran to the Commissioner General, August 6, 1923, IN File 54616/42; those resisting deportation are in IN Files

54616/39, /40, /42, /53, and /150. The alien represented in IN File 54616/145 accepted his expulsion.

116. Brief for the appellants, *U.S. ex rel. Brazier, et al., v. Commissioner of Immigration, New York*, PA File 41–641.

117. *Ibid.*; Assistant Commissioner Harry R. Landis to the Commissioner General, October 6, 1923, IN File 54616/42.

118. Learned Hand's dissent in *U.S. ex rel. Brazier, et al., v. Commissioner of Immigration, New York*, PA File 41–641.

119. Board of Review Memoranda of September 2, 1925, and June 15, 1927, IN File 54616/42.

120. The commission's work and recommendations and the Coolidge commutations may be found in PA File, Box 49, and PA Files 39–240, –241, and –242.

121. A. T. Seymour to Harry F. Ward, February 16, 1923, ACLU, LXXII.

122. Finch, Memorandum to Warren F. Martin, January 23, 1923, PA File 39–242. For other examples see R. P. Stewart to A. Mitchell Palmer, January 11, 1921, PA File 35–362; Stewart to Palmer, February 11, 1921, PA File 35–766; Finch to the Attorney General, December 10, 1921, PA File, Box 52, "Records of the Pardon Attorney" folder; Finch to Edith M. Chaplin, November 28, 1922, ACLU, CXCVIII.

123. Report of the Pardon Attorney on the Chicago I.W.W. and Count 4, December 20, 1922, PA File 39–240. See also this file, *passim*, for the penciled comments on individual cases; Attorney General William D. Mitchell to Calvin Coolidge, June 18, 1926, W. W. Husband to the Attorney General, May 24, 1926, PA File 44–152; IN Files 54616/43, /46, /50, /51, /51A, /60, and /69.

124. Finch to the Attorney General, December 13, 1923, PA File 39–240.

125. C. W. Anderson to Finch, March 23, 1923, PA File 43–105. Contrary to the generally accepted theory that persecution stiffens the ranks of those under fire, the wartime roundups and trials created a great deal of backsliding among radicals.

126. Bureau of Naturalization, Radio Release no. II, October 16, 1922, DJ File 38–0, sec. 8.

127. House Subcommittee of the Committee on Appropriations, *Hearings, Second Deficiency Appropriation Bill, 1920,* 66 Cong., 2 Sess. (1920), 463–465.

128. Commissioner Luther Weedin to the Commissioner General, September 25, 1922, IN File 53531/192B; IN File 54709/473; *U.S. v. Olsen,* 272 F. 706, and DJ File 209112–6; *In re Olsen,* 4 F. 2d 417.

129. *In re Olsen,* 4 F. 2d 417.

130. IN File 54379/525; R. P. Bonham to the Commissioner Gen-

eral, June 8, 1918, Decision of Judge Wolverton in *U.S. v. Carl Swelgin*, IN File 53531/192A.

131. The naturalized I.W.W.'s are in IN Files 54616/37, /47, /62, /63, /65, /66, /68, /147, /149, and 55264/13. The Rowan case is covered in IN File 54616/63, DJ File 210791, and PA File 39–240.

132. U.S. Department of Justice, Criminal Division, *Denaturalization* (Washington, 1943), 32.

133. *Ibid.*, 7, 34, 68, 70.

134. DJ File 210791, *passim*, especially H. S. Ridgely to U.S. Attorney Donald F. Kizer, Spokane, August 6, 1925 (210791–31).

135. *U.S. v. Rowan*, DJ File 210791–46, and 18 F. 2d 246.

136. F. G. Wixon to the Solicitor General, undated, DJ File 210791–48; W. W. Husband to John Sargent, May 7, 1927, H. S. Ridgely to O. R. Luhring, May 19, 1927, Solicitor General to O. R. Luhring, June 7, 1927, DJ File 210791–49.

137. Department of Justice, *Denaturalization*, 35, 70.

138. Finch, Memorandum of July 20, 1929, PA File, Box 52, "Records of the Pardon Attorney" folder.

139. Finch to Solicitor General Biggs, May 29, 1933, PA File, Box 52, "War Violators" folder.

140. Proclamation of December 23, 1933, DJ Circular 2514.

Epilogue

1. *U.S. v. Galvan*, in *Washington Post and Times Herald*, May 25, 1954.

2. Konvitz, *Civil Rights*, 97–103. The cases cited are *Carlson v. Landon* and *Butterfield v. Zydok*, 342 U.S. 524; *Harisiades v. Shanghnessy, Mascitti v. McGrath*, and *Coleman v. McGrath*, 342 U.S. 580.

3. *Whom We Shall Welcome*, Report of the President's Commission on Immigration and Naturalization (1953), 162.

4. Konvitz, 103.

5. Bureau of Naturalization, Radio Release No. II, October 16, 1922, DJ File 38–0, section 8.

6. Quoted in Post, *Deportations Delirium*, 304.

7. *San Diego Tribune*, March 4, 1912.

Index

Abercrombie, John W., 209, 217–218
Addams, Jane, 143–144
Alien and Sedition Acts of 1798, 21–22
Alien enemies: postwar policy toward, 246–247, 250–252; release of, 251–252; wartime internment, 106, 162, 170, 209, 249. *See also* Deportation law of May 1920
Aliens: I.W.W.'s stereotyped by Immigration Bureau, 165; stereotyped as radical, 4, 6, 21–26, 31
Allen, Clay, 156–157, 160, 162–163
American Alliance for Labor and Democracy, 142–143
American Civil Liberties Union, 262, 271. *See also* National Civil Liberties Bureau
American Federation of Labor, 36–38, 129, 142; amnesty policy, 259; and I.W.W., 129
Americanization, 45–46
American Union against Militarism, 143
Amnesty campaign, 239–240, 258–259, 262–264, 266. *See also* Political prisoners
Anaconda Copper Company, 94–95, 110–114, 232–233
Anarchism, 21, 25–27, 29–33
Antiradicalism: and business cycles, 3–4, 24–27, 34, 193–194; and deportation, 75–84; federal, 2–3, 5–6, 21–22, 24, 27–33, 60–61, 193–194, 239–241; I.W.W.'s role, 8, 92–98; and legislative pattern of 1917, 85–87; local, 3, 26, 30, 92–97, 107, 111–113, 115–116; and naturalization, 66–73; opposition to, 29, 32; state, 24, 27, 30, 50–61, 230–231, 239; and social and economic conditions, 22–27, 29, 34

Appropriations Committee, 209, 211

Baker, Newton D., 105, 266
Baldwin, Roger N., 143
Beard, Charles A., 143
Bill of Rights, 12, 18, 43, 143, 202, 221–222, 249–250
Bisbee deportation, 93
Borah, William E., 262, 264
Bourquin, George, 111
Burke, Frank, 216–217
Burleson, Albert S., 144, 146
Burnett, John L., 76, 78, 82
Businessmen: appeal for federal suppression of I.W.W., 5, 52–53; influence on federal policy, 52–55, 87, 98–99, 100, 103–105, 109–116, 122–127, 131, 135, 139, 231–232; labor policies: lumber, 95–97, 100, 103–105, 116, 154, migratory harvest, 56–59, 132, mining, 93–95, 110–114, 138–139, postwar, 191–192, 198, 230–231, Seattle, 154; local antiradical programs: Arizona, 93, Butte, 94, 111–113, 232–233, California, 132–135, Northwest, 96–97, 107, Seattle, 155–156, 160–161; proposals for dealing with I.W.W., 1917, 95, 97–100, 103–105, 123–127, 131, 135, 139, 155, 167; support deportation, 99–100, 166–167

California antiradical program: by Republicans, 50–55; by Progressives, 55–61
California Commission on Immigration and Housing, 57–60, 124
Caminetti, Anthony, 181–182, 193, 211, 213–214, 217–220, 223–226, 232
Chaplin, Ralph, 118

Churchill, Marlborough, 193
Class war, federal government's belief in, 239–240
Communist party, 1, 8, 180, 192,
212–213, 217, 220–221, 223, 241–
242, 273
Communist Labor party, 1, 192,
212–213, 217, 220–221, 223
Conditional commutation, judicial review of, 264–265
Coolidge, Calvin, 242, 256, 262,
266

Daugherty, Harry M., 241, 243, 259
Debs, Eugene V., 27, 48, 90, 259,
262
Denaturalization, 267–271
Densmore, John B., 136
Deportation: administration of, 13–
20, 32, 229–237; of aliens convicted during war, 252–265; for
crime involving moral turpitude,
19, 248–249, 254–255; due process
in, 11–13, 18, 212–219, 221–222,
273–275; as harassment of I.W.W.
defense, 149, 176; of I.W.W.'s arrested, 206–207; for liability to
become a public charge, 19, 177–
179; postwar opposition to, 195–
197, 199–201, 214–217; prewar,
18–20; proposed wartime use, 99–
103; and rule 22, 16, 212–214,
217–218; Seattle crusade, 163–
171; time limits, 81–83; telegraphic warrants, 164–165, 231–
233. See also Immigration; U.S.
Bureau of Immigration
Deportation law of 1917: department policy re-established, 168–
169; erroneous application at Seattle hearings, 173–179; judicial review, 185–186, 189–190, 204–
205; lack of definition, 84; origin
and debate, 73–85; provisions, 83;
reinterpretation by Seattle office,
163–164; reinterpretation by Immigration Bureau, 183–191; revision proposed, 182; theory of,
73–76, 84
Deportation law of 1918, 6–7; origin,

182–183, 193; provisions, 183; relation to Palmer raids, 207, 218;
in Seattle crusade, 189
Deportation law of May 1920: inconsistent enforcement, 252–265;
judicial review, 254, 261; origin
and passage, 238–239, 246–251;
provisions, 238–239, 252
Deportation law of June 1920: origin and passage, 226–229; provisions, 228
Depressions, 4, 24, 25
Draft Act, see Selective Service Act

Economic conditions: 1870's, 22–24;
1880's, 25–27; 1910's, 35–37; in
California, 56–57; postwar, 110,
191–192
Espionage Act, 60, 119, 143, 145,
147, 149, 151–152, 157, 194, 237,
239, 241, 247–250, 254–255, 258,
261, 263, 272. See also I.W.W.
trials

Farmer's Protective League, 58–59,
61
Federal trials, see I.W.W. trials
Fickert, Charles M., 133–136
Finch, James A., 239–240, 259, 263–
264, 271–272
Fong Yue Ting v. United States, 11,
273
Free speech, as issue: deportation
hearings, 173, 175–179; in immigration policy, 193–194, 227;
I.W.W. organizing, 43–44, 51–52;
naturalization hearings, 68–71;
wartime indictments and trials,
120–121, 136, 260, 267, 271–272
Free-speech fights, see I.W.W., free-
speech fights

Gill, Hiram, 153–156, 159, 171
Gregory, Thomas W., 60, 123, 127,
152–153, 160, 169–171, 258
Gompers, Samuel, 38, 129, 142

Hand, Augustus N., 204–205
Hand, Learned, 17, 265
Hanson, Ole, 171

Harding, Warren G.: opposition to amnesty, 240, 258; release of Debs, 259

Hardwick, Thomas W., 250

Haymarket riot, 25, 26, 27, 29

Haywood, William D., 35, 39, 41, 45, 48–49

Henshaw, Frederick W., 133–136

Hoover, J. Edgar, 193, 230; and antiradical roundups, 210–212; appointed head of Bureau of Investigation, 243; analysis of I.W.W., 72; opposition to due process in deportation, 223–227; on rule 22 and bail, 219–220

Immigration: attitudes toward, 74–75; judicial review, 11–13, 18, 273–274; literacy test, 31–32, 34, 74–76, 80, 83; restriction, 4, 7–8, 28–29, 73–74, 236, 271

Immigration laws: of 1798, 21–22; proposals of 1891, 1893, 1894, 28–29; of 1895 and 1897, 29; of 1903, 4, 24, 30–32; Immigration and Nationality Act of 1952 (McCarran-Walter Act), 1, 274

Immigration Committee, 226–227, 250

Industrial Workers of the World (I.W.W.): as alien enemies, 247, 249, 251–252; and anarchists, 72; at Butte and Tonopah, 1920's, 231–233; in California, 1912–1915, 50–61; Centralia massacre, 227; commutation of sentences, 259–267; denaturalization, 267–271; and deportation law of 1917, 61–62, 73–76; and deportation law of June 1920, 227–228; deportation for violations of war statutes, 252–265; direct action, 40, 44, 48; early history, 42–43; founded, 5, 39; free-speech fights, 43–44, 51–52; government raids, 118–119, 131–133, 135, 137, 139, 149; Immigration Bureau deportation decisions, 184–191, 201–206; Lawrence strike, 35, 44; military suppression, 103–117; naturalization,

67–73, 268; pardons, 262, 272; philosophy, 39–42, 45, 47–49, 51; as political prisoners, 8, 258–267; Seattle crackdowns, 152–180; and Socialist party, 46–50; wartime resurgence, 61, 91–97, 154; on World War I, 88–91, 129

I.W.W. defense, 140–151; appeals, 150–151; due process for, 144–150; financial support, 150

I.W.W. trials: Chicago, 123, 126–128; justice of, 249–250, 261; legal theory, 119–122, 126–127, 140–141; northern Minnesota, 138–139; number arrested and indicted, 150; Omaha, 136–138; Tulsa indictment proposed, 130–131; Sacramento, 120, 132–136, 140–141; Wichita, 131–132

Inter-Church World Movement, 221–222

Internal security: 8–9, 64, 274–276; and civil liberties, 9–10; crisis of 1798, 21–22

Internal Security Act of 1950, 1, 273–274

Japanese Immigrant Case, 11–12, 15

Jaques, Alfred, 139

Johnson, Albert, 74–75, 82, 227

Johnson, Hiram, 52, 55, 57, 60, 135

Judicial review, see Immigration; Deportation; Supreme Court

Juries, wartime eagerness to convict radicals, 122, 132, 135, 140–141, 150, 170

Lamar, William H., 148, 193

Lind, John, 99, 126–127, 139

Literacy test, see Immigration

Logan Act (sec. 5, Criminal Code), 241–242

Lowe, Caroline, 150

Lubin, Simon J., 58

Matthews, Mark A., 152–153, 155, 163, 167, 171, 180

McCarran-Walter Act, see Immigration laws

McKinley, William, assassination, 4, 30, 31, 66, 85
Most, Johann, 25–26, 48
Minute Men of Seattle, 155–156, 161, 167, 225–226
Mooney, Thomas, 133–136, 142, 198
Moral turpitude, defined, 248–249, 252, 254–255

National Civil Liberties Bureau, 129, 143, 148
National Labor Defense Council, 142
Nativism, 5–7, 21–34, 45, 50, 98, 159, 181, 192, 230, 236, 271; and internal security, 2; and naturalization, 64. *See also* Antiradicalism; Internal security
Naturalization: antiradical policy of courts, 64, 68–72, 268; denied socialists, 1891, 63–64; federal policy, 64–66, 71–73, 267–268
Naturalization laws: of 1790–1802, 65; of 1903, 66; of 1906, 65, 67
Neterer, Jeremiah, 189–190

O'Brian, John Lord, 258–259
Older, Fremont, 133–134

Palmer, A. Mitchell, 1–2, 193–194, 218–219, 223, 225–226, 238, 241, 243, 258
Palmer raids, 1–2, 7, 151, 180, 220–221, 227, 229; preparation for, 208–220; reaction to, 221–222
Parker, A. Warner, 181–182, 193
Pepper, George Wharton, 262
Political prisoners, 8, 151, 239–240, 249–250, 257–259, 262–267
Post, Louis F., 143, 201, 222–225, 234, 253; attempted impeachment, 226
Postal censorship, *see* U.S. Post Office Department
Progressive movement, 37, 55–58

Raker, John E., 76–77
Reames, Clarence L., 160–163, 167, 169–171, 180

Red scare, *see* Palmer raids
Red Special, 198–200, 212
Robertson, Fred, 131–132
Roosevelt, Franklin D., 8, 272
Roosevelt, Theodore, 31, 33
Rowan, James, 269–270
Rudkin, Frank H., 185–186, 188, 190
Rule 22 (Immigration Bureau), 16, 212–213, 217–218, 221–222, 235
Rules Committee, 226
Russian Revolution, effect of, 7, 192, 244–245

Sacramento Bee, 135
San Francisco, antiradicalism, 133–135
Saville, M. E., 159–160, 163
Seattle: antiradical lawlessness, 155–156, 158, 160–163, 171; appeals for federal suppression, 155, 163–164, 167, 169–170; belief in I.W.W.'s seditious conspiracy, 152–153, 155, 157–160; deportation roundups, 164–171; deportation hearings, 172–179; general strike, 1919, 197–199; Saville report, 159–160; wartime conditions, 152–163
Seattle Union Record, 154
Sedition laws: of 1918, 145; and peacetime, 195, 242
Seditious conspiracy (sec. 6, Criminal Code), 5, 53–54, 97–98, 119, 194–195, 241–242
Selective Service Act, 60, 90, 119, 138, 151, 157, 194, 237, 239, 241, 247–250, 252–254, 272. *See also* I.W.W. trials
Socialist party, 38, 46–47, 49–50; expulsion of Haywood and opposition to radicals, 46–50; on World War I, 88–90
Socialist Labor party, 25
Stone, Harlan Fiske, 242–243, 262
Strikes: 1877, 5, 24–25; Butte, 94, 110–111, 112–115; coal, 1919, 245; Homestead, 26–27; I.W.W. Everett, Washington, 96–97; I.W.W. Lawrence textile, 35–36,

44–45, 76; I.W.W. Northwest lumber, 95–96, 107, 116; I.W.W. wartime, 6, 92–95, 103–105, 107–108, 113, 114, 119, 121; I.W.W. Wheatland, 57–59; Pullman, 1894, 5, 27; Seattle general, 1919, 197–199; steel, 1919, 247; wartime, 98
Supreme Court, 11–13, 15–16, 261, 273

Taft, William Howard, 50, 53, 261
Trials, *see* I.W.W. trials
Truman, Harry S., 1

Union of Russian Workers, 1, 192, 212–213; raided, 216
U.S. Army: antiradical operations, 1920's, 243–246; in Arizona, 108–110; at Butte, 110–114, 232; constitutional provisions for use in domestic disturbances, 103–104; military intelligence, Seattle, 156, 171; in Northwest, 1917, 106–108; and Pullman strike, 1894, 27; Seattle general strike, 1919, 197–199; and strike of 1877, 24; "War Plans White," 245–246; wartime theories justifying use, 104–109, 112, 115–116
U.S. Bureau of Immigration, 13–20, 84–85, 99–103, 160, 191; cooperation with Department of Justice, 181, 209–214, 222–226; deportation decisions, 184–191, 201–206, 233–236; and I.W.W. aliens, 165, 172–177; special radical division, 181; support of guilt by association, 164–166, 170, 173, 183, 202–203; and war violators, 252–265
U.S. Bureau of Investigation, 118, 124, 126–127, 241; antiradical activities, 210–214; Coolidge-Stone reorganization, 242–243; and Communists, 1920's, 241–242; during Harding administration, 242; wartime expansion, 209–210
U.S. Bureau of Naturalization, 68–70, 267–268, 275
U.S. Department of Justice, 53–54, 59–60, 71–72, 99, 114, 149, 241,

246–247, 257–259, 267–271; alien enemy policy, 238–239, 247–252; alien radical investigation, 209–214; commutation policy, 260–266; General Intelligence Division, 243; I.W.W. prosecutions, 119–141; I.W.W. raids, 118–119, 131–133, 135, 137, 139, 149; Palmer raids, 220–221; postwar limitations, 194–195; reorganization, 1924, 242–243; Seattle cleanup, 160–163; Union of Russian Workers raid, 216–217
U.S. Department of Labor, 100–103, 202–203, 234, 239, 248, 253–257, 260–262, 264–266, 270–271
U.S. Navy, 162; naval intelligence operations at Seattle, 156, 161–162, 198
U.S. Pardon Attorney's office, 271–272; on amnesty of political prisoners, 257–260
U.S. Post Office Department: cooperation with express companies, 148–149; index of illegal radical ideas, 146–147; techniques of suppression, 144–145, 148; wartime censorship, 144–149
U.S. War Department, 105, 115, 239, 244, 251
U.S. v. W. D. Haywood, et al., 123

Vanderveer, George F., 155, 159, 196–197, 214–216, 220; "Notice to Aliens," 215–217
Villard, Oswald Garrison, 80

Wallace, Hugh Campbell, 158–159
Walsh, Frank P., 142
Walsh, Thomas J., 275
Wells, Hulet M., 156–157
Western governors: 1917 internment proposals, 124–126; request federal prosecutions, 60, 124–126
Wheatland riot, 57–59
Wheeler, Burton K., 111, 114
White, Henry M., 163–164, 167, 180, 198
Wilson, William B., 160, 164, 167–

168, 174, 180, 184–185, 201, 203, 210, 212, 217–218, 227–228, 230, 234, 248; and due process in deportation, 222–224; opposition to military suppression, 105; wartime I.W.W. policy, 101–103, 168–169, 189

Wilson, Woodrow, 60, 80–81, 83, 170–171; I.W.W. policy, 128–130; opposition to postwar amnesty, 258; on Seattle conditions, 153
World War I, effect on federal policies, 6–7, 36–37, 91, 97–98, 116, 119–122, 150–151, 194